Non-Traditional Export Promotion in Africa

Non-Traditional Export Promotion in Africa

Experience and Issues

Edited by

G. K. Helleiner
Professor Emeritus, Department of Economics
Distinguished Research Fellow, Munk Centre for International Studies
University of Toronto

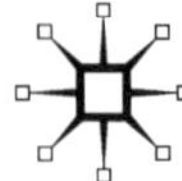

First published 2002 by
PALGRAVE
Houndmills, Basingstoke, Hampshire RG21 6XS and
175 Fifth Avenue, New York, N.Y. 10010
Companies and representatives throughout the world

PALGRAVE is the new global academic imprint of
St Martin's Press LLC Scholarly and Reference Division and
Palgrave Publishers Ltd (formerly Macmillan Press Ltd).

ISBN 0–333–96891–3 hardback

This book is printed on paper suitable for recycling and made from fully managed and sustained forest sources.

A catalogue record for this book is available from the British Library.

Library of Congress Cataloging-in-Publication Data
Non-traditional export promotion in Africa : experience and issues/edited by G.K. Helleiner.
    p. cm.
  Includes bibliographical references and index.
  ISBN 0–333–96891–3
    1. Foreign trade promotion—Africa. 2. Exports—Africa. 3. Africa—Commercial policy. 4. Africa—Economic conditions—1960– 5. Foreign trade promotion—Developing countries.
  I. Helleiner, Gerald K.

HF1611 .N66 2001
382'.63'096—dc21

             2001036927

10   9   8   7   6   5   4   3   2   1
11   10   09   08   07   06   05   04   03   02

Printed and bound in Great Britain by
Antony Rowe Ltd, Chippenham, Wiltshire

Contents

List of Figures

List of Tables

Notes on Contributors

Manuel Agosin, at the time of his contribution, was Professor of Economics and Director, Center on International Economics and Development, University of Chile. He holds a PhD from Columbia University and has published widely on issues related to international economics, macroeconomics and development. He now works at the World Bank.

Anthony Black teaches economics at the University of Cape Town. His research is in the area of industrial and trade policy, and in particular the automotive industry.

Jesimen Chipika teaches at the University of Zimbabwe. Her research currently focuses on issues of poverty and income distribution.

Beealasingh Dabee is an Associate Professor in the Department of Economics and Statistics at the University of Mauritius.

Rob Davies is a Senior Lecturer in the Department of Economics at the University of Zimbabwe, Harare.

Ibrahim A. Elbadawi, a Sudanese national, holds a PhD in Economics and Statistics from North Carolina State and Northwestern Universities. He has worked at the Policy Research Group of the World Bank since 1989, including five years of external service in Nairobi, from 1993 to 1998, where he served as the Research Director of the African Economic Research Consortium.

Gerald K. Helleiner is Professor Emeritus, Department of Economics, and a Distinguished Research Fellow, Munk Centre for International Studies, at the University of Toronto.

Brian Kahn, at the time of his contribution, was Professor and Director of the School of Economics at the University of Cape Town and a research associate at the Centre for Research into Economics and Finance in Southern Africa at the London School of Economics. He now works at the Reserve Bank of South Africa.

Sanjaya Lall is a Professor in Development Economics at the University of Oxford and a Fellow of Green College.

Ammon V. Y. Mbelle is a Lecturer in the Department of Economics, University of Dar es Salaam.
Francis Mwega is an Associate Professor of Economics at the University of Nairobi. He has written extensively on the Kenyan economy.

Benno Ndulu is a Lead Specialist with the Macroeconomic Division for Eastern Africa at the World Bank. He previously taught economics at the University of Dar es Salaam and served in the leadership of the African Economic Research Consortium.

Ennio Rodríguez, former Minister of External Finance and Debt of Costa Rica, holds a DPhil from the Institute of Development Studies, University of Sussex, and is a Professor at the University of Costa Rica. He is currently Senior Economist of the Integration, Trade and Hemispheric Affairs Division at the Inter-American Development Bank in Washington, DC.

Joseph J. Semboja is an Associate Research Professor, Economic Research Bureau, University of Dar es Salaam, Tanzania, currently on leave as Executive Director, Research on Poverty Alleviation (REPOA), Dar es Salaam, Tanzania.

Foreword

Giovanni Andrea Cornia
Director, UNU/WIDER

Sub-Saharan growth prospects have for long been at the centre of the international development debate. The protracted stagnation of the region has been alternatively attributed to its past interventionist policies, an erroneous approach to adjustment or 'geography'. While in part pertinent, none of these hypotheses is completely convincing. Other factors which offer deeper insights – such as the weakness of the African states or their inability to increase and diversify exports – are likely to be equally or more relevant.

Indeed, there is widespread agreement that a main development failure in Africa has been its inability to extricate itself from its traditional colonial export pattern. With the economy strongly dependent on foreign technology, energy, key inputs and food, the rate of growth of output – and people's well-being – are closely dependent on import capacity. In the long term, this depends on the ability to generate sufficient foreign exchange earnings through exports. In this regard, even an improved performance of African traditional exports cannot offer a long-term solution to the financing of essential imports: the long-term prices of traditional export commodities continue sliding gradually, their demand is characterized by low price and income elasticities and their markets are nearly saturated. Thus, while export recovery is an essential component of any African development strategy, this cannot focus on traditional exports alone.

In spite of much talk about the need to increase 'non-traditional exports' from Africa, there has been little empirical research on the degree to which such exports are emerging, the features of such goods and markets, the sustainability of such a policy approach, or even what precisely is meant by the term. In particular, solid research geared to the immediate needs of African people, entrepreneurs and policymakers has remained scarce, and disproportionate amounts of it have been undertaken by outsiders with strong 'priors' and a limited knowledge of local experience.

This study has consciously sought to fill this gap by developing the first serious cross-African analysis of its kind. Despite major data problems, it has been able to reach some important conclusions: that a few African countries have already come quite a long way in the development of non-traditional exporting, notably Mauritius and South Africa; that others undertaking adjustment programmes in the 1980s and 1990s have also had some modest success in this sphere; that the appropriateness and predictability of the real exchange rate has been a fundamental determinant of success; and that a variety of other export-supportive policy instruments, still weakly developed in most African countries, are also likely to be required if more African countries are to move significantly into non-traditional exporting.

This study has sought to build upon the research conducted in Africa primarily by Africans with considerable local expertise. These scholars participated fully in the design and execution of the research activities. The study has also seen the participation of researchers from Latin American and Asian countries which succeeded in expanding non-traditional exports and whose experience seemed potentially relevant for Africa. The process through which all these researchers have interacted directly with one another has been an important further product of this project which benefited also from the strong support and collaboration of the African Economic Research Consortium (AERC), UNCTAD, UNECA and, less directly, the Inter-American Development Bank. The Finnish Ministry for Foreign Affairs has generously contributed to this project and UNU/WIDER's work on Sub-Saharan Africa.

The original and innovative findings of this study can be extremely useful to African policymakers as they seek to expand their exports beyond their traditional base, practitioners and researchers in international agencies, and scholars interested in the development debate on Sub-Saharan Africa and in 'non-traditional exports' in developing countries. This volume, and the research processes that lie behind it, are also to be recommended as a model of how to conduct policy-relevant research to beleaguered policymakers in the world's poorest countries and for other development research institutions around the world. I therefore do warmly recommend this study to all these people mentioned above as well as to the general reader interested in African development issues.

Preface

This volume is the product of a collaborative project on 'Growth, External Sector and the Role of Non-Traditional Exports in Sub-Saharan Africa', sponsored and financially supported by the World Institute for Development Economics Research (WIDER) of the United Nations University. Initiated in mid-1996 at a planning meeting at WIDER in Helsinki, it involved collaboration with and inputs from the United Nations Conference on Trade and Development (UNCTAD), the African Economic Research Consortium (AERC), Nairobi, and the United Nations Economic Commission for Africa (UNECA). Project participants met twice – in Kampala, Uganda, in June 1997 and Addis Ababa, Ethiopia, in March 1998. We would like to thank Germina Ssemogerere and K-Y. Amoako, respectively, for their organizational inputs and warm hospitality on these occasions. We are most grateful for the firm support we have received throughout the life of the project from Giovanni Andrea Cornia, Director of WIDER; Janis Vehmaan-Kreula, our project secretary at WIDER; and Barbara Tiede, the project secretary and editor in Toronto.

G. H.

1
Introduction

G. K. Helleiner

In the vast literature on economic growth and development around the world the role of international trade occupies a prominent place. Trade and trade policies are seen by many as among the most important determinants of overall economic performance; and these views are widely believed to be supported by both theory and empirical evidence. In actual fact, however, the relationships between trade, trade policies and economic development are complex, and the empirical record is not unambiguous (Helleiner, 1995; Rodriguez and Rodrik, 1999; Rodrik, 1999; Buffie, forthcoming). What is beyond dispute is that export performance matters significantly to development in small low-income countries (Berge, Daniel et al., 1994), and that, for exports to expand sufficiently to make reasonable development targets attainable in such countries, traditional primary product exports are unlikely to be enough. It is also generally agreed that export performance is likely to be profoundly influenced by government policies, although which policies and which policy instruments are most important in this respect remains in some dispute. In the Sub-Saharan African context, in which most countries are small and economically very poor, trade and appropriate trade policies have always been seen as critically important to growth and development.

International trade played a major role in nineteenth- and twentieth-century African development, and it will undoubtedly continue to do so in the twenty-first century. International exchange has created the opportunity for greater specialization, increased use of capacity, and the import of productivity-increasing goods and services. Many speak of the economic development of African and other low-income countries, particularly the smaller ones, as actually or potentially export-led. It would be more accurate, however, to speak of such development as investment-led. Whatever its other requisites, African growth and development will certainly require increased investment. The key question is where such investment is likely to be privately and socially profitable. In small, poor countries, investment in production for export markets is obviously an area of greater potential than most. Hence the important historical and prospective roles of exports in African development.

Unfortunately trade and related policies must now be constructed in an international economic environment that is more hostile to many of Africa's traditional exports. Since Africa lost market shares in global markets for many of its traditional commodities in the past two decades, it could, with increased productivity and improved incentives, probably 'claw' some back. But the prospects for traditional export expansion, while certainly not zero, as is sometimes suggested, are somewhat limited, particularly in the important case of tropical beverages, which still make up over one-third of total exports in ten African countries, by low world price elasticities and the risks of rendering the already weak price prospects even bleaker. To make matters worse, traditional export markets are highly unstable and, in recent years, world market instability has even increased. The global economy seems likely to continue to be as turbulent as it was in the last two decades; possibly more so. African governments must probably learn to live within an even more unstable world.

Background

In the next decade or two, growth and development in Sub-Saharan Africa, if it occurs, will be driven primarily by efficient and profitable investment, both in physical and in human capital. With such investment comes more rapid total factor productivity growth and the prospect of a self-sustaining process of increased growth, increased voluntary savings and further increases in investment. Voluntary private investment obviously must play a major role. At present, however, private investment rates in Africa are far below those of other developing areas, or those necessary to generate adequate rates of growth. Even in the relatively successful 'adjusters', real private investment – whether domestic or foreign – has remained at disappointingly low levels (World Bank, 1994, 2000; Hadjimichael et al., 1995). There are various explanations: the possible low credibility of the policies and incentive structures introduced by 'adjusting' governments and other uncertainties in the investment climate; the weakness and small size of local entrepreneurial groups; constraints imposed by other factors, e.g. infrastructure, legal systems, credit, etc. The determinants, potential sources and possible composition of private investment in Africa all need to be more clearly understood. To make matters worse, the productivity of much of Africa's investment, for related reasons, has been low.

In the export sphere, African 'adjusters' have typically done relatively better; but here too the record has been spotty and disappointing. Weak export growth is linked to weak performance in private investment. In small, poor countries, opportunities for efficient and profitable investment in import-substituting or non-tradable activities are limited. Investment in production for export markets is an obvious area of greater longer-run potential. (Prospects in export-oriented mining – and, in some cases, forestry – depend heavily on the possibility of attracting fresh foreign direct investment which, in most instances, remains highly uncertain despite considerable current investment in exploration.)

Exporting provides foreign exchange with which to import capital goods, critical inputs, management and technology, all of which are likely to contribute to continuing growth in productivity. 'Openness' to international exchange may also stimulate increased efficiency via the competitive pressures that it typically brings. Exports have therefore played an important role in African economic progress in the past and they are bound to continue to do so in the future. Weak export performance, and consequent declining African market shares in traditional export markets, were important concomitants of the African crisis of the 1980s. Whatever else may divide current analysts of Africa's economic problems, they are virtually at one in their recognition of the need quickly to achieve more rapid export growth if hopes for more acceptable levels of economic and social development are to be realized in the medium term (Lyakurwa, 1991; Helleiner, 1992; Rodrik, 1997, 1999; Sachs and Warner, 1997; Elbadawi and Helleiner, 1998; Oyejide, 1998; UNCTAD, 1998; Collier and Gunning, 1999; Mkandawire and Soludo, 1999).

Yet dependence on exports has also created problems, particularly when, as in the past two decades, traditional African exports have faced severe real price deterioration in world markets. Economies that are small, poor and dependent upon primary exports are highly vulnerable to external influences and external shocks, particularly those from sharp changes in the terms of trade. Shocks are always costly to growth (Easterly et al., 1993). These economies' structural rigidity (or, in Killick's (1995) terminology, 'inflexibility') and limited access to offsetting credit result in particularly heavy costs from temporary adverse shocks which hit them, in any case, on average more severely. Sub-Saharan African countries experienced enormous adverse trade shocks in the 1980s – larger than those suffered in the 1930s – and the costs to their progress have been severe (Elbadawi and Ndulu, 1996; World Bank, 2000: 20–2). Nor have African governments recently managed their commodity booms and busts well (Collier and Gunning, 1998). In the absence of international reforms to stabilize commodity prices and/or primary exporters' import volumes (the prospects for such reforms at present look bleak), there must be increased attention to the management of shocks (both positive and negative), which seem likely to continue to be frequent as integration into the global economy proceeds, so as best to preserve prospects for longer-run development whatever the trend rates of export growth. Effective social institutions for mediating conflicts among social groups, especially in societies characterized by social cleavages emanating from high income inequality or ethnic diversity such as are found in most of Africa, are likely to be helpful in such management of shocks (Rodrik, 1999).

African export performance in recent decades has been disappointing, but it is important to understand the overall context for such poor performance. African failures have been *developmental* failures, not *export* failures per se. Export shares of gross domestic product (GDP) in Africa are within the usual norms for countries of equivalent size and income levels; and their trade ties, both with industrial countries and with one another, are similarly 'normal' (Foroutan and Pritchett, 1993; Rodrik, 1997; Coe and Hoffmaister, 1998). 'If anything', one study finds, 'Africa overtrades compared with other developing country regions in the sense that its trade is higher than would be expected from the various determinants of bilateral trade' (Coe and Hoffmaister, 1998). African countries' declining shares of world trade reflect their relatively slow growth of GDP (and, to some degree, others' increasingly outward orientation), *not* a decline in their trade or export shares of GDP.

It is also important to emphasize that there is great intercountry variation in Africa both in overall economic performance and in export growth. Cross-African generalizations can therefore be quite misleading about individual countries' experiences. To be most useful, analysis is best conducted at the national level, where trade policy is made and most statistics are kept.

Non-traditional exports and their problems

Steady deterioration in the terms of trade of the traditional export basket, such as was found in most Sub-Saharan African countries in the 1980s, *should* be met with a shift to new *non-traditional* activities, both exporting and efficiently import-substituting. In addition, with worldwide trade liberalization, market access for African non-traditional exports should be improving. Even temporary adverse shifts in the terms of trade, if handled well, may provide useful opportunities to restructure the economy towards non-traditional exports and other activities, as they did, for instance, in the case of Colombia's transition from primary exports to industrial development (Ocampo, 1991). Deterioration in the external terms of trade should, other things being equal, generate 'reverse Dutch disease' effects. As aggregate demand declines, the relative price of non-tradables should fall and there should follow some shift of resources into new exporting and import-competing activities.

Yet, despite an evidently increasing need for it, most Sub-Saharan African countries appear, at least until recently, to have achieved remarkably little diversification of their traditional primary export base. With a few obvious exceptions, e.g. Mauritius and South Africa (see Chapters 7 and 8), the shares of the top two or three traditional exports in individual African country export bills altered very little over the 1980s. Diversification increased in more African countries, though by no means all, in the 1990s (World Bank, 2000: 215).

In some cases, manufactured exports did respond somewhat to real devaluation and domestic demand restraint, but this response often amounted only to a once-and-for-all diversion of production capacity, which had not itself expanded, from the meeting of domestic demand to export markets. In others, production expanded in consequence of increased availability of foreign exchange and thus increased capital utilization, and some of the increase was exported. What are the principal constraints on the development of non-traditional exports – whether primary or manufactured – in Africa? Can such improvements as there have been be sustained? What is required to attract more private *investment* in this sector?

Rapid growth of the global economy and ready access to its markets are fundamental to Africa's non-traditional export prospects and indeed, since African economies are so 'open' and 'dependent', to African development more generally. African access to Northern markets has generally been relatively open (Amjadi et al., 1996); but in specific instances, Northern protectionism has been and remains a serious impediment (Kaplan and Kaplinsky, 1999). Neither rapid global growth nor market access can be assured. Still, on the basis of experience elsewhere (see Chapters 2–4), one would think that there is much that policies within Africa can do to raise the prospects of export success and there are important issues of development strategy and tactics in this regard that need to be addressed.

Sub-Saharan Africa's endowments of relatively abundant natural resources and relatively scarce human skills appear to offer almost all its countries little hope of developing significant manufacturing for export in the near future, except in some unskilled-labour-intensive primary processing activities (Lall, 1995; Wangwe, 1995; Lall and Wangwe, 1998). This familiar proposition has been buttressed by empirical research by Adrian Wood and colleagues on the roots of comparative advantage in a world of mobile capital and immobile resources and labour of different skills (Wood, 1994; Wood and Berge, 1994; Wood and Mayer, 1998). Investment in human capital has a very long gestation period so that even if Africa could accelerate it – and, under current constraints, it is unable to do so – it would be many decades before its relative factor endowments could significantly alter. Sub-Saharan Africa's (static) comparative advantage therefore lies unquestionably with primary production – agricultural and, where possible, mineral (and petroleum) production and related unskilled-labour-intensive activities; and this will continue to be so for decades to come. Again, exceptions are Mauritius and South Africa.

But what does this imply for Africa's longer-run development and its future role in the global economy? Unskilled-labour-intensive activities can be a technological 'dead-end', unconducive to the productivity enhancement and indigenous learning upon which ongoing development is now generally believed to depend. Analysts from Adam Smith to Grossman and Helpmann (1991) have called attention to the risks attendant upon specialization in activities with few 'dynamizing' possibilities. Import-substituting industrialization, which has attracted so much opprobrium from mainstream economists, and was so imperfectly implemented, was motivated significantly by such theoretical (and practical) considerations. Yet we still know remarkably little about the potential 'dynamic' properties of different economic activities, and different degrees and forms of specialization. There is a corresponding vacuum in the theoretical and empirical literature on the appropriate government policy stance in circumstances where static comparative advantage clearly rests with primary activities, but where these activities are likely to be weak in 'development' effects.

To shed light on the possibilities of different 'dynamic' effects from different types of production the most obvious approach is the analysis of learning, productivity growth, externalities, scale economies and the like in industries and countries that have a history to analyse (Pack, 1992; ul Haque, 1995; Wangwe, 1995, 1998; Mayer, 1996; Mytelka and Tesfachew, 1998; Tybout, 1998; UNCTAD, 1998).

Leaving the precise nature of export specialization entirely to the market imparts a significant degree of randomness to the eventual export composition and overall product-mix in countries with comparative advantage in primary activities. Scale economies in processing, transport and marketing – even if such scale effects are weak in production – would generate locational decisions on the part of private investors, if they are left to make them alone, that concentrate investments and production in relatively few places rather than *wherever* the objective conditions would make them profitable (Krugman, 1989). Externalities may further encourage processes of concentration in the evolution of the 'geography' of international trade (Krugman, 1991). The literatures on the economics of infrastructure and on the locational decisions of transnational corporations (including that on investment incentives) are certainly relevant here.

There is therefore an *a priori* case, powerfully argued in Chapter 2, for conscious and selective governmental non-traditional export promotion. Successes and failures of others' efforts at encouraging non-traditional exports deserve analysis in Africa. From the standpoint of Africa's interests, experience in countries that, in relatively recent times, have successfully diversified their exports and thus their overall economies is likely to be most relevant; and that is the rationale for the non-African case material presented in Chapters 2–4 of this volume.

Concepts and definitions

The basis for any statistical measurement of 'non-traditional exports' will vary depending on why one considers the non-traditional character of exports to be important. One can, for instance, distinguish at least four different reasons for policy interest in non-traditional exports:

- The hope of finding new export products that are not as vulnerable to deteriorating terms of trade and/or declining world demand as are the traditional bundle of exports (e.g. Delgado, 1995)
- The hope that diversification in the export portfolio will reduce export instability and, more broadly, risk; diversification may, for these purposes, be achieved either through a new mix of products or via an expanded range of markets (e.g. Alwang and Siegel, 1994)
- The belief that certain new export products may generate greater 'dynamic' effects – learning, positive externalities, etc. – than traditional exports (e.g. Wangwe, 1995; Ernst et al., 1998)
- The prospect of exporting products that were previously produced within the country but not exported.

Clearly the search for more dynamic products (either in the sense of stronger world markets or broader productivity-raising effects) will require a different categorization of exports than the search for a more diversified export portfolio. No doubt this ambiguity as to the purposes of diversification into non-traditional exports helps to explain the fact that many different definitions of 'non-traditional exports' can be found in the literature. A great many studies have used the term 'non-traditional exports' in a qualitative way without defining it in precise quantitative terms. Such approaches can generate *ad hoc* and arbitrary lists of non-traditional exports; sometimes analyses of the same country can employ quite different lists of so-called non-traditional exports.

It is certainly desirable to try to identify products with different degrees of developmental and productivity-increasing effects (and some attempt has been made in what follows to do so) but these are difficult and controversial issues. Wood and Mayer's categorization of African exports, shown in Figures 1.1a and 1.1b, shows not only the standard broad trade and industrial categories (and how they differ) but also eight subcategories that are intended to shed light on these issues. Davies and Chipika, in their study of Zimbabwe (Chapter 10), express particular concern over these questions and argue that dynamism may be reflected in new markets as well as new products in the export bill.

Efforts to get at the 'dynamic' properties of different exports have typically been forced to resort to fairly crude categorizations, complicated further by the arbitrary and often inconsistent trade and industrial statistical systems in most frequent use (the SIC (Standard Industrial Classification) and SITC (Standard International Trade Classification) systems). (See Wood and Mayer, 1998, for a good discussion of these statistical issues.) Some have defined traditional exports of developing countries as food and raw materials excluding fuels (SITC 1-digit commodity groups 0, 1, 2 and 4). Non-traditional exports, in this formulation, therefore consist of manufactures and machinery (SITC groups 6, 7, 8 and 9) (Love, 1983: 7–9). Such a categorization obviously excludes the possibility of non-traditional primary exports, and it categorizes fuels and chemicals (SITC groups 3 and 5) separately. UNCTAD's recent analysis of the share of such 'manufactures' in African exports (it is unusually small by international standards) is obviously predicated upon the assumption that such exports have particularly desirable developmental characteristics (UNCTAD, 1998). In the end, since we were unable to shed much light on the possible developmental attributes of alternative forms of export production (this is an obvious area for further research), we abandoned the effort.

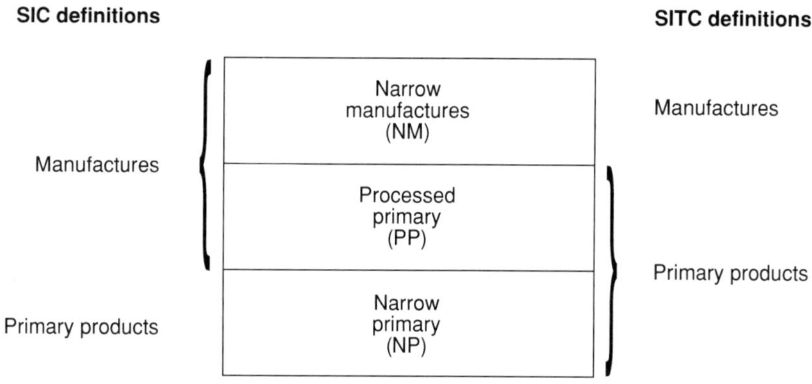

Figure 1.1a   Alternative export categorizations: three export categories

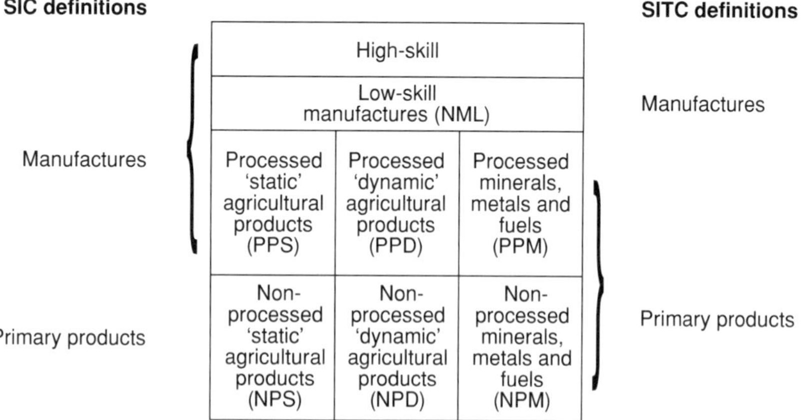

Figure 1.1b   Alternative export categorizations: eight export categories

Other attempts have been made to derive the dynamic *market* characteristics of different products based upon the growth of the Organization for Economic Cooperation and Development's (OECD) demands for different products (e.g. UNCTAD, 1996). In this approach, the most 'dynamic' products are those with both the most rapidly increasing OECD import demands and an increasing share in OECD imports, while the most 'stagnant' products are those with both lower rates of growth in OECD demand and a declining share therein. Such a demand-based definition has the major disadvantage of neglecting entirely the frequently important (and growing) trade with non-OECD members, not least other African countries. After some experimentation with this approach, we therefore also abandoned it.

Much less difficult and less controversial, although obviously also less useful, is the focus upon 'newness' of export products and/or market destinations. In the absence of agreed methodologies for assessing developmental and dynamic attributes of non-traditional exports, it is on the latter that the common approaches to this volume's African studies are based. We are painfully aware that sheer 'newness' is far from the whole story when it comes to the motivation for non-traditional export promotion.

Because of this agreed common approach, the definitions of non-traditional exports employed therein overlap to some degree with others' definitions of so-called 'minor' exports. Most quantitative analysts have employed *export share* thresholds to distinguish statistically between 'traditional' and 'non-traditional' exports. Agreement on such an approach still leaves lots of room for variation in detailed methodology. For instance, recent authors have defined non-traditional exports as those accounting for less than 1 per cent (Labys and Lord, 1990: 268), 5 per cent (de Vries, 1967: 9), 2 per cent (Balassa, 1977: 17), and 3 per cent (Balassa et al. 1971: 49–50). Most recently, in the World Bank's measurement of export diversification in its compendium of 'development indicators' (World Bank, 1997, and subsequent), it defines 'traditional exports' as the ten largest three-digit commodity groups in the country's exports in the base year (1983–4), unless those 10 do not account for at least 75 per cent of those exports, in which case more three-digit groups are added as necessary until at least 75 per cent is reached (1997: 259). Non-traditional exports are, by implication, all of the rest.

Following discussion among the project participants, it was decided that it would be most feasible to employ the following three measures of non-traditional exports (NTX):

- NTX1 – the definition of non-traditional exports as defined in conventional usage by the government within each country
- NTX2 – the World Bank definition of non-traditional exports described above
- NTX3 (our own somewhat arbitrary definition) – all goods exports accounting for less than 3 per cent of total exports in 1979–80 or 1980

plus exports of non-factor services (notably tourism). (Items not domestically produced were not included unless there was significant domestic value added; and in the case of South Africa, for some purposes gold was excluded from total exports.)

African data are notoriously unreliable and trade statistics are unfortunately no exception (Yeats, 1990). Export data, as recorded in African exporting countries, have generally been considered less reliable than the statistics of OECD member countries on their imports from African countries (Yeats, 1995). Intra-African trade data have no such checks on their reliability and are considered especially dubious in quality.

Despite much general discussion and even advocacy of the expansion of 'non-traditional exports', then, it seems that the precise meaning of this term is not agreed and the reasons for interest in them are varied. An important early conclusion of this study is that greater effort should be made to generate standardized definitions and measurement procedures if this term is to continue to be used in international discourse on trade and development. In particular, a clear distinction is required between 'minor' exports (those which are not of great relative size but may have a considerable history) and 'new' exports (which have no prior history in the country in question). Within the category of 'new' exports it is also important to distinguish between those previously produced only for home consumption and those which are truly innovative and presumably require new investments and skills. More fundamentally, many see 'non-traditional' activities as innovative in a deeper sense – involving a switch from primary or primary-based production to 'higher value added' activities involving more complex technology and skills; in short, as incorporating a shift to manufacturing activities and industrialization, and/or to exports with more dynamic demand prospects. It is small wonder, then, that a literature search uncovers so limited a yield of international studies of the development of non-traditional exports. Trade and development economists have not yet agreed on what exactly they are.

Objectives

The main objectives of the international research project of which this volume is the main product were twofold: (1) to draw on other developing countries' (specifically, East Asia, Chile and Costa Rica) experiences in the development of rapid and more diversified (non-traditional) export growth so as to inform today's African export policy discussion; and (2) to analyse recent experience in 'adjusting' Sub-Saharan African countries with a view to identifying key constraints on better export performance, particularly non-traditional export expansion, and policy requirements to overcome them. (There has been remarkably little written on individual African countries' experience in non-traditional exporting. An exception is Jebuni et al., 1992, on Ghana.)

The African case studies

With the limited availability of African data and the great variation in African experience it has proven extremely difficult to conduct detailed cross-country comparative analysis in the African context. Several proposed elements of the African country studies therefore had to be dropped.

Nine Sub-Saharan African countries were originally chosen for detailed analysis at the country level. Unfortunately, only five such analyses could be included in this volume. Burkina Faso had to be dropped because of severe data limitations there. Côte d'Ivoire, Ghana and Uganda were eventually dropped as well; in the case of Ghana, the existence of the earlier (Jebuni et al., 1992) study compensates somewhat for this.[1] The five countries retained for analysis in this volume are the following: Kenya, Mauritius, South Africa, Tanzania and Zimbabwe.

The basic characteristics of these economies are shown in Table 1.1. They are obviously *not* a random sample of African countries. They exclude countries severely affected by war or civil disturbance. They are all countries that have undertaken economic stabilization and structural adjustment to some degree, with a fairly wide range of success (or failure). Their initial conditions, e.g. per capita income, vary widely, with South Africa and Mauritius at the top and Tanzania at the low end. Total exports grew more rapidly in the 1990s than in the 1980s in three of the five countries; but gross national product (GNP) growth also fell in three of the five countries (obviously not the same three) in the 1990s. The quality of investment and savings data is often weak but it is clear that of these five countries only Mauritius had savings and investment rates that might sustain rapid economic growth.

The base period for all of these African analyses is 1980, immediately after the second oil price shock and prior to the widespread adoption of structural adjustment programmes in Africa. Export promotion and trade liberalization have been prominent features of these programmes (Soludo, 1998). Each African country's analysis undertakes to explain the record of recent export performance, particularly performance in non-traditional exporting, in the context of this recent policy experience (as well as other elements of policy), and to analyse the current constraints on such performance. Particular attention is devoted to the distinction between incentive systems and other supports and supportive institutions, e.g. credit, for the expansion of non-traditional exports (Nissanke, 1998). Special efforts have been made to understand the role of new investment, if any, in such non-traditional export expansion as has taken place. (Among the important findings of this research

Table 1.1 Basic economic characteristics, selected African countries

	Annual average GNP per capita (constant US$)[a]		Annual average GDP growth rate, real (%)			Annual average growth rate of total exports (constant US$) (%)		Annual average GDI[b]/GDP (%)			Annual average GDS[c]/GDP (%)	
								Total	Total	Private		
	1975–84	1990s	1975–84	1985–9	1990–9	1980–90	1990–9	1990–6	1999	1990–6	1990–6	1999
Kenya	340	315	4.7	5.9	2.2	4.4	0.4	20.2	20	11.0	18.1	14
Mauritius	1,073	3,154	3.6	7.7	5.2[d]	24.5[e, f]	7.0[d, f]	28.8	n.a.	19.2	24.2	n.a.
South Africa	2,119	3,278	2.6	1.6	1.9	1.9	5.3	16.4	16	12.4[e]	19.3	18
Tanzania	n.a.	178	n.a.	n.a.	3.1	1.6[e, f]	9.5	23.4	18	n.a.	–0.5	14
Zimbabwe	865	750	3.0	4.2	2.4	4.3	11.0	22.2	18	19.3	19.1	15

Notes:

[a] 1987 prices.

[b] Gross domestic investment.

[c] Gross domestic savings.

[d] 1990–6.

[e] 1985–9.

[f] Current US$.

Sources: World Bank, *African Development Indicators, 1998*; World Bank, *World Development Report, 2000*.

12

has been that data on such investment, or on firm-level performance in the export sector more generally, are very hard to come by.)

Organization of this volume

The analysis of non-traditional export promotion and performance is presented in this volume in two parts. Part I begins with three chapters on non-African countries' experience and the key issues raised. In particular, attention is devoted to the lessons from the East Asian experience and those from Chile and Costa Rica. In these analyses, attention is directed not only to the general policy approaches to the encouragement of non-traditional exports but also, most importantly for the African debate today, the more selective policies for export promotion that have been pursued. Part I concludes with an original cross-country econometric analysis of the role of the real exchange rate and other influences in the development of non-traditional exports (NTX2) in a wide sample of developing countries.

Part II is devoted to the performance of five African countries in the export sector from 1980 onwards, with particular attention to policies and experience with respect to non-traditional exports. Here, local authors employ elements of a common framework developed through discussions among themselves, and discussed in part above, but also introduce particular country-specific elements to their individual chapters.

Summary and conclusions

Non-African experience

What do the studies of other developing countries in Part I have to say that may be relevant to Sub-Saharan Africa's export, particularly non-traditional export, prospects? In East Asia, Chile, Costa Rica and other developing countries, non-traditional export success was associated with a number of aspects of economic experience and policy that are worth noting.

- An appropriate and stable real exchange rate, typically itself associated with relatively stable macroeconomic conditions, has been associated with rapid growth in non-traditional exports both in the East Asian and Latin American case studies and in the econometric analysis of the experience of a much larger sample of developing countries. (The same result was found in our analytically comparable analysis of *total* exports but the details are not reported here.) The need for this maintenance of an appropriate real exchange rate argues against complete capital account liberalization.
- The East Asian and Latin American case studies do not support the proposition that generalized import liberalization, of itself, is

necessarily important to non-traditional export success. The degree of anti-export bias, on the other hand, typically *is* important to such success. Special incentives to non-traditional exports, including import duty drawbacks or rebates, undoubtedly *were* usually associated with success.

- In East Asian, Chilean and Costa Rican experience, conscious governmental policies were implemented to strengthen indigenous capacities to produce potential new exports competitively. These took the forms both of general factor market interventions (e.g. strengthened infrastructure, technological training, research support, etc.) and of unique institutions, incentives and arrangements specifically to assist exporters, and particularly non-traditional exporters. The econometric investigation of a larger sample of developing countries also found evidence suggestive of the importance to non-traditional export success of supply-side (capability) factors, over which policy may have influence, such as the quality of human capital (schooling), investment in machinery and well-functioning factor markets.

- Selective governmental intervention in support of particular forms of non-traditional exporting activity – both through special incentives and through other types of encouragement and support, including specific training and research, credit, and marketing assistance – were important to the development of non-traditional exports in East Asia, Chile and Costa Rica.

- The role of multinational corporations and their direct investments varied greatly in the non-traditional export experience of the East Asian and Latin American cases studied in this volume. They played a major role in non-traditional export development in Malaysia, Singapore and Costa Rica. Foreign direct investment (FDI) played a part in Chile, Hong Kong, Indonesia and Thailand but was less important (though foreign buying firms still usually played an important role) in Korea and Taiwan. To attract FDI, governmental policies were 'friendly' but that is not to say that they were *laissez-faire*. Except in Hong Kong, governments were active in attempting to encourage FDI into 'priority' sectors while restricting it elsewhere.

- While non-traditional export experience in Asia and Latin America may be highly relevant to Africa's future, clearly it offers no 'quick and easy' lessons. The initial conditions differ markedly across countries. The capabilities of potential exporters and the supportive infrastructure in Sub-Saharan African circumstances are often uniquely weak. Investment rates are typically low. Governmental capacity for sustained and effective economic development policymaking is also often lacking; and aid donors and international financial institutions, with agendas of their own, frequently 'drive' the development policymaking process.

African experience

As noted above, the five African countries studied here are not intended to portray the full range of African experience.

- Non-traditional exports, however defined, grew at rapid rates in each of the five African countries studied here. Kenyan NTX3 grew at 20 per cent per annum from 1980 to 1996; NTX1 grew at 15.6 per cent annually in Mauritius from 1981 to 1997, and at 17 per cent annually in Tanzania from 1986 to 1997. Non-traditional exports increased significantly in relative importance, both in total exports and in total GDP, in each of these African countries from the early 1980s onward. By the second half of the 1990s, NTX3 was valued at 24.6 per cent of GDP in Kenya, 41 per cent in Mauritius and 14.1 to 16.8 per cent in South Africa (depending on whether gold is included in the export total in the definition of NTX3 in that country). (Value added in non-traditional exporting activity is much less than suggested in these numbers where, as in Mauritius, imports make up an important share of gross export value.) In Tanzania, however, NTX1 was still only 5.2 per cent of GDP in the 1990s. In South Africa and Zimbabwe NTX3 by this time made up half or more of total export value. Overall export concentration fell after 1980, both in terms of commodities and of country destinations, in all five countries.
- In Mauritius, South Africa and, to some extent, Zimbabwe there was considerable non-traditional exporting of manufactured products which may potentially have more 'dynamic' characteristics. The bulk of the non-traditional exporting in Kenya and Tanzania was found in primary production, primary processing and tourism.
- The real exchange rate was associated with successful non-traditional export performance in African countries as elsewhere. In the Tanzanian case study, time series econometric analysis found a statistically significant relationship between real devaluation (and also reduction in anti-export bias) and non-traditional export growth. In the other African countries (including Kenya, where no statistical relationship between the real exchange rate and non-traditional exports could be found) the real value of the currency was sustained at or near its 'fundamental' value throughout periods of non-traditional export growth. None of the five African countries could be said, however, to have engaged in conscious real currency undervaluation, as might be indicated, for instance, by accumulation of foreign exchange reserves.
- All of the five African countries offered general incentives specifically to encourage non-traditional exports. These took a variety of forms including direct subsidies, more liberal foreign exchange retention allowances, import duty rebates, income tax concessions, ready and/or

subsidized credit and the establishment of export processing zones (EPZs). Generalized import liberalization formed an element in all of these countries' adjustment programmes but, as elsewhere, it seems to have been, of itself, only sporadically important (e.g. in Kenya in 1993–5) to the creation of relevant incentives for non-traditional exports. More directed export incentives were typically of greater significance in this respect.

- African governments have typically *not* developed strong supply-side supports, either general or selective, to encourage *investment* in non-traditional exports, comparable to those employed in South-East Asia or Latin America. Overall investment rates, averaging 16–23 per cent of GDP in the 1990s, remain well below those necessary for sustained rapid overall economic growth in all of these African countries except Mauritius; and even in Mauritius the investment rate has recently fallen (to around 25 per cent of GDP). Weak infrastructure, limited access to credit, and limited support for relevant human capacity-building have undoubtedly inhibited African success with non-traditional exports, as with other dimensions of growth and development.

- Relative to the East Asian and Latin American cases studied in this volume, the five African countries do not appear to have made as much effort at *selective* non-traditional export promotion. But there are nevertheless, as noted above, examples of such selective promotion in these African studies, e.g. special supports for tourism in all five countries, for particular elements of processing and manufacturing in South Africa, etc. Again, limited resources and human capacities undoubtedly constrained the efficacy of public policies in Africa, whatever may have been governmental intentions; particularly was this so in such extremely poor countries as Tanzania.

- Export processing zones were *not* important contributors to non-traditional export success, except in the dramatic case of Mauritius where they were a dominant influence. Other constraints evidently limited their attraction to investors in the other four African countries, each of which experimented with EPZs (albeit somewhat hesitantly) with, at least so far, only very limited effect. It is possible to argue, however, as some do, that EPZs will have greater potential if they are given both more support and more time.

- When major non-traditional 'success' was realized, as in Mauritius, there was a long lag between the policy changes that appear to 'explain' it and their positive effects. In Mauritius it took many years from the initiation of the explicit 'export push' before rapid non-traditional export expansion began.

- Foreign direct investment has not as yet made a particularly important contribution to African non-traditional export expansion. Even in the Mauritius EPZ experience domestic investment was dominant.

Elsewhere there is little firm evidence of significant long-term private investment, whether domestic or foreign, in non-traditional exporting; but, as noted above, the absence of good firm-level investment data seriously inhibits analysis of this question.

From the experience described in Parts I and II of this volume, there is room for considerably greater optimism about African non-traditional export prospects than has customarily been expressed in analyses of Africa's economic problems. (A recent, more optimistic, assessment, however, may be found in World Bank, 2000: 212–21.) Non-traditional exports are obviously not a development panacea. Without minimizing the extent of the many current constraints on Africa's economic growth and development, or overstating the representativeness of the five African countries studied in this volume, it is possible to say not only that non-traditional exports *can* respond to official policies that support and promote them, but also that in many African countries they have already done so.

For the effective promotion of non-traditional exports African governments will have to pursue policies that are not merely 'permissive' – a stable macroeconomic framework, an appropriate level and stability of the real exchange rate, adequate export incentives, a friendly investment climate (but caution with capital account liberalization), etc. They will also have to pursue more 'activist' policies to overcome continuing weaknesses in infrastructure and human capital and, more particularly, to offer selective further support for those non-traditional exports with the most promising developmental and market prospects. Such activist policies require knowledge and resources; and in Africa these are both usually in short supply. To maximize effectiveness, it is likely to be fruitful for governments to work closely with potential investors in the private sector as they develop strategies and policies for non-traditional export expansion. African governments can also benefit from information-sharing and other forms of regional cooperation, including trade and exchange liberalization among themselves, at the regional or subregional levels. Needless to say, and as noted earlier, access for African export products on world markets will also be essential for sustained non-traditional export success.

With appropriate national and international policies, increased investments (both public and private) and improved overall domestic capacities, one should be able to expect better and more widespread non-traditional export success in Africa in the future. Sustained private investment will clearly be critical to long-run success. In the meantime it will be important for policymakers that more research be undertaken on the developmental advantages of different kinds of export activity so as to increase conceptual clarity as to what non-traditional exports it may be most efficacious to promote.

Acknowledgements

For comments on earlier drafts I am grateful to Anthony Black, Ibrahim Elbadawi, Francis Mwega, and two anonymous WIDER-appointed referees, none of whom are responsible in any way for the contents of the final version.

Note

1. Draft studies of Côte d'Ivoire and Uganda can be obtained from WIDER on request.

References

Alwang, J. and Siegel, P. B. (1994) 'Portfolio Models and Planning for Export Diversification: Malawi, Tanzania and Zimbabwe', *Journal of Development Studies*, 30, 2 (January).

Amjadi, A., Reinke, U. and Yeats, A. (1996) 'Did External Barriers Cause the Marginalization of Sub-Saharan Africa in World Trade?', Policy Research Working Paper 1586, World Bank International Economics Department (March).

Balassa, B. (1977) *Export Incentives and Export Performance in Developing Countries: A Comparative Analysis*, World Bank Staff Working Paper No. 248, Washington, DC.

Balassa, B. et al. (1971) *The Structure of Protection in Developing Countries*, Baltimore, MD: Johns Hopkins University Press.

Berge, K., Daniel, P. et al. (1994) 'Trade and Development Strategy Options for the Poorest Countries: A Preliminary Investigation', Working Paper 12, Institute of Development Studies, Sussex (December).

Buffie, E. (forthcoming) *Trade Policy in Developing Countries*.

Coe, D. and Hoffmaister, A. W. (1998) 'North–South Trade: Is Africa Unusual?', IMF Working Paper 98/94, Washington, DC.

Collier, P. and Gunning, J. W. with associates (1998) *Trade Shocks in Developing Countries: Theory and Evidence*, Oxford: Oxford University Press/Clarendon.

Collier, P. and Gunning, J. W. (1999) 'Explaining African Economic Performance', *Journal of Economic Literature*, 37, 1 (March): 64–111.

Delgado, C. L. (1995) 'Agricultural Diversification and Export Promotion in Sub-Saharan Africa', *Food Policy*, 20, 3 (June).

de Vries, Barend A. (1967) *The Export Experience of Developing Countries*, World Bank Staff Occasional Papers No. 3, Washington, DC.

Easterly, W., Kremer, M., Pritchett, L. and Summers, L. (1993) 'Good Policy or Good Luck? Country Growth Performance and Temporary Shocks', *Journal of Monetary Economics*, 32: 459–83.

Elbadawi, I. and Helleiner, G. K. (1998) 'African Development in the Context of New World Trade and Financial Regimes: The Role of the WTO and its Relationship to the World Bank and the IMF', African Economic Research Consortium, Nairobi, mimeo.

Elbadawi, I. and Ndulu, B. J. (1996) 'Long-Run Development and Sustainable Growth in Sub-Saharan Africa' in M. Lundahl and B. J. Ndulu (eds), *New Directions in Development Economics*, London: Routledge.

Ernst, D., Ganiatsos, T. and Mytelka, L. (eds) (1998) *Technological Capabilities and Export Success in Asia*, London: Routledge.

Foroutan, F. and Pritchett, L. (1993) 'Intra-Sub-Saharan Trade: Is it Little?' *Journal of African Economies*, 2, 1.

Grossman, G. and Helpmann, E. (1991) *Innovation and Growth in the Global Economy*, Cambridge, MA: MIT Press.

Hadjimichael, M. T., Ghura, D., Mühleisen, M., Nord, R. and Uçer, E. M. (1995) 'Sub-Saharan Africa: Growth, Savings and Investment', IMF Occasional Paper 118, Washington, DC.

Helleiner, G. K. (1992) 'Structural Adjustment and Long-Term Development in Sub-Saharan Africa' in F. Stewart, S. Lall and S. Wangwe (eds), *Alternative Development Strategies in Sub-Saharan Africa*, London: Macmillan, pp. 48–78.

Helleiner, G. K. (1995) 'Trade, Trade Policy and Industrialization Reconsidered', *World Development Studies*, 6, WIDER, Helsinki.

Jebuni, C. D. et al. (1992) *Diversifying Exports, the Supply Response of Non-Traditional Exports to Ghana's Economic Recovery Programme*, Overseas Development Institute and University of Ghana.

Kaplan, D. and Kaplinsky, R. (1999) 'Trade and Industrial Policy on an Uneven Playing Field: The Case of the Deciduous Fruit-Canning Industry in South Africa', *World Development* (October).

Killick, T. (1995) 'Flexibility and Economic Progress', *World Development* (May).

Krugman, P. (1989) 'New Trade Theory and the Less Developed Countries', in G. Calvo, R. Findlay, P. Kouri and J. De Macedo (eds), *Debt, Stabilization and Development, Essays in Memory of Carlos Diaz-Alejandro*, Oxford: Basil Blackwell and WIDER, pp. 347–65.

Krugman, P. (1991) *Geography and Trade*, Cambridge, MA: MIT Press.

Labys, W. C. and Lord, M. J. (1990) 'Portfolio Optimisation and the Design of Latin American Export Diversification Policies', *Journal of Development Studies*, 26, 2 (January): 260–77.

Lall, S. (1995) 'Structural Adjustment and African Industry', *World Development*, 23, 12 (December).

Lall, S. and Wangwe, S. (1998) 'Industrial Policy and Industrialization in Sub-Saharan Africa', *Journal of African Economies*, 7, supp. 1 (June).

Love, J. (1986) 'Concentration, Diversification and Earnings Instability: Some Evidence on Developing Countries' Exports of Manufactures and Primary Products', *World Development*, 11, 9: 787–93.

Lyakurwa, W. L. (1991) 'Trade Policy and Promotion in Sub-Saharan Africa', AERC Special Paper 12 (May), African Economic Research Consortium, Nairobi.

Mayer, J. (1996) 'Implications of New Trade and Endogenous Growth Theory for Diversification Policies of Commodity-Dependent Countries' *UNCTAD Discussion Paper No. 122* (December).

Mkandawire, T. and Soludo, C. C. (1999) *Our Continent, Our Future*, Dakar; Ottawa; Trenton, NJ: CODESRIA; IDRC; Africa World Press.

Mytelka, L. K. and Tesfachew, T. (1998) 'The Role of Policy in Promoting Enterprise Learning During Early Industrialization: Lessons for African Countries', UNCTAD, African Development in a Comparative Perspective, Study No. 7 (September).

Nissanke, M. K. (1998) 'Financing Enterprise Development and Export Diversification in Sub-Saharan Africa', UNCTAD, African Development in a Comparative Perspective, Study No. 8 (September).

Ocampo, J. A. (1991) 'The Transition from Primary Exports to Industrial Development in Colombia' in M. Blomström and P. Meller (eds), *Diverging Paths, Comparing a Century of Scandinavian and Latin American Economic Development*, Washington, DC: Inter-American Development Bank.

Oyejide, T. A. (1998) 'Using Trade and Industrial Policies to Foster African Development: Some Perspectives on Issues and Modalities', *Journal of African Economies*, 7, supp. 1 (June).

Pack, H. (1992) 'Learning and Productivity Change in Developing Countries' in G. K. Helleiner (ed.), *Trade Policy, Industrialization and Development: New Perspectives*, Oxford: Clarendon Press, for World Institute for Development Economics Research, pp. 21–45.

Rodriguez, F. and Rodrik, D. (1999) 'Trade Policy and Economic Growth: A Skeptic's Guide to the Cross-National Evidence', University of Maryland and Harvard University, mimeo.

Rodrik, D. (1997) 'Trade Policy and Economic Performance in Sub-Saharan Africa', Harvard University. Paper prepared for the Division of International Cooperation of the Ministry for Foreign Affairs, Sweden (November).

Rodrik, D. (1999) *The New Global Economy and Developing Countries: Making Openness Work*, Policy Essay No. 24, Washington, DC: Overseas Development Council; Baltimore, MD: Johns Hopkins University Press.

Sachs, J. D. and Warner, A. M. (1997) 'Sources of Slow Growth in African Economies', *Journal of African Economies*, 6: 335–76.

Soludo, C. C. (1998) 'Trade Policy Reforms and Supply Responses in Africa', UNCTAD, African Development in a Comparative Perspective, Study No. 6 (September).

Tybout, J. (1998) 'Manufacturing Firms in Developing Countries: How Well Do They Do and Why?', Working Paper No. 97–19R, Georgetown University, Department of Economics (June).

ul Haque, I. in collaboration with others (1995) *Trade Technology and International Competitiveness*, Economic Development Institute of the World Bank, Washington, DC.

UNCTAD (1996) *Trade and Development Report*.

UNCTAD (1998) *Trade and Development Report*.

Wangwe, S. M. (1995) *Exporting Africa: Technology, Trade and Industrialization in Sub-Saharan Africa*, UNU/Intech Studies in New Technology, London and New York: Routledge.

Wangwe, S. (1998) 'How African Manufacturing Industries Can Break Into Export Markets with Lessons from East Asia', UNCTAD, African Development in a Comparative Perspective, Study No. 5 (September).

Wood, A. (1994) 'Skill, Land and Trade: A Simple Analytical Framework', IDS Working Paper 1 (February), Sussex.

Wood, A. and Berge, K. (1994) 'Exporting Manufactures: Trade Policy or Human Resources?' IDS Working Paper 4 (July), Sussex.

Wood, A. and Mayer, J. (1998) 'Africa's Economic Structure in Comparative Perspective', UNCTAD, African Development in a Comparative Perspective, Study No. 4 (September).

World Bank (1994) *Adjustment in Africa: Reforms, Results, and the Road Ahead*, Oxford: Oxford University Press.

World Bank (1997) *World Development Indicators, 1997*, Washington, DC.

World Bank (1998) *African Development Indicators, 1998*, Washington, DC.

World Bank (2000) *Can Africa Claim the Twenty-First Century?*, Washington, DC.

Yeats, A. J. (1990) 'On the Accuracy of Economic Observations: Do Sub-Saharan Trade Statistics Mean Anything?', *World Bank Economic Review*, 4: 135–56.

Yeats, A. J. (1995) 'Are Partner-Countries Statistics Useful for Estimating "Missing" Trade Data?', Policy Research Working Paper 1501, World Bank International Economics Department (August).

Part I
Non-African Experience and Issues

2
Selective Policies for Export Promotion: Lessons from the Asian Tigers

Sanjaya Lall

Introduction: setting the scene

This chapter considers the rationale for and limitations to selective export promotion policies in developing countries. It draws upon the experience of the most successful exporters in the developing world – the Asian 'Tigers' and 'new Tigers' – to illustrate the policy needs of upgrading and 'dynamizing' comparative advantage. It then considers the practical difficulties in designing and implementing selective policies. The focus here is on *manufactured* exports (a reflection of the background of the author, not a belief that these are preferable to other non-traditional exports).

In theory, export promotion policies, like all interventions, are justified by the presence of market failures.[1] Export promotion policies can, however, be divided into two groups according to the nature of the failure: first, to *remove distortions created by policies that deter exporting*, and, second, to *overcome structural market deficiencies in the creation of new advantages*. The distinction between them may not always be firm or clear, but it is useful for analysing the case for selective promotion policies to make it. Each set of policies can be further subdivided according to different interpretations placed on the efficiency of markets and governments.

1. The first group essentially comprises policy reforms (we may call these *'permissive' policies*) to reduce macro policy mismanagement and uncertainty, make exporting profitable and minimize transactions costs to exporters. Typically, these involve removing or offsetting overvalued exchange rates or high rates of domestic protection (though not necessarily moving to free trade); policy volatility and uncertainty; inflation and high interest rates; price ceilings or taxes on, and inefficient marketing of, exportable primary products; cumbersome or biased procedures on entry, exit, finance or trade;

segmented or poorly functioning labour markets, and so on. There are two ways to interpret these policies. The first is simply to treat permissive policies as the reduction of biases against exports and improvement in macro management. This is uncontroversial, and has no further implications for other policies on industry, exports or factor markets – in this broad sense, such policies are accepted by everyone concerned with export promotion.

However, it is possible to take the argument further, and to suggest that permissive policies are *all* that is required by way of export promotion: governments should eschew all interventions in resource allocation, implement free trade and practise minimalism. This is the 'strong' neoclassical position, based on assumptions that markets are efficient and that 'getting prices right' is necessary *and sufficient* for an economy to reach optimality in world trade. In this strong position, since this 'optimum' represents the ideal level and structure of a country's exports at each point of time, no further export promotion policies are needed. Neither functional nor selective measures are therefore justified.

This extreme position has been held by some economists, but is unlikely to appeal today to most analysts of trade or to policymakers. Most would accept that failures do exist in many product and factor markets, and that governments often need to mount more positive measures to promote export expansion and diversification (in addition, obviously, to having the necessary permissive policies). This brings us to the second set of 'positive' promotion policies.

2. *'Positive' policies* intend to tackle the costs and deficiencies in stimulating new areas of competitive export activity: raising the quality, technology and cost competitiveness of existing or new activities; helping smaller enterprises to enter international markets; enhancing the domestic content of exports; lowering the information costs on new markets and of setting up marketing and distribution systems; creating a good 'image' of a country's products in world markets, etc. These 'positive' policies can be subdivided into *functional* and *selective* interventions. Functional (or 'market friendly') interventions remedy market failures without influencing resource allocation between specific activities. These include actions, for instance, to improve the physical infrastructure, capital markets or general human capital, or to provide information and technical support to potential exporters.[2] Selective policies do intend to influence resource allocation, by protection or export subsidies, credit direction, creation of specific skills or technologies, promoting large firms or particular types of small firms, attracting specific investors and the like.

At first sight, functional policies are, like permissive ones, also fairly uncontroversial. All analysts would agree with the need to strengthen infrastructure and other factor markets in developing countries. It is selective policies that arouse controversy, part of the larger industrial policy debate between the 'market friendly' and structuralist or 'revisionist' schools.[3] It is important, in this context, to note that the *market friendly approach* (as an approach) is different from a case for functional policies as part of a larger strategy. The approach is a moderate version of the strong neoclassical philosophy described above. It accepts that *some* markets function imperfectly and thus are deficient, but takes a particular view of which of such market failures are important and can or should be addressed in policy. It tends to interlace its economic analysis with political judgement on what governments are or are not capable of doing (Shapiro and Taylor, 1990). It concludes that only the failures that call for functional interventions should be addressed, i.e. that failures that require selectivity are either unimportant or cannot be remedied, and/or that where selectivity is required governments are incapable of devising or implementing the remedies. In other words, either the cost of market failures 'of the selective kind' is low enough not to matter, or the cost of government failures invariably outweighs them. The structuralist approach, by contrast, is that market failures, of both functional and selective kinds, are important and pervasive, that remedies to both can be devised and implemented and that, therefore, governments have a more crucial role to play than accepted in the market friendly approach.

The market friendly approach represents the mainstream view of development. On trade policy, its stance is described as follows by Helleiner:

> Trade policy in this dominant view, which was effectively summarized in World Bank, 1991 and 1987, is a fundamental determinant of economic performance, and it functions best when it attempts the least ... Domestic goods prices should closely approximate world prices, except in a narrowly limited range of cases, notably where countries possess market power (are not 'small') in the world markets for their principal exports. Government interventions should be few and, where they are made, should be unselective as between different forms of economic activity, leaving their impact as 'neutral' as possible. They should, in general, employ 'market friendly' policy instruments, like subsidies or taxes, rather than administrative instruments, like quantitative controls. These trade policies are assumed to be universally appropriate and should be introduced as rapidly as possible. Liberal policies regarding the inflow of services, technology and capital are also recommended as part of this universally applicable set of appropriate policies. (Helleiner, 1995b: 2)

This chapter has to consider some of the more general arguments for selectivity as part of the analysis of selective export promotion policies. The approach adopted is deductive. We look first at the *evidence* of effective export promotion, and at the literature on enterprise development and 'learning' in developing countries, to infer the nature of market failures that affect export development. This is because received theory, with an oversimplified view of how competitive advantages are developed, offers little *a priori* guidance on the processes and market failures concerned. We then consider qualifications to the case for intervention: government failure, the limited transferability of experiences across countries, and the changing international rules of the trade and investment game that increasingly constrain the use of selective instruments.

Export promotion policies in the Asian Tigers

The effectiveness of export promotion policies can be judged only by their effects. Thus, the most effective were presumably in the countries with the most rapid recent growth and diversification of exports: the 'Tiger' economies of Asia. This chapter looks at seven of these – the four 'Tigers' (Hong Kong, Singapore, Korea and Taiwan) and the three 'new Tigers' (Malaysia, Thailand and Indonesia). It is important to note that, while all these countries were 'export oriented' in a broad sense, they had very different approaches to export promotion. This reflected their governments' different objectives, which led them to identify different constraints (i.e. market failures) and to employ different strategies to overcome those constraints. The following two subsections sketch the main differences in their achievements and the strategies used.

Export growth and related efforts

Export growth and structure

Here I present export data to illustrate the technological and other efforts underlying the growth and diversification of manufactured exports from East Asia. Several indicators of export dynamism are used to bring out the inter-country differences. This is followed by data on different measures of domestic effort related to competitiveness development.

Let us start with aggregate figures on merchandise and manufactured exports by seven Asian countries.

Table 2.1 shows that in 1994 the largest exporters, both of merchandise and manufactures, were Korea, Taiwan, Malaysia and Singapore.[4] The fastest rates of growth in 1990–4 were for Thailand, Indonesia, Malaysia and Singapore. Hong Kong was the only country in the group with declining exports (re-exports excluded), a dramatic deterioration on its earlier performance. Of the larger Tigers, Korea had a stronger performance than Taiwan. The general dynamism of exports suggests considerable and widespread underlying capability development. However, this is misleading.

These data reveal little about the *nature* and *determinants* of export dynamism. They do not, for instance, distinguish between different export structures, or differing levels of technology within given product groups. Nor do they distinguish between exports by foreign and domestic firms. All these are important in that they may be based upon different local technological efforts and competence, which in turn may involve different market failures and policy needs. Let us try to remedy these as best we can, by looking at the structure, local technological content of exports and the role of FDI in trade.

Table 2.1   Merchandise exports from selected Asian countries (1994)

| Country | Merchandise Exports | | | Manufactured Exports |
	Value (US$m)	Growth rate (1980–90)	Growth rate (1990–4)	Value (US$m)
Hong Kong*	28,739	11.5	–0.3	27,302
Singapore*	57,963	12.1	10.9	56,224
Korea	96,000	13.7	7.4	89,280
Taiwan	92,847	11.6	5.9	86,348
Indonesia	40,054	5.3	21.3	21,229
Malaysia	58,756	11.5	17.8	41,129
Thailand	45,262	14.3	21.6	33,041

*Excluding re-exports.

Sources: Asian Development Bank, *Key Indicators of Developing Asian and Pacific Countries*, 1994; *Hong Kong External Trade*, February, 1996; *Singapore Trade Statistics*, 1996; World Bank, *World Development Report*, 1996.

Let us start with the *technological composition* of manufactured exports. There are numerous ways to categorize this. The most frequently used one, 'high' and 'low' technology, is too aggregated and can conceal interesting differences between developing countries that are largely exporting simple products. A breakdown by technological characteristics, as shown in Table 2.2, is more useful.

Table 2.2   Technological basis of manufactured exports

Activity group	Major competitive factor	Examples	OECD exports 1985 (%)
Resource-intensive	Access to natural resources	Aluminium smelting, oil refining	13.5
Labour-intensive	Costs of unskilled or semi-skilled labour	Garments, footwear, toys	9.8
Scale-intensive	Length of production runs	Steel, chemicals, auto-mobiles, paper	33.8
Differentiated	Products tailored to varied demands	Machinery, power equipment	27.3
Science-based	Rapid application of science to technology	Electronics, biotechnology, medicines	15.5

Source: OECD, 1987.

The breakdown is far from perfect. Categories may overlap (resource-based activities can be very capital-intensive) or be very broad (many electronics exports are labour-intensive). However, the classification is plausible and helpful if carefully used. Labour-intensive products are generally at the low end of the technology and skill spectrum. Products in the scale-intensive group tend to use complex, capital-intensive technologies, but are generally not at the cutting edge of technology. Here we should distinguish between process (e.g. chemicals) and engineering (e.g. automobiles) industries; the latter tend to have more difficult learning requirements, be very linkage-intensive, and involve a larger variety of skills. 'Differentiated' products are sophisticated capital goods involving advanced design, research and manu-facturing skills, while 'science-based' products use leading edge technologies. We classify the last three categories as *technologically advanced*, and the last two as *high-tech*, products.

Table 2.3 gives the technological breakdown of manufactured exports for these countries since 1980. The highest ratio of labour-intensive exports (primarily textiles and garments) is currently in Hong Kong (54 per cent), followed by Indonesia (49 per cent) and Thailand (38 per cent). With industrial development there is a general tendency for the share of labour-intensive products to decline, but in Indonesia this share has risen over time (because of a rapid relocation of garment and plywood processing activities from the newly industrializing economies (NIEs) in response to rising costs, with Indonesia offering by far the lowest wages in the group).

Acknowledging the inherent problems of aggregation and categorization, the results are still plausible and useful, supporting prior impressions about technological capabilities in these countries. However, some adjustments have to be made to these indicators to assess the *domestic technological and other effort* involved in upgrading exports – this is what is needed in order to understand the relevant policies and market failures. We have to look, in particular, at the level of technology involved and the role of multinational corporations (MNCs) in exports, as well as local technological activity and human resource development.

Level of technology

The local technological content of similar exports can vary between countries, according to the level and extent of local inputs of components, equipment and technical knowledge. A 'high-tech' export from one country may come from assembled imported components, with few local inputs, physical or technological; in another, it may have substantial local equipment, components, design, development and engineering. These show different capabilities, and may have very different policy implications. The Tigers differ greatly in this respect. Malaysia's high-tech exports are driven primarily by electronics and electrical assembly activity in export enclaves; while there has certainly been upgrading in process and product technology,

Table 2.3   Distribution of manufactured exports by technological categories, selected Asian countries, 1980 and 1993/4 (%)

	Hong Kong		Singapore		Korea		Taiwan		Malaysia		Thailand		Indonesia	
	1980	*1994*	*1980*	*1994*	*1980*	*1994*	*1980*	*1994*	*1980*	*1993*	*1980*	*1993*	*1980*	*1993*
Resource-based	2.0	3.7	6.5	3.3	7.3	3.8	9.4	6.8	11.0	5.4	53.9	20.1	14.7	29.5
Labour-intensive	65.8	54.3	16.9	8.5	49.5	27.8	53.9	32.7	18.4	17.4	28.4	38.3	28.9	48.7
Scale-intensive	1.2	4.2	20.9	10.5	25.8	27.2	9.4	13.9	4.9	5.3	4.3	5.6	20.2	7.6
Differentiated	16.7	21.4	50.3	46.3	14.7	35.6	23.7	30.9	60.1	29.6	13.4	15.7	19.0	7.6
Science-based	14.3	16.4	5.4	31.4	2.7	5.6	3.6	15.8	3.8	42.3	0.0	20.3	0.0	0.9
Subtotals														
Tech. advanced	32.2	42.0	76.6	88.2	43.2	68.4	36.7	60.6	68.8	77.2	17.7	41.6	39.2	16.1
High-tech	31.0	37.8	55.7	77.7	17.4	41.2	27.3	46.7	63.9	71.9	13.4	36.0	19.0	8.5

Note: Singapore and Hong Kong data are for total manufactured exports including re-exports; the UN data do not allow own exports to be distinguished from re-exports. The last year for Malaysia, Thailand and Indonesia is 1993.

Source: UN trade data. The classification is at the two-digit SITC level.

there are still few domestic linkages and very low local technological inputs (World Bank, 1996). Singapore's exports are also driven by MNCs, but processes and products are at a higher level of sophistication, using more advanced skills and involving greater local technological activity. However, Singapore's levels of design and development are still low, with the critical elements done overseas by the MNCs involved.

By contrast, high-tech exports from Korea and Taiwan have significant local supply linkages (both for equipment and components) and technological inputs to basic design stages. Korea is ahead of Taiwan, with a more diverse and 'heavier' industrial structure and greater research and development (R&D) effort. Of the Tigers, Hong Kong has the lowest technological input, remaining specialized in light consumer goods (though within these there has been upgrading); in addition, even its 'high technology' exports are simpler than in the other Tigers (consisting largely of electronic items like games and watches). Thailand is also basically at the assembly stage in technologically advanced products, but its rate of growth in such activities is impressive, and in more traditional activities there is a lot of local 'depth'. Indonesia remains at the lowest end of assembly activity, though there are signs of recent export growth in sophisticated engineering activities like automobile engines.

Role of MNCs

MNCs have played very different roles in promoting exports and upgrading capabilities in the Tigers (Table 2.4). Singapore is the most FDI-intensive economy in the region, while at the other end, Korea has very low levels of foreign reliance with the others ranged in between. This reflects differences between the Tigers in perceptions of FDI and desired modes of technology transfer: Korea and Taiwan, particularly the former, emphasized 'externalized' technology transfer (via licensing and other arm's-length transactions), while Singapore strongly targeted 'internalized' modes (via direct investment) and Hong Kong had a *laissez-faire* attitude (Lall, 1996). The first two had selective policies on entry, restricting FDI where domestic capabilities were adequate. Once allowed in, investors were induced to share their knowledge and diffuse technologies.

Singapore also used selectivity, to attract investors into targeted activities and to induce technological upgrading. Only Hong Kong left FDI and technology transfer entirely to market forces. Malaysia has adopted some elements of the Singapore strategy, with an increasing effort by its investment promotion agency to gear incentives to technology levels, local content and R&D effort (instead of, as earlier, just export orientation). Thailand was more liberal on export-oriented FDI, but, like Malaysia, exercised selectivity on domestic market-oriented investments. Indonesia followed a similar path, but from an initial hostility to MNCs and with larger discretionary elements (its public sector controls large areas of technologically advanced industry).

Table 2.4   Inward FDI, selected Asian countries, 1984–94/5

Country	Annual FDI inflows (US$ million)							FDI as % of GDI[*]	
	1984–9	*1990*	*1991*	*1992*	*1993*	*1994*	*1995*	*1984–9*	*1990–4*
Hong Kong	1,442	1,728	538	1,918	1,667	2,000	2,100	12.2	6.7
Singapore	2,239	5,575	4,879	2,351	5,016	5,588	5,302	28.3	28.4
Korea	592	788	1,180	727	588	809	1,500	1.4	0.7
Taiwan	691	1,330	1,271	879	917	1,375	1,470	3.3	3.0
Indonesia	406	1,093	1,482	1,774	2,004	2,109	4,500	1.6	3.5
Malaysia	798	2,333	3,998	5,183	5,006	4,348	5,800	8.8	22.4
Thailand	676	2,444	2,014	2,116	1,726	640	2,300	4.4	4.3

[*]GDI stands for gross domestic investment. The figures are simple annual averages.

Source: UNCTAD, *World Investment Report 1996*, Geneva.

The export contribution of FDI corresponds to its role in domestic capital formation. According to available estimates, MNCs account for around 25 per cent of manufactured exports from Hong Kong, 70 per cent from Malaysia, 90 per cent from Singapore, 17 per cent from Taiwan (Ramstetter, 1994). Thailand and Indonesia probably lie between Hong Kong and Malaysia, and Korea has a much lower figure than Taiwan.

What do these differences imply? Korea's low dependence and selective restrictions on FDI, along with its strong performance in technologically demanding exports (and its own outward FDI), reflect strong indigenous capabilities, driven by its giant conglomerates, the *chaebols*. Taiwan is similar, but lagging where large-scale, capital-intensive production and marketing are involved. Hong Kong's strong indigenous base in exporting (and large outward FDI) along with its *laissez-faire* policies on FDI also reflects well-developed local capabilities, but its specialization in low technology activities means that these capabilities are not as deep or complex as those in Korea and Taiwan (and foreign investors have remained in relatively simple manufacturing activities). Singapore remains highly dependent on foreign sources of technology and marketing, but its success in moving into the most advanced technologies means that it has been able to use MNCs by a series of highly targeted policies.

The new Tigers have relatively lower levels of indigenous capabilities, and FDI dominates export activity in both low and high technology activities. While they have been selective in FDI entry into domestic-oriented activities, they have been fairly liberal on export-oriented FDI; in the latter, they have yet to develop the kind of selective targeting that Singapore has mounted so effectively.

Indigenous technological activity

Though these countries are, like developing countries generally, highly dependent on imported technologies, they undertake increasing amounts of technological activity, to absorb complex technologies, adapt and improve upon imported knowledge, and even to create new technologies. Formal R&D does not capture the full extent of technological activity, but it is something on which comparable data are available. Moreover, with growing industrial maturity, as more routine technological capabilities become standard, formal research activity may become a more accurate measure of inter-country technological differences.

Table 2.5 shows R&D as a proportion of GDP in these countries. The clear leader is Korea, which spent 2.3 per cent on this activity in 1993 (and 2.6 per cent in 1996 according to Kim, 1997). This is just behind the technological leaders in the OECD, though in per capita terms it is still one-third of the US and one-quarter of Japan. Some 85 per cent of Korean R&D is financed by enterprises rather than the government, making its private R&D/GDP ratio of 1.7 per cent (now 2.2 per cent) one of the world's highest: this may be regarded as a better indicator than total R&D of technological effort directly relevant to industrial competitiveness. Taiwan comes next, with per capita spending slightly higher than Korea. However, more than half of Taiwanese R&D comes from the government: its dominant small and medium sized enterprise (SME) sector is unable to undertake expensive research. The government compensates with an extensive infrastructure of public institutions that offer extension, contract R&D and productivity improvement services (Lall, 1996).

Table 2.5   R&D expenditures, selected Asian and OECD countries, 1990s

Country	Year	As % of GDP		R&D
		Total	By enterprises	per capita (US$)
Hong Kong	1995	0.1	n/a	19.8
Singapore	1992	1.0	0.6	153.6
Korea	1993	2.3	1.98	176.2
Taiwan	1993	1.7	0.8	179.6
Malaysia	1992	0.4	0.17	11.2
Thailand	1991	0.2	0.04	3.1
Indonesia	1993	0.2	0.04	1.5
Memo item: some OECD countries				
Japan	1992	3.0	1.9	762.9
France	1991	2.4	1.0	512.7
Germany[*]	1989	2.8	1.8	427.3
UK	1991	2.1	1.1	365.7
USA	1988	2.9	1.5	540.9

[*]Figures for the former Federal Republic.

Sources: UNESCO, *Statistical Yearbooks*, and national sources.

Private industrial R&D is relatively weak in the other countries. Singapore has increased enterprise R&D in recent years as a result of strong government incentives and targeting, but much of it is located in foreign affiliates and does not reach the depth that has been achieved in Korea and Taiwan. Hong Kong, in line with its specialization in low-technology activities, lacks a significant R&D base. Of the new Tigers, only Malaysia has some R&D capability, but this is largely confined to the product engineering units of a few large MNCs; the bulk is in 25 electronics firms (World Bank, 1996).

Human resource development

Human resource development is most readily measured by educational enrolments, but it is not an ideal measure. Formal education is only one way to create skills: on-the-job learning and training are often more important. Nevertheless, formal education is a basic condition for industrial skill acquisition, and enrolment data serve as a reasonable proxy (though there are differences in definition, quality and dropout rates between countries, which we cannot correct for).

Table 2.6   Educational enrolments and literacy rates, selected Asian countries (1990–2) (% of age group)

Country	Primary	Secondary	Tertiary	% Tertiary abroad[*]	% Adult literacy
Hong Kong	117	75	20	32	91
Singapore	107	71	9	25	90
Korea	105	90	46	2	97
Taiwan	100	88	38	–	–
Malaysia	93	58	7	38	82
Thailand	97	33	19	1	94
Indonesia	115	38	10	2	83

[*]1987–8.

Sources: Government of Taiwan, *Taiwan Statistical Data Book*, 1994; World Bank, *World Development Report*, 1994, 1995; UNDP, *Human Development Report*, 1995; Ministry of Education, Singapore; UNESCO, *Statistical Yearbook*, various.

Table 2.6 shows *general enrolments* at the three levels, as well as tertiary students abroad and the adult literacy rate. Secondary enrolment rates are very high in the Tigers, with Korea and Taiwan now reaching developed country levels. Hong Kong and Singapore are slightly behind, followed by Malaysia, Indonesia and Thailand.

At the tertiary level, Korea and Taiwan are again at developed country levels. Then come Hong Kong and Thailand, with around 20 per cent. Indonesia, Malaysia and Singapore have tertiary enrolments of 5–10 per cent.

There are high proportions of students studying overseas from Hong Kong, Singapore and Malaysia. Korea, Taiwan and Singapore have in place attractive incentives for nationals studying or working overseas to return, and these have provided an important input into their capability development. Singapore places more emphasis than other countries on non-university technical education.[5]

Conclusion on performance and capabilities

What may we conclude from the evidence presented above? Of the Tiger economies, Korea stands out as the clear technological leader on almost every criterion. Its industrial sector has considerable depth and integration, with competitive export capabilities over a very wide range of activities (including practically all heavy producer goods industries) which have been developed largely as a result of *indigenous* learning, skills and R&D effort. Its leading *chaebols* are now multinationals in their own right, challenging established MNCs on their home ground in complex industries (such as automobiles) where it was believed that developing country firms could not play an independent role. Korea is followed by Taiwan, which has a narrower industrial base and a preponderance of small and medium-sized enterprises (SMEs). This gives it more flexibility, but perhaps less depth in technology generation. As its industrial sector approaches technological frontiers this may prove a disadvantage (and may account for the fact that Taiwanese manufacturing output and exports have been growing more slowly than Korea's over the past decade). Nevertheless, some of its largest firms are world leaders in their technologies; a superlative network of technology institutions gives Taiwanese SMEs some of the support they need to keep up with technological change.

The smaller Tigers have narrower spheres of competence. Singapore is distinctly ahead of Hong Kong in technological terms. Despite its smaller size and higher wages, which may be expected to lead to faster 'deindustrialization', Singapore continues to register high rates of industrial and export growth, while Hong Kong is suffering a rapid contraction of its manufacturing sector and falling (own) exports. Their industrial structures have also diverged over the past four decades, Singapore transforming itself into a centre for high-tech electronics and chemicals production, Hong Kong remaining in activities with low technological content. The Hong Kong economy continues to grow by moving into services largely directed at the mainland, but its rate of growth is lower than that of Singapore, which has also increased its service sector without running down industry. However, Singapore's edge lies in providing an efficient, high skill and well-located base for MNC activity rather than in its own technological capabilities. These capabilities are growing, partly as MNCs are induced to set up research facilities there, but they are not comparable to the larger Tigers.

The new Tigers have relatively shallow industrial structures, with Thailand the most advanced in terms of indigenous capabilities and Indonesia the least. Malaysia provides an interesting combination of a very high-tech MNC sector with a weak indigenous industrial base; however, the domestic sector has built up a range of competitive capabilities in resource processing, services and infrastructure which it is exploiting in its own FDI overseas, and some advanced suppliers to MNCs have also emerged.

These contrasts provide the base from which we can assess the role of government policies in promoting export growth and diversification. *Do government policies in any form help to explain these differences? If so, was it purely 'market friendly' functional policies that were responsible? Or were selectivity and targeting also important?*

Export promotion strategies

The Tigers adopted a mixture of permissive and positive (both functional and selective) policies to promote the growth, diversification and upgrading of their manufactured exports. It is not easy to draw clear distinctions between these in practice, since the same set of policy instruments can be used in different ways. As noted, different Asian governments did indeed use very different combinations of policies and employed similar tools in different ways.

A useful point of departure is the summary of main export policies in the HPAEs, the 'high performing Asian economies' (the seven above, plus Japan) provided by the World Bank, based on its *East Asian Miracle* study:

Trade policies in all the Asian economies (except Hong Kong) passed through an import-substitution phase with high and variable protection of domestic import substitutes. In all cases, however, policies that strongly favoured the production of import substitutes to the detriment of exports were abandoned. And governments of high-performing Asian economies (HPAEs) ... adopted strategic pro-export policies that established a free trade regime and offered a range of other incentives for exports. This approach provided a mechanism by which industry moved rapidly toward international best practice, despite highly imperfect world markets for technology.

In the HPAEs that intervened selectively to promote exports, a contest based on performance in global markets played the allocative role that is normally ascribed to neutral exposure of both import-substituting and exporting industries to international competition.

Export targets provided a consistent yardstick to measure the success of market interventions. When protected sectors interfered with the exports of other sectors, the latter could seek redress and were successful ...

The more recent export-push efforts of the Southeast Asian newly industrializing economies – Indonesia, Malaysia, and Thailand – have relied less on highly specific incentives and more on gradual reductions in import protection, coupled with institutional support of exporters and a duty-free regime for inputs for exports.

The close link between successful macroeconomic policies and trade liberalization can be seen in the experiences of Indonesia, Korea, and Taiwan (China) ... The three economies used deliberately undervalued exchange rates to assist exporters. Exchange rate policy and the fiscal and monetary tools to carry it out became part of an overall export-push strategy.

One can see a fairly clear relationship between devaluations in these economies and export growth in the 1980s ...

Each of the eight HPAEs contributed to one or more of the four elements of a successful export push: access to imports at world prices; both long- and short-term financing; market penetration; and flexibility.

Access to imports at world prices. HPAE governments have found numerous ways to grant exporters access to imports at world prices: free trade zones, export processing zones, bonded warehouses, duty drawbacks, or tariff exemptions.

Export financing. Expansion into new export activities often requires financing, both long- and short-term. Nearly every HPAE has had some program to ensure access to credit, often at subsidized prices.

Market penetration. Nearly all governments recognized the difficulty exporters face in cracking into foreign markets, and again chose various means to encourage exporters to overcome the hurdles. Some directly subsidized export activity (direct income tax incentives), some subsidized market penetration (through exporter associations), some subsidized small and medium-size exporters to offset their difficulties in market penetration, and some promoted the creation of international trading companies.

Flexibility. Pragmatism and policy flexibility proved important because hitting the right strategy is not easy, for three reasons. The right strategy depends on the circumstances. It changes as the economy changes. And it is not always obvious. (World Bank, 1993b)

While we may quibble with the interpretation by the Bank of some policies (e.g. did selective interventions to promote exports using 'contests' play a neutral allocative role?), this gives a reasonable picture of the kinds of policies used to directly promote exports. However, this does leave out some policies that were critical in indirectly raising competitive capabilities.

'Permissive' policies

The Asian Tigers all had macroeconomic policies and trade regimes that favoured exports, in some cases strongly so, making them more profitable than domestic sales (and, in some cases, as in Korea, essential for survival). Exporters had confidence that favourable policies would be maintained. Most governments emphasized export promotion as a national objective and gave various awards or marks of recognition to successful exporters. The exchange rate and trade regimes were generally stable and predictable; devaluations were used to further improve export profitability.

Export incentives, by means of tax privileges and subsidies, were often given.[6] Where the economy had trade barriers, inputs were made available at world market prices to exporters (in export processing or free trade zones or bonded warehouses, or by duty drawback schemes). Transactions costs in trade were reduced by efficient, streamlined administration of imports, exports, customs clearance, shipping facilities and the like (the original Tigers did so early, while the new Tigers improved these over time) (see Keesing, 1988). Labour markets generally functioned efficiently, and wage rises were generally kept moderate, or in line with productivity increases.

'Positive' functional policies

Functional support was given to exporters to meet several types of factor market failure, without targeting particular activities or firms:

Physical infrastructure: The public goods characteristics of infrastructure, in conjunction with deficient capital markets and private sector capabilities, meant that the state often had to invest in improving the infrastructure for export activity. Many governments concentrated this on export processing zones, though in the original Tigers (and Malaysia) there was a tendency to improve the industrial infrastructure more generally.

General skills: Market failures in the provision of education, arising from information gaps and asymmetries, risk, poor institutional capabilities and bad income distribution, are widely accepted by analysts, especially at the basic levels. The original Tigers started with a fairly high base of literacy and general skills, found that this was insufficient to sustain their industrialization drive and invested massively in it over time (but a significant part of higher skill creation was of a *selective* nature, taken up later).

The new Tigers started from a lower human capital base (in particular Indonesia), and invested heavily in upgrading education and worker training. In general, however, the newcomers still have considerable skill gaps *vis-à-vis* the established Tigers: their enrolment rates are far lower, as are the quality and relevance of their education systems. Firms train their employees to compensate (this is especially marked in the case of the electronics industry in Malaysia), aided by incentives and training levies. However, this is mainly aimed at creating basic operational rather than more advanced skills (partly because of the cost and partly because turnover rates of employees are very high), and is not enough to sustain an upgrading of the export structure into more demanding technologies. Their exports have grown well so far because they are concentrated in simple technologies, but it is widely acknowledged in all these countries that a massive improvement in the skill base is needed if growth is to be sustained in the face of rising wages and growing competition from cheaper countries.

Capital markets: The market failures that afflict capital markets in developing countries, arising from asymmetric information and moral hazard, and from more general market deficiencies that drive a wedge between social and private returns, are well known (Stiglitz, 1989). The Tigers ensured credit access to all exporters, often on subsidized terms (while this was 'functional' in that it did not favour particular export activities, it was selective to the extent that it helped export over domestic market-oriented activities). Credit direction and subsidization, often highly selective, were strongest in Korea, followed by Taiwan (for a recent review of capital market interventions in East Asia see Stiglitz and Uy, 1996). Singapore used credit allocation to build up infrastructure and give signals to foreign investors. The new Tigers provided general support for credit to exporters, but with relatively little targeting (World Bank, 1993a). Hong Kong did not use this tool, though it gave land and housing cheaply to manufacturing industry in general.

SME support: Small and medium-sized enterprises face a variety of market failures, arising from segmentation in the various markets in which they compete with larger firms. These are recognized by governments at all levels of development and addressed by a variety of functional as well as selective measures – to 'level the playing field', favour SMEs over larger enterprises (if they provide social, locational, employment or other benefits) or to favour SMEs in some activities over others. All the Tiger governments mounted special measures to help SMEs, in particular Taiwan and Hong Kong, where these enterprises account for the bulk of manufacturing activity and exports.[7] Singapore and Korea also have strong SME support systems, though their industrial and export drive has been led by large companies, foreign in the first case and domestic in the second (Singapore by encouraging subcontracting by MNCs under its Local Industries Upgrading Programme (LIUP), and by providing subsidized technical and other assistance to help SMEs upgrade, Korea by reserving over 1200 products for SMEs, giving tax incentives to large firms to subcontract, and by providing subsidized credit and a range of assistance to help SMEs to upgrade and export).

The new Tigers also have a number of institutions for SME support, but these appear to be less dedicated, skilled and effective than in the above countries; the procedures tend to be more cumbersome, and the management is far more passive in reaching out to SMEs. In addition, SMEs themselves tend to be less well-organized in representing their interests and seeking assistance. The most advanced is perhaps Malaysia, with its various schemes to subsidize and assist Malay-owned (*bumiputra*) SMEs.

Export market information: New exporters, especially smaller ones, invariably face high costs in obtaining necessary information on export markets. The Tigers have invested considerable effort in helping them to overcome this deficiency (Keesing, 1988). The Hong Kong Trade Development Council, set up in 1966, is highly regarded for its 'matchmaking' between foreign buyers and exporters. Taiwan's China External Trade Development Council (CETDC), set up in 1970, is perhaps the most effective; however, a substantial proportion of Taiwan's exports are handled by Japanese trading companies and US buyers. The Singapore Trade Development Board (STDB) started later, in 1983, and was doing extremely well within five years; again, its scope is fairly limited because over 80 per cent of manufactured exports are from MNC affiliates that do not need such assistance. The Korean Trade Promotion Council (KOTRA) started in 1962, modelled upon the Japan External Trade Research Organization; it seems to be regarded as less effective than its Hong Kong and Taiwanese counterparts. Most Korean exports are handled by its giant trading companies that buy from smaller enterprises, or else emanate directly from the *chaebols*.

The main contribution of these organizations has been to help SMEs establish contacts with foreign buyers and break directly into new markets. They are highly skilled and professional. For instance, in the first three organizations 'most of the officials … come from overseas-Chinese communities that are business-oriented in the extreme and highly sophisticated in international trade. Many of their higher officials have MBAs, postgraduate degrees in practical fields such as engineering or design, or substantial previous business experience. Most have degrees from first-rate universities. Each gives its staff excellent training' (Keesing 1998: 9–10).[8] All four have large computerized information bases, and actively help enterprises in establishing contact, participating in trade fairs and missions, conducting research and often providing industrial and packaging assistance.

Again, the new Tigers have similar agencies but they appear to be less effective. Most of the marketing information and assistance comes from overseas investors or buyers and from large (generally foreign) trading companies.

To sum up: functional export promotion policies have been generally pervasive, and well-managed, in the old Tigers, but of more limited range and effectiveness in the new Tigers. The latter did have trade regimes that were conducive to exporting, and their location and relative costs enabled them to expand manufactured exports rapidly in less demanding products over the 1980s. They relied more on large firms (domestic but particularly foreign) and foreign buyers and trading houses, rather than on policies and institutions, to overcome information and other market failures. However, their functional support weaknesses have to be remedied if export growth is to deepen like those of the larger Tigers.

'Positive' selective policies

While conducive trade regimes and functional support were necessary for the Tigers' export growth, they are only part of the explanation for the differences in their export patterns and capabilities. For the original Tigers, these were the result more of their (different) selective rather than (fairly similar) functional policies. The selective policies that affected export performance were not confined to those dealing directly with exports but included the whole gamut of industrial policies that led to the evolution of the industrial structure and capabilities. Table 2.7 lays out the outline of the selective policies adopted by the Tigers.

It is apparent that Hong Kong was the exception to the general picture of selective interventions: in a sense, it was the special case rather than the rule (Lall, 1996). Its exports grew rapidly but because of low cost literate labour combined with certain unique advantages – its location and entrepôt experience, the presence of the British trading, finance and other *Hongs*, and the influx of experienced entrepreneurs and engineers from Shanghai (where they had already undergone a 'learning' process). However, these advantages did not prevent its deindustrialization and relative stagnation in technological terms. Let us therefore look at the selective policies that explain the differing patterns sustaining export growth and deepening in the other Tigers.

Selective industrial promotion   With the exception of Hong Kong, all the Tigers and new Tigers protected their infant industries. Singapore switched to free trade after a brief period of import substitution. The two larger Tigers practised extensive selective trade interventions from the start of their industrialization process; the intensity of the interventions diminished over time as the economic system grew more complex and efficient but has never vanished altogether. They sought to promote new areas of activity considered to be in the long-term national interest – the selection was directed at products that would have the maximum technological and export potential and build up domestic linkages and capabilities. Korea had relatively high, prolonged and variable levels of effective protection (ranging from nil to several hundred per cent), by quantitative and tariff-based measures. Taiwan used similar measures, with somewhat less intensity. These policies were, however, implemented flexibly, and, unlike typical import substituting regimes, changed as circumstances demanded.

The period of strongest trade interventions in the larger Tigers was over the late 1960s and 1970s; this was followed by liberalization, but this was slow and controlled (there are complaints even now about hidden restraints on, and government exhortations against, consumer goods imports by Korea). A comparison of price 'distortions' compiled by David Dollar shows that Japan, Korea and Taiwan had larger distortions, in terms of deviations of domestic from international prices, than 'classic' import substituting economies like India, Brazil, Mexico, Pakistan or Venezuela (World Bank, 1993a: 301). The East Asian economies with the largest 'distortions' were precisely the ones with the strongest strategies to develop indigenous technological bases in advanced industrial activities.

Table 2.7 Selective industrial policies in the Asian tigers

	Deepening industrial structure	Raising local content	FDI strategy	Raising technological effort	Promotion of large local enterprises
Hong Kong	None.	None.	Passive open door.	None except technology support for SMEs.	None.
Singapore	Very strong push into specialized high-skill/tech industry for export markets, but without protection.	None, but subcontracting promotion for SMEs.	Aggressive targeting and screening of MNCs, direction into high value-added activities.	None for local firms, but MNCs targeted to increase R&D.	None, but some public sector enterprises enter targeted areas.
Taiwan	Protection and subsidization of capital, skill and technology intensive industry. Incentives for exports of more advanced products.	Pressures for raising local content, technology diffusion by MNCs and local subcontracting.	Screening FDI, entry discouraged where local firms strong. Local technology diffusion pushed.	Intense support for local R&D and upgrading of SMEs. Government targeted and orchestrated high-tech development.	Sporadic; to enter heavy industry by public sector enterprises.
Korea	Strong trade and credit interventions to push into capital, skill and technology intensive industry, especially heavy intermediates and capital goods. Selective export targeting and promotion.	Stringent local content rules, creating support industries protection of local suppliers, subcontracting promotion.	FDI kept out unless necessary for technology access or exports; joint ventures and licensing encouraged.	Ambitious plans for R&D in advanced industry; heavy investment in technology infrastructure. Targeting of strategic technologies.	Sustained drive to create giant private conglomerates to internalize markets, lead heavy industry, create export brands.

The most intensive form of trade intervention in East Asia was in *Korea*, in its Heavy and Chemical Industry (HCI) drive in the 1970s. During the HCI drive, a range of electrical, electronic, steel, chemicals, heavy engineering and automobile industries was built up behind high and variable import protection at a speed and with an intensity unmatched in recent economic history. While this created macroeconomic problems which led to stabilization measures in the early 1980s, the HCI industries 'took off' in export markets in the mid-1980s, and, after some restructuring of the activities (Kim, 1994), now provide Korea's most dynamic exports. With the benefit of hindsight, and despite the criticism at the time that the HCI drive had failed, this concentrated set of selective interventions proved to be the foundation of industrial deepening and upgrading in Korea. Of course, the learning period involved was long, and probably underestimated by the government (Kim, 1997); but given the inherent problems involved in mastering such advanced technologies and the experience of other developing countries in building up equivalent levels of capability, it was surprisingly short rather than long.

Korean industrial targeting and promotion was pragmatic and flexible, and developed in concert with private industry. Moreover, only a relatively small number of activities were supported at a given time, and the effects of protection were offset by strong export orientation (below). These features strongly differentiate its interventions from those in typical import substituting countries, where infant industry protection was sweeping and open-ended, non-selective, inflexible and designed without consultation with industry (Westphal, 1997).

In *Taiwan*, according to the World Bank (1993a: 131–3), early trade policies had 'extensive quantitative restrictions and high tariff rates [that] shielded domestic consumer goods from foreign competition. To take advantage of abundant labour, the government subsidized some light industries, particularly textiles.' As import substitution started to run out of steam by 1960, 'a multiple exchange rate system was replaced with a unitary rate, and appreciation was avoided. Tariffs and import controls were gradually reduced, especially for inputs to export. In addition, the Bank of Taiwan offered low-interest loans to exporters. The government also hired the Stanford Research Institute to identify promising industries for export promotion and development. On the basis of Taiwan's comparative advantage in low-cost labour and existing technical capabilities, the institute chose plastics, synthetic fibres and electronic components. Other industries subsequently promoted included apparel, consumer electronics, home appliances, watches and clocks.'

In the 1970s, the Taiwanese government again drew upon foreign advice, now from consultants Arthur D. Little, to upgrade the industrial structure and enter into secondary import substitution.[9] These interventions included the setting up of 'capital-intensive, heavy and petrochemical industries to increase production of raw materials and intermediates for the use of export industries'. In the 1980s, as its light exports lost competitiveness, Taiwan's government 'again moved to restructure the economy. After extensive consultation with domestic and foreign advisors, the government decided to focus on high-technology industries: information, biotechnology, electro-optics, machinery and precision instruments, and environmental technology industries. The shift to a high-technology economy has necessitated the close coordination of industrial, financial, science and technology, and human resource policies.' Individual tariff rates still varied widely, with widespread quantitative restrictions in use: the use of these protective instruments was made conditional on prices moving towards international levels in two to five years. The average legal tariff rate in 1984 was as high as 31 per cent, higher if additional charges are added; in total this was higher than the 34 per cent prevalent in the developing world (Wade, 1990: 127).

Apart from promoting new infant industries, both the Taiwanese and Korean governments used selective interventions to strengthen existing, mature industries that were facing growing competition from new entrants. In part, and in particular in the 1990s, this comprised measures to help labour-intensive industries to locate in cheaper areas (all the Tigers except for Singapore are now net FDI exporters). More generally, however, it comprised selective measures to assist firms to restructure, improve their technological levels, raise quality and design, and invest in new equipment and skills.[10]

In Singapore, the promotion of new activities was conducted via FDI targeting and incentives and factor market interventions rather than by trade policy. This does not mean that the government was not selective – the identification and targeting of areas of dynamic comparative advantage was firmly in the hands of the Economic Development Board (EDB) rather than market forces. The EDB formed industrial strategy (a series of strategic plans have been devised and implemented over time) and used all the incentives available to catalyse investment. The government announced in 1997 that the EDB was to set up an Economic Resources Division to undertake 'proactive planning, development and organization of key economic resources for present and future needs, i.e. specialized infrastructure and specialist manpower'. This was supported by a grant of S$4.3 billion (US$3.1 billion).[11]

The *new Tigers* had extensive infant industry protection, though large parts of the export-oriented sectors were kept insulated in export processing zones or similar facilities. According to estimates collected by the World Bank (1993a: 138), effective rates of protection (ERP) in the import substituting phase came to around 45 per cent for Malaysia, 75 per cent for Indonesia and 90 per cent for Thailand; these rates fell to 18 per cent, 57 per cent and 65 per cent respectively in their export-push phase. Over time, several of the protected activities 'matured' and moved into export markets, often (like

Korea) keeping domestic markets fairly protected – this is the case, say, with the Malaysian automobile industry, Thai food processing and Indonesian textiles and garments.

Credit allocation and subsidization   Stiglitz and Uy categorize financial market interventions in Asian Tigers into three types: 'creating markets and financial institutions; regulating them; and providing rewards (subsidies or access to credit or foreign exchange, often on preferential terms) to firms, groups, or industries that undertake priority activities or perform in an exemplary manner' (Stiglitz and Uy, 1996: 250). After considering the first two types and analysing why several of these apparently 'market unfriendly' measures (such as financial 'repression' and restricting bank competition) succeeded, they go on to consider the case for directed credit.

> All East Asian countries have directed credit in varying degrees to support industrial policies or social objectives ... Like other economies, high-performing East Asian economies use two broad types of intervention. First, the government directs credit to priority firms, groups, industries and activities (such as exports or high-technology projects). Second, the government directs credit for social reasons, often to small farmers, small and medium-scale enterprises, or a specific ethnic group. In both cases the government directs credit by investing in public enterprises, using its development banks to lend to priority areas (and to signal to other financial institutions what these areas are), and compelling commercial banks to lend to designated activities. (ibid.: 270)

Of the Tigers, *Korea* 'most pervasively directed credit to promote specific firms and industries' (ibid.: 271), with mixed results during the HCI drive. According to the World Bank (1993a: 280), as much as 60 per cent of loans by its commercial banks were directed during 1973–81. As with Japan, most of the targeted activities were 'associated with large optimum scales and increasing returns to scale'. In the context of enhancing competitiveness, we may note that the government provided and directed large amounts of *technology finance* in Korea.[12] In addition to this, there were a number of schemes at commercial banks to provide technology loans and credit guarantees. Korea has the largest venture capital industry in the developing world to support local innovation.

Taiwan also used directed credit extensively. The curb market for loans was very large, but significantly more expensive than the commercial banking system, which was largely government controlled. According to Wade:

> In addition to concessional credit for export production ... the government has also indicated priority industries for bank lending ... During the 1950s and the early 1960s the banks received credit allocation

targets for rather broadly defined sectors, supplemented by more detailed case-by-case instructions from the planners. By the mid-1960s the banks were receiving lists of six to twelve industries to which priority attention should be given. These lists were drawn up by the planning agency, with the Ministries of Finance and Economic Affairs and the central bank having opportunities to suggest modifications. During the 1970s the banks themselves began to participate more in drafting the lists. Each bank was required to select five or six areas it wished to focus upon for the coming year ... (Wade, 1990: 166–8)

Singapore also directed and subsidized credit to its public enterprises that were set up to catalyse activity in areas that were too risky for private investors. This direction continues today, for instance in setting up industrial estates and export processing zones overseas (e.g. in the 'Growth Triangle' with Indonesia and Malaysia, and in India and China).

The new Tigers, with the apparent exception of Thailand, also used a variety of forms of directing and subsidizing credit, though often with less success than the old Tigers (World Bank, 1993a: 280). Over time, Indonesia and Malaysia reduced their capital market interventions, though Indonesia continues to offer substantial financial support to its 'strategic' industries which are to spearhead its drive into high technology.

Industrial structure and FDI   All the Tigers started their export drives with small indigenous enterprises operating in relatively simple technologies. Thereafter their strategies differed. Taiwan and Hong Kong had exceptionally strong SMEs and a relatively arm's-length stance on the direction of firms – they did not act directly to change the structure of the private industrial sector. However, Taiwan used public enterprises to enter heavy industry where the private sector was reluctant to step in, and to coordinate technological activity.[13] Its industrial structure remains dominated by SMEs, and these are, as with Hong Kong firms, relocating massively in lower-cost areas as costs rise.

By contrast, Korea created large industrial firms in the belief that large size was necessary to fulfil its ambition of entering difficult technologies at world levels of competitiveness, building up its own know-why capabilities and building its own MNCs and brand names in world markets. It encouraged firms selected on the basis of their export performance to grow large, using the whole battery of selective measures. The implicit objective was to allow them to internalize defective markets for capital, skills, technology and entrepreneurship and to act as interlocutors for government policies towards the industrial sector as a whole. This was also part of its strongly nationalistic strategy of industrialization – large firms were necessary to replace foreign investment in heavy and high-tech industry, and to undertake the R&D required to absorb and create advanced technologies. The Korean government wielded considerable power to discipline the conglomerates, and in the early days several *chaebols* were closed down when they failed to meet the export targets set by the government (Kim, 1997). However, over time this strategy led to a highly concentrated industrial structure, with economic power located in the hands of a small number of firms; this worked well in creating industrial capabilities and going into very demanding activities, but it had its social costs. Nevertheless, the Korean *chaebols* are today the technological leaders in the developing world, its most powerful exporters and multinationals.

Singapore chose the opposite route, deliberately targeting and attracting foreign investors, with large state-of-the-art facilities and technologies, to lead its drive into more advanced export activities. Its industrial structure is thus also fairly concentrated, but with control dispersed over a large number of affiliates with overseas head offices.[14] This structure was necessitated by an export strategy that was driven by integration into the globalized production structure of multinational firms, with continued reliance on the transfer of research and development conducted overseas and on the marketing networks of the parent companies. Interestingly, Singapore drew extensively upon the managers of foreign affiliates in designing its industrial policy, one of the few countries that involves foreigners in its highest levels of policymaking.

The new Tigers have also intervened in the industrial structure: Malaysia has targeted large MNCs and set up a large public sector holding company for heavy industries (now being privatized to Malay entrepreneurs close to the Prime Minister); Indonesia has favoured large local conglomerates, again with close connections to the President, and has created giant public sector 'strategic' industries; Thailand has supported large local conglomerates. These interventions have not directly affected their export performance very noticeably in the past, but with the upgrading of comparative advantage they should become more significant in the future. Each is becoming more selective in its FDI policies, using incentives to promote upgrading and local linkages.

Human resource development   General human resource development strategies in the Tigers have already been dealt with earlier. The main point to note here is that a large part of the investments in education and training was not 'market friendly' – above a certain level, these policies were also highly selective. In the three Tigers with industrial policy, in particular, the creation of high level technical manpower was geared closely to the activities being targeted by the government. Selvaratnam (1994) describes in detail how the Singapore government changed the orientation and structure of its higher education system from a liberal arts-based one to a very technological one, using its powers over finance and appointments. In Korea and Taiwan, the Japanese legacy of technical orientation in education was reinforced by subsequent policy. Korean education planning was explicitly based on comparisons with Japan, Germany and the US, on the assumption that its long-term skill needs would be very similar as its industrial policies led to the development of heavy and high technology activities.

The Tigers have also created strong industrial training systems. Singapore has one of the world's strongest structures for pre-employment and employee training.[15] Korea has enforced a training levy on large firms of 5 per cent of payroll, very much higher than the norm of 1 per cent. The education of high-level technical manpower has been promoted by the setting up of institutions like the Korea Advanced Institute of Science and Technology at the postgraduate level, and the Korea Institute of Technology at the undergraduate level. These were aimed at exceptionally gifted students, while the normal university system catered for the normal run of science and engineering training. Taiwan has numerous institutions to support training for its myriad SMEs.

The new Tigers have invested much less, and less selectively, in their human resource development. As noted, this has not held back their export growth, mainly because of the low demands of the technologies they are operating and their reliance on foreign investors to transfer technology. However, they are acutely conscious of their need to upgrade their skill levels if they are to sustain their export growth in the future, and have made this a high policy priority.

Technology support   The Tigers have launched several selective policies to upgrade their quality, design, productivity and R&D activity. Hong Kong has an excellent support system for SMEs in the form of the Hong Kong Productivity Centre, which imports, adapts and diffuses advanced manufacturing technologies. One of its few selective support schemes is to provide the textile and garments industry with designers; it has set up a world class design training centre to upgrade this industry.

Singapore goes much further. Two aspects of Singapore's technology infrastructure programmes are worth noting, each with selective aspects tied in with its general policies of technology upgrading. The first is its policies on SMEs. In 1962 the EDB launched a programme to fund SMEs to modernize equipment. In the mid-1970s, it launched several other schemes for financial assistance; of these the most significant was the Small Industries Finance Scheme to encourage technological upgrading in SMEs. The 1985 recession induced stronger measures, and a Venture Capital Fund was set up to help SMEs acquire capital through low interest loans and equity. A Small Enterprises Bureau was established in 1986 to act as a one-stop consultancy agency; this helped SMEs with management and training, finance and grants, and coordinating assistance from other agencies. In 1987, US$519 million was provided for eight SMEs programmes, including product development assistance, technical assistance to import consultants, venture capital to help technology start-ups, robot leasing, training, and technology tie-ups with foreign companies.[16]

Singapore also undertakes technology dissemination activities among SMEs, provides information on foreign technical requirements and how to meet them, and management and technological advice and consultancy. The EDB encourages subcontracting to local firms through its Local Industries Upgrading Programme, under which MNCs are encouraged to source components locally by 'adopting' particular SMEs as subcontractors. In return for a commitment by the MNCs to provide on the job training and other assistance to subcontractors, the government provides a package of assistance to the latter, including cost-sharing grants and loans for the purchase of equipment or consultancy and the provision of training.

The second element of Singapore's support system consists of direct government support of R&D and new technologies. For instance, the government decided actively to promote *biotechnology* as an area of future comparative advantage.[17] In December 1996, the Singapore government set up a US$500 million Innovation Development Scheme to be administered by the EDB. This scheme will 'typically defray 50 per cent of the costs involved when undertaking or developing capabilities for innovation projects in products, processes, applications and services' in both manufacturing and service activities.[18]

Korea promoted local R&D and other forms of technology development by a series of measures (Lall, 1996). We have already noted the strongly nationalistic stance of the government in importing technology by 'externalized' means, not involving foreign ownership and control. Thus, the main forms of technology inflows were by capital goods, licensing, subcontracting and imitation (Rhee et al., 1984). The government intervened in these transactions to ensure that local technological capabilities were well served.[19] In the early years, the emphasis was on building basic mastery of imported technologies, but R&D was promoted from the early years, first in public technology institutions and later in private firms. The startling rise in industrial R&D noted earlier led to a reversal of the relative funding of these expenditures in Korea, from three-quarters public in the early 1970s (which is typical of most developing countries today), to over 80 per cent private by the mid-1990s. The main thrust of private R&D was, of course, the *chaebols*, which were forced to raise their technological effort to be internationally competitive in the high-tech areas the government had chalked out for them; however, these pressures were reinforced by a range of R&D incentives offered by the government.[20]

In 1966 the government set up KIST (Korea Institute of Science and Technology) to conduct applied research of various kinds for industry. In its early years, KIST focused on solving simple problems of technology transfer and absorption. In the 1970s the government set up other specialized research institutes (on machinery, metals, electronics, nuclear energy, resources, chemicals, telecommunications, standards, shipbuilding, marine sciences, etc.), largely spun off from KIST. By the end of the decade there were 16 R&D institutions; in 1981 the government decided to reduce their number and rationalize their operations. The existing institutes were merged into nine under the supervision of the Ministry of Science and Technology.

The government launched a series of 'National R&D Projects' in 1982, large-scale projects regarded as too risky for industry to tackle alone but considered to be in the country's strategic industrial interest. These were conducted jointly by industry, public research institutes and the government, and covered activities like semiconductors, computers, fine chemicals, machinery, material science and plant system engineering. National Projects were a continuation of the strategy of identifying and developing the country's dynamic comparative advantage, orchestrating the different actors involved, underwriting a part of the risks, providing large financial grants, and directly filling in gaps that the market could not remedy. Strategic technological activities are still targeted and promoted today.

Since the early 1980s a number of measures have promoted SMEs, leading to a perceptible rise in their share of economic activity (over 1975–86, the share of SMEs in employment, sales and value added rose by 25 per cent). Policy support has covered SME start-up, productivity improvement, technology development and export promotion. A host of tax incentives has been provided to firms participating in these programmes, as well as finance at subsidized rates for using support services, credit guarantees, government procurement and a specialized bank to finance SMEs. A number of other institutions have been set up to help SMEs, such as the Small and Medium Industry Promotion Corporation to provide financial, technical and training assistance and the Industrial Development Bank to provide finance. The government has greatly increased its own contribution to the programme, though SMEs also had to pay a part of the costs of most of the services provided.

To promote subcontracting by the *chaebols*, the Korean government enacted a law designating parts and components that had to be procured through SMEs and not made in-house. By 1987 about 1200 items were so designated, involving 337 principal firms and 2200 subcontractors, mainly in machinery, electrical, electronic and shipbuilding. By this time, subcontracting accounted for about 43 per cent of manufacturing output and 65–77 per cent of the output values of the electrical, transport equipment and other machinery industries. Generous financial and fiscal support was provided to subcontracting SMEs, to support their operations and process and product development. In addition, subcontracting SMEs were exempted from stamp tax and were granted tax deductions for a certain percentage of their investments in laboratory and inspection equipment and for the whole of their expenses for technical consultancy. Subcontracting promotion councils were set up by the industrial subsector and also within the Korea Federation of Small Business to help SMEs in the contractual relationship, arbitrate disputes and monitor contract implementation. The government put pressures on the *chaebols* to establish vendor networks; such pressures were very effective and led to a rapid expansion of localization of components among subcontractors.

As for Taiwan, we have already noted the measures for supporting SMEs. We now note some more selective policies for promoting technological effort. A series of Science Plans have been launched since 1959, each targeting technologies important for future industrial development. For instance, the 1979 Programme targeted four areas for technology development: energy, production automation, information science and materials science, to which biotechnology, electro-optics, hepatitis control and food technology were added in 1982. The S&T Development Plan (1986–95) continued the targeting of strategic areas of technology. Private sector R&D has been relatively weak in Taiwan because of the preponderance of SMEs, though some firms have now grown sufficiently large to perform substantial R&D, and are induced to do so in order to maintain competitiveness in international markets. In the late 1980s, some 43 per cent of total R&D expenditures went into eight national strategic programmes for R&D, of which the bulk (62 per cent) was carried out by private enterprises; engineering accounted for 73 per cent of this.

Export marketing   As noted in the section on functional interventions, all the Tigers supported their exporters in overcoming the costs and risks of entering unfamiliar, risky and demanding international markets. However, the countries that had selective industrial policies also had (and had to have) selective policies to promote exports. This was partly in order to offset the differential entry costs facing exporters from different activities, and partly to achieve different levels of international marketing capabilities and a national marketing presence. Korea had the strongest ambitions to build up its own marketing capabilities, trading houses, international brand names and its own multinationals; these ambitions grew over time as the constraints imposed by exporting through foreign buyers and by original equipment manufacture (OEM) arrangements began to chafe. Taiwan remained more dependent on buying and OEM arrangements, and on foreign general trading houses, though its small number of giant firms also decided to build up their own brand names and distribution networks. Singapore essentially relied on foreign investors to market its exports, though government organizations took the lead in certain kinds of overseas activities such as the setting up of EPZs. Hong Kong had no selective measures for export promotion apart from the information and matchmaking service noted above.

It is important to reiterate that the strong measures of export promotion undertaken by the interventionist Tigers were essential to ensure that protected 'infants' were forced to mature and move into the export arena.[21] In effect, this was the discipline that ensured that selective trade and other interventions were effective – without such export promotion, these interventions would have gone the way of other developing countries that adopted protection. It is also important to note that several measures were selective and went well beyond reproducing a 'neutral' trade regime.

In Korea, in particular, export promotion became a compelling system to force firms into export activity. Korea's export targeting system is well known. Targeting was practised at the industry, product and firm levels (Rhee et al., 1984), with the targets set by the firms and industry associations in concert with the government. There were monthly meetings between top government officials (chaired by the President himself) and leading exporters. These targets were also enforced by several punitive measures: access to subsidized credit and import licences; income tax audits; and a number of other measures of suasion, publicity and prizes. On a long-term basis, moreover, bureaucrats were held responsible for meeting export targets in their respective industries, and had to keep in close touch with enterprises and markets. These measures were supported by regular studies of each major export industry, with information on competitors, technological trends, market conditions, etc. The selectivity of these measures mirrored the selectivity of interventions to promote infant industries.

Korea set up its own large trading houses (owned in turn by the *chaebols*) on the Japanese model, with strong government support in the form of preferential loans for stocking products and higher ceilings on foreign exchange holdings overseas. By 1976 there were eleven general trading houses that met specified criteria of export volumes, paid-up capital and number of overseas branches. By 1982 these houses accounted for about half of Korean exports and had an average of 23 offices overseas (Rhee et al., 1984: 53). The initial heavy reliance on foreign buyers was reduced as local marketing capabilities were built up. Today, the *chaebols* have a massive international presence in practically all foreign markets and are investing enormous sums in building up an 'image'.[22]

Taiwanese exporters were given preferential tax treatment and access to credit on favourable terms (above). According to Wade (1990), they were encouraged to form cartels and provided with quality assistance, marketing information and prizes. Local enterprises, predominantly SMEs, led the export drive, first by using the 'Chinese connection' in Asia and then, as their horizons widened, by tapping Japanese trading companies and American mass-market buyers. In the 1960s, about 60 per cent of textile exports were sold through Japanese *sogo shosha*, and even today these companies handle one-third to half of Taiwanese exports. US buyers grew more important over time, with the government facilitating contacts with small suppliers and with aggressive assistance from industry associations and other private organizations. In addition, there also emerged large numbers of relatively small local trading houses, which proved valuable sources of technical, design and marketing information to Taiwanese exporters.

In general, however, there was considerably less selectivity in promoting exports in Taiwan than in Korea; in particular, there was no targeting of specific products, industries or firms. While the Taiwanese government gave strong general incentives for its firms to go multinational and relocate uncompetitive facilities overseas or tap new markets, these were more functional than selective in nature.

The new Tigers also have some selective export marketing strategies: Malaysia is promoting the Proton car in overseas markets, while Indonesia has ambitious plans to sell its passenger planes. Malaysia also wants to promote a 'Made in Malaysia' campaign, but differentiated manufactured products made by indigenous enterprises are a very small part of its total exports and it is not clear that this will have much effect. On the whole, however, selectivity has not played much of a role in export marketing in these countries.

The institutional setting

It is important to bear in mind the political economy which made this array of interventions feasible. The most interventionist economies had well-managed macro economies, strong and stable governments clearly committed to export development, efficient and relatively honest bureaucracies insulated from daily political pressures, a fair degree of economic equity and national consensus on economic goals.[23] The interventions themselves were pragmatic and flexible, and evolved in consultation with business. The governments always had the power to punish enterprises that failed to meet their performance criteria. They were not saddled with ideological predilections on free markets versus planning – they did whatever was considered necessary to improve national competitiveness and export performance. Ideologies were important in setting the national objectives of industrial deepening, local ownership and technological development: relatively practical matters on which each Tiger evolved its own approach and instruments, with very different degrees of selectivity and different results in terms of industrial structure and depth.

Selective interventions could work so well only because of these conditions, and, most importantly, because of the discipline exercised by export orientation. However, the design of the selective policies was also much better than in most other countries. Only a relatively few activities were promoted at a time, with mistakes corrected fairly quickly. Interventions in product markets were integrated with those in factor markets, allowing firms access to the inputs they needed in order to become efficient in the activities they were being encouraged to undertake. Information was shared between the policymakers and economic actors, and a great deal of effort went into having up-to-date market and technological intelligence. The financial and educational systems were geared to meeting the long-term industrial objectives of the government. While the Tigers learned from each other, they maintained their different objectives and approaches. However, over time, there has been policy convergence as the extent of selective interventions has been reduced and external 'rules of the game' have changed.

The importance of these international 'rules of the game' has increased greatly in recent years. In the 1960s and 1970s, pervasive government intervention was the accepted norm and there were practically no external pressures against the kinds of selective policies undertaken by the Tigers. Today, many of these policies are ruled out of court: selective import protection, local content requirements, export subsidies, directed credit and differential interest rates, performance and entry rules for foreign investors and copying of foreign products are either unacceptable to the World Trade Organization (WTO) and major OECD trading partners or are fast becoming so. In fact, practically all these tools were used at critical stages of development by the presently industrialized economies, but the perception of what constitutes a 'level playing field' has changed so much, and the simple acceptance of the theoretical benefits of free markets is so ingrained, that these are often now relegated to the attic of obsolete ideas. We shall return to these issues later; let us first look briefly at the theoretical case for selectivity.

Market failures and selective interventions

The export success of the Tigers suggests that they 'did something right' in mounting the selective interventions described above. But what is the theoretical rationale for such interventions? What does theory have to say on the market failures that call for selectivity? And what does recent research on enterprise development suggest on the nature of these market failures?

The neoclassical approach

We can contrast two (simplified) approaches to these issues: neoclassical and evolutionary (also termed 'capability'). In neoclassical theory, apart from the classic cases of monopolies, public goods and externalities, there may be four types of market failures in resource allocation that justify selective government interventions (World Bank, 1993a: 90–2). The four market failures are:

- capital market deficiencies (caused by information gaps, asymmetries and moral hazard)
- lumpiness of investment (scale economies)
- the imperfect appropriability of firm-level investments in technological innovation and skills
- the inability of individual actors to invest rationally when there are interdependent investments (i.e. in intermediate inputs) that enjoy scale economies and cannot be replaced by trade.[24]

This list of market failures is based on an oversimplified framework of technology and information. At the level of theory, the very nature of information and innovation are such that it is difficult to conceive of a static market-clearing optimum which is given by free markets.[25] At the more empirical level of development policy, it essentially ignores the slow, costly, risky and unpredictable process by which firms in developing countries become efficient and learn to compete in world markets. This process poses important additional market failures, and provides some of the most critical arguments for selective intervention.

The neoclassical depiction of enterprise development assumes that technology is freely available from a known 'shelf' on which there is full information. Firms choose from this shelf according to their factor and product prices, and any intervention in these prices necessarily leads to harmful 'distortion' in resource allocation. The technology selected is then absorbed costlessly and risklessly by the enterprise and used at efficient ('best practice') levels. There is no need for intervention to support the process: the assumptions ensure that any observed industrial inefficiency *must* be due to interventions in efficient markets. The removal of such interventions then becomes the necessary and sufficient condition for restoring efficiency. Only 'good' and 'bad' firms exist, since there are none that are in the process of becoming efficient – the good can only be sorted out from the bad by free markets.

If there is any lag in efficiency it can, at most, only be for a brief period in which scale economies are fully realised or costs fall in an automatic 'learning by doing' process. However, these lags are predictable (scale economies are given by technical design parameters, while the learning curve is known) and a simple function of the quantity of output. Again, there is no need for intervention because firms can anticipate the process and raise money in efficient capital markets to finance the learning process. If capital markets do fail, the correct theoretical solution is to improve their functioning rather than to intervene selectively to support particular activities. Thus, capital market failures and scale economies do not provide grounds for selective intervention in resource allocation. The only second best case for selectivity exists when these failures cannot be remedied readily, and protection or subsidies are used as intermediate solutions.

The evolutionary/capability approach

There is a large and growing literature on technological learning by developing countries which suggests that this analysis is oversimplified and misleading.[26] Technology has many 'tacit' elements and cannot be transferred like a physical product. Its mastery and use require the recipient to invest in new skills, technical information, organizational methods and external linkages. The process varies greatly by technology. It may be relatively short, cheap and predictable in 'easy' technologies where the equipment involved is simple, the range of skills limited, and the operation relatively self-contained. In technologies that have complex processes and sophisticated equipment, the range of skills is large, there are many differing stages of production, and large numbers of enterprises have to interact in the production chain, mastery may be prolonged, costly, unpredictable and uncertain. When firms are undergoing such learning, it is difficult to sort out 'good' and 'bad' firms, since there is a large intermediate category.

More important, the process of learning may be distorted and curtailed if firms do not *know* how to go about learning, how long it will take, how much it will cost, or where to look for information and skills. There may be a 'learning to learn' process which firms may be unwilling to undertake if they face free competition from those that have already undergone the process. Dropping the assumptions on perfect information in technology markets and full transferability of technology gives rise to market failures in resource allocation. Given the cost, risk and information gaps within the firm in learning, firms in free markets will tend to under-invest in technologies that have costly, prolonged and risky learning periods. This will also affect the process of technological deepening: entering complex technologies, increasing local content, or doing more demanding technological tasks (moving from simple final assembly technology to design and development).

The capability approach clearly does not suggest that *no* industry will take root in free markets. Where there is a modicum of skills, good infrastructure and low labour costs, simple labour-intensive activities will start (though in modern industry even the simplest of industries require advanced technical and management skills). However, upgrading into more complex and demanding technologies may be limited in the absence of interventions to overcome learning costs. Such interventions cannot be functional – since technologies differ in their learning needs, they *have* to be selective.

The protection of infant industries is one, and historically the most popular and effective, means of selective intervention. However, protection is a dangerous tool. Apart from the cost to the consumer, it dilutes the incentive to invest in capability development, the very process it is meant to foster. Firms are very sensitive to competitive pressures in deciding to invest in capabilities, and the protection offered in typical import-substituting regimes tended to detract from costly and lengthy investments in competitive skills and knowledge. There may be many solutions: offer only limited protection; impose performance requirements; or enforce early entry into export markets while maintaining domestic protection. The last has the added advantage that it taps information externalities of export activity, and was the one used widely by the larger NIEs.

Firms do not learn on their own. They draw upon other firms and factor markets for a variety of skills, information, finance and inputs. All these markets may suffer from failures, and protection of final products can only *partly* remedy market failure impediments to firms becoming efficient.

Offering protection without remedying factor markets can be wasteful, while simply improving factor markets without offsetting market failures to learning within firms can lead to narrow and shallow technological development. An ideal policy requires an integrated set of interventions addressing all the interlinked market failures affecting industrial growth. As noted, interventions in factor markets are not necessarily functional; they can be as selective as offering protection to 'winners'.

A further issue in selectivity relates to promoting *dynamic groups* of activities. The coordination problem caused by technological linkages between firms, when each link in the production chain is undergoing its own learning process and so is unable to anticipate correctly what the others will do, is noted in the *Miracle* study (World Bank, 1993a). The policy issue, however, goes beyond simply coordinating individual investment decisions. Where some activity 'clusters' generate stronger benefits for the economy (in terms of technological learning, spillovers and dynamism) than others, there is a case for promoting them selectively. The case for such 'strategic' sectors is noted by some endogenous growth theorists, who distinguish between patterns of specialization that lead to technological stagnation or dynamism (Rodrik, 1996).

Industrial strategy has to distinguish the *ownership* of enterprises. Market failures are particularly binding for *local* enterprises, particularly small and medium sized ones. Foreign investors, especially affiliates of large multinational firms, face fewer failures in developing countries. Their *raison d'être* lies in the internalization of many intermediate markets, especially for capital, skills and technology. This is why multinationals can be a powerful means of launching industrialization in developing countries (as long as some complementary factors exist). Their significance is greatest where technologies are changing rapidly, production is tightly linked across nations, and export market access is difficult for new entrants. However, the advantages offered by foreign direct investment do not mean (as neoclassical theory suggests) that the best way to develop is to adopt passive 'open door' policies that leave matters entirely to free markets.

There can be two important types of market failures in the foreign investment process. First, a passive liberal policy may only attract MNCs into areas of static comparative advantage. Selective and functional interventions then need to be used to guide investment into more dynamic and complex activities (as in Singapore). Second, multinationals tend to transfer operating know-how rather than complex technological functions like design and research to developing host economies. The R&D process remains largely in advanced countries, near sophisticated markets, established suppliers, advanced science systems and universities. However, as countries industrialize it becomes important for them to develop local R&D capabilities, to keep abreast of and absorb technologies, deepen industrial activity and reduce the cost of importing technology. Interventions may be needed either to induce

MNCs to deepen local technological activity (as in Singapore), or to restrict foreign entry and encourage local firms to establish their own innovative base, to develop *indigenous* R&D capabilities and so capture the externalities and dynamic benefits that this may offer (as in Korea and Japan).

This is all concerned with basic production capabilities – entry into *export* markets, given such capabilities, involves a further learning process. Information on foreign markets, tastes, specifications, marketing systems and regulations is generally costly and difficult to acquire for a newcomer. The costs rise inversely with the size of the exporter, and tend to be highest when demand patterns are changing constantly and rapidly, as with labour-intensive consumer goods, or where highly differentiated and customized products, such as sophisticated engineering goods, are involved. It is for this reason that most new entry into manufactured exports, in the former category, is handled by foreign buyers who take care of the marketing and transmit all the necessary information to the producer. Bypassing buyers is therefore a difficult and expensive process, and few exporters in developing countries have been able to reach this stage.

In engineering products, the equivalent is OEM production, where the local firm manufactures to specifications provided by an established firm in the importing country and sells under the latter's brand name and through its own retail and service outlets. Again, bypassing OEM arrangements to set up an independent brand, with after-sales service and customer relations, is a very expensive undertaking, and few firms have accomplished this.[27] It is therefore not surprising that export marketing has attracted the range of functional and selective interventions noted above.

The case for selective interventions

Theory thus provides valid grounds for interventions, once more realistic assumptions are introduced on the process by which competitive advantages are developed. Market failures can take three forms: within firms, in inter-firm relations and *in factor markets*. These failures are inter-related, and their remedy calls for a range of integrated interventions. Those within firms have to be dealt with by providing a 'cushion' for learning (as by protection), and by the provision of information and other support; those between firms by the coordination of investments (partly by protection), geographical clustering and promotion of linkages; and those in factor markets by direct interventions to remedy the failure. Note that protection meets only a small part of the need (within firms and in inter-firm relations); used by itself, it can be harmful for technological development because it leaves other failures untouched. Protection can only be used effectively if its deleterious incentive effects are fully offset by such means as strong export orientation and if other factor market failures are addressed.

The capability approach suggests that import-substitution strategies failed and export orientation worked, not because of 'getting prices right' and realising static comparative advantage, but by providing a setting in which selective interventions could promote a healthy and dynamic learning process. It offers the following generalizations:

- Interventions in factor and product markets have to be closely coordinated and integrated; one without the other may be ineffective, even counter-productive. Factor market policies as recommended by new growth theories cannot provide a complete explanation of rapid industrial development by indigenous enterprises, since they ignore the costs of learning and the variety of market failures faced.
- Distortions introduced by interventions must be offset. In particular, protection must be accompanied by competitive pressures to enter world markets. This is what traditional import substitution strategies failed to provide.
- Since intervention resources are limited, only a few activities should be supported at any time. Intervening in a large number of unrelated activities risks waste and failure.
- Since learning is a cumulative and incremental process, interventions must aim to support activities that have a base in existing skills and knowledge in a country. New technological 'leaps' must be modest, based on realistic assessment of what is feasible within reasonable periods of time.
- The line between market friendly and selective interventions is almost impossible to draw. Each market may be subjected to a combination of functional and selective policies.

Limitations to selective interventions

While it is possible to establish a theoretical case for government interventions to promote dynamic comparative advantage, and to show that some countries have been able to use selective policies successfully, it is vital to bear in mind the risks of government failure. After all, the history of development policy is replete with cases of failed policies, and the current trend to liberalization is partly a reflection of such failure. The failure of some interventions does not, of course, mean that *all* interventions are undesirable: as long as market failures exist, a wholesale reliance on free markets will be inefficient compared to a situation where policy can improve or create markets. However, as long as governments are prone to failure, it is vital to ascertain the conditions under which selective interventions of different types can be undertaken. The issue is, then, not a black-and-white one of free markets versus wholesale intervention, but of deciding which type and level of intervention it is desirable to undertake in different product and factor markets.

Main constraints

Lack of clarity of objectives: Governments often have unclear or conflicting objectives in their economic and trade policies. This makes it difficult, or impossible, to design and implement a strategy of selective interventions, which calls for a strong, unambiguous pursuit of efficiency and competitiveness and a sharing of these objectives with the main actors involved. 'Leaving it to the market' at least has the advantage that it imposes a clear set of priorities on policy makers and is easily understood by the actors, but in the presence of market failures it may not be the best strategy for development (and even here governments have to make compromises with equity and other social needs, select between market friendly interventions and cope with pressure groups). Clarity of objectives is, of course, a matter of political leadership and commitment rather than of economic analysis. There may nevertheless be different degrees of clarity and commitment. Korea, for instance, was very different in its political economy from Taiwan, where relations between government and business were much more arm's length – in the former, the government could therefore exercise a much greater degree of selectivity. But both shared the commitment to achieving export competitiveness, as do the very different regimes in the new Tigers. Given the other demands of selectivity (below), it would seem to be a basic condition that any government that undertakes industrial policy have a clear and well-publicized set of objectives where efficiency and export growth have top priority.

Lack of information: A government wishing to use industrial policy needs information on technological and market parameters, and on local capabilities and institutions – this is often posed as one of the main constraints to selectivity. The government may not have access to better information than industrial firms, even if such information exists somewhere (for existing technologies, say, in more industrialized countries); where the choice involves new technologies the necessary information is unlikely to exist anywhere. While it is clearly better placed than individual agents to tackle coordination problems and externalities, these may involve even more difficult issues of information. There are very real dangers, calling for caution in devising selective export promotion strategies. However, it is possible to over-stress the information problems of 'picking winners'.

Neoclassical economists, in particular, with their concern for finding a 'unique' equilibrium solution, find it difficult to conceive how governments can ever obtain and process adequately the requisite information of the endless array of choices and combinations; at the same time, they tend to overlook how their simplifying assumptions minimize the problems that private agents face in this respect – when information is imperfect, the future uncertain and risks cannot be insured (Stiglitz, 1996). In any case, the issue facing governments in the real world is not to solve a gigantic optimization problem which yields a unique solution. Given the various market failures and possibilities of multiple equilibria, they have to decide upon which path they set the economy without being able to evaluate in detail the costs and benefits of different outcomes. As Stiglitz notes, 'Good decision-making by the government necessarily involves making mistakes: a policy that supported only sure winners would have taken no risks. The relatively few mistakes speak well of the government's ability to pick winners' (ibid.: 162). In the real world, the government does not replace a perfect market – it acts more as a venture capitalist who takes risks.

Most developing countries choose between technologies that are established elsewhere and, with some effort, they can obtain full information on the technological and skill parameters involved. This is much easier than 'picking winners' at the frontiers of innovation, the problem of industrial policy in advanced industrial countries. In effect, between a reasonable range of technological choices, it does not matter very much exactly which particular activities developing countries choose to promote. By mounting a coherent and integrated series of interventions it is possible to create winners. This is precisely what the governments of the interventionist Tigers did. Each defined its own set of favoured activities (within the different strategic objectives it had chosen). Having done this, it mobilized factor and product markets with appropriate trade, industrial and other policies to guide enterprises and industries, imposing export discipline to ensure that the privileges granted were not wasted or abused. Mistakes were made, as with all private investments, but flexible and rapid response ensured that the costs were not very high. None of this was done, as far as we can tell, on the basis of sophisticated quantitative models or calculations, but by using simple guides – 'follow Japan' or the immediate competitors, increase backward integration, tap high income elasticities of demand for exports, maximize technological 'spread' effects, or establish a foothold in important new technologies. Their choices also at times reflected strategic rather than economic priorities.

This does not mean that *any* choice of activities would have worked equally well. The choices have, as noted, to be 'reasonable' – what does this mean? Given the incremental and cumulative nature of technological learning, the activities promoted had to be based on the existing base of skills and capabilities and the rate at which these could realistically be increased. The technologies developed had to have commercial applications, and the private sector that was to use them had to have the financial wherewithal to mount the necessary investments. The main demands were organizational rather than informational.

As far as information goes, the real challenge to developing countries lies in finding out the basic parameters of new technologies (efficient scales, sources of know-how and equipment, skill needs, international market size and access) and in predicting the availability of the local capabilities and suppliers. The mistake import substituting governments made was to ignore efficiency requirements and international markets, and to assume away local capability problems. In effect, they believed that the necessary capabilities existed within the country, or would be created automatically and without extra cost. The Tigers, on the other hand, tended to look carefully at scales, skills, supplier structures, technological effort, quality, market needs, etc., and to intervene to help firms develop the necessary capabilities. The procedure was not easy, but it was systematic and rational, unlike that pursued by import substituting regimes. The need to export forced technological jumps not to be too large or non-commercial (though some, particularly in Korea, appear highly risky).

How can governments collect information? Purely technological data can be obtained from a variety of sources: larger local firms, MNCs, capital goods suppliers, consultants and the published literature. Market data can be obtained, where necessary, from MNCs, sales outlets, buyers, consultants, embassies, publications, etc. The best guide to the design of economic strategies is the strategies and results in countries that are further along the road of industrial development, and that have pursued what each country regards as feasible and desirable policies. The latter qualification is important, since not every country has the ability nor the desire to mount Korean-style interventions (this apart from its legality under present rules, considered below). Many governments firmly believe in market oriented policies and wish to undertake minimal selectivity. Many others that do wish to have selective policies lack the political economy to direct industry in the Japanese or Korean tradition: Taiwan may be a much more useful model for them. Singapore provides pointers to how foreign affiliates can be persuaded to conform to selective policies (and its EDB is now actively selling consultancy services to help other countries set up similar institutions).

Skills: The strategy just described is clearly very demanding of technical and administrative skills, often in short supply in developing countries. The skills are needed to understand and devise strategies with strong technical content, and, more importantly, to implement and improve them over time, to communicate with the industrial sector, and to ensure that agency problems (below) are overcome. Of course, the need for skills is not uniform, and depends on the level of industrial development and the degree of selectivity aimed for. The more advanced the industrial base and the more detailed and adventurous the strategy, the higher the levels of skills involved. In countries with small and simple industrial activities, the strategies can be devised far more easily and their implementation may need a smaller range of technical skills. The degree of selectivity itself can be geared to the capabilities of the bureaucracy and the pace at which its information and training can be improved. In this context, it is important to note that administrative capabilities are not required only for selective strategies; it is just as important for the success of 'market friendly' policies, that they provide for education, competition policy, infrastructure, etc.

Government skills are not a given; they can be improved by training, better selection, competitive salaries, appropriate promotion schemes and performance incentives (see the World Bank, 1993a, on the lessons of East Asia in this regard). The social status of the civil service is an important determinant of its confidence and ability to liaise with the private sector. All these considerations are fairly obvious and mundane, but they are important nevertheless – it is surprising how many governments tend to overlook them when demanding that their bureaucrats surmount difficult and demanding tasks.

Agency problems: Principal-agent theory suggests that policymakers have to devise suitable incentives and monitoring mechanisms to ensure that the (implicit) 'contract' between them and agents (mainly in the private sector) is enforced. While theoretical solutions often appear very complex and difficult, it is possible to devise simpler practical ones. The Tigers did this in different ways: the most important and common one was, as noted, the use of export performance as the monitoring and allocation device (what the World Bank, 1993a, calls 'creating contests'), but there were others. Banks acted as agents of monitoring and implementing export policy. Regular meetings between industry and government permitted the inter-flow of information, backed by detailed industry and strategy studies. Close contact between the bureaucracy and industry was promoted, with personnel moving between the two. In Korea promotion of a relatively few *chaebols* allowed the government to limit the number of agents it had to deal directly with, and to use them as interlocutors with the rest of the industrial sector. Industry associations also played vital roles as interlocutors in all three interventionist countries.

Within the bureaucracy itself, there are means of ensuring better compliance. As noted, skills and information can be enhanced; internal incentive structures can also be improved to ensure that general objectives are met efficiently. Again, making bureaucrats responsible for meeting export targets can be an effective way of improving their commitment and incentives. Adequate reward and promotion systems are another.

Resource constraints: Most intervention requires financial resources as well as human ones. Tariffs are an exception. The creation of skills, technology institutions and marketing support systems can be expensive propositions – the market friendly approach does not escape these – as are industry specific programmes for restructuring, technology upgrading, training or design. Unless the government has ensured that its budget can provide the necessary resources to carry through the interventions it has selected, the results can be very negative: again, an obvious point but often forgotten in practice.

Coordination with the private sector: The importance of close coordination between government and the private sector has been noted at several points above. The World Bank study (1993a) also comments on the need for mechanisms to ensure regular interaction, and describes how the new Tigers are setting up new institutions for this purpose. The exact form differs, of course, from country to country, but the general principles are similar across countries.

Inflexibility: Many interventions turn out to be costly not so much because they are poorly designed (private business makes huge mistakes all the time) but because often changing course is difficult for governments and there is little accountability for the outcome. Clearly, all interventions have to be designed flexibly and monitored constantly so that mistakes can be rectified as they appear. There are precedents in the private corporate sector on how this can be done, but the use of export performance as the check is perhaps the best way to monitor export policies.

Sectional interests: While the 'hijacking' of policies by sectional interests is a danger in most countries, regardless of the nature of policies, the danger is greater where the government has selective as opposed to functional interventions. It can be offset only by strong leadership, the setting up of appropriate institutions and internal checks on the allocation of favours: again we step outside the realm of economic analysis. That sectional interests can be dominated by national ones is illustrated by the Asian experience. Whether or not this is feasible in a particular set of circumstances, however, cannot be said *a priori*. What we can say is that the danger of hijacking of national policies in sectional interests is a good argument against selectivity where there are strong vested interests facing a weak government.

Corruption: There may be several levels of official corruption: the higher the level the more difficult it is to solve. At lower levels, changes in monitoring, employment conditions, salaries and incentives may help reduce rampant corruption. At the top levels, however, if there is no one able to impose sanctions on wrongdoers and there is no genuine commitment to economic development, there is really no way of mounting selective, or indeed any useful development, policies. Venality at the top will also tend to breed and condone that lower down the scale, and it follows that the greater the risk of corruption the less selectivity should be exercised.

The degree of selectivity

It is difficult for an economist to take this sort of discussion much further. There are clearly very real dangers of selectivity when government capabilities are weak in a broad sense. Neoliberals may argue that *all* governments are inherently weak and corruptible, and that selectivity can never succeed: this is a matter of ideology and has no base in either theory or fact. What we suggest is that there are certainly risks that have to be acknowledged and faced. We also argue that government capabilities can be improved, that the level of selectivity can be geared to capabilities if the leadership is clearly committed to competitive development and that governments can be helped to intervene efficiently.

It is important, therefore, to distinguish between different intensities or degrees of selective intervention. There is a common tendency to treat all selectivity as equal in intensity, a selective industrial strategy being something like Korea's, and to dismiss the feasibility of a selective strategy if government capabilities do not match up to those in Korea. This is mistaken. Selectivity can be exercised at very different degrees, from relatively mild to very intense. A low degree of selectivity would be involved, say, in favouring technical education over liberal arts, giving uniform protection to all manufacturing over agricultural activities, or providing privileged access to credit for all exporters. At the other end, a high degree of selectivity would resemble early Korean-style direction of investment at the firm and product level, control of technology imports at the detailed level or the creation of hand-picked giant firms. In between, we can think of a multitude of interventions of different degrees of selectivity, defined by the intent and the impact. But they are all selective in their own way.

The lower the capabilities of the government, the lower the degree of selectivity that it can safely be entrusted with. The lower the level of selectivity, the lower also the risks involved as well as the possible 'payoff' in terms of transforming the competitive structure. If there were the possibility of a rational choice of strategy differentiated by country, then the optimal one would take into account present and future government capabilities. This is in theory – in reality governments do not choose strategies on a realistic assessment of their own capabilities and limitations. External advisers or analysts may be able to provide such an assessment, but there is little guarantee that a government will base its strategy on such advice. If strategies of more general applicability were to be recommended, what would they be?

If governments were really intent on copying what they regarded as each other's 'best practice' without regard to their own failures and weaknesses, the best general strategy may be the one aimed at the lowest common denominator of capabilities, i.e. one with a fairly low level of selectivity. The implicit assumption here would be that the cost of government failure at all higher levels of selectivity would outweigh the costs of market failures left untreated, and that this balance could not be altered by improving government capabilities. In this case, the rational strategy would be to persuade governments that non-selectivity was economically the ideal strategy they should aim at under all circumstances. Arguments in favour of selectivity would then be dismissed on economic rather than political or administrative ones, as part of a general persuasion campaign, and no attempt would be needed to improve capabilities to undertake selective intervention.

Conclusions

This sounds rather like the present situation: the awesome weight and authority of the Washington consensus and the WTO, backed by the major aid donors, combining some sensible policy advice on macroeconomic management with strong neoliberal advice on the inherent desirability of free markets. However, whether this is due to a strong belief in free markets, the interplay of pressures from powerful governments or a considered judgement based on the above reasoning is not clear.

What is evident is that the scope for selective interventions has been considerably narrowed by the new rules of the game of international trade and finance. This constitutes today the single most important constraint to the use of the tools that were deployed so successfully by the two larger Tigers: import protection and export subsidies, credit subsidies and direction, local content rules, discriminatory treatment of FDI, interventions in technology transfer and lax intellectual property protection.

While there is no doubt that this wholesale move to liberalization has many desirable effects, reducing the scope for inefficient interventions and corruption that past policies have exhibited, our argument suggests that by ignoring the legitimate and important role of selectivity it goes too far. The genuine constraints that exist on the use of selective instruments need to be addressed directly, since it is possible to remedy them. They are presently going by default, crushed by the Washington juggernaut and the impenetrable mantras of formal neoclassical economics.

Conclusions

In the absence of selective policies, export growth and diversification are likely to be slow and shallow. A domestic enterprise based strategy of technological deepening calls for the most pervasive interventions, but even a foreign investment driven strategy needs targeting if it is to go beyond the basic labour based activities. This chapter has drawn upon the East Asian experience to illustrate the range of possible policies and strategies, providing the rationale for selectivity and the role of 'vision' or national objectives in defining the relevant market failures. It has noted the limitations to selective policies, posed partly by the risk of government failures and weak capabilities and partly by external constraints and governments' own ideological perceptions. When all is said and done, there does remain some scope for the use of selective policies to promote exports, but its exact scope still has to be delineated.

In the meantime, governments continue to worry about their international competitiveness in an era of liberalization, and competitiveness studies are a major industry in the most mature industrial to the least developed countries. Most studies are unfortunately poorly done, using current fads like 'cluster' analysis, with little analysis of the economic issues or of market failures. It is important that they be well done, based on sound economics and on the experience of successful exporters. This chapter has simply highlighted some of the important issues in this context.

Notes

1. Though it is convenient to use the market failure terminology to discuss the role of government interventions, it may not be the most appropriate framework for analysing policy, especially where technological change is concerned. 'Market failure' in neoclassical theory is a deviation from a market clearing equilibrium under conditions of perfect competition, and the remedy is to return to (a theoretically achievable) static optimum. This may not be possible, or even desirable, in the markets that characterize modern industry. Some authors argue that perfect competition is undesirable *as a theoretical construct* under conditions of increasing returns and uncertain and unpredictable technological change (Richardson, 1996). Information economics suggests that whenever information is imperfect, externalities 'diffuse' and markets incomplete (including all future markets for risk), invariably the case with technical change, free markets cannot in principle meet the strict requirements of optimality in resource allocation (Stiglitz, 1996, 1997). It is misleading to think of market failure as something that can, or should, be 'remedied' in order that the economy can be brought back to a desired (static) optimum (Lipsey, 1994). In developing countries, where technological learning is essential to industrial development, externalities are rife and markets highly imperfect – indeed, when new markets, agents or endowments are being created – it is difficult to describe policy as 'remedying market failure' in the neoclassical sense. Where economies of scale exist in intermediate products, leading to multiple equilibria (Rodrik, 1996), government policy should aim to move from low to high productivity/technology paths. Again, this is not really dealing with 'market failure' since equilibrium could in theory be reached in any of the multiple possibilities. However, this chapter cannot deal with such fundamental issues. We continue to use the market failure terminology for purposes of exposition, but remind the reader that strategic interventions may have little to do with achieving static resource optimization.
2. Some proponents of 'market friendly' policies (e.g. the World Bank, 1993a) also recommend an element of selectivity, in terms of favouring exports over domestic sales to capture the special externalities that exports generate. Even this element of selectivity concerns export activities in general, rather than selected export activities. For a review of the arguments for a pro-export bias, see Helleiner (1995a).
3. Of the large, and burgeoning, literature on this see Pack and Westphal (1986), Amsden (1989), Wade (1990), World Bank (1993a), Lall (1996), Rodrik (1996), Stiglitz (1996).
4. Note that the data for Singapore and Hong Kong exclude re-exports, which account for 40 per cent of total merchandise exports for the former and 81 per cent for the latter.
5. The tertiary enrolment figures for Singapore would be higher if polytechnics were included – polytechnic enrolment in Singapore is nearly double that of universities.
6. Helleiner describes the direct and indirect subsidies to exports as follows: 'import and excise duty exemptions and drawbacks for inputs (often extended to local suppliers of inputs to exporters); subsidized credit; corporate tax concessions (reductions or refunds); preferential exchange rates; preferential foreign exchange retention rights or allowances; and direct cash subsidies' (Helleiner, 1995b: 19). Some of these fall under our category of 'positive' rather than 'permissive' promotion policies and are noted below.

7. Taiwan has around 700 000 SMEs, accounting for 70 per cent of employment, 55 per cent of GNP and 62 per cent of manufactured exports.

8. Most of these institutions have substantial government financial support.

9. According to Wade, the use of quantitative restrictions on imports was more widespread than of tariffs, and senior policymakers believed that it was more flexible and effective. Local content rules were used to foster backward linkages in several sectors, though their use lessened in the 1980s; the information industry was, unlike Korea, not subjected to local content rules (Wade, 1990: 137–8).

10. One example of the Taiwanese government's support for industrial restructuring is for the textile industry. Textile exports, Taiwan's second largest foreign exchange earner, consist mainly of synthetic fibres, since labour-intensive garments have been largely relocated to lower wage countries. Faced with rising labour costs and intensifying competition from cheaper countries, the government embarked in the late 1980s on a major programme of restructuring and upgrading the industry. The Industrial Development Bureau of the Ministry of Economic Affairs developed a programme of grants to private firms to speed up technological renovation, encourage R&D, improve design capabilities and train technical and managerial personnel. Over 250 textile plants were to receive financial and technical assistance under this programme.

11. 'Towards a Developed Economy: EDB Sets Bold Targets for the Year 2000', EDB website.

12. The main technology finance schemes in Korea are as follows: (1) The Designated R&D Programme which, since 1982, supported private firms undertaking research in core strategic technology development projects in the industrial areas approved by the Ministry of Science and Technology. It funded up to 50 per cent of R&D costs of large firms and up to 80 per cent for SMEs. (2) The Industrial Technology Development Programme, started in 1987 to subsidize up to two-thirds of the R&D costs of joint projects of national interest (National Research Projects) between private firms and research institutes. (3) The Highly Advanced National Project (HAN) launched in 1992 to support two activities: the development of specific high-technology products in which Korea could become competitive with advanced industrial countries in a decade or two (Product Technology Development Project), and the development of 'core' technologies considered essential for the economy in which Korea wanted to achieve an independent innovative base (Fundamental Technology Development Project).

13. For instance, when the Taiwanese government found that it lagged behind Korea in semiconductor production, and local private firms were too small to set up the capital-intensive facilities entailed, it took the initiative directly. The Electronic Research and Service Organization (ERSO) started to import and develop process technologies for very large integrated circuits (VLSI) in the late 1970s. A decade later the government set up a joint venture for wafer fabrication, the Taiwan Semiconductor Manufacturing Company (TSMC), with Philips of the Netherlands and local private participants. TSMC also orchestrated the design and manufacturing activities of numerous small electronics firms. Once TSMC was established, private companies started producing semiconductors, microprocessors and related products.

14. There are 4000 foreign firms located in Singapore, about half of them being regional headquarters. The government is targeting the attraction of such headquarters as a major plank of its FDI policy.

15. The Vocational and Industrial Training Board (VITB) has established an integrated training infrastructure which has trained and certified over 112 000 individuals, about 9 per cent of the existing workforce, since 1979. Its Full-Time Institutional Training Programme provides pre-employment skills training for school leavers. Its Continuing Skills Training Programme comprises part-time skills courses and customized courses, offered to workers based on requests from companies and specifically tailored to their needs. Its Continuing Education Programme provides part-time classes for working adults. Its Training and Industry Programme offers apprenticeships to school leavers and ex-national servicemen. The government has collaborated with MNCs to jointly set up specialized training centres, funding a large part of employee salaries while they are being trained. The government has also worked with the governments of Japan, Germany and France to provide technical training. Under the Industry-Based Training Programme, employers, with VITB input, conduct training courses for their specific needs. VITB also provides testing and certification of its trainees and apprentices as well as trade tests for public candidates. Using various grant schemes, the National Productivity Board's Skills Development Fund (SDF) created 405 621 training places in 1990. The SDF is responsible for various financial assistance schemes to help SMEs finance their training needs and to upgrade their operations. The Training Voucher Scheme supports employers in augmenting training resources. It enabled the SDF to reach more than 3000 new companies in 1990, many of which had 50 or fewer employees. The Training Leave Scheme encourages companies to send their employees for training during office hours. It provides 100 per cent funding of the training costs for approved programmes. In effect, Singapore penalizes firms that do not invest in employee training on a continuous basis (information from the EDB website).

16. During 1976–88, the total value of government financial assistance to SMEs amounted to S$1.5 billion, of which 88 per cent was in the Small Industries Financing Scheme (Soon, 1994).

17. It set up an Institute of Molecular and Cell Biology (IMCB) within the National Biotechnology Program, which was started in 1988 to strengthen the national R&D base and fund biotechnology development. Supporting this effort is a strong push in basic research at the National University of Singapore (NUS), which houses the IMCB. The University conducts one-third of Singapore's R&D, and NUS scientists have made their mark in several areas including materials technology, microelectronics and information technology. To nurture this industry, the EDB established Singapore Bio-Innovation (SBI) Pte Ltd. which by 1991 had invested S$41 million in 12 local biotech start-up firms making health care, food, and agricultural products. SBI also invests in overseas companies that might be strategic allies.

18. 'Towards a Developed Economy: EDB Sets Bold Targets for the Year 2000', EDB website.

19. In the field of plant and process engineering, for instance, the government stipulated that foreign contractors transfer their design knowledge to local firms, which quickly absorbed design technologies in some process industries. The government intervened in technology licensing to lower prices and strengthen the position of local buyers, but in a way that did not constrain access to know-how. Licensing policy was also liberalized over the 1980s as the need for advanced technologies increased. The *chaebols* soon developed sufficient international

presence to manage their technology imports, but the SME sector had to be assisted in buying technologies overseas.

20. Incentives for private R&D in Korea included tax exempt Technology Development Reserve funds, tax credits for R&D as well as for upgrading human capital related to research, and setting up industry research institutes, accelerated depreciation for investments in R&D facilities, a tax exemption for 10 per cent of cost of relevant equipment, reduced import duties for imported research equipment, and a reduced excise tax for technology-intensive products. The Korea Technology Advancement Corporation helped firms commercialize research results; a 6 per cent tax credit or special accelerated depreciation provided further incentives. The import of technology was promoted by tax-deductible costs of patent purchase and other technology import fees. Income from technology consulting was tax-exempt. Foreign engineers were exempt from income tax. Grants, long term low interest loans and tax privileges were granted to participants in National Projects. Technology finance was provided by the Korea Technology Development Corporation.

21. However, domestic markets in Korea were kept protected long after an industry had become export competitive, as in garments earlier and automobiles more recently. This seems to have been intended to afford an extra cushion to firms for cross-subsidizing their export expansion or upgrading. Taiwan liberalized faster when activities matured, though analysts note considerable redundancy in tariff rates.

22. The success of this can be judged from the fact that LG Group's proposed investment in a semiconductor plant in the UK was greeted by the British press as an injection of 'Eastern high technology', and was promised a subsidy by the UK government of over £300 million.

23. In Korea, for instance: 'Underlying the effectiveness of Korea's system of export promotion has been the single-minded commitment of the country's political leadership to an outward-looking development strategy based on international competitiveness. That commitment did more than foster an efficient bureaucracy. It unified all economic agents in Korea in a common identifiable undertaking' (Rhee et al., 1984: 73).

24. This leads to the possibility of multiple equilibria in which government policy can shift an economy from a low-growth to a high-growth path (Rodrik, 1996).

25. As Stiglitz notes in criticism of the neoclassical assumption of 'efficient' markets: 'whenever information was imperfect or markets were incomplete, government could devise interventions that filled in for these interventions and that could make everyone better off. *Because information was never perfect and markets never complete, these results completely undermined the standard theoretical basis for relying on the market mechanism.* Similarly the standard models ignored changes in technology; for a variety of reasons markets may under-invest in research and development ... Because developing economies have underdeveloped (missing) markets and imperfect information and because the development process is associated with acquiring new technology (new information), these reservations about the adequacy of market mechanisms may be particularly relevant to developing countries' (Stiglitz, 1996: 156; emphasis added). G. B. Richardson argued essentially the same thing about the undesirability of a neoclassical optimum in the 1960s, but with little impact on mainstream thinking (see his reflections in Richardson, 1996).

26. For a review see Lall (1996).

27. On the electronics industry and the role of OEM and own-brand exports from the Tigers, see Hobday (1995). The greatest success in moving to independent branding, design and sales has been in Korea.

References

Amsden, A. (1989) *Asia's Next Giant: South Korea and Late Industrialization*, New York: Oxford University Press.

Helleiner, G. K. (ed.) (1995a) *Manufacturing for Export in the Developing World: Problems and Prospects*, London: Routledge.

Helleiner, G. K. (1995b) *Trade, Trade Policy and Industrialization Reconsidered*, UNU/WIDER, World Development Studies 6.

Hobday, M. G. (1995) *Innovation in East Asia: The Challenge to Japan*, Cheltenham: Edward Elgar.

Keesing, D. B. (1988) 'The Four Successful Exceptions: Official Export Promotion and Support for Export Marketing in Hong Kong, Singapore, Taiwan and the Republic of Korea', World Bank: Trade Policy Division, draft.

Kim, K. S. (1994) 'Trade and Industrialization Policies in Korea: An Overview', in G. K. Helleiner (ed.), *Trade Policy and Industrialization in Turbulent Times*, London: Routledge, 317–63.

Kim, L. (1997) *Imitation to Innovation: The Dynamics of Korea's Technological Learning*, Boston, MA: Harvard Business School Press.

Lall, S. (1996) *Learning from the Asian Tigers: Studies in Technology and Industrial Policy*, London: Macmillan.

Lipsey, R. G. (1994) 'Markets, Technological Change and Economic Growth', Quaid-I-Azam Invited Lecture, *Pakistan Development Review*, 33, 4: 327–52.

Organization for Economic Cooperation and Development (OECD) (1987) *Structural Adjustment and Economic Performance*, Paris.

Pack, H. and Westphal, L. E. (1986) 'Industrial Strategy and Technological Change: Theory versus Reality', *Journal of Development Economics*, 22, 1: 87–128.

Ramstetter, E. (1994) 'Employment-Related Characteristics of Foreign Multinationals in Selected Asian Economies', Background paper for UNCTAD, *World Investment Report 1994*, Geneva.

Rhee, Y. W., Ross-Larson, B. and Pursell, G. (1984) *Korea's Competitive Edge: Managing the Entry Into World Markets*, Baltimore, MD: Johns Hopkins University Press, for the World Bank.

Richardson, G. B. (1996) 'Competition, Innovation and Increasing Returns', Aalborg: Danish Research Unit for Industrial Dynamics, DRUID Working Papers, No. 96–10.

Rodrik, D. (1996) 'Coordination Failures and Government Policy: A Model with Applications to East Asia and Eastern Europe', *Journal of International Economics*, 40: 1–22.

Selvaratnam, V. (1994) *Innovations in Higher Education: Singapore at the Competitive Edge*, Technical Paper No. 222, World Bank, Washington, DC.

Shapiro, H. and Taylor, L. (1990) 'The State and Industrial Strategy', *World Development*, 18, 6: 861–78.

Soon, Teck-Wong (1994) 'Singapore' in S. D. Meyanathan, *Industrial Structures and the Development of Small and Medium Enterprise Linkages: Examples from East Asia*, World Bank, Economic Development Institute.

Stiglitz, J. E. (1989) 'Markets, Market Failures and Development', *American Economic Review Papers and Proceedings*, 79, 2: 197–202.

Stiglitz, J. E. (1996) 'Some Lessons from the East Asian Miracle', *World Bank Research Observer*, 11, 2 (August): 151–77.
Stiglitz, J. E. (1997) 'Market Failures, Public Goods, and Externalities', in E. Malinvaud (ed.), *Development Strategy and the Market Economy*, Oxford: OUP (forthcoming).
Stiglitz, J. E. and Uy, M. (1996) 'Financial Markets, Public Policy and the East Asian Miracle', *The World Bank Research Observer*, 11, 2: 249–76.
Wade, R. (1990) *Governing the Market*, Princeton, NJ: Princeton University Press.
Westphal, L. E. (1997) 'Government–Business Relations: Experience of the Republic of Korea', Background note prepared for UNCTAD Expert Group Meeting.
World Bank (1993a) *The East Asian Miracle*, Oxford: Oxford University Press.
World Bank (1993b) 'East Asia's Export Push', *Development Brief Number 23*, October.
World Bank (1996) *Made in Malaysia: Technology Development for Vision 2020*, Study prepared for the Ministry of Science, Technology and the Environment, Government of Malaysia.

3
Export Performance in Chile: Lessons for Africa

Manuel Agosin

Introduction

For good and bad reasons, Chile has come to be identified in academic and policymaking circles as one of the foremost examples of the successes that await countries that are bold enough to carry out and stick to policy reforms in favour of market forces. In the period 1974–9, the military government that overthrew President Allende in 1973 implemented a thorough trade liberalization, freed domestic financial markets, and opened up the capital account of the balance of payments (Ffrench-Davis et al., 1991, 1993; Agosin and Ffrench-Davis, 1993; Meller, 1996, chapter 3). These reforms had the objective of bringing down the curtain on the import substitution model of industrialization that had served as the main developmental paradigm since the 1940s and that had been upheld by governments of very different stripes. The reforms of the period 1974–9 were guided by the idea that, once market forces were given full reign, resources would be reallocated (costlessly) to export industries in which the country had a comparative advantage and that this would lead to rapid growth not only of exports but also of aggregate output.

Therefore, in any evaluation of Chilean policy reforms, special interest attaches to the behaviour of exports. It is certainly true that exports rose rapidly after 1974, and that they have continued to do so up to the present. Thus one of the key ingredients in the Chilean success story, it is claimed, has been outstanding export performance.

This chapter looks at the performance of exports over a long period: 1960–95. It seeks to identify the main trends in the growth of exports and attempts to assign responsibility to various factors for export performance. We provide answers to the following questions: Was trade liberalization responsible for the evident export success that Chile has had since the mid-

1970s and has been able to maintain up to the present? What weight can one assign to other government policies that are less known outside of Chile? Were there specific factors at work at a sectoral level? And last but not least, what should the governments of other countries that have not yet opened their economies do in order to jump-start a process of export-led growth?

The chapter is organized in the following way. First, we develop (very briefly) an analytical framework for evaluating policies and their impact on export growth. Besides the need to change market incentives in favour of export-led growth, which requires trade liberalization-cum-depreciation of the exchange rate, we emphasize that the strength of the supply response will depend on policies to overcome a number of constraints that are endemic to developing economies and that are related to market failures in key sectors – financial markets, human capital formation, and technology and market information acquisition.

Next, we deal with export and GDP growth trends in the Chilean economy in the long term. It is certainly true that export growth has been impressive since the mid-1970s and that the Chilean economy has undergone a remarkable process of opening up to trade. However, one can speak of sustained export-led growth only since the mid-1980s, when policymaking became more pragmatic and real exchange rate depreciation gave a big boost to exports.

We then describe the trade liberalization of 1974–9 and other policies with a bearing on its results and argue that the restructuring of the economy was needlessly costly because an important share of installed capacity in manufacturing was destroyed rather than gradually redeployed toward the export sector. Although we do not have a counterfactual against which we can evaluate the degree of success of the reforms, it is argued that a different policy package that would have assisted the restructuring of the manufacturing sector would have been more successful. The lessons of the Chilean reforms are very relevant for policymakers elsewhere who are evaluating different routes to opening up the economy.

We then look at other policies that affected exports and at specific policies and factors at the sectoral level. We conclude that it is not possible to ignore other policies and initial conditions that increased the strength of the supply response and that were very important in explaining the export successes at the sectoral level.

We then move on to estimate a supply function for the exports of manufactures. It is shown that tariff reductions, real exchange rate depreciation, and excess capacity in manufacturing have all had a role to play in the growth of manufacturing exports. Excess capacity was particularly important during the depressed economic conditions of the 1970s in giving exports their initial push. But the permanent change in incentives associated with trade liberalization and steep real exchange rate depreciation became increasingly important in the 1980s. As excess capacity wound down in the second half of the 1970s, investments for the export market and export-led growth took hold.

Finally, we wrap up the policy discussion and derive policy implications for other developing countries. It is clear that trade liberalization is a necessary but not sufficient condition for export success. The manner in which the Chilean trade liberalization was undertaken, together with its supporting policies (i.e. exchange rate policies, policies toward domestic and international finance), imposed unnecessary costs and delayed the positive effects of the change in relative prices. In fact, a better designed trade liberalization package-cum-measures to strengthen the competitiveness of manufacturing would have led to even faster rates of growth of manufacturing exports and would have avoided significant decreases in output and losses in productive capacity in that key sector. In other sectors, in spite of its neoliberal leanings, the authorities instituted policies which gave strong signals to exporters and worked to correct the market failures that blunt supply responses. After the crisis of 1982, policies became more pragmatic and exporters were assisted by a combination of drawbacks, export subsidies, steep real exchange rate depreciation, and reasonable interest rates. These policies are also fundamental in explaining Chilean successes in promoting exports.

The analytical framework

The central idea that underlies the analysis of this chapter is that the launching of export-oriented growth requires not only a well-designed trade liberalization, as well as supporting policies with regard to key macroeconomic variables (e.g. the exchange rate and interest rates) but also overcoming barriers that inhibit a strong supply response to price signals. These constraints are not spontaneously removed by the operation of market forces and require more purposive policy action by governments or by other institutions that are able to internalize the externality or to correct the market failure involved.

The objective of trade liberalization is to change market signals from favouring import-competing and non-tradable sectors towards encouraging the production of exports and import substitutes that do not require high protection to be profitable. Usually, conventional trade policy advice (which always advocates liberalization, without bothering to look at a country's institutional set-up) relies on a simple two-sector trade model with one exportable and one importable *and no non-tradables*. In such a model, it is possible to ignore the exchange rate, since it disappears from relative prices. However, in the real world non-tradables loom large in the economy and, moreover, there are many tradables, with various levels of protection for importables. Likewise, there is a set of potential exportables, which can be ranked from lowest to highest according to their average costs.

Ceteris paribus, the real value of the currency must depreciate as a result of import liberalization; therefore, those sectors which initially had effective rates of protection below the percentage real depreciation induced by the reduction of import barriers would *benefit* from the package of trade liberalization-cum-depreciation. Thus, they cannot be considered to have been inefficient and, therefore, candidates for the block, just because prior to import liberalization they enjoyed higher effective protection than post-liberalization rates. In addition, the depreciation will generate (with a lag) new exports, as the economy moves further down the list of potential exports ranked according to costs. In fact, some of these new exports may come from sectors previously protected at higher rates than those prevailing after liberalization.

As a result of the trade liberalization, it can be shown that the compensating depreciation[1] must be as follows (see appendix for a formal derivation):

$$\hat{e} = \frac{\hat{t}}{\varepsilon_x / \varepsilon_m - 1}$$

where e is the exchange rate, t the average tariff, a hat over a variable is percentage change, and ε_x and ε_m are (average) export and import price elasticities, respectively. In the Chilean case, the average tariff went from 94 per cent in 1973 to 10 per cent in 1979, implying an induced decline in import prices of 43 per cent. Assuming a price elasticity of export supply of 0.5 and a price elasticity of import demand of (minus) unity, the compensating depreciation would have been 29 per cent. This means that any importable with initial tariff of up to 29 per cent was, indeed, internationally competitive and that, with a final tariff of 10 per cent it should have been able to compete with imports and/or become an exporter.

Even if price signals are favourable to exporting, there are, as already noted, important constraints to a swift and strong supply response. Some of them are of an informational nature. Domestic producers do not have adequate information about (1) technologies for producing goods or services that will sell in foreign markets or that will help them to compete with foreign producers at home; (2) marketing and distribution channels in overseas markets; or (3) consumer tastes or producer needs in potential markets. Successful countries, such as those of East Asia, have been able to overcome these barriers (Lall, 1994). The peculiarity about information is that it is both costly and in the nature of a public good: on the one hand, it is a non-rival good, in the sense that its consumption by one agent does not reduce its value to another; on the other, it is non-excludable – i.e. individual agents find it difficult to keep others from using it.[2] This gives the policymaker an important role in the process of opening up the economy: subsidizing the gathering of information on technologies, foreign markets, and foreign tastes; subsidizing the establishment of reputation for domestic producers (what in recent years has been called 'creating a country image'); and assisting existing firms to retool, orienting their activities towards foreign markets and becoming better able to compete in domestic markets with foreign producers.

A less direct way of dealing with this evident form of externality, and one that makes use of the market, is to create institutions or firms to internalize it. For example, associations of exporters may find it profitable to gather information on markets or technologies on behalf of their members. Thus the role of government can be to assist in the formation of such associations.

In most developing countries, capital markets are non-existent or very shallow. As emphasized by an abundant literature (e.g. Stiglitz and Weiss, 1981), there are important informational asymmetries that make capital markets imperfect in any part of the world. In developing countries, these imperfections are magnified (Stiglitz, 1994). Supply responses are blunted if potential entrepreneurs have inadequate access to long-term investment finance. Therefore, policies to deepen domestic financial markets and to improve their operation (e.g. by better regulation or disclosure requirements) are complements to trade liberalization. Even these policies are unlikely to be enough: formal financial markets, no matter how developed, tend to discriminate against small producers and firms without reputation or collateral. Therefore, it will be necessary to supplement private financial markets with appropriate public action. For example, Díaz-Alejandro (1985) advocates the use of development banks to provide credit, at positive and market-related rates of interest, to projects with high social and private returns but which are rationed out of private markets.

Other supply-side bottlenecks are related to low levels of human capital formation and to lack of adequate infrastructure. In these areas, public policy is also indispensable. Education and training have strong externalities; therefore, private market solutions will underproduce them. In addition, human capital formation is an investment for which capital markets are particularly unwilling to supply funds. The planning, design, and, despite current fashion, the construction of infrastructure continues to be a priority task of governments.

If one accepts this view, trade liberalization acquires a more limited, although still important, role in the process of launching export-oriented growth. Trade liberalization is a means for altering relative prices in the economy and making it more likely that producers will allocate resources to activities in which the country has a current comparative advantage. Since it does nothing to correct the market failures associated with the factors mentioned above, it is a rather blunt tool for encouraging producers to create new comparative advantages. In fact, some countries – e.g. Korea or Taiwan – launched very successful processes of export-oriented growth *without* trade liberalization (Wade, 1990; Amsden, 1993, 1994; Rodrik, 1995). In spite of its free market rhetoric, there were a few instances of industrial policy in post-

1974 Chile – notably in the forestry sector. In addition, prior to 1974, history and policies had created the precondition for adequate supply responses.

Export and GDP growth, 1960–95

Chile is a small, middle-income, open economy with a population of 14 million inhabitants, at present exporting about a third of its GDP (Table 3.1).[3] The share of exports in GDP has risen about two and a half times since 1973, the year in which the import liberalization programme was launched. Although GDP growth has been strong since the mid-1980s, per capita GDP is still below US$5000. The World Bank (1997: 215) estimates that, in purchasing power parity terms, Chile's per capita GDP in 1995, at US$9520 (current international dollars), put the country at the top of the middle income group and just below what it classifies as 'high-income economies', whose per capita GDPs began at US$11 450 (Korea).

Table 3.1   Basic data on the Chilean economy, 1960–95

	GDP per capita *(in 1995 US$)*	*Population* *(thousands)*	*Exports* *(% of current GDP)*
1960	2,293	7,607.6	13.8
1973	2,758	10,006.5	13.9
1981	3,232	11,318.6	16.4
1989	3,590	12,882.8	35.1
1995	4,727	14,210.4	29.3

Source: Author's calculations, based on data of the Central Bank of Chile.

The stylized facts of the growth process in Chile can best be understood by dividing the period since 1960 into five subperiods. The period from 1960 to 1970 was characterized by steady (albeit unremarkable) economic growth. While copper dominated the export basket, there was significant growth in non-traditional exports. In the second half of the decade, economic policies had already begun to shift from unrestricted support for import substitution to greater emphasis on export promotion.

The period 1971–3 corresponds to the upheavals of the socialist experiment. In a radical break with the past, the Allende government nationalized large segments of the economy, including the copper mines (which at the time had 49 per cent foreign ownership), the banks, and most large and even medium-sized industrial firms. There were widespread price controls, high tariffs, various sorts of non-tariff barriers, and multiple exchange rates. Non-traditional exports declined steeply during this period.

After the military coup of September 1973, there ensued another attempt at radical departure from the past, this time in a neoliberal direction. The military regime can be divided into two subperiods, 1974–81 and 1982–9. The first begins with the reorganization of the economy and ends with the boom of 1981; as a response to the banking and balance of payments crises of 1982, the second subperiod is marked by strict prudential regulation of the banking system, sharp exchange rate depreciation, and a greater pragmatism with respect to measures in support of non-traditional exports. In spite of the fact that positive growth resumed in 1984, per capita GDP in 1988 had not surpassed its 1981 level. The growth of GDP and exports, and export diversification, was very brisk beginning in 1984.

The final period, which begins in 1990, is associated with the return to democracy. During this period, the growth of GDP has been strong, the investment rate has risen steadily, and non-traditional exports have become the most dynamic sector of the economy. In contrast to what happened in the 1970s and 1980s, the growth of exports has pulled the rest of the economy in its train. Government policies have been supportive of such growth. In the face of large inflows of foreign capital, exchange rate policies have aimed at preventing a massive appreciation of the exchange rate. Finally, policies in support of technological innovation and marketing products abroad have been introduced or strengthened.

Since 1974, export growth has led GDP growth (Table 3.2). However, it is only since 1989 that the growth in non-traditional exports has been accompanied by strong and sustained GDP growth. During 1974–89, not only did GDP growth trail export growth, but growth and investment rates were substantially below those achieved during the 'golden age' of the 1960s.[4]

Table 3.2   Growth and export performance, Chile, 1960–95 (%)

	GDP growth	*Gross investment*[a]	*Total export growth*[b]	*Non-copper export growth*
1960–70	4.2	25.1	5.6	4.6
1971–3	0.5	16.9	–4.4	–11.9
1974–81	3.7	22.2	12.0	20.9
1982–9	2.4	19.8	6.5	8.2
1990–5	6.7	28.5	9.0	9.8

Notes: [a]As a percentage of GDP in 1986 constant prices.
          [b]Goods only.

Source: Central Bank of Chile and author's calculations.

Even so, as already shown, the degree of openness of the Chilean economy has increased dramatically since 1974. In a sense, one of the objectives of the trade liberalization policies can be said to have been achieved: the economy has gone from a situation in which producing either non-tradables or importables was its mainstay to another in which exports are its leading sector. In the process, large patches of the manufacturing sector (e.g. textiles, machine tools) disappeared. Others eventually emerged, mainly oriented towards external markets.

Since 1974, export growth has been very fast indeed, and the growth of non-mineral exports has been spectacular. We have divided goods exports into seven categories: copper, other minerals, agricultural products (which are mainly fresh fruit and vegetables), fishmeal and extractive fishing products, wood and wood products (including a growing but small item of furniture), pulp and paper (mostly pulp), and other manufactures. This last category consists of about 3000 items of the most varied nature. It comprises, among others, confectionery, fruit juices, processed food, canned and frozen fish, cultivated salmon, wine, auto parts, sanitary equipment and metal products. What these products have in common is that they are either natural-resource intensive or use standardized technologies. Their main markets are in other Latin American countries, but they are an increasing component of exports to developed countries.

Exports of non-factor services have also risen dramatically. It has not been possible to disaggregate services exports by category. Nonetheless, available qualitative information indicates that some new service industries have begun to export successfully in recent years (software and engineering services, for example). These are sectors where the country has been able to acquire comparative advantage through long-term policies of human resource development, which, parenthetically, suffered serious setbacks during the military regime.

Thus exports have not only grown, but they have become increasingly diversified. In 1971–3, copper represented almost 80 per cent of total goods exports. If we add other minerals, the share of minerals was almost 90 per cent. By contrast, in the 1990s the share of copper has fallen to under 40 per cent and that of all minerals to under 50 per cent.[5] On the other hand, the share of 'other manufactures' has risen from 5 per cent in 1971–3 to almost 30 per cent in the 1990s. If we add pulp and paper, fishmeal, and wood products, total exports of manufactures and semi-manufactures comprise over 40 per cent of total exports, as compared to 10 per cent in 1971–3 (Figure 3.1).

For all of these seven categories of products, we calculated price indices with which we could derive export volume growth rates by category.[6] Non-mineral exports have grown rapidly in volume terms since 1974 (Table 3.3). The rates of growth of export volumes during the first period under military rule (1974–81) are particularly impressive, but this is due mainly to their small (and depressed, in the case of manufactures) levels in 1973.

Moreover, to a large extent, the growth of exports of 'other manufactures', which include items that are produced both for export and for domestic markets, was induced during this period by the huge excess capacity created by the trade liberalization policies. Fiscal adjustment in order to reduce a fiscal deficit that had grown to almost 20 per cent of GDP, together with very

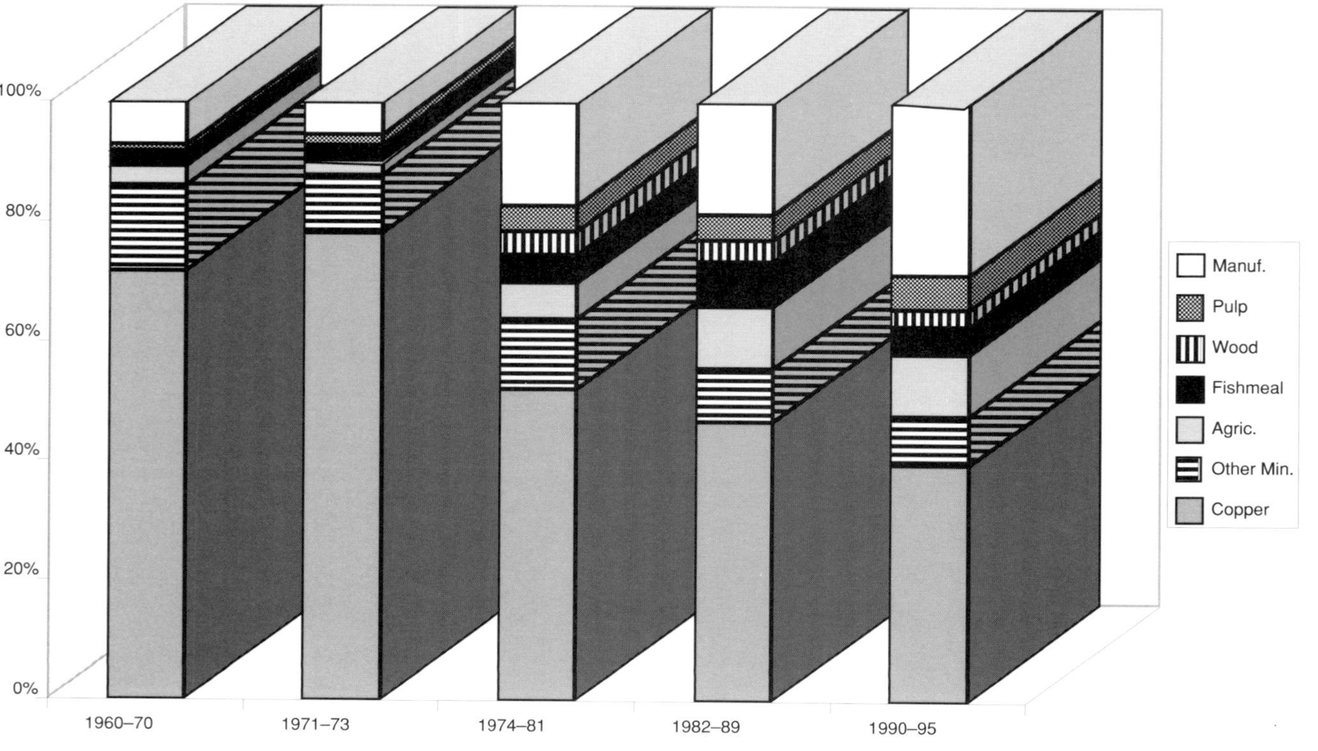

Figure 3.1 Sectoral distribution of exports, Chile, 1960–95

high interest rates (resulting from financial liberalization without adequate regulation) also contributed to the depression in aggregate demand and to the contraction in GDP in 1975, which bordered on 13 per cent. One way in which domestic producers of manufactures defended themselves was to seek foreign markets for the goods they could not sell at home (Ffrench-Davis, 1979). The manufacturing sector shrank in absolute terms, manufacturing output did not recover its 1972 levels until 1987 (Figure 3.2), and the share of manufacturing in GDP contracted from 26.6 per cent in 1972 to 20.8 per cent in 1987.[7]

Table 3.3   Average annual rates of growth of export volume, by type of good, Chile, 1960–95

	1960–70	*1971–3*	*1974–81*	*1982–9*	*1990–5*
Copper	6.2	–1.0	7.8	4.6	7.8
Other minerals	1.6	–2.6	6.7	6.5	3.4
Agricultural products	2.4	–27.5	32.6	11.8	7.0
Fishmeal and fish products	18.7	–31.1	45.8	11.1	3.0
Wood and wood products	15.9	–25.1	41.0	7.3	4.3
Pulp and paper	16.7	–7.6	18.5	0.8	22.7
Other manufactures	7.1	–28.0	38.6	9.2	12.7
Total non-copper	4.6	–11.9	20.9	8.2	9.8
Total goods	5.6	–4.4	12.0	6.5	9.0
Services	–	–	18.8[*]	0.1	8.0

[*]1976–81.

Source: Author's calculations and Central Bank of Chile.

Excess capacity also played a role in the expansion of manufacturing exports in the 1982–9 period. Once again, there was a severe economic contraction in 1982–3, with GDP falling about 15 per cent. It was not until after 1985 that one can speak of export-led growth with positive net investment in this sector. By contrast, during the period since 1989, output has been close to potential output, investment has grown sharply, and exports have led a rapid increase in overall manufacturing production.

Therefore, it is only since the mid-1980s that export-led growth has become firmly based. Non-traditional exports have become the most dynamic component of the economy, investment rates have been rising from Latin American toward East Asian standards, and overall growth has been high and steady. Since 1989, excess capacity in manufacturing (and in the economy as a whole) has been close to zero and, therefore, cannot explain the increase in manufacturing exports.

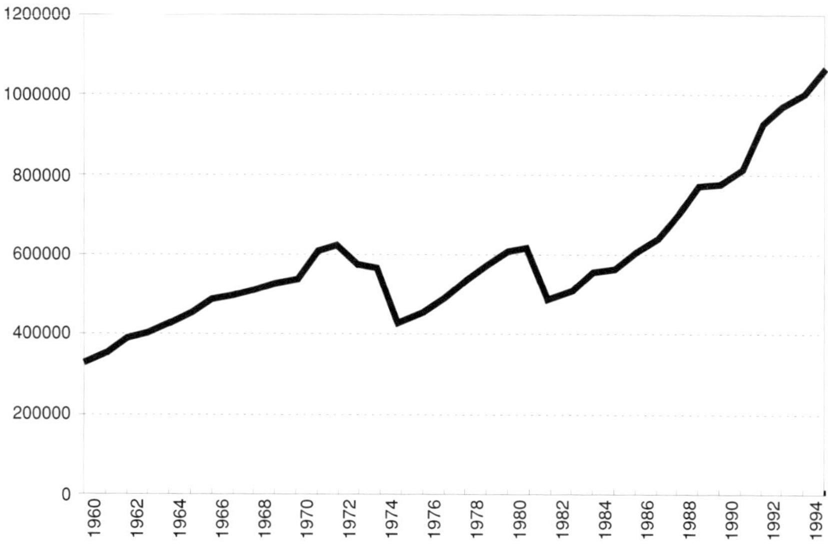

Figure 3.2   Real manufacturing output, Chile, 1960–95 (in millions of 1995 pesos)

The role of trade liberalization

One of the first measures of the military government after the September 1973 coup was to announce a trade policy reform. Indeed, at that time trade policy can best be described as chaotic: the (unweighted) average tariff was 94 per cent; there were 57 different tariff rates, ranging from zero to 220 per cent (plus surcharges on a number of items); there were many non-tariff measures (prior import deposits, prohibitions, quotas, etc.) and a multiple exchange rate system with eight rates, where the highest price for the dollar was ten times the lowest. This *ad hoc* system of protection served no development purpose at all. The disorganization of the Allende period had led to stagnation in manufacturing, the disappearance of economic growth, and a strong contraction of a fledgling non-traditional export sector (which included several manufactures).

The trade liberalization announced in late 1973 involved the elimination of all non-tariff barriers, the gradual reduction of tariff rates and their consolidation into three tariff levels (with a maximum rate of 60 per cent), the unification of the exchange rate, *and a devaluation to compensate the reduction in the average tariff.* In effect, the real exchange rate did depreciate in real terms during the two and a half years following the introduction of the reform. In the absence of capital flows, this was the outcome of market forces:

the opening up of the economy led to an import surge which caused the currency to depreciate sharply (Figure 3.3).

Several events induced a change in the course of the reform. As the trade liberalization programme progressed, it was radicalized. In 1975, the authorities announced a new tariff range of 10–35 per cent, to be reached in gradual steps by 1978. Toward the end of 1977, the objective of reaching a 10 per cent tariff by mid-1979 for all imports was set, with monthly tariff reductions. In addition, prospects for tapping international financial markets changed for the better by mid-decade. This made it possible for the authorities to assign exchange rate policy to the objective of slowing down inflation

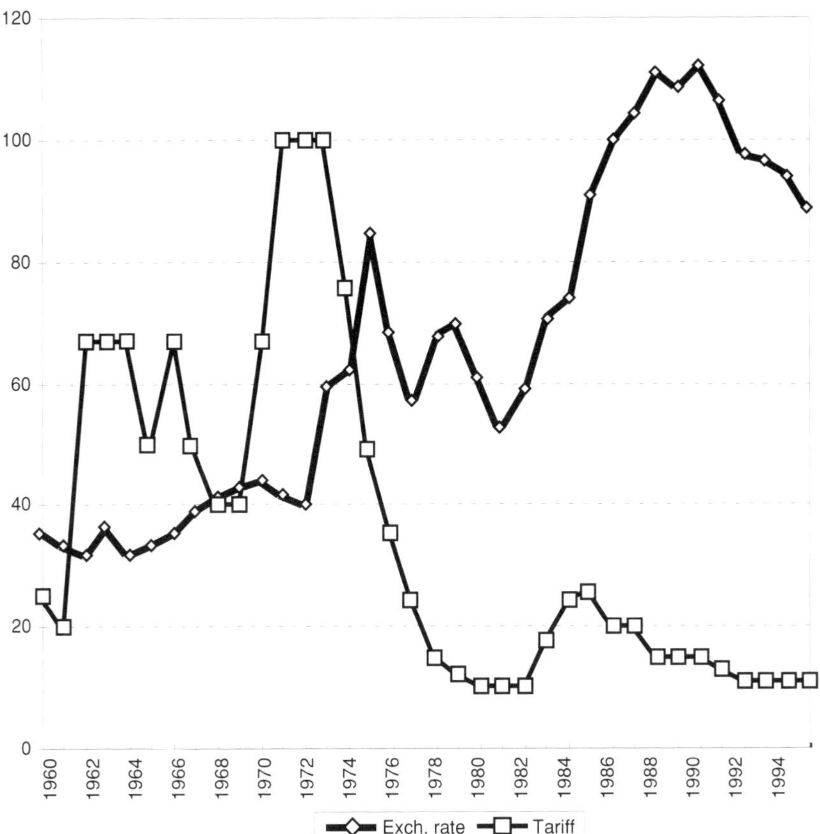

Figure 3.3 Real exchange rate and tariffs, Chile, 1960–95 (Exchange rate 1986 = 100;[*] tariffs in %)

[*] Increase denotes real currency devaluation.

(essentially, by appreciating the real exchange rate). As a consequence, beginning in 1976, limitations to international capital movements were steadily lifted.[8] At the same time, a strict crawling peg was abandoned, and nominal exchange rate changes began to lag past inflation. Finally, the nominal exchange rate was fixed in mid-1979. Since inflation wound down slowly, considerable real exchange rate appreciation accumulated in the period 1976–81. This was made possible, of course, by large capital inflows. Real currency appreciation, together with the liberalization of imports, implied a negative shock to the entire tradable sector. Rather than reconversion and the orientation of tradables towards international markets, the tradable sectors of the economy shrank and non-tradables expanded.

The way domestic financial markets were liberalized also had an important bearing on the poor initial results of the trade liberalization programme. The situation in domestic financial markets before the coup was one of extreme financial repression: the banks had been nationalized; ceilings on interest rates were set which bore no relationship to domestic inflation, resulting in extremely negative real rates and financial disintermediation; and the monetary authorities intervened heavily in the allocation of credit, with a proliferation of special credit lines which, *in toto*, did not amount to anything close to an industrial policy. The reforms instituted in 1975 included the privatization of banks, the lifting of interest rate ceilings, the reduction of reserve requirements, and the elimination of any restrictions on credit. At the same time, with the aim of encouraging competition, entry barriers to the banking and finance industry were lowered significantly. There were no prudential regulations on the activities of banks or other financial institutions; no considerations of moral hazard in banking and finance deterred the reformers. As a consequence, the financial sector grew enormously, financial operations crowded out real investments, and interest rates went from very negative to extremely high in real terms (Figure 3.4).[9] The retooling of firms producing for the domestic market, or their transformation into exporters, was rendered well-nigh impossible.

In order to deal with the consequences of the drying up of foreign capital inflows and a rapidly worsening domestic crisis, in mid-1983 the flat tariff was raised to 20 per cent and in September 1984 to 35 per cent (the level bound by Chile in 1979 at the end of the Tokyo Round of the General Agreement on Tariffs and Trade (GATT) multilateral trade negotiations). Surcharges on automobiles and consumer electronics were also introduced. As the crisis abated, the flat tariff was again reduced in gradual stages beginning in 1985. In 1989, at the end of the military regime, it stood at 15 per cent, from where it was lowered in 1991 to 11 per cent by the democratic government. During the 1980s, policies favourable to the expansion of exports were introduced: duty drawbacks for exporters, a subsidy for small exports, and foreign direct investment policies favouring non-mineral exports (more on all of these below). In addition, owing to stringent prudential

Figure 3.4   Real interest rate, Chile, 1960–95

regulation of financial institutions, interest rates settled down to more reasonable levels in real terms, which favoured investment and technology acquisition. Last but not least, a binding foreign exchange constraint produced steep real exchange rate devaluations in the period 1982–8.

Figure 3.3 shows data for the evolution of the real exchange rate and the average tariff rate.[10] Broadly speaking, the relationship between the real exchange rate and the average tariff (for the period before 1979, a crude but probably accurate indicator of trade policy) behaves as one would expect: the much lower tariffs since the mid-1970s have been accompanied by a lower real value of the currency. As theory would predict, this relationship holds in a long-run context. However, between 1976 and 1981, dramatic tariff reductions were associated with a sharp real currency appreciation.

The exchange rate trends noted above, together with very high real interest rates prevailing after the freeing of domestic financial markets in 1975, meant that the spurt of export growth after 1974 was not sustainable. In fact, the upward movement in exports was partially reversed in 1979–83.

Other policies

Other policies have been just as important as, or probably more important than, trade liberalization in explaining the sustained growth of non-copper exports. These policies can be categorized into two broad groups: general policies affecting all exports and sector-specific policies and factors. Here, we also deal with preferential trade agreements, which in the 1990s superseded unilateral trade liberalization as the major tool in the strategy for international economic integration.

General policies

Exchange rate policy

In a world with many tradables (which have widely different initial levels of protection) and a large non-tradable sector, the real exchange rate and policies towards its determinants are crucial to the success of a trade liberalization, if success is gauged by (a) the speed with which the economy adjusts its production structure, and (b) the strength of the underlying growth process. As already noted, exchange rate policies were not conducive to self-sustained outward-oriented growth in the 1970s. After several experiments with exchange rate policy in 1982–3, the market exchange rate was allowed to fluctuate within a narrow band (initially set at 1 per cent around the central rate and later gradually widened). The central rate began to be devalued on a daily basis according to the difference between domestic and foreign inflation during the past month. In addition, beginning in 1982, the severe balance of payments situation forced several discrete devaluations. As a consequence, the real value of the currency more than halved between 1981 and 1988 (Figure 3.3). These trends in the real exchange rate were undoubtedly one of the factors that account for the rapid and sustained growth of non-traditional exports after 1982.

During the 1990s, the Chilean economy has been faced once again with an abundance of foreign capital resources. This time, the management of the capital account has been more flexible than during the last episode of foreign capital abundance. Policymakers responded to the increased supply of foreign capital by discouraging the inflows of short-term capital while maintaining liberal access for FDI (Agosin and Ffrench-Davis, 1996). Essentially, this has been done by placing a 30 per cent unremunerated reserve requirement (which has to be maintained for one year, regardless of the maturity of the financial instrument) on foreign borrowing and on foreign financial investments (including investments in the Chilean stock market). The scheme is very onerous for short-term flows and has a low cost for flows that have a time horizon longer than one year. While effective in reducing short-term credits and portfolio inflows in the period 1993–5, in 1996 and 1997 medium- and long-term credits bulged, and portfolio inflows returned on a massive scale. Banks appear to have shifted their borrowing toward longer maturities, and portfolio investors may have tended to view the cost of the reserve requirement as akin to taking an option on possible future capital gains.

In addition, the exchange rate band within which the price of the US dollar is allowed to float was broadened (it now stands at 12.5 per cent around the benchmark price), with the Central Bank practising within-band dirty floating. The reference exchange rate is no longer the US dollar only, but a basket of currencies made up of the dollar, the yen and the Deutschmark. These moves have had the purpose of creating greater uncertainty for short-term operators while giving the long-term participants in the market (most importantly, exporters) greater certainty as to where the Central Bank believes the price of the US dollar will be in the long run. However, even this more flexible exchange rate policy has tended to lose its efficacy over time. Since the market exchange rate has remained close to the bottom (expressed as the peso price of foreign exchange) of the band for a couple of years now, the Central Bank has, in effect, been guaranteeing a fixed real exchange rate for foreign investors. Considering that the odds are more in favour of real currency appreciation (through a lowering of the floor of the band) than depreciation, the differential in interest rates in favour of the peso is hard to resist, particularly if one considers that the tax equivalent of the reserve requirement diminishes very rapidly with the time the funds remain in Chile.

Thus the authorities are now in a quandary as to how to prevent a greater real currency appreciation, which would undoubtedly threaten the viability of the export-led model. Several solutions have been proposed, including taxing interest remittances abroad, hiking the reserve requirement rate or extending its duration (particularly for portfolio inflows), and imposing an additional tax on mining exports or profits thereon, which would discourage FDI and capture for the government a portion of natural resource rents. As regards the exchange rate mechanism, the effectiveness of managed floating with a band depends on the authorities' willingness to keep the market exchange rate well within the band through dirty floating and to prevent it from going to the extremes of the band, which only invites one-way speculation.

Drawbacks

Since the mid-1980s, two drawback schemes have been in use. One is a regular drawback, which has been in force since 1988, by which duties on imported inputs used by exports are recovered after the fact. This programme has some weaknesses. It requires paperwork and has a financial cost for the firm, since it has first to pay the duty, which it recovers with considerable delay. The other system is the so-called 'simplified drawback', introduced in 1985. For exports of less than US$20 million for a given tariff item, all exporters receive a cash subsidy of 3, 5 or 10 per cent (depending on the value of exports for the entire tariff line) on their export value in lieu of a regular drawback. Although the scheme has been sold domestically and internationally on the grounds that it simplifies life for small exporters for whom it is costly to do all the paperwork needed to apply for the regular drawback, it does in fact contain a subsidy element, with a maximum rate of around 6 per cent, corresponding to the 10 per cent drawback rate (which applies to exports below US$10 million for the entire tariff line).[11]

This scheme has become increasingly important as an export incentive. In 1994, the state paid a total of US$150 million on these subsidies, compared to just US$26 million on the regular drawback. Approximately 13 per cent of the value of exports (and 70 per cent of the number of exported products) obtained the simplified drawback that year (Ffrench-Davis and Sáez, 1995: 79, 89).

What the Chilean experience shows in this regard is that modest incentives can have a powerful effect if they are well-administered. Although there have been no careful econometric studies of the impact of the simplified drawback on the emergence of new exports, it may be no coincidence that after the introduction of the scheme the number of exported manufacturing products, and the values exported, grew rapidly. In fact, this kind of incentive is close to economic optimality: new exports are certain to have strong externalities related to information gathering; as the exports of an item grow, the externalities disappear. Thus, the automatic extinction of the subsidy is a particularly attractive feature of this scheme.

In addition, importers of capital goods pay duties on a deferred schedule of up to seven years, and exporters are exempted from those payments. This undoubtedly encourages investment for exports. Both this provision, as well as the simplified drawback, which are considered subsidies by the World Trade Organization (WTO), will have to be eliminated by the end of 2002.

Policies towards foreign direct investment

Policies towards FDI have played a direct and indirect role in stimulating exports. The FDI regime was completely liberalized in 1974. The new Decree Law (DL) 600 of that year gave national treatment to foreign investors, opened most of the economy to FDI, made approval of FDI projects automatic once simple conditions were met, and guaranteed unrestricted remittance of profits at any time and repatriation of capital after three years (reduced to one year in 1992). All performance requirements (with the exception of one in the automobile sector, see below) were also abolished (Riveros et al., 1996).

FDI did not increase until 1987, but since then, its growth has been uninterrupted. About 60 per cent of all new investments through DL 600 have gone to the mining sector. These investments were made for a combination of reasons. In the first place, the comparative advantage of Chile in copper, molybdenum, iron ore, and other minerals is well-known. Second, the liberalization of FDI rules and regulations allowed investment to take place. Third, a Mining Law passed in the 1970s authorized private property in mining and made it very difficult for the state to expropriate mining concessions.

Other FDI policies have had the result of encouraging non-mining exports. In 1985, the authorities instituted a debt-equity swap programme whose objectives were to decrease the burden of external debt and to encourage FDI at the same time. But this channel for investing in Chile did not have the neutrality and automaticity of DL 600. As noted by Ffrench-Davis (1990), the debt-equity swap programme involved a heavy subsidy to FDI; however, projects had to be approved on a case-by-case basis. Mining projects were banned from using the instrument; and projects involving technology transfer and new exports received priority. Thus, the authorities made of necessity a virtue and practised industrial policy by another name. During the years in which it was in operation (1985–91), about 60 per cent of the investments made under the programme went into manufacturing and agriculture, the largest components of which were forestry and pulp and paper operations. Roughly 40 per cent of all FDI during this period was made with swaps. As a consequence of a new interest in investing in Chile, investments through DL 600 continued to rise *pari passu* with investments through swaps. Therefore, the swap programme is unlikely to have substituted investments that would have been made anyway through DL 600. Because of the increase in the market value of Chilean debt, swaps stopped being used by foreign investors in 1992, and the programme was formally abolished in 1996.

Although quantitatively much less important than investments in mining, several foreign investments in the agroindustrial sector have been very important in the development of new exports. For example, US fruitpacking firms have brought new storage and transport technology and opened new marketing channels for Chilean products; as will be discussed below, an investment by a Spanish winemaker was responsible for the introduction of new technology into the wine industry. Emulation by traditional Chilean producers made exports soar. Such investments would not have been made if FDI regulations had not been as liberal as they were and incentives had not been favourable to producing for export markets. At the same time, it is important to emphasize the information component that FDI brought, with regard to both technology and markets.

Market information

As already noted, information gathering on foreign markets is a costly activity in which social returns are far superior to private returns. Since 1974, the Chilean government has made a significant investment in the gathering of information on foreign markets. With the assistance of 32 commercial offices abroad, a trade promotion division of the Ministry of Foreign Affairs (ProChile) has been in the business of conducting market studies and gathering commercial information relevant to exporters. Recently, it has engaged in an aggressive campaign to create a positive country image. It is about to become an independent semi-public corporation with substantial private sector participation.

During the 1990s, publicly subsidized trade promotion activities have been intensified. Groups of firms have been encouraged to form associations and to promote their products and carry out market intelligence activities jointly. The financing of the foreign activities of these Export Committees is subsidized on a decreasing scale for a maximum period of six years. The Chilean Development Corporation (CORFO, a public agency established in the 1940s which played a key role in the country's industrialization during the import-substituting period) runs a similar programme with the assistance of trade associations and subsidizes for a limited time a share of the groups' management costs.

Technological development

The problem of underinvestment in technological development has been handled in an ingenious way. Fundación Chile, a profit-making but (until now) publicly subsidized institution whose capital is owned in equal shares by the Government of Chile and ITT,[12] has developed new technologies that are appropriate for export products and has set up new firms which it has later sold to the private sector. As any venture capital outfit, it has had many failures, but some notable successes, of which the development of the salmon export industry has been the most remarkable. The encouragement of R&D in the broadest sense (including the development of new products for export markets) is an important component of an organic export promotion effort. In fact, it can be argued that sustained export growth and diversification in the future will require a much larger allocation of resources to R&D, and that the combined efforts of the private sector, the government, and institutions such as Fundación Chile are still quite insufficient.

Infrastructure and human resource development

Although Chile's inadequate infrastructure of roads, ports, airports, tunnels, etc., constitutes at present a serious bottleneck to the intensification of its export-led growth process, the existence in the mid-1970s of (for the time) adequate infrastructure was certainly an important facilitating element in the export take-off. In other words, without the infrastructure that existed at the time (e.g. several large ports, a new international airport inaugurated in 1967, a North–South highway finished in the 1960s, essentially with foreign aid), changes in price signals alone would have elicited a weaker supply response.

Likewise, human resources were adequate to the task of reorienting the economy toward export markets. By the early 1970s, Chile could count on a large pool of engineers and managers formed in good state universities over the previous decades. The import substitution period and active state entrepreneurship since the 1940s had also left a legacy of industrial and management skills that could be put to use in the export drive. As discussed below, state universities had begun to turn out forestry engineers in the 1950s. In the 1960s, there were important programmes for creating sector-specific human capital in agriculture which later turned out to be essential in the development of fruit and vegetable exports. In 1964, a semi-autonomous agricultural research institute (INIA) was created with public funds. In 1965, a ten-year programme between the University of Chile (the country's main public university) and the University of California at Davis was established to train Chilean agricultural economists and agronomists. This relationship became an important mechanism for the transfer of technology between two regions with similar climate and soil conditions (Meller, 1994).

Sectoral policies

There have also been important sectoral policies and special factors that have had a direct bearing on the expansion of particular export products. Some of these are described below.

The forestry cluster

An important contributor to the increase in exports has been the forestry cluster (logs, chips, processed wood, pulp and paper, and, recently, furniture). In 1995 prices, from 1973 to 1995, the exports of this group of industries have increased seventeenfold, from US$105 million to US$1.8 billion.

Public forestation and reforestation programmes date back to the 1960s. In 1974, a subsidy of 75 per cent of tree planting costs was instituted (Decree Law 701). At the same time, privately planted land was declared unexpropriable, a prohibition on cutting trees of under 18 years of age was repealed, and exports of raw wood in any form were authorized. These legal changes made vertically integrated operations possible and very profitable (Rossi, 1995). In addition, between 1975 and 1979, the Central Bank provided private commercial banks and the State Bank (a public commercial bank catering to the needs of small depositors and business firms) with a special line of credit for on-lending to forest development projects, with particularly favourable conditions for Chilean nationals and small firms.

It had long been known that Chile has a comparative advantage in forestry. Climate and soil conditions ensure the rapid growth of certain species of trees, particularly radiata pine. In view of this natural resource endowment, during the 1950s, two public universities began to offer degrees in forestry engineering, so that, when the sector began to develop, the industry had at its disposal a significant corps of specialists in the field. When conditions were favourable, a large number of these professionals became entrepreneurs in the forestry and wood sector. In more recent years, forestry engineering programmes at public universities have grown, and they have started to be offered at many private universities.

In spite of Chile's natural resource advantages in this sector, an industrial policy was necessary to give it the 'big push' to become a major industry. This is perhaps the only instance of industrial policy on a big scale – and a very successful one – since 1974. It included special incentives for the development of the sector, a legal framework favourable to private enterprise and exports, removing the liquidity constraint to investment, and the accumulation of human capital specific to the sector. Perhaps the most compelling trait of this policy package has been its transparency and simplicity, something that can be emulated by countries at a lower stage of development.

The cultivated salmon industry

Cultivated salmon exports went from almost nothing in 1986 to US$520 million in 1996. At present Chile holds about 15 per cent of the world market for cultivated salmon and trout and is the second world exporter behind Norway. Thus the salmon industry constitutes a real success story and one in which technological adaptation and development played a key role.

Fundación Chile began experimenting with cultivated salmon technology in the second half of the 1970s. In the early 1980s it set up a firm to produce cultivated salmon in Lake Llanquihue using floating cages, a technology developed in Norway and Scotland and which, it was thought, could be adapted very successfully to the natural conditions of the Chilean lake district. The firm, Salmones Antártica, was later sold to Nippon Suisan, a Japanese company that is one of the largest fishing companies in the world. The example of Salmones Antártica attracted many other investments by domestic entrepreneurs and by foreign companies (Achurra, 1995).

This industry is very interesting for a number of reasons. One of them is that it combines technological change induced by a semi-public institution with the country's natural advantages. Second, salmon exports represent the exploitation of a niche export market. Their success shows that it is not necessary to follow the Asian model of penetrating mass markets for consumer goods in which the main comparative advantage of a developing country is its low wages. These sectors are very vulnerable to protectionism, and, at present, different approaches may have greater pay-off. Last but not least, the salmon industry has many positive backward linkages. It has spawned local industries for floating cages, nutrients, fish nets, packing materials, and transport services. Since it employs highly skilled profession-als (engineers, technicians in aquaculture, biologists), it has also had a positive impact on the demand for construction, education and retail trade in the region.

Wine

Chilean wine exports have risen meteorically over the last ten years, from US$10 million in 1985 to US$290 million in 1996. Winemaking is a traditional economic activity in Chile that goes back to colonial times.

However, wine exports took off only in the mid-1980s. The kinds of wines produced by Chilean winemakers were not acceptable to consumers in developed countries, and technological change on a large scale was needed for Chilean wines to sell abroad. These included the introduction of stainless steel vats, the use of small and new wood vats (rather than large used ones) for ageing wine, and investments in new cooling equipment and machinery for pressing and mashing. Although it was known that Chilean wines could be very advantageously produced with the new technologies being used in Europe and the US, a demonstration effect was needed. In 1981, the Spanish firm of Miguel Torres bought large tracts of land in the Central Valley (Curicó) and began to produce wines with the new technology. This firm's success led to the rapid introduction of the new methods by Chilean firms.

The openness of the economy aided the process of importing new machinery. In addition, many of the traditional wine producers are large firms by European standards and are also active in other export sectors (particularly fruit). Therefore, they do not face severe liquidity constraints on investment. In more recent years, there have been investments by other large European and US firms (e.g. Rothschild, Larose Trintaudon, Grand Marnier, Robert Mondavi and Christian Brothers). Also, several new 'boutique' wineries are producing new products for the export market and are trying to position their wines at a higher price and quality range than traditional vineyards. These producers, with less financial muscle than that of the large wineries and the foreign investors, rely on associations of new winemakers to market their exports (Bordeu, 1995).

The automotive industry

Automotive parts have been a small but significant component of manufacturing exports for over a decade. They have been stimulated by the only performance requirement that remains in Chilean investment policy. A special programme (called the Automotive Statute) allows assemblers duty-free imports of completely knock down (CKD) or semi knock down (SKD) kits to the extent that imports are compensated with exports of nationally produced components of an equal value. The statute also grants assemblers a tax credit on components that are domestically produced or exported. In order to qualify for the tax credit, a component must have a domestic value added of at least 70 per cent if it is for domestic use or of 50 per cent if it is for export. These incentives are incompatible with the WTO's trade-related investment measures (TRIMS) agreement and had to be struck off the books by the end of 1999. The tax credit expired at the end of 1998.

Preferential trade agreements and regional integration

With the return to democracy, there has taken place a significant change in the country's internationalization strategy. While in the 1970s and 1980s the favoured approach was one of unilateral trade liberalization, in the 1990s priority has been given to the signing of free trade agreements; thus, policy-makers have come to give priority to reciprocal liberalization with specific partners over unilateral integration with the world economy without reciprocity. Perhaps the single most important reason for this change of emphasis has been that the Chilean tariff at the end of the 1980s (15 per cent, lowered to 11 per cent in 1991) was already low, so that large efficiency gains were unlikely to be reaped by further unilateral liberalization. At the same time, Chile's main trading partners maintained high tariffs or other trade barriers for products in which Chilean producers had attained (or could attain in the short or medium term) comparative advantage.

In Chile's case, the country's highly geographically diversified foreign trade by region of origin and destination (Table 3.4) appears to suggest that the optimal strategy is one of negotiating free trade agreements with all of its main trading partners. Success in doing so would also minimize the major cost of bilateral free trade agreements, which is trade diversion. This was, roughly, the strategy adopted. At the same time, the authorities sought admission for Chile into the North American Free Trade Agreement (NAFTA, made up of Canada, Mexico and the US), negotiated a free trade agreement with Mercosur (a customs union between Argentina, Brazil, Paraguay and Uruguay), took the first steps toward a free trade agreement with the European Union, and signed a host of other free trade agreements with less important trading partners (Mexico, Venezuela, Ecuador, Colombia, Canada, Bolivia).[13] Chile has been participating actively in the Asia Pacific Economic Cooperation (APEC) forum, but it is unclear what direction that grouping will take. So far, of the free trade agreements sought with major trading groups (NAFTA, European Union and Mercosur), only the association with Mercosur has met with success, the association agreement having gone into effect in October 1996.

Table 3.4   Composition of exports by market, Chile, 1986 and 1993 (%)

Destination	Natural resources		Processed natural resources		Other industrial products	
	1986	*1993*	*1986*	*1993*	*1986*	*1993*
World	66.1	1.7	29.4	35.6	4.5	12.7
US	68.0	50.1	27.1	37.1	4.9	12.8
EU	73.6	65.9	24.5	29.6	1.9	4.5
Japan	78.9	53.3	20.2	45.8	0.9	1.0
LAIA	51.6	26.7	0.6	38.3	7.8	34.7
Argentina	51.2	21.6	34.5	36.2	14.3	41.5
Bolivia	14.0	3.7	65.0	24.9	21.0	71.6
Brazil	81.7	55.4	17.1	27.6	1.3	17.0
Peru	14.1	13.3	74.6	46.2	11.3	40.5

Source: Ffrench-Davis and Sáez (1995: 89).

While Chilean export successes of the past two decades owe nothing to free trade agreements, they are likely to play an important role in the continuation of outward-oriented growth and in the development of new and more sophisticated export products. In this respect, the association with Mercosur is crucial. Even without a free trade agreement, a large share of Chile's exports of manufactures go to other Latin American countries, with Mercosur countries being the main buyers. Moreover, almost 60 per cent of the increase in the exports of manufactures since the mid-1980s has been absorbed by regional partners. Trade with Argentina has grown particularly rapidly, in spite of the Argentinian crisis of 1995 and the poor infrastructure hampering commercial relations between the two countries. Exports to Argentina rose by 172 per cent in the 1992–6 period. In 1991, exports to Argentina represented 3 per cent of total Chilean exports; in 1996, this share had risen to almost 5 per cent.

High tariffs are an effective impediment to exports to Mercosur countries. While the average trade-weighted tariff affecting Chilean exports to Mercosur before the entry into force of the association agreement was 8.2 per cent, some exports faced much higher tariffs. Tariffs for exports to Argentina of clothing, metallic products, and paper were 19.6, 14.4 and 14.2 per cent, respectively. Hachette (1994) has estimated that, as a consequence of import liberalization in Chile's favour, exports of clothing to Argentina ought to increase by 45.9 per cent, while the exports of metallic products should rise by 33.7 per cent.

Immediately upon the entry into force of the association agreement, the average trade-weighted tariff faced by Chilean exports declined to 3.2 per cent. The agreement calls for the gradual liberalization of all trade between Chile and Mercosur on a reciprocal basis. Products have been classified into five categories. A general list includes all products that are to receive duty-free treatment over a period ranging from two to eight years. The initial tariff cut from the Most Favoured Nation (MFN) rate is 40 per cent. Products on this list account for about 50 per cent of all bilateral trade. The other four lists include products with increasing degrees of sensitivity for both parties. In the two most restrictive categories, Chile has placed some traditional agricultural products, (e.g. beef, sugar, wheat and wheat flour), which will reach duty-free treatment only after 15 and 18 years, respectively.

The benefits for Chile of the agreement with Mercosur are twofold. On the one hand, Mercosur, as well as other regional trading partners, are the main markets for the exports of Chilean manufactures, and this will become even more so as trade barriers are reduced. Quality requirements in these markets are more in line with Chilean supply capabilities than those of developed countries, and distance to markets is also a factor in favour of exports from Chile. On the other hand, Mercosur is internationally competitive in agricultural staples, while Chile is not. In other words, Chile and Mercosur countries (as well as other countries in the Latin American region) are potentially much more 'natural' trading partners than their current reciprocal trade flows suggest. Trade barriers, poor transport links and almost non-existent infrastructure have prevented the emergence of more significant trade flows among the countries in the region. But, as the example of Mercosur clearly indicates, once trade barriers begin to come down, trade flows can increase very rapidly indeed.

Explaining the increase in manufacturing exports

Perhaps the single most important feature of the Chilean export success story is the emergence of a diversified group of manufactures for export comprising a great variety of products, most of which are light manufactures or are natural resource intensive. And it is this group of products – their further growth and continued diversification – that provides the greatest hope for future growth in exports and in the economy in general. Therefore, great interest attaches to explaining the factors that are behind the growth of these exports.

There have been two studies of the behaviour of Chilean exports in the past. Using a partial adjustment approach, De Gregorio (1984) estimates supply functions for Chilean non-copper exports and finds positive and statistically significant price elasticities of export supply. Within an error-correction framework, Moguillansky and Titelman (1993; henceforth 'MT') estimate supply functions for several categories of non-copper exports. They conclude that long-term price elasticities are consistently higher than short-term elasticities (and that both are statistically significant). In their supply functions for manufacturing exports, tariffs, which are entered as an additional explanatory variable, turn out to be negatively associated with the exports of manufactures.

MT apply a more advanced econometric technology than De Gregorio. However, for our purposes, their study has a number of shortcomings which justify yet another try at econometric estimation. In the first place, MT do not include an excess capacity variable, in a context where recession and idle capacity played a key role in the initial spurt of export growth in the mid-1970s. Second, their relative price of exports variable uses the CPI as *numeraire*, which misspecifies the model: importables represent a large component of the CPI, so that tariffs appear as a separate variable *and* in the denominator of the relative price of exports. In our model, we avoid this problem by using nominal wages as the *numeraire* of export prices. Third, we have a longer time series, 1960–95, as compared with 1962–90 for MT.

Here we use a different technique than MT. With a single-equation vector autoregression analysis, we study the role of various factors – tariff reductions, real currency depreciation, and excess capacity – in explaining the growth of manufacturing exports. The underlying model is also a supply function. The small country assumption being appropriate in the case of Chile, we can safely assume that Chilean manufacturing exports do not affect world prices of those goods, and this entitles us to ignore feedback effects from export volumes to relative export prices.

In this exercise, manufacturing exports (XM) are a function of the real price of manufactures for the export market (PM, defined as the price index for manufactures in dollars multiplied by the nominal peso price for the dollar and deflated by nominal wages in manufacturing), the unweighted average tariff (TR), and an index of excess capacity in manufacturing (EX, defined as the percentage by which potential manufacturing output, calculated by the peak-to-peak method, exceeds observed output). The basic idea of the model is that there are two groups of manufactures: products for the domestic market and which could be exported under certain circumstances, the relative price for which is the tariff rate; and goods produced largely for export markets because the domestic markets for them are small. The relative price of these goods is expressed in terms of non-tradables, here proxied by the nominal wage rate. All variables except excess capacity are expressed in logs.

According to MacKinnon tests, the log of manufacturing exports turned out to be a stationary variable with a deterministic trend. EX is also stationary (without trend). All other variables have unit roots.[14] This means that we cannot explain the level of manufacturing exports by recourse to our price variables or by excess capacity. We are left with the possibility of explaining the rate of growth of manufacturing exports, using as explanatory variables dln PM, dln TR, and EX. The general procedure employed was to start with a generalized structure with two lags and reduce the model by eliminating variables that were not significant. The final equation obtained was:

$$dLXM = 0.083 - 0.47^{*}dLTR_{-1} - 0.28^{*}dLPM + 0.45^{*}dLPM_{-1}$$
$$ (2.0)\ (-4.27) \qquad (-2.17) \qquad\quad (3.31)$$
$$ + 0.008^{*}EX - 0.42^{*}dLXM_{-2} \tag{1}$$
$$ (3.03) \qquad (-3.64)$$

$R^2 = 0.758$; AR (1) = 1.67 [0.208]; ARCH 1 = 0.0005 [0.981]; Normality χ^2 = 0.55 [0.761]; X_i^2 = 0.89 [0.560]; $X_i^{*}X_j$ = 0.69 [0.757]; RESET =2.07 [0.161]. (Figures in parenthesis are *t*-ratios, and the figures in brackets are the probabilities of not rejecting the null hypothesis involved.)

The results are good from an econometric point of view, and all variables are significant at standard statistical levels. Signs are as expected, except that contemporaneous changes in the rate of change of relative export prices are associated with declines in the rate of growth of manufacturing exports. However, the lagged effect of price changes is positive and higher in absolute value than the contemporaneous effect. Therefore, the long-run static equation shows the expected positive association. In the steady state, the rate of growth of manufacturing exports is the following:

$$dLXM = 0.058 - 0.33^*dLTR + 0.12^*dLPM + 0.006^*EX \qquad (2)$$

This equation tells us that the long-run trend rate of growth of manufacturing exports in the period 1960–95 was 5.8 per cent and that tariff and peso export price changes produced deviations of the expected signs from this trend rate of growth. Changes in excess capacity also were important contributors to the growth of exports: each percentage point increase in excess capacity was associated with a 0.6 percentage point increase in the rate of growth of exports.

We carried out an exercise to gauge the importance of excess capacity in generating exports over the periods 1975–7 and 1982–5, when the indicator of excess capacity averaged 36 and 25 per cent of potential output, respectively. We compared the levels of exports yielded with the rates of growth predicted with equation (1) with those that would have occurred had the levels of the excess capacity indicator remained at 10 per cent, which is about the average for the whole period 1960–95. The results of this exercise are quite interesting. During 1975–7, above-average excess capacity in manufacturing is estimated to have generated about 38 per cent of manufacturing exports; in the period 1982–5, a similar calculation yields 12 per cent.

Conclusions

What then, are, the main causes of Chile's export successes? Undeniably, the trade liberalization of 1974–9 radically altered relative prices and increased the profitability of exporting *relative to producing tradables for the domestic market*. However, the liberalization was faulty in many respects. The concurrent liberalization of the capital account beginning in mid-1976, in a context of very liquid international financial markets, made real currency appreciation inevitable. This meant that, until the exchange rate correction that took place after 1982, price signals encouraged non-tradables rather than exportables and efficient import-competing sectors. In addition, the sky-high interest rates of the second half of the 1970s made it all but impossible for manufacturers to adjust to the new set of relative prices. That is why it took until the second half of the 1980s, when interest and exchange rates were more favourable, for exports to become the engine of growth envisaged by the liberalizing paradigm.

Other policies were also important. Generic export promotion in the 1980s certainly contributed. So did the evolution of the exchange rate after 1982 and more pragmatic exchange rate policy in the 1990s. Sharp and premature real currency appreciation in 1996–7 attests to the difficulties of maintaining an export-led strategy on course in the face of present-day capital mobility. Countries that are successful in achieving long-term export-led growth ought to experience currency appreciation. In fact, the appreciation is but one manifestation of rising per capita incomes. In the case of Chile, however, the appreciation has come at a very early stage in the export-led growth process. And, anyway, the appreciation has had little to do with the current account and much with the huge inflows of foreign capital that the economy has been experiencing.

Sectoral industrial policy in favour of the forestry and wood cluster was instrumental in that sector's take-off. Policies toward FDI also aided in the growth of non-traditional exports. The activities of information gathering and technology development by public or semi-public agents assisted in improving supply responses. Prior human resource development and prior investments in physical infrastructure enabled export sectors to grow rapidly.

What should African countries desiring to foster export-led growth do? In the design of a comprehensive policy package dealing with the structure of incentives as well as with improving the supply responses of economic agents, the Chilean experience has much to teach, both in a positive sense of what to do and in a negative sense of what to avoid or correct. We highlight seven lessons.

In the first place, countries should embrace trade liberalization *in conjunction with* policies that ensure that relative prices will be favourable to export industries (and not just to non-tradables) and that interest rates will support investment and economic restructuring. This implies *not liberalizing* the capital account of the balance of payments. The proper dosage of capital inflows is thus very important to the eventual success or failure of the trade liberalization exercise, and this is something to be seriously considered by African countries when designing policies of integration into the international economy. It is also important for countries to maintain some control (particularly of a prudential nature) over domestic finance in order to ensure that potential exporters obtain financial resources for investment at reasonable interest rates.[15]

Second, temporary subsidies can be a powerful tool for stimulating the growth of non-traditional exports. New exports have important informational externalities that amply justify subsidization. Chile's 'simplified drawback' should be of interest to African countries: it involves moderate and self-extinguishing subsidies for genuinely new exports. Some countries will come up against the WTO's prohibition on export subsidies. However, all least developed countries and other developing countries with per capita incomes of less than US$1000 (listed in Annex VII of the Uruguay Round's Subsidies and Countervailing Duties Agreement) can still apply export subsidies if their exports of a particular good represent less than 3.25 per cent of world imports of such goods (Agosin et al., 1995: 10). This is a criterion that is not hard to meet for these countries. Other countries must rely on subsidies to information gathering for groups of producers, such as those used by Chile in recent years, or subsidies to R&D, both of which are still allowed, since they are either precompetitive or do not affect export prices.

Third, FDI policy can be used to attract desired investments. A liberal, and steady, policy framework is best for FDI. However, this does not mean that countries must renounce an active policy. Rather than prohibiting investments in sectors with low priority or following a project-by-project approval procedure, it is possible to design a system of incentives that favours investments that open up new export possibilities or introduce new technologies to the country.

Fourth, infrastructure and human resource development are important preconditions for the success of pro-export policies. For countries with deficits in these areas, foreign financial and technical assistance is essential.

Fifth, a strategy of growth spearheaded by a few niche exports can pay handsome dividends. In Chile, one of those sectors was the forestry–wood cluster of industries. The task of selecting the industries to be fostered is easier than the detractors of industrial policy would have us believe. Common sense about a particular country's comparative strengths in world markets will go a long way. Niche exports are also less likely to come under attack by protectionists in importing countries. Such choices are important in orienting technology and information gathering policies. Since human capital is particularly scarce in poor countries, it is important to exercise great selectivity with regard to human resource development and to ensure that policies in this area are harmonious with the development strategy adopted.

Sixth, the growth of these exports must be supported by the provision of financial resources at positive but reasonable real interest rates (perhaps through the active participation of development banks or similar agencies) and by public action to encourage the formation of producer associations to overcome the small scale problem, which makes meeting foreign orders a difficult task and information gathering too costly.

Finally, a policy of regional integration makes sense. It is easier to export manufactures to regional partners who have similar consumer tastes than to the developed countries. Learning to produce and to export products in demand in foreign markets is a precondition for expanding and diversifying exports. Regional integration, in the context of more open national economies than in the past, can play an important role in this respect.

Appendix

Deriving the compensatory depreciation

Assume that, to start out, the economy is in balance of payments equilibrium. Letting F^* be equilibrium capital flows, the balance of payments equilibrium can be described as follows:

$$p_m^* * q_m(p_m) - p_x^* * q_x(p_x) = F^* \tag{A1}$$

where asterisks denote international prices (assumed to be independent of the levels of trade of our country).

We can differentiate (A1) to obtain:

$$p_m^* \star dq_m - p_x^* \star dq_x = 0 \tag{A2}$$

Under the small-country assumption, the prices for the importable and exportable are, respectively:

$$p_m = e \star (1 + t) \star p_m^*$$
$$p_x = e \star p_x^* \tag{A3}$$

where t is the (*ad valorem*) tariff and e is the nominal exchange rate.

By the definition of elasticity, we obtain expressions for dq_m and dq_x:

$$dq_m = q_m \star \varepsilon_m \star [\hat{e} + \hat{t}]$$
$$dq_x = q_x \star e_x \star \hat{e} \tag{A4}$$

where a hat over a variable denotes percentage change.

Replacing (A4) and (A1) into (A2) and collecting terms, one obtains the value of the compensatory depreciation:

$$\hat{e} = \frac{\hat{t}}{\varepsilon_x / \varepsilon_m - 1} \tag{A5}$$

Acknowledgements

The author wishes to thank Gustavo Crespi, Gerry Helleiner, and Leonardo Letelier for their suggestions on an earlier draft. Useful comments were made by participants at the UNU/WIDER Workshop on Growth, External Sector, and the Role of Non-Traditional Exports in Sub-Saharan Africa, Kampala, 16–20 June 1997. He also thanks Julio Cáceres for able research assistance. The usual disclaimers apply.

Notes

1. In this chapter, we follow the Latin American convention of expressing the exchange rate as units of domestic currency per unit of foreign currency.
2. These characteristics of information tend to be ignored by standard trade theory and conventional trade policy advice, which assume that all relevant information is costlessly available to all agents. The consequence of relaxing this assumption will be that trade liberalization is rendered more costly, as agents are less able to reallocate resources towards export-oriented activities. Therefore, complementary

Table 3.A1   Volume of exports of goods and services, Chile, 1960–95 (millions of 1995 US dollars)

	Copper	Other mining	Agricultural	Fishmeal	Wood	Pulp and paper	Manufactures	Services	Total*
1960	951.9	370.4	77.5	6.4	7.0	25.1	106.7	–	1545.0
1961	1044.7	368.3	93.9	12.0	14.1	36.9	104.8	–	1674.6
1962	1080.1	405.8	84.6	20.3	12.3	31.1	67.1	–	1701.2
1963	1123.7	369.4	79.6	27.6	10.9	27.0	69.5	–	1707.7
1964	1071.2	462.1	79.8	42.7	13.2	28.9	177.0	–	1874.9
1965	991.7	525.2	76.1	18.6	14.9	42.8	251.9	–	1921.2
1966	1176.2	537.1	60.6	60.1	15.0	75.1	202.6	–	2126.7
1967	1804.0	488.7	59.6	46.9	9.6	105.5	160.3	–	2674.5
1968	1691.6	460.6	88.3	60.9	13.0	114.6	180.8	–	2609.6
1969	1852.9	437.5	84.1	45.5	28.2	129.1	184.5	–	2761.8
1970	1744.1	434.2	98.0	35.4	30.5	117.4	211.6	–	2671.3
1971	1904.5	433.7	62.5	72.9	26.9	104.5	163.1	–	2768.1
1972	1800.2	229.3	38.7	33.4	16.5	85.1	92.4	–	2295.5
1973	1692.7	401.2	37.3	11.6	12.8	92.7	78.9	–	2327.2
1974	2358.8	325.0	76.1	44.0	21.9	206.3	166.1	–	3198.2
1975	2111.0	455.7	111.6	52.7	39.1	115.3	504.3	699.6	4089.1
1976	2605.6	448.7	204.4	77.1	54.7	183.5	639.9	828.6	5042.4
1977	2658.2	370.4	237.8	86.4	136.1	222.9	656.2	1078.9	5446.9
1978	2730.1	329.5	361.5	124.8	206.7	343.1	875.1	1098.5	6069.4
1979	2822.3	520.8	380.4	201.1	311.4	370.2	1212.3	1536.9	7355.5
1980	2888.1	674.4	368.7	237.9	345.2	377.1	1164.2	2207.0	8262.5
1981	2885.1	674.3	356.0	236.7	200.2	360.3	1075.8	1963.9	7752.4
1982	3426.5	474.3	474.5	369.8	209.0	373.1	1228.3	1644.1	8199.6
1983	3452.2	584.6	494.0	321.2	233.8	394.5	1191.6	1442.4	8114.4
1984	3415.5	514.3	539.5	361.9	256.5	393.0	1360.3	1192.6	8033.6
1985	3700.2	507.1	747.1	432.7	269.9	313.6	1929.3	1267.4	9167.4
1986	3761.7	525.9	901.7	420.0	306.3	411.1	2049.5	1744.3	10120.6

1987	3679.1	563.1	943.9	403.8	430.1	414.5	2103.4	1591.7	10129.7
1988	3852.7	660.1	1083.5	393.1	516.0	398.4	1719.9	1515.4	10139.1
1989	4141.5	1113.1	870.2	549.1	352.4	385.1	2172.9	1983.5	11567.8
1990	4212.5	970.8	994.7	433.0	370.3	353.5	2477.9	2221.4	12034.0
1991	4625.8	1031.2	1108.9	428.3	343.2	406.0	2924.8	2512.0	13380.3
1992	5266.7	1214.5	1166.2	422.9	278.4	834.3	3661.3	2760.2	15604.5
1993	5380.7	1052.2	1106.7	427.9	361.7	915.7	4148.3	2936.4	16329.6
1994	5728.2	1401.9	1180.4	431.5	335.8	1309.6	4582.8	3079.9	18050.1
1995	6487.1	1363.0	1306.0	654.0	452.8	1315.9	4459.8	3155.2	19193.8

*Until 1974, goods only.

Source: Central Bank of Chile and author's calculations.

policies become indispensable in order to ensure strong supply responses to changed price signals within a reasonable time period.

3. Obviously, the share of exports of goods and services in GDP depends on two key variables: the exchange rate and the terms of trade. The real exchange rate has fluctuated widely in Chile over the last few decades. In 1986 prices (a year in which the Chilean peso was severely undervalued), exports of goods and services represented 37 per cent of 1995 GDP. In 1995 prices (with an overvalued currency), exports represent 29 per cent of 1995 GDP.

4. The 1960s can be rightfully called a 'golden age': steady growth was achieved in a context of political democracy and social change. The Frei government (1964–70) introduced a land reform without expropriation, bought for the Chilean state 51 per cent of the ownership of the large (and foreign-owned) copper companies, and initiated many innovative economic and social programmes (Ffrench-Davis, 1973). This period was succeeded by two dramatically contrasting economic and social experiments that disrupted the economy and destroyed long-established traditions of political and ideological pluralism.

5. However, large investments by foreign copper companies over the last decade may reverse these trends in the coming years, when the output generated by these investments comes on stream.

6. There are no long time series on export volumes and prices available in Chilean official statistics. For the period from 1960 to 1989, as deflators of the value statistics we used the export price indices calculated by Sáez (1991). For the period 1990–5, Central Bank estimates for export prices and volumes are available. Unfortunately, there are no data for 1990 with which to splice together the two data sets. Therefore, price indices for 1990 were forecast with the Sáez (1991) data using an autoregressive scheme with seven lags. Since both the Sáez and Central Bank price index for manufacturing prices include pulp and paper, fishmeal, and wood products, and we wished to estimate export prices and volumes for an aggregate excluding these items, we proceeded to calculate an export price index for manufactures of our own. A price index was constructed for these three items using moving yearly weights. In spite of the flimsiness of the price series, the volume series obtained with them behave reasonably.

7. Data drawn from Central Bank of Chile, *Indicadores Económicos y Sociales, 1960–88*, Santiago, 1989, p. 30. The ratios cited in the text are calculated with data in 1977 constant prices.

8. Ironically, the process ended in 1981, shortly before the onset of the debt crisis, with the complete freeing up of international capital flows.

9. In his last published article, Carlos Díaz-Alejandro (1985) provides a masterly description and a devastating critique of the Chilean financial liberalization.

10. The real exchange rate is estimated as the nominal price of the US dollar deflated by the consumer price index (CPI) and multiplied by an index of external prices (IEP) relevant to the Chilean economy calculated by the Central Bank. For the period 1977 onward, the Central Bank series was used. For earlier periods, we constructed our own series using the IEP estimated by Ffrench-Davis (1984). Our numbers for 1974–6 correct for official underestimation of the rate of increase in the CPI. As regards average tariffs, for 1974 onward the series is an unweighted average. Since there were no non-tariff barriers after 1975, the average tariff rate is a fairly accurate representation of the restrictiveness of the trade regime. No data are available for the period before 1973, which was marked by high tariffs, considerable tariff dispersion, and many non-tariff restrictions. We used an index

of trade liberalization developed by De la Cuadra and Hachette (1992: 79) and applied the ratio of that index to its value in 1980 to the average tariff that year (10 per cent) in order to obtain a tariff equivalent of all trade restrictions for the period 1960–73. It is appropriate to use the 1980 tariff because that was the first full year of application of a unified tariff of 10 per cent.

11. Given the current flat tariff of 11 per cent, the 10 per cent 'drawback' would not involve a subsidy if imported inputs constituted 90 per cent of the value of exports. The actual number is more likely to be in the 30–40 per cent range.

12. The genesis of Fundación Chile is interesting. When the military government set out to repay ITT for the nationalization of the Chilean Telephone Company, it was agreed to establish Fundación Chile, with the ITT share paid in by the government.

13. The economic rationale of these agreements is doubtful, given the small trade volumes involved. They would make considerably more sense within the framework of a South American Free Trade Association that multilateralizes the myriad agreements signed bilaterally or plurilaterally between individual countries of the region.

14. Results are not shown, but are available on request.

15. Stiglitz and Uy (1996) argue that in the East Asian countries mild financial repression, the main traits of which were the maintenance of positive but controlled real interest rates and credit allocations that favoured exporting sectors, was an important factor explaining export success.

References

Achurra, M. (1995) 'La Experiencia de un Nuevo Producto de Exportación: Los Salmones', in P. Meller and R. E. Sáez (eds), *Auge Exportador Chileno – Lecciones y Desafíos Futuros*, Santiago: CIEPLAN/Domen Editores.

Agosin, M. R. and Ffrench-Davis, R. (1993) 'Trade Liberalization in Latin America', *CEPAL Review*, 50 (August).

Agosin, M. R. and Ffrench-Davis, R. (1996) 'Managing Capital Inflows in Latin America', in M. ul Haq, I. Kaul and I. Grunberg (eds), *The Tobin Tax – Coping with Financial Volatility*, New York: Oxford University Press.

Agosin, M. R., Tussie, D. and Crespi, G. (1995) 'Developing Countries in the Uruguay Round: An Evaluation and Issues for the Future', in UNCTAD, *International Monetary and Financial Issues for the 1990s, Research Papers for the Group of Twenty-Four*, Vol. VI, United Nations: New York and Geneva.

Amsden, A. H. (1993) 'Trade Policy and Economic Performance in Korea', in M. R. Agosin and D. Tussie (eds), *Trade and Growth – New Dilemmas in Trade Policy*, Houndmills and London: Macmillan.

Amsden, A. H. (1994) 'Why Isn't the Whole World Experimenting with the East Asian Model to Develop?: Review of *The East Asian Miracle*', *World Development*, 22, 4.

Bordeu, E. (1995) 'Exportaciones de Vino: La Importancia del Mejoramiento de la Calidad', in P. Meller and R. E. Sáez (eds), *Auge Exportador Chileno – Lecciones y Desafíos Futuros*, Santiago: CIEPLAN/Domen Editores.

De Gregorio, J. (1984) 'Comportamiento de Exportaciones e Importaciones en Chile', *Colección Estudios CIEPLAN*, 13 (June).

De la Cuadra, S. and Hachette, D. (1992) *Apertura Comercial: Experiencia Chilena*, Editorial de Economía y Administración, Universidad de Chile, Santiago.

Díaz-Alejandro, C. F. (1985) 'Goodbye Financial Repression, Hello Financial Crash', *Journal of Development Economics*, 19, 1/2 (September–October).
Ffrench-Davis, R. (1973) *Políticas Económicas en Chile, 1952–1970*, Santiago: Ediciones Nueva Sociedad.
Ffrench-Davis, R. (1979) 'Exportaciones e Industrialización en un Modelo Ortodoxo – Chile, 1973–8', *Revista de la CEPAL*, 9 (December).
Ffrench-Davis, R. (1984) 'Indice de Precios Externos: Un Indicador para Chile de la Inflación Internacional', *Colección Estudios CIEPLAN*, 13 (June).
Ffrench-Davis, R. (1990) 'Debt–Equity Swaps in Chile', *Cambridge Journal of Economics*, 14 (March).
Ffrench-Davis, R., Leiva, P. and Madrid, R. (1991) *La Liberalización Comercial en Chile*, Estudios de Política Comercial No. 1, Geneva and New York: UNCTAD.
Ffrench-Davis, R., Leiva, P. and Madrid, R. (1993) 'Trade Liberalization and Growth: The Chilean Experience', in M. R. Agosin and D. Tussie (eds), *Trade and Growth – New Dilemmas in Trade Policy*, Houndmills and London: Macmillan.
Ffrench-Davis, R. and Sáez, R. E. (1995) 'Comercio y Desarrollo Industrial en Chile', *Colección Estudios CIEPLAN*, 41 (December).
Hachette, D. (1994) 'Argentina: ¿Un Socio Posible?', *Cuadernos de Economía*, 94 (December).
Lall, S. (1994) '*The East Asian Miracle*: Does the Bell Toll for Industrial Strategy?', *World Development*, 22, 4.
Meller, P. (1994) 'Chilean Export Growth, 1970–90: An Assessment', in G. K. Helleiner (ed.), *Manufacturing for Export in the Developing World – Problems and Possibilities*, London: Routledge.
Meller, P. (1996) *Un Siglo de Economía Política Chilena (1890–1990)*, Santiago: Editorial Andrés Bello.
Moguillansky, G. and Titelman, D. (1993) 'Estimación Econométrica de Funciones de Exportación en Chile', *Estudios de Economía*, 20, 1 (June).
Riveros, L. A., Vatter, J. and Agosin, M. R. (1996) 'La Inversión Extranjera Directa en Chile, 1987–93: Aprovechamiento de Venatjas Comparativas y Conversión de Deuda', in M. R. Agosin (ed.), *Inversión Extranjera Directa en América Latina: Su Contribución al Desarrollo*, Santiago and Mexico City: Fondo de Cultura Económica.
Rodrik, D. (1995) 'Getting Interventions Right: How South Korea and Taiwan Grew Rich', *Economic Policy*, 22 (April).
Rossi, I. (1995) 'Desarrollo y Competitividad del Sector Forestal-Maderero', in P. Meller and R. E. Sáez (eds), *Auge Exportador Chileno – Lecciones y Desafíos Futuros*, Santiago: CIEPLAN/Domen Editores.
Sáez, S. (1991) 'Indicadores para las Exportaciones Chilenas: 1950–89', *Notas Técnicas 138*, CIEPLAN, Santiago.
Stiglitz, J. E. (1994) 'The Role of the State in Financial Markets', *Proceedings of the World Bank Conference of Development Economics, 1993*, The World Bank, Washington, DC.
Stiglitz, J. E. and Weiss, A. (1981) 'Credit Rationing in Markets with Imperfect Information', *American Economic Review*, 71, 3 (June).
Stiglitz, J. E. and Uy, M. (1996) 'Financial Markets, Public Policy, and the East Asian Miracle', *The World Bank Research Observer*, 11, 2 (August).
World Bank (1997) *World Development Report, 1997*, Washington, DC.
Wade, R. (1990) *Governing the Market – Economic Theory and the Role of Government in East Asian Industrialization*, Princeton, NJ: Princeton University Press.

4
Costa Rica: Policies and Conditions for Export Diversification

Ennio Rodríguez

Antecedents

A few antecedents, even if outlined in broad strokes, are needed to assess Costa Rica's experience in export diversification, to understand both the results and why certain policies have been implemented.

Costa Rica is a middle-income developing country with a total population of 3.5 million in 1997. Population density was 67 persons per square kilometre in 1995, and will reach 103 by 2020. Since the human development index began to be calculated, Costa Rica has been one of the top two Latin American countries. Moreover, life expectancy at birth of 76 years in 1995 surpassed that of the US.

Although historians argue about the date at which a democratic form of government was firmly established, 1889 has been cited. In any case, important developments in the last third of the nineteenth century also include the abolition of capital punishment in 1870; the separation of State and Church; the reduction of the military budget (the army was formally disbanded in 1948); an increase in public education expenditure, with the declaration of free and compulsory elementary education; and the strengthening of the judicial system. By the end of the nineteenth century, consensus-creating institutions had been firmly established.

Soon after independence in 1821 coffee was introduced. From 1832 onwards the expansion of coffee was extraordinary. The more specialized activities of processing and international marketing underwent, almost immediately, a process of concentration. Meanwhile the process of land concentration seems to have been much slower in manifesting itself and its timing is still subject to debate. The absence of large contingents of workers on the one hand, and of strong concentration of capital on the other, in the face of the intensive but seasonal requirements of labour in the cultivation of coffee, checked the development of large *haciendas* to some extent. A symbiosis between the *haciendas* and the surrounding family plots developed, thus ensuring the survival of small producers, who even today account for a significant share of total coffee production.

Banana production developed as a result of the construction of railroads for the increasing foreign trade towards the end of the nineteenth century. A system of plantations was developed by the builders of the railroads, as land had been granted to them in partial payment for the investments made. On the other hand, the finalization of the construction of the railways had left idle a large contingent of workers brought mainly from Jamaica for their construction.

Large tracts of arable land in the hands of the state became the escape valve for the periodic crises resulting from fluctuations in coffee and banana prices. Spontaneous and organized colonization of the agricultural frontier absorbed displaced farm workers and brought new areas into production. This mechanism operated throughout the nineteenth century and up until the limit of the agricultural frontier was exhausted in the early 1970s. Following that, a more organized programme of distribution of untilled land was developed on the basis of the experiences of the colonization process, which played an important part in providing rural employment until the export diversification of the second half of the 1980s. To some extent, Costa Rica has been likened to a case of the 'staple theory of economic growth' (Rodriguez, 1982).

Export diversification was slow and so was the development of industrial activities. Primary export-led growth provided for a fast growing population. To outside observers, change in Costa Rica appears to have been slow, but this reflects its past successes. In general, the case for change, in the absence of major crises, has had to be made carefully and the costs of the transition carefully weighed. Indeed in 1940 coffee accounted for 53 per cent of total exports, bananas for 25 per cent, and cocoa 8 per cent. From 1950 until 1954, bananas and coffee accounted for 88 per cent of total exports; from 1955 to 1959, for 84 per cent. In the late 1950s and early 1960s new export commodities included beef and sugar, supported by subsidized credit programmes as well as increasing research and technical assistance. The banking system had been nationalized in 1949, and credit allocation and subsidized interest rates were normal tools of economic policy.

Over the last 35 years Costa Rican exports (in dollars) have grown at an average annual rate of 10.8 per cent. In the context of an import-substituting industrialization and subregional integration, exports grew at increasingly higher rates through the 1960s and 1970s, but the severe external debt crisis in the early 1980s led to export stagnation. In the late 1980s and through the 1990s, there has been a substantial recovery, which shows to some extent the effect of a second generation of export promotion policies.

Subregional integration and import-substituting industrialization

The high growth rates of the 1960s and 1970s are associated with the import-substitution strategy[1] and regional integration with the other Central American countries (in the Central American Common Market – CACM). The first generation of export incentives were devised as incentives for manufactured exports within the framework of subregional integration, accompanied by some efforts to diversify primary exports to third countries. The incentives included high common external tariffs and tax rebates on imports of capital goods and raw materials. Exports to the rest of Central America rose from less than 5 per cent to 20 per cent of total exports in just a few years in the 1960s. They remained stable afterwards, reaching a peak in 1980. However, due to a combination of internal conflicts in the region and the payments crisis arising from the debt crisis, Central American markets lost dynamism during the 1980s, while non-traditional exports to other markets became increasingly important.

In 1954 a moderate tariff for industrial protection was introduced, and in 1959 it was replaced by the Law of Protection and Industrial Development. In the 1950s the manufacturing sector consisted mainly of traditional consumer goods; firms were small and family owned. Food processing, beverages, tobacco, textiles, shoes, clothing, lumber and wooden furniture and accessories accounted for about 80 per cent of industrial output in 1955. The pressure from the Chamber of Industry in favour of an import-substituting strategy had met with some resistance. However, a decline in coffee prices meant a 40 per cent decline in the barter terms of trade between 1954 and 1962. There was a growing perception that the limits to staple growth had been reached. The agricultural frontier was rapidly being exhausted and attempts to diversify agricultural exports had achieved only limited success. Industrialization was then seen as the alternative. At the time, the recommendation of the United Nations Economic Commission for Latin America and the Caribbean to tackle the limitations imposed by the small size of the internal market was regional integration. Further pressure for regional integration came from the US Alliance for Progress. Costa Rica joined the CACM in 1963.

Free regional trade was established for industrial products behind a high common external tariff. Protection was high for consumer goods and low for intermediate and capital goods, resulting in high nominal and effective levels of protection. In 1962, the five CACM member countries signed the Central American Agreement of Fiscal Incentives for Industrial Development, which included total or partial exemptions from import duties for capital goods, intermediate products and raw materials; and an income tax deduction for certain investment expenditures. Other instruments included: an overvalued exchange rate; subsidized interest rates that were sometimes negative in real terms; other extraordinary tariffs and surcharges; and higher selective consumption taxes for imported goods from outside the region. A vocational training institute was created (Instituto Nacional de Aprendizaje), funded by a surcharge on the payroll of both the private and the public sectors, largely dedicated to the training of technicians in demand for the industrial activities. A high-level technical university was also established (Instituto Tecnológico de Costa Rica).

Industrial production soared, and manufacturing increased its share of GDP from 14 per cent in 1962 to 20 per cent in 1973; employment in manufacturing increased its share of total employment from 11 to 12 per cent; and industrial exports, which represented 14 per cent of total exports in 1962, increased to 25 per cent in 1973. The overall rate of growth of the economy was 7.1 per cent per annum from 1962 to 1974. Although the share of traditional exports had dropped to 73 per cent in 1972, down from 85 per cent in 1963, only 7 per cent of non-traditional exports were sold outside the CACM in 1972.[2]

During the 1970s, trade within the CACM lost dynamism. The oil shocks in 1974 and 1978 and the wide fluctuations in commodity prices, especially coffee and beef, generated payments problems. The limits to the 'easy phase' of import-substitution were becoming apparent. From 1974 to 1978 Costa Rican exports to the CACM grew at the lower rate of 7 per cent per annum. However, industrial GDP still grew at the slightly higher rate of 7.4 per cent per annum.

The most significant internal determinant of the limits of import-substituting industrialization was the highly skewed income distribution of the region (excluding Costa Rica, it is among the worst in Latin America). The internal market is thus smaller than population figures might suggest. Nevertheless, while the CACM as a whole was witnessing a decline in the rate of industrial investment in the 1970s compared with the 1960s, Costa Rica saw an increase in the rate of capital formation throughout the decade from under 20 per cent in the 1960s to over 25 per cent at the end of the following decade. Part of the explanation is the financial reform of 1972 which allowed private financial intermediaries to tap savings and lend for consumption purposes; that in its turn led to a consumer durables boom. This later exhaustion of import-substituting possibilities in Costa Rica, as compared with the other members of the CACM, may also be explained by the different patterns of specialization of their industrial sectors. Costa Rica had specialized in consumer durables (metal goods and electrical equipment); its neighbours had concentrated on the traditional manufacturing sectors (textiles/clothing and leather/shoes) (Bulmer-Thomas, 1978). To the extent that income elasticity of demand is higher for durables than for traditional manufactured goods, it was to be expected that Costa Rican industry still showed growth while its partners might have already exhausted the possibilities of the regional market.

From 1978 to 1982 exports to the CACM grew at an annual rate of 1.3 per cent and GDP at 2.3 per cent. Costa Rica had a severe debt crisis in August 1981. The factors leading to the crisis include: a severe decline in the terms of trade; a crisis of the CACM as all members faced a difficult external environment;[3] and internal policy mismanagement leading to increasing foreign indebtedness, until the sharp increase in international interest rates made the situation untenable.[4]

Although intended as a transitory phase leading to the eventual development of third-market exports, import-substituting industrialization had left an industrial sector generating less than half of the exports needed for imports of capital and intermediate goods, and raw materials. A decrease in tariff protection never took place until after the crisis, when the distortions introduced by currency overvaluation and subsidies for capital investment were also corrected. The system of incentives had been biased against export diversification for sales outside the CACM, particularly against agricultural exports. Again the relative success of the strategy and the interests of those favoured by its implementation kept it in place until the payments crisis; after more than two decades of record high growth rates, the crisis forced change.

However, industrial development brought about a new more dynamic entrepreneurial group, new technological knowledge, more efficient financial and professional services, and a better trained labour force. Competition within the CACM also reduced potential inefficiency levels as some initially relatively similar and protected industrial sectors were made to compete. Additionally, the 'second phase' of import substitution including the development of a capital goods sector under heavily subsidized and protected conditions was never attempted. All these elements later facilitated the transition towards a more open economy.

It is also worth mentioning that some efforts to diversify exports outside the CACM were undertaken during the 1970s. The Export Promotion Law of 1972 included: tax certificates (*certificado de abono tributario* – CAT) for exports with a 35 per cent or higher value added domestically by firms of at least 60 per cent Costa Rican capital and producing from a list of preselected products, which consisted of a 12–15 per cent subsidy on the value of exports (a higher subsidy the greater the value added); reimbursement of taxes paid on raw materials and intermediate goods used to produce exports; the 'increase in export' certificates (*certificados de incremento de las exportaciones* – CIEX), providing a one-year subsidy of 1–10 per cent paid on the increase in value of exports from one year to the next; and, finally, a drawback system for the promotion of the *maquila* industry. The impact of the Export Promotion Law was limited as its application was cumbersome, export taxes remained, export procedures were complicated, and the currency was highly overvalued.

Export diversification and structural change

The transition to a more open, less distorted economy has been gradual and carefully avoided recessions and massive unemployment after the 1981 crisis. The initial emphasis was on a more appropriate and stable exchange rate, and subsidies to compensate for the anti-export bias, targeted on promoting non-traditional exports to third markets. As export diversification gathered momentum tariffs have been reduced and other distortions removed. Shock treatment of the external sector has been avoided. External support to the export diversification strategy came mainly from USAID, following the debt crisis, which took place one year before the Mexican crisis. Support from the International Monetary Fund (IMF) and the World Bank only came after some success in macroeconomic stabilization and export diversification had already been achieved.

Here, first, we describe trade policies and export incentives in the 1980s and the first half of the 1990s; second, some export diversification achievements are analysed.

Exchange rate policy

Prior to and during the import-substituting phase, there was a fixed exchange rate system to which several adjustments in parity had to be made. In 1981, after a speculative attack on the currency, a floating exchange rate system was temporarily adopted, which was then followed by a crawling peg. Some modifications have been introduced since then, but it is basically the same system that is still in place. The rate of depreciation has been mostly determined by purchasing power parity considerations, though the behaviour of capital flows has also been taken into account. Exchange rate policy has been key to the promotion of exports by contributing to the creation of competitive conditions.

In the 1980s, the exchange rate policy actively sought to promote exports, while in the 1990s, it has aimed at maintaining purchasing power parity. From 1980 to 1990, the real effective value of the currency depreciated by 55 per cent, but it has remained fairly stable since then. It is also noticeable that Costa Rica was one of the first countries in Latin America that had important real depreciations in the first part of the 1980s. Then in the 1990s, while there has been a trend towards real appreciation in many countries, Costa Rica's real effective exchange remained fairly stable.

Tariffs

Tariff reduction has been gradual, and has allowed for an adaptation of firms to the more competitive environment. The exchange rate policy contributed to smoothing the transition. There never was a process of generalized closures or reduction in employment levels in the manufacturing sector. High tariffs were not used as a result of regional competition. The first tariff reduction programme of the CACM in 1986 revealed the presence of 'water' in the tariffs. Initially, there was a simplification and reduction of maximum tariffs, which did not lead, however, to a generalized reduction in effective protection (Mange, 1987). Central America was among the first to start liberalizing trade in Latin America. By 1990 its tariffs were reduced to within a range of 5–40 per cent. In 1993, a further reduction of tariffs took place, still leaving the maximum tariff at 40 per cent. Finally, in 1996 another planned reduction was agreed, a comon external tariff (CET) range of 0–15 per cent by the year 2000.

Direct subsidies to non-traditional exports

In February 1984, the Public Sector Financial Equilibrium Law was passed in Congress. Its main objective was to reduce fiscal imbalances by creating new taxes and granting new powers to Central Government to control the fiscal deficit. It imposed taxes on traditional exports (coffee, bananas, sugar cane and meat), which were deemed to be realizing windfall profits after a 500 per cent exchange rate devaluation in 1982. At the same time, this law approved the following incentives to non-traditional exports under an 'export contract':

- Duty-free intermediate goods importing
- Income-tax exemption
- Tax-saving certificates (CAT).

The right to *ex ante* duty-free importing was granted to exporting companies, in the absence of a duty drawback system. It is not a subsidy so much as a mechanism to facilitate trade for exporters. The income-tax exemption benefit appears to have been significant, but there are no firm data to confirm this. According to informal estimates by the Ministry of Finance, the fiscal cost of this benefit in 1996 could have been around 0.25 per cent of GDP.

The CAT had existed since 1972, but it was enhanced by the 1984 Law. It is a subsidy granted initially for a period of ten years as a way to compensate exporters for domestic distortions that impair competitiveness and as a way to cover possible costs of entry to new markets with new products. It is intended for non-traditional exports only. The CAT is equivalent to 15 per cent of the FOB value of exports, when they are destined to the Western Hemisphere, or 20 per cent, when destined elsewhere. The entitlement itself has a maturity period of 18 months.

It can be argued that as a subsidy, the CAT has not been efficient because it does not address specific distortions. Rather, it has been general (the only exception being traditional exports) with only some minor restrictions in terms of value added requirements and other qualifications. However, it seems to have been very effective according to Agosin et al. (1996), who studied the impact of CAT on export growth. In their work, the growth of US imports from the Caribbean Basin countries, excluding oil, is compared to the growth of Costa Rican non-traditional exports destined to markets other than Central America from 1985 until 1994, on the assumption that the difference in growth rates is due to the subsidy. They also assume that the average added value of exports is 40 per cent, which allows them to estimate an increase in the value added due to the CAT. Finally, they compare the value of the CAT granted to the increase in the exports' value added. This leads them to conclude that for each US$1 of subsidy the increase in value added was between US$1.42 and US$2.05. This would mean that, in spite of its fiscal cost, the CAT subsidy has been very successful in promoting export growth. However, it is hard to argue that the difference in growth rates between the Caribbean Basin countries and Costa Rica can be attributed solely to the CAT incentive. For instance, some of the countries in the region were experiencing political turmoil that impeded their exporting capacity. Costa Rica did respond faster and more vigorously than its neighbours to the incentives of the Caribbean Basin Initiative, in particular the United States' Caribbean Basin Recovery Act, but this could also be related to longer-term competitiveness advantages such as the education and health levels of the work force, and the credibility of macroeconomic and trade policies.

Hoffmaister, on the other hand, concludes that export subsidies had little effect on Costa Rica's impressive export growth rates on the basis of his estimate of exports in the absence of CATs. Using quarterly data for the years 1970 to 1989, Hoffmaister fits a regression model in which export volume is a function of: CAT subsidies, relative prices, nominal exchange rate and real GDP. Based on his simulation of a scenario without CATs, Hoffmaister concludes that each dollar of subsidy appears to have increased exports only by US$1.35 (Hoffmaister, 1992). The estimated model, however, has serious limitations. Due to data limitations, the dependent variable is the volume of all non-traditional exports including very large categories not eligible for CAT subsidies: export processing zones and exports to the CACM.

A more simple approach, undertaken by Willmore (1997), allows him to conclude that for each dollar of subsidy exports increased by US$3.70 for the 1984–90 period. Willmore fits a linear trend to non-traditional exports for the years 1970 through 1983 and projects for the subsequent period 1984–94. The projection is only 2.5 per cent above the actual exports. However, if non-traditional exports are separated into exports to CACM and Panama, and those destined to the rest of the world, interesting results can be observed. Actual intraregional exports drop sharply while the projected trend is positive. The result is the reverse for exports to the rest of the world, for which no positive trend is projected and actual exports mushroom. CAT subsidies would explain the expansion in non-traditional exports to the rest of the world. In fact, much of the increase in extra-regional exports is offset by a decrease in intraregional sales.

From a fiscal perspective, the CAT may indeed have had an excessive opportunity cost. In 1989, 1990 and 1991, export subsidies represented more than 1 per cent of GDP. These high costs led Congress to pass a new law in 1992 extending the maturity of CATs from 12 to 18 months, which caused a reduction in costs in 1993. It also eliminated the possibility of granting export contracts to new companies. The existing contracts began to expire in 1996, which has also meant the end of the income-tax exemption benefit to some exporters, but CAT issuance did not end until the year 2000. In contrast, the remaining taxes on traditional exports were removed in 1995. The taxes on coffee exports were transformed into an income-tax equivalent, while the tax on banana exports was drastically reduced and was completely eliminated in 1998.

Limits to the second generation of incentives were reached both from fiscal considerations and because of the implementation of Uruguay Round agreements. A third generation of export incentives is currently under consideration.

Credit

Following the financial reforms of 1972, before which the banks were state-owned, private sector financial institutions were increasingly able to tap into private savings, and in the 1980s were quite prepared to finance the rapidly expanding foreign trade.[5] Additionally, commercial banks had access to special credit lines made available by the Central Bank, to finance both working capital and fixed capital investments. These programmes have been specifically targeted on non-traditional exporting firms. Most of the time, interest rates on loans in these programmes have been lower than on regular credit lines.[6]

International trade agreements

On 1 January 1984, the Caribbean Basin Economic Recovery Act (CBI) came into effect in the United States granting duty-free access to US markets for exports from beneficiary countries for 12 years. It was later extended for an indefinite period and some improvements added, such as exemption from the cumulation clause.[7] However, important products were excluded; namely, textiles and apparel, canned tuna, petroleum and byproducts, leather goods and footwear. Sugar was subject to quotas. Eligibility for duty-free access is relatively lax, including a requirement of 35 per cent of value added in one or more of the beneficiary countries, of which up to 15 per cent can be US components, and that the product be 'substantially' transformed whenever foreign components are included.

The CBI has provided a good opportunity for Costa Rican exports. Macroeconomic stabilization started as early as 1982 and export promotion of non-traditional exports in 1984, the first country in Central America to embark upon it. However, the exceptions to the CBI are important. More than 50 per cent of Costa Rican exports to the US are excluded from CBI benefits (Mange and González, 1988). Indeed, the fast growing sector of textiles and apparel was excluded from the CBI. On the other hand, more intangible benefits may have been derived from the CBI, notably the increased attention of potential investors to an area very close to the US and of some political importance to the US government.

As part of the efforts to increase its participation in international markets, Costa Rica joined the World Trade Organization and subscribed to a free-trade agreement with Mexico, which began gradually to be implemented in 1995.

Costa Rica is actively engaged in the Free Trade for the Americas (FTAA) process, initiated at the Miami Summit of 1995, which is to achieve its goal of a free trade area by the year 2005. Costa Rica chaired the FTAA during 1997. Moreover, Costa Rica has agreed to have joint and/or coordinated trade negotiating positions with the other CACM members in future FTAA negotiations.

Science and technology

The Costa Rican development strategy has included the provision of innovation finance in some predefined sectors and training in renowned universities overseas (Rodríguez and Grinspan, 1983). Many of the success stories of new exports with a technological component developed locally benefited in early stages of product development from the innovation financing facility (Viceministerio de Ciencia y Tecnología, 1996). This facility is characterized by interest rates only slightly lower than those in the market. The important difference from the market is in the collateral required, as the project itself has normally been accepted for this purpose. Additionally, the link between universities and the productive sectors has been actively promoted by strengthening research and service centres which sell their services. The Center for Food Technology and the Post-Harvest Institute of the University of Costa Rica have been of particular importance for the support of non-traditional agricultural exports.

Investment promotion and institutional development

Prior to the reforms of the early 1980s, the private sector was already well-organized, particularly in the industrial sector but also in agricultural and commercial activities. Private sector organizations participated actively both in policy dialogue and in the setting up of new export organizations, such as in textiles and the exporters' chamber, which have also been very active in international trade negotiations, especially fighting against quotas and, when unavoidable, in their administration.

Of particular importance was the creation of a private sector foundation financed by USAID called CINDE (Costa Rican coalition for development initiatives). CINDE spent its first two years defining its role, but from 1985 onwards three of its most successful programmes included attraction of foreign investment, a training programme (PROCAP), and the Private

Agricultural and Agroindustrial Council (CAAP). In 1988, CINDE also started to promote tourism (Camacho, 1996).

CINDE's current programmes are: (i) the economic environment programme, which organizes seminars and promotes studies; (ii) foreign investment attraction; (iii) promotion of export investment projects; (iv) the intelligence system (data bases and trade related studies); (v) the agricultural services programme, which provides quality certification services and has a laboratory to respond to agricultural and agroindustrial technical demands; (vi) the supply of university texts; and (vii) the training programme (ibid.: 16).

The investment programme has been targeted on specific activities considered important given the macroeconomic environment. During the first stage (1984–90), rising unemployment and a difficult Central American climate due to political and military conflicts in the subregion were the context in which a decision was made to promote light assembly operations, particularly apparel *maquila*. The second stage (1991 onwards) included higher technology and skill-intensive industries, such as electronics, metal mechanics and health care products. The economy was by then closer to full employment and the highly educated and flexible labour force was already being recognized abroad. The investment attraction strategy was based on the Irish model of targeting potential companies in the US, Europe and later in Asia in those sectors in which Costa Rica was considered internationally competitive.

Independent evaluation of CINDE's impact on investment attraction has been positive. It was concluded that CINDE had positively influenced 61.3 per cent of the US$556 million of FDI flowing into Costa Rica between 1986 and 1990, and that 42 per cent of the decisions to invest overseas had not yet even been made when CINDE approached the company to promote Costa Rica (Lanza, 1994).

CINDE's training programme was targeted on the human resource needs of non-traditional exports, including managers and top-level administrators, university lecturers, and personnel from private financial institutions and the Central Bank. The training programmes emphasized practical information and strategy formulation, through 'hands on' observational learning.

The evaluation showed it had a greater impact on small and medium-sized firms than on larger ones, and seems to have been more effective in the industrial and tourism sectors than in the agricultural sector. CINDE's programme was the first training programme targeted on the non-traditional export sector. Today many organizations offer training programmes to help solve export problems.

CAAP emphasized its relationship with universities and research centres and with producer organizations on the one hand, while on the other, it performed its own product selection, constraint identification and technical assistance. By 1987, 12 potential crops had been identified (cut flowers, ornamental plants, cocoa, macadamia, black pepper, asparagus, melons, root and tuber crops, papaya and pineapples), and by 1994, six new products were added (plantain, blackberries, vegetables, industrial tomatoes, hot peppers and onions). In general, two types of constraints were identified: those affecting a group of products, such as general economic policies, and those affecting a particular product, such as diseases. The programme surpassed the initial goals in terms of hectares assisted, investment, and foreign exchange generated (Camacho, 1996).

Another important institutional simplification was the development in 1988 of a one-stop window for exporters, the whole process taking only a few hours; in the 1990s, the time imports spend in customs was reduced to an average of half a day.

Export diversification results

Non-traditional exports have exceeded the value of traditional exports in the 1990s. Overall export growth rates averaged 12.3 per cent from 1987 to 1995 and are among the highest in Latin America for that period. Moreover, while from 1980 to 1983 exports of non-traditional products to markets outside the CACM accounted for only 15–18 per cent of total exports, they doubled from 1984 to 1987, and by 1995 represented 46 per cent of total exports.

The manufacturing sector increased its participation in total exports outside the CACM from a similar share to that of agriculture before 1985 to 63 per cent of total non-traditional exports in 1995. Exports from *free trade zones* increased at an average annual rate of 30 per cent during 1993–6. Higher value added industries are being attracted to free trade zones, as reflected by increasing investment per worker ratios.

Agricultural export diversification has also been successful. Non-traditional agricultural exports which accounted for less than 8 per cent of total exports during 1981–3 increased to 17 per cent in 1992, hovering around 15 per cent thereafter. Interestingly, four of the 'winners' picked by CAAP (ornamental plants; foliage, leaves and plant parts; pineapples; and melons) accounted for more than half of total non-traditional agricultural exports. Other important crops include flowers, chayotes, yucca, root and tuber crops and *raicilla*, three of which were also originally preselected. Though it is difficult to quantify the effect of CAAP (Camacho, 1996: 23–5), the technological packages designed and constraints overcome, including lobbying for policy and administrative change, undoubtedly had a decisive impact in the initial diversification efforts. In particular CAAP was effective in the case of root and tuber crops, in which there is major participation of small producers, many in the areas of land redistribution programmes of the 1970s and early 1980s. The research centres in the universities and their service orientation also proved important in areas such as disease diagnosis and treatment, and post-harvest management of perishable crops.

Moreover, in the 1990s, part of the export promotion effort has been undertaken in areas that are not included in Costa Rican data on 'exports':

maquila and *free trade zone* exports, and tourism. The value added of *maquila* exports has been less dynamic in recent years due to quota restrictions, rising competition and the end of some export incentives. Nevertheless, this sector contributed value added of US$126 million in 1995, which is 11 per cent of traditional exports. On the other hand, the value added of free trade zone exports has increased very rapidly, from US$25.4 million in 1990 to US$142.1 million in 1995, an average annual growth rate of 41.9 per cent. Local purchases from free trade zones increased at an annual rate of over 30 per cent during 1993–5, albeit from a small base. Average investment per firm increased 10 per cent per annum and average wages in US dollars increased at a rate of 21 per cent. Tourism has also risen, which is explained in part by fiscal incentives. Revenues have gone up from US$275 million in 1990 to US$661.3 million in 1995, an annual growth rate of 19.7 per cent, making tourism the single most important foreign exchange earning activity in the country, ahead of coffee or bananas.

It is interesting to note that the structural change in total industrial production is evident in some of its most promising sectors. The share of research and development-intensive activities has increased in industrial sector total production. The participation of 'Science Based Industries' increased from 5.7 per cent in 1989 to 14.1 per cent in 1995, and 'Differentiated Products Industries' increased from 4.8 to 8.5 per cent; while 'Natural Resources Based Industries' and 'Labour Intensive Industries' both decreased, from 59.4 to 51.0 per cent and from 10.8 to 9.0 per cent, respectively (Central Bank, based on OECD definitions).

Another indicator of rising competitiveness is the increase in locally designed computer software, which in 1996 reached US$11 million, the highest in Latin America (CEFSA). Moreover, a recent study has concluded that Costa Rica is competitive in the electronics sector (FIAS, 1996). Foreign investment in this sector has come in three waves: the first during the second half of the 1970s, the second during the late 1980s and early 1990s, and the third since 1995. The first wave seems to be explained by particular circumstances, such as the instability in neighbouring countries. Firms mainly produced electrical products and only two manufactured electronic components, and served mainly the CACM.

In the second wave there was a surge in investment for the production of electronic components, particularly power conditioning components. There also were the first investments in highly sophisticated sensors for industrial and medical applications. Sensors and power conditioning components have production processes in which Costa Rica has a comparative advantage. They are produced in low volumes for niche markets with unique specifications and require a large amount of testing. Therefore, skilled labour is a major production cost, with which the country is relatively well-endowed.

The third wave of investments reflects a greater concentration in power conditioning components and sensors. Recent investments include more sophisticated power conditioning components. The United States is by far the most important market for electronics exports of Costa Rica. Four-fifths of the companies export to US markets, most of them exclusively to their parent companies.

CINDE has played an active role in attracting many of these firms to Costa Rica. The factors these companies cited for locating in Costa Rica include: (i) a well-educated and low-cost labour force with considerable dexterity (clearly the main factor); (ii) the fact that a large number of Costa Ricans speak English;[8] (iii) the speed for setting up a plant and starting operations, in some cases within six to nine months, revealing the absence of bureaucratic hurdles; (iv) cost savings of around 35 per cent over their operations in the US; (v) the long tradition of political stability and clean business environment; (vi) the flexibility of the free trade zone legislation; (vii) duty-free access to US markets under the CBI; (viii) the relative ease with which firms can bring in technical and managerial staff; and (ix) proximity to the US. In general it was found that companies were attracted to Costa Rica because it is seen as a location enabling continuing improvement in productive processes and productivity (FIAS, 1996: 13).

For the future, instead of picking *product* winners, FIAS proposes to select *firms* from selected technology areas as they are not subject to the relatively short lifecycles of products. The characteristics of the technological processes should include: (i) high value but low volume production; (ii) product lines with many different models or part numbers, requiring a large number of set ups; and (iii) products in which final testing constitutes a relatively large part of total costs (ibid.: 22).

In 1997, INTEL started setting up a plant for the assembly and testing of microchips, with an investment of between US$300 and US$500 million, and expected sales of US$5000 million.

New export or other incentives

As many of the existing export incentives are expiring, there is growing consensus that the 'third generation' of such incentives should concentrate neither on non-traditional exports, nor on global exports, but rather should assist both tradables and non-tradables as appropriate to increase overall competitiveness. The areas mentioned include among others: further economic deregulation; an increase in infrastructure investment, including greater private sector participation; opening up of trade in services sectors; promotion of innovation, strategic alliances, technological transfers and foreign direct investment; support for market intelligence; and efficient institutions (Alonso, 1995).

Social results

Many observers agree that during the process of market opening (1986–90) inequality and poverty levels were reduced in Costa Rica in contrast to other such processes in Latin America such as in Chile. Parts of the explanation are the non-recessionary path of reform and the initial conditions prior to the crisis of 1980–2. Also important were explicit poverty reduction programmes. Moreover, better than pre-crisis levels were soon achieved thereafter (Morley and Alvarez, 1992; Céspedes and Jiménez, 1994).

Export diversification and competitiveness

Another way to evaluate the impact of export promotion policies is through a Competitiveness Analysis of Nations (CAN), which is a methodology developed by the United Nations Economic Commission for Latin America and the Caribbean (ECLAC) to assess a country's relative position in international trade. It employs the OECD trade database, containing information for 88 countries. It is, however, limited in that the methodology uses only imports to OECD countries, excluding, particularly, South–South trade.

Methodology

CAN methodology is based on several types of indicators, as described in Agosin et al. (1996), who applied it to the case of Costa Rica. Among them, two indicators are used to construct a competitive matrix for the country:

1. *Sector participation*:

$$\frac{M_i}{M} * 100$$

where M_i is the OECD's sector 'i' imports from all countries and M is the OECD's total imports from all countries.

This shows the weight of a specific sector in global markets. A 'dynamic' sector is one with an increasing share in OECD trade, while a 'stagnant' one has a declining share. A given country is said to be 'better positioned' the larger is the weight of 'dynamic' sectors in total exports.

2. *Market participation*:

$$\frac{M_{ij}}{M_i} * 100$$

where M_{ij} is the OECD's sector 'i' imports from country 'j' and M_i is the OECD's sector 'i' imports from all countries.

This shows the national share in the international sector market. An increase in market participation is associated with an increase in national sector competitiveness, particularly when it is compared to a rival country's market participation. A given country is 'more competitive' the larger is the proportion of sectors with increasing participation in the world market.

A three-year average for each of these indicators is used to classify all sectors of a given country in a competitive matrix, showing a country's relative position in international trade, according to the following four categories:

- Rising stars (optimal situation): Dynamic sectors in the global economy (increasing share in world trade) and in which the country is competitive (increasing its participation in the world market).
- Declining stars (vulnerable situation): Declining sectors in world trade (decreasing share in world trade) and in which the country is competitive (increasing its participation in the world market).
- Lost opportunities: Dynamic sectors in world trade (increasing share in world trade) and the country is not competitive (decreasing its participation in the world market).
- Setbacks: Declining sector in world trade (decreasing share in world trade) and the country is not competitive (decreasing its participation in the world market).

| | | *Sector participation* | |
		Increase	*Decrease*
Market	*Increase*	Rising stars	Declining stars
participation	*Decrease*	Lost opportunities	Setbacks

A third indicator is used for the construction of an 'adaptability' index:

3. *Contribution*:

$$\frac{M_{ij}}{M_i} * 100$$

where M_{ij} is the OECD's sector 'i' imports from country 'j' and M_j is the OECD's total imports from country 'j'.

This shows a sector's relative weight in the country's total trade volume. An increase in this index reveals a change in trade structure, which may be used to point towards possible trends, such as an increase in the relative importance of dynamic or declining sectors or a trend towards diversification of the export structure.

In addition, there are two 'adaptability' indices that show the extent to which a country is moving towards more dynamic sectors:

(1)

$$MPAI = \frac{RP_j}{DP_j}$$

where

$MPAI$ is the market participation adaptability index, which shows the gains in competitiveness,

RP_j: Competitive sectors of country 'j' in terms of OECD market participation,

DP_j: Declining sectors of country 'j' in terms of OECD market participation;

and (2)

$$SCAI = \frac{RS_j}{DS_j}$$

where

$SCAI$ is the sector contribution adaptability index, which shows the gains in 'position' or country dependence of dynamic sectors in the world markets,

RS_j: Dynamic sectors, in terms of their OECD sector contribution, of country 'j',

DS_j: Declining sectors, in terms of their OECD sector contribution, of country 'j'.

The competitiveness matrix and adaptability indices of Costa Rica

Table 4.1 shows the competitiveness matrix of Costa Rica, Chile and Korea for 1985 and 1994 in terms of percentages of contribution to total exports (measured by OECD imports), as calculated by Agosin et al. (1996).

Since 1985, the 'rising stars' sectors of Costa Rica have increased their contribution from 15.3 per cent to 41.5 per cent, which is greater than Chile's but less than Korea's. The dynamic and competitive sectors in Costa Rica are: clothing (men and children), underwear, vegetables, jewellery, domestic appliances, fresh fish and medical instruments.

The importance of the 'declining stars' sectors in Costa Rica has fallen from 65.3 per cent in 1985 to 49.8 per cent in 1994, while in Chile and Korea this type of sector has increased in importance, but it is less than what it still is in Costa Rica. In the case of Costa Rica, these sectors are fruits and nuts (fresh or dry), coffee, fruit preserves, alcohol and alcohol derivatives, textile fibres, gold, leather, aluminum, animal products and photographic equipment.

Table 4.1   Competitiveness matrix: Costa Rica, Chile and Korea, 1985 and 1994

| | Costa Rica | | Chile | | Korea | |
Sector	*1985*	*1994*	*1985*	*1994*	*1985*	*1994*
Rising stars	15.3	41.5	6.4	20.1	23.0	48.4
Declining stars	65.3	49.8	41.1	48.8	10.5	12.2
Lost opportunities	15.3	7.7	3.0	2.5	57.5	35.0
Setbacks	4.1	1.1	49.6	28.7	8.9	4.5

Source: Agosin et al. (1996).

The 'lost opportunities' sectors have fallen from 15.3 per cent in 1985 to 7.7 per cent in 1994. Chile and Korea follow a similar trend, but with very different values. In 1994 these sectors represented 2.5 per cent and 35 per cent in Chile and Korea, correspondingly. In the case of Costa Rica these sectors are clothing for women, meat, crustaceans, electric appliances, electricity conductors, cereals, telecommunications equipment, metal manufactures, canned foods and other processed foods, and woods.

Table 4.2   Costa Rica: rising stars, market participation and sector contribution, 1985 and 1994

| | Market participation | | Sector contribution | |
	1985	*1994*	*1985*	*1994*
Clothing (men and children)	0.4	1.3	1.3	1.8
Underwear	1.1	2.2	0.6	0.9
Vegetables	0.7	1.5	0.9	1.0
Jewelry	0.1	0.4	0.4	0.4
Domestic appliances	0.0	0.2	0.6	0.7
Fresh fish	0.2	0.2	0.5	0.6
Medical instruments	0.0	0.3	0.2	0.4

Source: Agosin et al. (1996).

The setback sectors represented 4.1 per cent of total exports in 1985, but fell to 1.1 per cent in 1994. Chile and Korea follow a similar trend, but with higher values, 28.7 per cent in Chile and 4.5 per cent in Korea. In the case of Costa Rica, these sectors are sugar, cocoa, boats and ships, minerals, skins.

The adaptability indices show an increase in market participation for Costa Rica, that is, sectors with an increasing market share have grown relative to those with a declining market share. This is also the case of Chile. Korea has already achieved a high index, but it fell. The dependence of these countries on dynamic world markets, as opposed to declining markets, has increased according to the sector contribution index.

Table 4.3   Adaptability indices: Costa Rica, Chile and Korea, 1985 and 1994

	Costa Rica		Chile		Korea	
Sector	*1985*	*1994*	*1985*	*1994*	*1985*	*1994*
Market participation	0.36	0.40	0.08	0.12	3.36	2.07
Sector contribution	0.44	0.97	0.10	0.29	4.14	5.00

Source: Agosin et al. (1996).

Summary and conclusions

Over the last 35 years Costa Rican exports have grown in dollars at an average annual growth rate of 10.8 per cent. In the context of an import-substituting industrialization strategy and subregional integration, exports grew at increasingly higher rates through the 1960s and 1970s, but the severe external debt crisis in the early 1980s led to export stagnation. In the late 1980s and through the 1990s, there has been a substantial recovery, which shows to some extent the effect of a second generation of export promotion policies. The transition to a more open less distorted economy has been gradual and carefully avoided recessions and massive unemployment after the 1981 crisis. The initial emphasis was on a more appropriate and stable exchange rate, and subsidies to compensate for the anti-export bias, targeted on promoting non-traditional exports to third markets. As export diversification gathered momentum tariffs have been reduced and other distortions removed. Shock treatment of the external sector has been avoided. Some of the success with export diversification in non-traditional agriculture was the result of 'picking winners' and solving technological and marketing problems. Selectivity has also been employed in relatively successful investment attraction programmes.

Longer-term factors enabling export diversification include a well-educated labour force with high health and living standards; a relatively good distribution of income; the managerial and entrepreneurial experience accumulated during the import-substituting industrialization; the investment in physical infrastructure, and in research and development centres. Finally, close location and access to the US market has also been a factor.

Export diversification results are reflected in the growth of non-traditional exports. Non-traditional exports have exceeded the value of traditional exports in the 1990s. Overall export growth rates averaged 12.3 per cent from 1987 to 1995 and are among the highest growth rates in Latin America for that period. Moreover, while from 1980 to 1983 exports of non-traditional products to markets outside the CACM accounted for only 15–18 per cent of total exports, they doubled from 1984 to 1987, and by 1995 represented 46 per cent of total exports. The manufacturing sector increased its participation in total exports outside the CACM from a similar share to that of agriculture before 1985, to 63 per cent of total non-traditional exports in 1995. Another indicator of rising competitiveness is the increase in locally-designed computer software, which in 1996 reached US$11 million, the highest in Latin America. Also, the electronics sector is one of the fastest growing sectors and has been very successful in attracting foreign investment.

Agricultural export diversification has also been successful. Non-traditional agricultural exports which accounted for less than 8 per cent of total exports during 1981–3 increased to 17 per cent in 1992, hovering around 15 per cent thereafter.

Moreover, in the 1990s, part of the export promotion effort has been undertaken in areas that are not included in 'exports'. The value added of *maquila* exports has been less dynamic in recent years due to quota restrictions, rising competition and the end of some export incentives. Nevertheless, this sector contributed value added of US$126 million in 1995, which is 11 per cent of traditional exports. On the other hand, the value added of free trade zone exports has increased very rapidly, from US$25.4 million in 1990 to US$142.1 million in 1995, an average annual growth rate of 41.9 per cent. Local purchases from free trade zones increased at an annual rate of over 30 per cent during 1993–5, albeit from a small base. Average investment per firm increased 10 per cent per annum and average wages in US dollars increased at a rate of 21 per cent. Tourism has also risen, which is explained in part by fiscal incentives. Revenues have gone up from US$275 million in 1990 to $661.3 million in 1995, an annual growth rate of 19.7 per cent, making tourism the single most important foreign exchange earning activity in the country ahead of coffee or bananas.

It is interesting to note that the structural change in total industrial production is evident in some of its most promising sectors. The share of research and development-intensive activities has increased in industrial sector total production. The participation of 'Science Based Industries' increased from 5.7 per cent in 1989 to 14.1 per cent in 1995, and 'Differentiated Products Industries' increased from 4.8 to 8.5 per cent; while 'Natural Resources Based Industries' and 'Labour Intensive Industries' both decreased, from 59.4 to 51.0 per cent and from 10.8 to 9.0 per cent, respectively.

Increasing competitiveness of Costa Rican exports is also reflected in a report following the 'Competitive Analysis of Nations' methodology. It shows an increase in the participation of Costa Rica in OECD trade in dynamic sectors (those increasing their share in OECD trade) when comparing 1985 and 1994, and the dependence on dynamic OECD markets, as opposed to declining markets, has also increased.

Finally, as many of the existing export incentives are expiring, there is growing consensus that the 'third generation' of such incentives should concentrate neither on non-traditional exports, nor on global exports, but rather should assist both tradables and non-tradables as appropriate to increase overall competitiveness. The areas mentioned include among others: further economic deregulation; an increase in infrastructure investment, including greater private sector participation; opening up of trade in services sectors; promotion of innovation, strategic alliances, technological transfers and foreign direct investment; support for market intelligence; and efficient institutions.

Acknowledgements

The author wishes to thank Eddy Rodríguez for his support in preparing this paper. Also thanks to Gerry Helleiner for helpful comments.

Notes

1. Although the highest growth rates, achieved in 1976–8, are explained by a boom in coffee prices.
2. Non-traditional exports are comprised of all exports except coffee, bananas, beef and cocoa. (All other exports are considered 'non-traditional' except 'maquila' and 'free-trade zone' exports which are registered as services.)
3. Political and military conflicts added strain to the already faltering dynamism of the CACM. Consequently, far from counterbalancing external shocks, the CACM added to them.
4. For a detailed account of the factors leading to the debt crisis, as well as of its management and ensuing reform, see Rodríguez (1988).
5. The final reform enabling private banks to offer current accounts was approved in 1995, although several financial instruments had been devised prior to this formal approval.
6. It has been argued that the weight of this benefit has not been important relative to export value (Corrales and Mange, 1990).
7. This exemption means that the US will not add exports from CBI countries to those from other countries when determining injury to US producers.
8. For example, this is one of the reasons why Acer chose to establish its Customer Service Call Operations in Costa Rica.

References

Agosin, M., Gitli, E. and Vargas, L. (1996) 'La promoción de exportaciones en Costa Rica: Diagnóstico y recomendaciones para la próxima etapa', COMEX, San José (February).

Alonso, E. (1995) 'Tercera generación de incentivos', Ministerio de Comercio Exterior, San José.

Bulmer-Thomas, V. (1978) 'Trade Structure and Linkages in Costa Rica. An Input–Output Approach', *Journal of Development Economics*, 5.

Camacho, E. (1996) 'Trade Policy and Instruments', USAID impact on Costa Rica´s development during the last 50 years, San José.

Céspedes, V. H. and Jiménez, R. (1994) 'Apertura comercial y mercado laboral en Costa Rica', Academia de Centroamérica and Centro Internacional para el Desarrollo Económico, San José.

Corrales, J. and Mange, R. (1990) 'Exportaciones no tradicionales en Costa Rica', ECONOFIN, San José.

FIAS (Foreign Investment Advisory Service) (1996) 'A Strategy for Foreign Investment in Costa Rica's Electronics Industry', Washington, DC: International Finance Corporation and World Bank.

Hoffmaister, A. (1992) 'The Cost of Export Subsidies: Evidence from Costa Rica', *IMF Staff Papers*, 39, 1.

Lanza, K. E. (1994) 'Institutionalizing Export and Investment Promotion Organizations: The Case of Costa Rica's CINDE', North Carolina, Center for International Development Research, Sanford Institute of Public Policy (June).

Mange, R. (1987) *La Reform arancelaria: El caso de Costa Rica*, San José: Prodesarrollo.

Mange, R. and González, C. (1988) 'Políticas de protección e incentivos a la manufactura, agroindustria y algunos sectores agrícolas en Costa Rica', ECONOFIN, San José.

Morley, S. and Alvarez, C. (1992) 'Poverty and Adjustment in Costa Rica', *IDB Working Paper No. 123*.

Rodríguez, E. (1982) 'Costa Rica: How Far Can Primary Production Take a Small Economy?' in M. Bienefeld and M. Godfrey (eds), *The Struggle for Development: National Strategies in an International Context*, London: Wiley.

Rodríguez, E. (1988) 'Costa Rica: A Quest for Survival' in S. Griffith-Jones (ed.), *Managing World Debt*, London: Wheatsheaf.

Rodríguez, E. and Grinspan, R. (1983) 'Selección de acitividades estratégicas del sector industrial', Universidad de Costa Rica, Instituto de Investigaciones en Ciencias Económicas.

Viceministerio de Ciencia y Tecnología (1996) 'Sí se puede! Casos exitosos de investigación y desarrollo de Costa Rica', San José.

Willmore, L. (1997) 'Promotion of Exports in Central America: An Analysis of Second-Best Policies', United Nations, Department for Economic and Social Information and Policy Analysis, Working Paper No. 14, ST/ESA/1997/WP14.

5
Real Exchange Rate Policy and Non-Traditional Exports in Developing Countries

Ibrahim A. Elbadawi

Introduction

As a development strategy, export orientation has been credited for the phenomenal economic transformations of the East Asian economies over the last 30 years or so, as well as for other more recent remarkable economic successes in other places, such as Chile. Successful and sustained export orientation policies have usually led to significant export diversification, and therefore a much higher rate of growth of non-traditional exports than the overall growth rate of the economy or of aggregate exports. In particular, it is argued that export diversification through promotion of manufactured exports (considered non-traditional exports for many developing countries) could support sustained overall economic growth for at least three reasons: (i) compared to primary goods exports, manufactured exports are likely to grow faster when the global economy is expanding because their income elasticity of demand is higher; (ii) because of the relatively higher price elasticities of demand and supply for manufactured compared to primary goods exports the former are less susceptible to price variability; and (iii) the prospects for dynamic productivity gains are much higher in the manufacturing sector (Sekkat and Varoudakis, 1998).

Despite the differences between orthodox and revisionist views about the relevant set of policies/interventions that are responsible for the success of export orientation strategies, the two schools of thought, nevertheless, agree on the central role of some such strategy in the development process of recent 'success' stories (e.g. Rodrik, 1994). Moreover, exchange rate policy-induced competitiveness is also broadly accepted as – at least – one of the key instruments of this 'winning' strategy. Indeed, despite considerable differences about the relevance of some of the sectoral and microeconomic components of the 'Washington Consensus'[1] economic reform measures (such as trade liberalization, privatization and deregulation of markets), there is a strong and unanimous acceptance of the centrality of macroeconomic stability, fiscal discipline and real exchange rate competitiveness for the success of any reform programme (Rodrik, 1992, 1996; Helleiner, 1994).[2] Specifically, the exchange rate policies of these successful countries (most notably the high performing East Asian countries[3] and Chile), which made it possible for these countries to maintain very low real exchange rate risks, to minimize real exchange rate volatility and above all to avoid real currency overvaluation, have been among the major factors behind their economic success. The relevance of the real exchange rate (RER) (generically defined as the relative price of tradables to non-tradables)[4] to export promotion and generation of an optimal output and employment path can be shown in rigorous behavioural models based on optimization of welfare or expenditure functions (e.g. see Mussa, 1974; Edwards, 1986, 1987, 1989; Edwards and van Wijnbergen, 1986, 1987).[5]

The experiences of successful exporters have shown that responsiveness of exports to appropriate incentives depends crucially on the extent of weakness or market failure in key sectors such as financial markets, human capital formation, technology and market information. The notable experiences of East Asia make clear that successfully addressing problems of market failure can dramatically boost export expansion and especially export diversification (e.g. Rodrik, 1994). Even Chile, one of the more recent world class success stories, which adopted a much less 'statist' development strategy than those of East Asia, pursued very proactive policies in support of its export orientation drive (e.g. Agosin, Chapter 3, this volume). These experiences corroborate the policy recommendations of the literature on information asymmetries and market imperfection (e.g. Stiglitz and Weiss, 1981; Stiglitz, 1994).

Because of these non-price constraints, even if macroeconomic stabilization, exchange rate adjustment and trade liberalization policies have successfully delivered the appropriate structure of incentives for exports, a timely and adequate supply response may still not be forthcoming. The most subtle forms of these constraints are those related to incomplete or absent information in such areas as appropriate technology for producing competitive goods and services for both international and domestic markets following trade liberalization; requirements for penetrating overseas markets and creating a niche in new and high pay-off markets; and market intelligence regarding consumer tastes and producers' needs in overseas markets. These market imperfections clearly suggest an important role for the state in the process of opening up the economy, by directly subsidizing activities aimed at 'internalizing' these externalities, or by supporting creative institutional designs (such as associations of exporters) to achieve the same goals.

In addition, underprovision of development finance may require policies and regulation to deepen financial markets as well as competitive public financial institutions to complement the private financial system. The same also applies for the areas of human capital and infrastructure, especially in the most basic areas such as primary education and rural infrastructure where the leading role of the state is unavoidable.

The experiences of the above-mentioned successful countries contrast very sharply with the relatively weak export performance (especially in terms of diversification and growth of non-traditional exports) in many other developing countries, notably most Sub-Saharan African countries, even after many of them have embraced reforms for almost two decades. Against this background, it is not surprising that a lot of academic and policy interest in the region has been attached to the issue of what is the appropriate mix of policies and institutional designs that could jump-start the economies of Sub-Saharan Africa into self-sustaining export-led growth (e.g. World Bank, 1995).

This chapter contributes to this debate by specifying and estimating an empirical model of non-traditional export performance (World Bank definition, NTX2) for 60 developing countries over three periods (1980–5, 1986–9, 1990–5).[6] The empirical framework is based upon two different theoretical models of export determination. Motivated by the experiences of Korea and Taiwan, Dani Rodrik (1994) developed a model to explain the phenomenal expansion of exports in the two countries as driven by a sustained boom in capital goods investment (or import) demand. Based on Latin American experiences, Paredes (1988) developed an alternative model that predicts a significant role for real exchange rate competitiveness (as a proxy for profitability of exporting) and for RER stability in the determination of export supply. The unifying empirical framework of this chapter attempts to account for profitability of the export sector (measured by real exchange rate misalignment, relative to a notional RER equilibrium); macroeconomic stability relevant for export performance (stability of the RER); investment in or imports of capital goods; as well as a range of factors affecting technical capabilities and the effectiveness of strategic interventions.

As an input to the estimation of the non-traditional export model, a dynamic panel regression model of the RER is estimated and analysed. The estimation results allow the derivation of three key indicators of RER policy for 63 developing countries: the equilibrium RER (ERER) index; the index of RER misalignment (RERMIS); and a measure of RER variability (RERVAR) (a proxy for anticipated real exchange rate instability). The novelty of this approach is that it provides a systematic and model-consistent method for disentangling the channels through which the RER affects exports as well as estimating the relative orders of magnitude for the influences of each of the three channels.[7]

Below, I undertake a country-specific analysis of the evolution of non-traditional exports and some of the key variables of relevance to export behaviour over the 1980s and 1990s. Following this there is an overview of the theoretical framework that underlies the empirical model for non-traditional exports. I then move on to the estimation results and analysis of the determinants of the RER, the RER indexes and the non-traditional export performance model. The chapter ends with some conclusions.

Non-traditional exports (NTX2) in developing countries

Table 5.1a shows recent export performance (1994/5 relative to 1984/5) in the ten countries studied in this volume, five of which are African. The five non-African countries represent highly successful experiences in terms of export growth and export diversification.

The best performers among the African countries in terms of the growth rates of non-traditional exports (NTX2) relative to GDP are Tanzania (387 per cent) and Zimbabwe (209 per cent). (NTX made up 4.8 and 7.1 per cent of GDP, respectively, in these countries by 1994/5.) Kenya, Mauritius and South Africa initially had higher shares of NTX (at 2.8, 3.0 and 5.7 per cent, respectively) but rather modest growth performances (at 61, 52 and 45 per cent, respectively). Except for Zimbabwe and South Africa, the shares of NTX in the economies of these African countries are rather small relative to the five non-African countries. The real challenge for these countries is to sustain the growth of non-traditional exports as their share grows to higher levels. This was achieved by the 'world class' performers in the international export market – such as Chile, Costa Rica, Indonesia, Malaysia and Thailand – which managed to increase NTX ratios (to GDP) by, respectively, 68, 48, 261, 120 and 78 per cent, even though the share of NTX in their national economies was already quite high. The degree of export diversification achieved in Costa Rica, Indonesia and especially Malaysia was particularly remarkable: the shares of NTX in GDP for these three countries in 1994/5 were, respectively, 10 per cent, 9.8 per cent and 25 per cent.

NTX growth has often been associated with considerable real currency depreciation, which reached more than 100 per cent for the cases of South Africa, Tanzania, Zimbabwe and Chile (Table 5.1b). In terms of overall macroeconomic stability, South Africa, Mauritius and Chile managed to reduce inflation between the 1980s and 1990s as well as maintaining its level at single digits. On the other hand, inflation rose between the two periods, to reach 15 per cent or more in 1995, in Kenya, Zimbabwe and Costa Rica. Also inflation was high in Tanzania (more than 30 per cent in 1995) even though it declined by more than 10 per cent from its 1984/5 level. Despite substantial increases in their inflation rates between the two periods (including 120 per cent for Malaysia and 206 per cent for Thailand), the three Asian countries' inflation rates remained very low: at 4.8 per cent for Malaysia, 5.1 per cent for Thailand and 8.9 per cent for Indonesia.

Table 5.1a   Non-traditional exports in selected developing countries

		Aggregate exports (current US$m)	Non-traditional exports (NTX2) (current US$m)	% Share of total exports to GDP	% Share of non-traditional exports (NTX2) to GDP
African Countries					
Kenya	1994/5 Average	1305.0	227.64	15.82	2.76
	Growth Rate (%):				
	1994/5 relative to 1984/5	44.94	115.05	8.28	60.67
Mauritius	1994/5 Average	1447.56	110.02	39.04	2.97
	Growth Rate (%):				
	1994/5 relative to 1984/5	225.21	343.50	11.35	51.86
South Africa	1994/5 Average	17493.31	7294.59	13.56	5.66
	Growth Rate (%):				
	1994/5 relative to 1984/5	76.12	192.28	−12.66	44.94
Tanzania	1994/5 Average	547.56	168.85	15.69	4.84
	Growth Rate (%):				
	1994/5 relative to 1984/5	37.71	192.03	129.89	387.49
Zimbabwe	1994/5 Average	1321.11	437.19	21.46	7.10
	Growth Rate (%):				
	1994/5 relative to 1984/5	96.60	296.15	53.47	209.25
Non-African Countries					
Chile	1994/5 Average	14161.12	3662.31	23.71	6.13
	Growth Rate (%):				
	1994/5 relative to 1984/5	280.26	463.27	13.51	68.13
Costa Rica	1994/5 Average	3605.11	873.82	41.08	9.96
	Growth Rate (%):				
	1994/5 relative to 1984/5	213.58	243.12	35.50	48.27
Malaysia	1994/5 Average	73086.43	19716.02	93.66	25.27
	Growth Rate (%):				
	1994/5 relative to 1984/5	315.14	429.05	73.28	120.83
Thailand	1994/5 Average	46180.11	11128.64	29.78	7.18
	Growth Rate (%):				
	1994/5 relative to 1984/5	610.82	585.14	84.98	78.30
Indonesia	1994/5 Average	42599.13	18323.67	22.81	9.81
	Growth Rate (%):				
	1994/5 relative to 1984/5	114.52	673.35	0.31	261.62

Note: For various countries, due to the unavailability of data, the nearest available years have been used.

Notwithstanding efficiency considerations, the share of gross investment to GDP is a useful broad indicator of an economy's potential to sustain high rates of export (as well as overall economic) growth. On this score the African countries are lagging. Except for Mauritius and Tanzania – which have investment ratios comparable to those of Chile and Costa Rica, between 26

Table 5.1b   Economic variables relevant to non-traditional exports in selected developing countries

		Terms of trade (1987 = 100)	Terms of trade variability (%)	Real exchange rate[a] (1980 = 100)	Real exchange rate variability	Inflation rate (%)	Ratio of gross domestic investment to GDP	Roads paved (%)	Telephone mainlines (per 1000 people)
African Countries									
Kenya	1994/5 Average	100.88	8.46	128.42	5.14	14.94	18.92	13.70	8.88
	Growth Rate (%):								
	1994/5 relative to 1984/5	−19.33	426.99	29.73	149.94	27.99	−18.96	4.98	5.24
Mauritius	1994/5 Average	103.13	5.52	120.85	2.40	6.64	28.77	93.00	124.19
	Growth Rate (%):								
	1994/5 relative to 1984/5	33.50	36.15	14.28	103.29	−5.53	26.43	0.00	44.83
South Africa	1994/5 Average	106.62	3.18	134.23	0.15	8.65	18.01	32.50	92.65
	Growth Rate (%):								
	1994/5 relative to 1984/5	4.42	226.75	12.30	−82.20	−37.64	−21.31	7.97	4.71
Tanzania	1994/5 Average	83.95	2.50	253.67	24.16	30.97	31.17	4.20	3.05
	Growth Rate (%):								
	1994/5 relative to 1984/5	−34.69	9.18	381.25	276.38	−10.45	82.85		1.32
Zimbabwe	1994/5 Average	86.50	1.71	200.32	3.36	22.29		18.50	13.15
	Growth Rate (%):								
	1994/5 relative to 1984/5	−15.77	−57.84	98.08	−27.18	55.79		27.59	9.05

Non-African Countries

Chile	1994/5 Average	99.05	2.25	173.11	1.80	9.97	27.07	13.80	110.00
	Growth Rate (%):								
	1994/5 relative to 1984/5	9.27	−19.46	31.86	7.89	−60.80	75.52	0.00	16.49
Costa Rica	1994/5 Average	92.05	1.34	165.12	4.22	18.48	25.79	16.30	121.39
	Growth Rate (%):								
	1994/5 relative to 1984/5	−18.07	−55.34	14.92	647.61	37.18	6.15	6.54	17.38
Malaysia	1994/5 Average	93.50	2.35	132.92	8.97	4.76	39.62	75.00	119.58
	Growth Rate (%):								
	1994/5 relative to 1984/5	−23.45	−59.17	50.44	267.49	120.44	29.60		
Thailand	1994/5 Average	102.70	1.47	126.05	3.21	5.13	42.17	91.25	34.74
	Growth Rate (%):								
	1994/5 relative to 1984/5	−4.24	−48.58	27.26	26.62	206.06	46.11		
Indonesia		84.00	2.76	215.97	4.04	8.91	36.04	46.70	9.47
	Growth Rate (%):								
	1994/5 relative to 1984/5	−43.55	−55.63	96.71	187.38	16.79	36.70		

Notes: For various countries, due to the unavailability of data, the nearest available years have been used.
For definitions and sources, see Data Appendix.
[a] An increase indicates real currency devaluation.

and 31 per cent (and much of Tanzania's investment was notoriously inefficient and/or underutilized) – the African countries have investment rates lower than 20 per cent. The three Asian countries, on the other hand, managed to increase their investment shares by 30 per cent or more to register staggering rates of 40 per cent for Malaysia, 42 per cent for Thailand and 36 per cent for Indonesia in 1994/5. The three Asian countries have further distinguished themselves through their vastly superior capacity to support the export sector through telecommunications, transport and electric power generation. Chile, South Africa, Mauritius and to some extent Zimbabwe also have fairly substantial capacity in these areas.

An analytical framework for export performance

To motivate the empirical model for analysing the performance of non-traditional exports by developing countries, I review two interesting, but quite different, theoretical models of export determination. Dani Rodrik (1994) argues that, at least in the cases of the very successful development experiences of Korea and Taiwan, spectacular and sustained export growth was achieved with little increase in the profitability of exports – as measured by real currency depreciation. Rodrik developed a model to explain the phenomenal expansion of exports in the two countries as driven instead by a sustained boom in capital goods investment (and import) demand. On the other hand, Paredes (1988) developed a model that predicts a significant role for real exchange rate competitiveness (as a proxy for profitability of exporting) and for real exchange rate stability in the determination of export supply. He then uses the case of manufactured exports from several Latin American countries to corroborate his model.

Paredes' model

The breakdown of the Bretton Woods exchange rate regime in 1973, and the subsequent emergence of more flexible exchange rate arrangements, triggered a lot of concern about increased exchange rate risk and what it might do to exports. Most studies found fairly systematic evidence on the increased variability of real exchange rates in both developing and developed countries alike. However, while RER variability was found to be linked to export supply in developing countries, the evidence for developed countries is at best tenuous. The main explanation for the latter findings is that the presence of futures markets in the case of developed countries has effectively delinked the export supply markets from RER risks in these countries, while in developing countries futures markets either do not exist or could only be accessed at very high cost.

Paredes (1988) develops a behavioural model of export supply under uncertainty that formally justifies the inclusion of expected RER and RER risk as a determinant of manufactured export supply in developing countries.

According to this model, firms are assumed to maximize expected utility of profits under uncertainty, where the only source of this uncertainty is provided by exchange rate risk, which is proxied by various measures of RER variability. The firms are assumed to have some monopoly power in the domestic market but they are pure price takers in the international market. The technology for producing exports is such that maximization of profits equates marginal and average costs. The model assumes a two-period contract where firms get orders and are required to purchase the required inputs, which are assumed to be denominated in the importer's currency, in the first period; and these produce output for delivery in the second period. This contract design, which is very plausible in the developing world's environment, strongly emphasizes the role of exchange rate risk as a determinant of export supply.

Rodrik's model

In a very persuasive paper Rodrik (1994) argues that the emphasis on export orientation as the explanation for the 'miracle' growth performance of Korea and Taiwan, in both orthodox and revisionist approaches, is both incomplete and quite misleading. He shows that the increase in export profitability in both countries around the mid-1960s was too modest to fully account for the initial jump of the export/GDP ratio or for its steady rise thereafter. According to Rodrik, a more plausible explanation is that the economic take-off of the two countries was caused by a sharp increase in investment after the 1960s. This, argues Rodrik, was made possible by a sustained increase in private returns to capital engineered by the two governments through a range of strategic interventions, not only to enhance capability but also to resolve coordination failures that usually characterize modern sector production. Moreover, Rodrik argues that the effectiveness of these rather extensive interventions – which included investment subsidies, administrative guidance, and the use of public enterprise – very much depended on the initial conditions of favourable human capital endowment and relatively equal income and wealth distribution in the two countries.

Dani Rodrik's model thus assumes an exogenous increase in the profitability of investment, followed by an increase in the share of investment in GDP. Also the model assumes that the country in question has a comparative *dis*advantage in producing capital goods and that international borrowing is not unlimited. The increase in investment demand is represented, in a two good (exportables and importables) model, as a shift in preferences towards more capital-intensive importables and a proportionate decrease in *domestic* demand for exportables, leading to a net rise in aggregate consumption. Since in the short-run, with the external terms of trade fixed and the transformation frontier unchanged, aggregate production remains unchanged, exports increase simply as a result of reduced domestic demand for exportables. This model, therefore, suggests that the impact effect of an increase in investment is to render the economy more open to trade, even though the relative price of exportables remains unchanged. This result of the basic Rodrik model applies in the short-run only, where the transformation frontier is assumed to remain unchanged. However, Rodrik demonstrates that the qualitative prediction of this basic model remains basically intact in the longer-run when the transformation frontier moves outward in response to the expansion in the economy's capital stock. Moreover, in a more recent paper (Rodrik, 1995), it is shown that the above predictions are plausible even in a context of a more general model of exportables, importables and non-tradables.

An empirical framework for analysing non-traditional exports

A unifying empirical framework based on the above two models should account for: profitability of the export sector (measured by the evolution of the RER and RER misalignment); macroeconomic stability relevant for export performance (stability of the RER); investment and imports of capital goods; as well as a range of factors affecting technical capabilities and the effectiveness of strategic interventions. The latter group of variables should include the initial stock of human capital, the income distribution profile, an index of institutional quality and the capacity of infrastructure (such as power generation, telecommunications, road and port facilities).

In addition to controlling for the above non-price factors, this chapter's empirical analysis of non-traditional exports (NTX2) will particularly emphasize the role of RER-based profitability and stability variables. In this connection, the empirical model will extend Paredes' work by explicitly linking export supply both to equilibrium RER and to the degree of RER disequilibrium. The relevance of RER *misalignment* relative to its equilibrium as a determinant of export supply is straightforward, given the tradability of exports. In addition, the *level* of equilibrium RER also matters for exports. It has been argued that even though a country may manage to avoid massive overvaluation, it could nevertheless trap itself in a sub-optimal export growth path by maintaining a 'low' equilibrium RER, due for example to adopting a less open trade regime (e.g. Valdés, 1985; Edwards, 1992). However, it is important to distinguish between overvaluation due to less openness (as in many high performing East Asian economies during their IS phases) and currency overvaluation caused by unsustainable macroeconomic policy (as in Chile before the reform). This distinction is emphasized by Helleiner (1992) who argues that while the latter is harmful, the former amounts to a choice of a development strategy or a response to a practical necessity (e.g. foreign trade taxes in Sub-Saharan Africa).

Empirical analysis of RER and non-traditional exports

Here, there are three main empirical exercises. First, I discuss the estimation results of a real exchange rate model, using panel data from 63 countries covering three periods (1980–5, 1986–9, 1990–5). Second, the estimation of the long-run model will subsequently be combined with 'sustainable' values of the long-run fundamentals to generate indexes of the equilibrium real exchange rates, real exchange rate misalignment and real exchange rate instability for these countries. Third, the derived RER indexes will be combined with other non-price variables – as suggested by the analytical framework described above – to estimate a model of non-traditional export performance (NTX2) for the 60 countries.[8]

The RER econometric analysis

The empirical analysis of RER in this chapter is motivated by a theoretical model that emphasizes the interplay of the long-run (flow) fundamentals of current account balance and the determinants of the longer-term propensity for accumulation (or de-accumulation) of net foreign assets (NFA). Following Faruqee (1995), this model extends the less-developed countries' (LDCs) version of the empirical real exchange rate model (e.g. Edwards, 1989; Elbadawi, 1994; Elbadawi and Soto, 1997a, 1997b) to incorporate, in addition to the traditional current account fundamentals of the RER, three stock variables relevant for the determination of the capital account equilibrium. Moreover, this model also accounts for the effect of official development assistance (ODA), which constitutes an important current account variable for the determination of RER in many low income developing countries.

A fuller discussion of the model is contained in Elbadawi, 1998. In this section we estimate a simple dynamic version of the model using panel data. The following equation is estimated:

$$\text{Log } q_t = \alpha + \beta'F1 - \gamma_1 oda_t - \gamma_2 nfi_t + \gamma_3(\Delta resv_t - nki_t) + \delta \log q_{t-1} - \theta_1 \text{MACRO}_t + \theta_2 \text{DEVAL}_t \tag{1}$$

where q is the RER (defined as the ratio of the price of tradables to non-tradables).

F is a vector of four trade balance fundamentals (terms of trade (Log TOT), government consumption ratio (Log GCON/GDP), trade openness (Log OPEN), productivity (PROD)). Theoretically, the terms of trade influence on the RER cannot be signed *a priori*, depending on whether income or substitution effects dominate, with the former leading to real currency appreciation (decrease in RER) and the latter to real currency depreciation (increase in RER). However, most empirical evidence suggests that the income effect tends to dominate the substitution effect. Government consumption is expected to carry a negative sign, openness a positive sign and productivity a negative sign. The measure of openness (OPEN) is the residual of a panel regression of log (X + M/GDP) on GNP and GNP squared; this measure adjusts the trade ratio for the size of the economy. Productivity is proxied by the log of the ratio of real GNP per worker to that of the G7. The fifth current account fundamental is oda = ODA/GNP, which is predicted by the model to be negatively associated with RER. One capital account variable, Δresv (ratio of change in international reserves to GNP), is expected to have a positive long-term effect on RER (i.e. accumulation of reserves requires a real currency depreciation). The other two capital account variables, nki (ratio of net foreign capital inflows to GNP) and nfi (ratio of net foreign income to GNP), are expected to have negative long-run effects on the RER.[9]

The inclusion of capital account variables, in addition to the standard trade balance fundamentals, in the above equation permits interesting interpretations of the effects of ODA and other capital account stock determinants of the RER in the long run:

- Should a country successfully achieve a higher sustainable level of net foreign income in the very long run, the real currency value in this country will eventually converge to a more *appreciated* equilibrium level (lower RER)
- However, in the medium-to-long runs (when the stock of net foreign assets, NFA, is less than the desired level), this country may have to depreciate its real currency value (increase RER) (i.e. run a current account surplus – which is the counterpart of accumulating reserves) to allow the building of assets to desired levels
- The required magnitude of the real currency depreciation may be ameliorated by the extent of 'sustainable' levels of private capital flows or foreign aid, both of which support a more appreciated long-run path for the real currency value (lower RER) *if* they could be sustained in the future.

The above equation also incorporates two short-run determinants of RER. DEVAL refers to the rate of nominal exchange rate devaluation (where the exchange rate is defined in terms of domestic currency per unit of the foreign currency). The second variable, MACRO, the ratio of the change in domestic credit to initial stock of broad money, is an indicator of macroeconomic (monetary) policy. The short-run impact effect of nominal devaluation is expected to be real currency depreciation, and monetary expansion is expected to lead to real currency appreciation. As pointed out by Edwards (1989) a nominal devaluation will help the adjustment process only to the extent that the initial situation is one of overvaluation, and if the nominal exchange rate adjustment is accompanied by supporting macroeconomic policy. Finally, the partial adjustment term (given by the coefficient of log q_{t-1}) reflects the self-correcting mechanism that calls for future depreciation in real currency value, given initial overvaluation. The speed by which this automatic adjustment operates depends on the parameter δ, which falls in the interval (0,1). A value of δ equal to one signifies prompt adjustment over just one period, while the smaller the value of δ, the slower the adjustment will be.

The estimation results of equation 1 are reported in Table 5.2. Two sets of results are reported; each set contains two regressions of the same equation, one based on a fixed-effects model and the other on a random-effects model. The first set includes, in addition to the long-run fundamentals, the effects of macroeconomic policy (MACRO) as well as the devaluation effect (DEVAL). The second set excludes DEVAL. The Hausman test suggests that the random effects model is uniformly superior to the fixed effects model. In addition, perhaps due to the relatively long time horizon of the estimation the DEVAL effect was not found to be significant. Therefore, further analysis will be confined to the results of the random effects model of set #2 (i.e. regression #4).

The results of the regressions strongly corroborate the theoretical predictions of the model. Starting with the five long-term current account fundamentals, our results show that they are robustly and significantly associated with RER in all of the four regressions. The terms of trade has a negative and significant effect, with an elasticity of about –0.54. The degree of openness of the economy (appropriately adjusted for economic size) has a positive long-run elasticity of about 0.48. This result suggests that a more liberalized and open trade regime requires a more depreciated equilibrium real currency value (higher RER). The implication of this finding is that trade liberalization is not sustainable without commensurate real currency depreciation. The third current account fundamental, the government consumption/GDP ratio, was also found to be significantly associated with RER with a negative elasticity of about –0.30. Given the dominance of non-tradable goods in government consumption, an increase in the latter will lead to real currency appreciation. The fourth current account fundamental, productivity, is found to have a negative and significant effect at –0.55. This result is consistent with the theoretical prediction of the model that 'sustained' productivity enhancement should lead to a more appreciated equilibrium real currency value (lower RER). Finally, foreign aid (given by the ratio of ODA to GNP), which is associated with real currency appreciation, had an estimated effect of –0.91.

The model suggests that the capital account position influences the long run behaviour of the RER through three channels: the very long-run effect of the income from net foreign asset position (expressed as a ratio to GNP), which together with the net capital inflows/GNP ratio should lead to a more appreciated equilibrium real currency value (lower RER) in the long run; and the ratio of the change in reserves to GNP, which should force a real currency

Table 5.2   An empirical model of the real exchange rate in developing countries

Dependent variable log RER	Equation 1 Fixed		Equation 2 Random		Equation 3 Fixed		Equation 4 Random	
	Coeff	t-stat	Coeff	t-stat	Coeff	t-stat	Coeff	t-stat
Log (TOT)	−0.549	−3.654	−0.54	−3.911	−0.561	−3.658	−0.541	−3.91
Log (OPEN)	0.452	1.796	0.486	2.19	0.443	1.693	0.481	2.174
Log (GCON/GNP)	−0.551	−2.651	−0.294	−1.935	−0.388	−1.844	−0.304	−2.102
PRODUCTIVITY	−0.774	−2.203	−0.55	−2.042	−0.599	−1.994	−0.554	−2.059
NFI/GNP	−0.465	−0.657	−0.772	−1.58	−0.623	−0.887	−0.771	−1.572
ODA/GNP	−0.366	−0.750	−0.920	−2.475	−0.452	−0.930	−0.908	−2.470
DRNK/GNP	3.786	2.393	3.223	2.86	3.56	2.208	3.191	2.84
MACRO	−0.021	−0.319	−0.08	−1.687	−0.038	−0.653	−0.081	−1.713
DEVAL	0.7E−03	1.049	−0.9E−04	−0.238				
Log RER(−1)	0.096	1.069	0.274	2.958	0.144	1.566	0.27	3.005
CONSTANT			−0.327	−0.863			−0.346	−0.935
Adjusted R Squared	0.6485		0.4372		0.6457		0.4397	
R Squared	0.7831		0.6527		0.7795		0.6513	
P Value	0.01831				0.0003			
Number of observations	189							
Number of countries	63							
Period of Estimation	1970–5, 1976–9, 1980–5, 1986–9, 1990–5							

Notes:

TOT	Terms of Trade
OPEN	(Real Exports + Real Imports)/Real GNP
GCON	Government Consumption
PRODUCTIVITY	Ratio of the country's GNP per worker to OECD average GNP per worker
GNP	Gross National Product at market prices
NFI	Net Foreign Income
ODA	Overseas Development Assistance
DRNK	(Change in Reserves/GNP) – (Net Capital Inflows)
MACRO	(Change in domestic credit)/(lagged broad money supply)
DEVAL	Nominal Devaluation
RER	Real Exchange Rate
P Value	Refers to the Hausman test for Fixed vs. Random Effects Model

depreciation. In the restricted version of the model – estimated in this chapter – the last two variables are replaced by the difference between the change in reserve ratio and the net capital inflows ratio (DRNK). As predicted by the model, net foreign income was found to be negatively associated with RER with an estimated coefficient of –0.77. The effect of the composite variable (the change in reserves minus net capital inflows) is appreciable (at 3.19) and significant in all of the four regressions.[10] This result suggests that accumulation of reserves could be an effective instrument for minimizing undesirable effects of temporary capital flows on the real exchange rate.

The coefficient of the lagged dependent variable (Log q_{t-1}) has a highly significant estimated elasticity of 0.27, which indicates the importance of inertia in RER evolution over time. The model's estimate of automatic adjustment is much larger than the 0.19 obtained by Edwards (1989) for a different group of developing countries in an earlier period using a similar partial adjustment model. Finally, the short-run effect due to macroeconomic policy was found to be significant, though with a small impact coefficient at -0.08.

Real exchange rate equilibrium, RER misalignment and RER instability

Now we proceed to compute the indexes for ERER using the derived long-run elasticities based on the estimates of Table 5.2 (regression #4)[11] for given 'sustainable' or 'permanent' values of the fundamentals. Williamson (1994b: 187) recommends an *ex ante* approach for estimating, 'the set of real effective exchange rates (or paths) needed to achieve simultaneous internal and external balance by some date in the medium-run future, and to maintain balance thereafter'. The so-called 'fundamental equilibrium exchange rate' (FEER) concept, therefore, calls for assuming behavioural specifications for the fundamentals and using the real exchange rate equations in the context of a bigger model to derive a path (paths) for the equilibrium real exchange rate, given the assumed path(s) for the fundamentals. By and large, our approach for estimating 'sustainable' fundamentals resembles the FEER approach.[12] In particular, the capital account fundamentals are obtained using a model that links sustainable net capital flows and net foreign income to sustainable current account balance (Edwards, 1997) and sustainable change in reserves to long-term import requirements. In addition, sustainable foreign aid ratios are linked to levels that are judged to be consistent with avoiding excessive aid dependency.

Three pivotal series are derived for all of the 63 countries considered: the equilibrium RER (ERER) indexes; RER misalignment indexes (computed as (RER – ERER)/ERER)*100 per cent); RER variability (RERVAR) computed as a three-year moving standard deviation of the change in the log of the RER index. Table 5.3 contains estimates of ERER, RERMIS and RERVAR for the countries selected for study in this volume. In these countries, the ERER indexes – which do vary over time – suggest that at least part of the observed

Table 5.3   Equilibrium RER (ERER), RER misalignment (RERMIS) and RER variability (RERVAR) in selected developing countries

Country	Year	ERER (1980=100)[a]	RERMIS %	RERVAR %
African Countries				
Kenya	1978–9	89.40	4.63	4.11
	1980–5	101.83	–0.28	1.97
	1986–9	125.19	–0.31	0.97
	1990–5	130.13	3.38	2.71
Mauritius	1978–9	93.69	2.98	3.25
	1980–5	103.06	–0.62	1.15
	1986–9	112.07	3.27	2.90
	1990–5	88.75	14.11	2.92
South Africa	1978–9	88.75	8.49	2.43
	1980–5	96.94	2.78	0.92
	1986–9	98.24	14.82	0.26
	1990–5	99.51	11.70	0.27
Tanzania	1978–9	113.29	1.05	162.29
	1980–5	81.90	–9.12	5.89
	1986–9	77.02	27.57	6.18
	1990–5	226.29	8.59	14.71
Zimbabwe	1978–9	93.58	0.86	3.75
	1980–5	104.33	–2.72	2.99
	1986–9	105.42	7.77	2.01
	1990–5	122.35	19.01	3.10
Non-African Countries				
Chile	1978–9	94.61	8.76	5.51
	1980–5	126.80	–7.08	3.29
	1986–9	112.68	21.94	1.51
	1990–5	124.70	16.90	4.34
Costa Rica	1978–9	117.51	–4.26	2.66
	1980–5	125.53	6.95	2.58
	1986–9	148.68	3.67	1.47
	1990–5	165.76	0.07	3.91
Indonesia	1978–9	187.18	–17.16	5.12
	1980–5	166.02	–21.96	2.54
	1986–9	196.21	–2.73	1.45
	1990–5	220.12	–1.45	3.05
Malaysia	1978–9	88.49	4.24	1.18
	1980–5	99.41	–2.61	2.09
	1986–9	125.63	–2.53	1.71
	1990–5	302.65	–32.93	5.73
Thailand	1978–9	82.82	12.23	2.38
	1980–5	99.20	–1.01	2.16
	1986–9	80.13	19.04	1.19
	1990–5	93.08	13.24	2.39

Note: [a] Increase indicates real decline in the equilibrium value of the currency.

RER variability is related to changing equilibria, and that analyses of real exchange rate misalignment based on historical comparisons of observed RER levels (i.e. the purchasing power parity (PPP) approach) may lead to erroneous conclusions. In addition, the indexes of RERMIS are generally fairly successful in reproducing overvaluation (and undervaluation) 'episodes' that are consistent with other aspects of the recent macroeconomic history of these countries.

The experiences with RER adjustment of the five high-performing non-African countries in Table 5.1 provide interesting lessons for reforming African countries. First, Chile and Thailand both maintained highly undervalued currencies from the second half of the 1980s onward. In Chile the currency was undervalued by 22 per cent per annum in 1986–9 and by 17 per cent in 1990–5, while the annual rate of undervaluation in Thailand was equally dramatic at 19 and 13 per cent, respectively, for the two periods. Second, the experiences of Costa Rica and Indonesia, and especially Malaysia, suggest that countries that were able to keep RER close to its equilibrium for an extended period could also achieve substantial export growth, especially in the case of Malaysia, where RER policy was supported by other effective export-promoting measures. Following a small undervaluation of about 7 per cent per annum during the first half of the 1980s, the currency in Costa Rica remained in equilibrium thereafter. In Indonesia, following very large real overvaluation (by more than 19 per cent per annum) prior to 1986, the RER remained in equilibrium for the subsequent periods. For Malaysia the adjustment was somewhat different, where the RER remained in equilibrium throughout the 1980s following a small degree of currency undervaluation (of about 4 per cent per annum) for the late 1970s.

Third, contrasting the experiences of Chile to those of Indonesia and especially Malaysia might help shed some light on the challenge of stemming the adverse effects of capital flows on RER competitiveness. Chile was able to recover from the highly publicized overvaluation episodes of the early 1980s, which were mainly caused by excessive capital inflows,[13] by instituting explicit rules requiring the Central Bank of Chile to seek to prevent the current account deficit from exceeding 4 per cent of GDP on average (Williamson, 1997). To execute this rule – which basically committed Chile to a policy of sustained export orientation based on RER competitiveness – the Central Bank of Chile has aggressively and apparently successfully discouraged the inflow of unsustainable and speculative capital inflows. On the other hand, and as revealed by the recent Asian financial sector crisis, both Indonesia and Malaysia failed to exercise adequate prudential and regulatory measures in the face of massive capital inflows in the 1990s. This is manifested in the substantial real currency overvaluation in Malaysia throughout the 1990s (at an average annual rate of about 33 per cent), and the smaller but steady real overvaluation in Indonesia since 1992, which reached almost 8 per cent in 1995.

The determinants of non-traditional exports in developing countries

Table 5.4 provides estimates of a non-traditional export performance equation for the panel of the 60 developing countries over 1989/90 and 1994/5.[14] The estimated equation, the rationale for which was discussed earlier, is:

$$\text{Log XNTY}_t = \propto + \beta_1 \text{ RERMIS}_t + \beta_2 \text{ RERVAR}_t + \beta_3 \text{ Log MM}_t/\text{GNP}_t + \beta_4 \text{ Log TOT}_t$$
$$+ \beta_5 \text{TOTVAR} + \beta_6 \text{ log SCH}_t + \beta_7 \text{ OECYB}_t + \gamma_1 \text{ DSSA} + \gamma_2 \text{ DEA} + \gamma_3 \text{ DLAC} \qquad (2)$$

where XNTY is the ratio of non-traditional exports to GDP (both in current dollars); RERMIS and RERVAR are as described earlier;[15] MM is machinery imports; TOTVAR is variability in the terms of trade (standard deviation of the change in Log TOT); SCH is an index of schooling (the average of the primary and secondary enrolment ratios); OECYB is OECD countries' GDP per worker (in constant dollars) a proxy for external demand; and DSSA, DEA and DLAC are dummies for Sub-Saharan Africa, East Asia and Latin America (proxying for differing supply conditions). To avoid picking up spurious effects, the dependent variable is given by the log of the ratio of non-traditional exports to GDP and all right hand side variables (other than relative prices) are expressed relative to appropriate scale variables (see notes to Table 5.4).

The table contains results for three random effects regressions. (The full set of results, including both random and fixed effects, are contained in Elbadawi, 1998). The random effects results are stronger and more consistent with theoretical predictions. Moreover, in two of the regressions (#1 and 2), a formal Hausman specification test suggests that random effects results are superior to the results based on the fixed effects regressions.) All of the three regressions appear to fit the data very well, with more than 80 per cent of the variation in the non-traditional export/GDP ratio explained by the model. Regression 1 incorporates the full set of variables, while regression 2 excludes imports of machines, and regression 3 excludes RERMIS (the measure of export profitability).

In regression 1, two of the RER-based variables (RERMIS, RERVAR), terms of trade variability, the schooling variable and imports of machinery are all very significantly and robustly associated with export performance, and their effects are consistent with theoretical predictions. However, GDP per worker in the OECD countries is only marginally significant. Interestingly, neither the level of RER nor the equilibrium RER were significantly related to exports, when RERMIS is included; if anything, the results improve considerably when *only* the RERMIS is employed as a proxy for profitability of exporting. This suggests that what matters for exports is that the currency should not be allowed to become overvalued in real terms and that real currency depreciation relative to its equilibrium (i.e. undervaluation) will enhance export performance; whereas the absolute level of RER (or its equilibrium level) is irrelevant to export performance.

Table 5.4   An empirical model of non-traditional exports in developing countries

Dependent variable: log (XNTY)	*Equation 1*		*Equation 2*		*Equation 3*	
	Random		Random		Random	
	Coeff	*t*-stat	Coeff	*t*-stat	Coeff	*t*-stat
RERMIS	0.546	2.674	0.649	3.22	–	–
RERVAR	–4.401	–3.844	–5.921	–5.798	–3.547	–3.186
Log (MM/GNP)	0.175	3.007	–	–	0.2	3.436
Log (TOT)	–1.611	–4.243	–1.702	–4.496	–1.093	–3.27
TOTVAR	–2.462	–3.48	–2.578	–3.646	–2.232	–3.112
Log (SCH)	1.191	5.771	1.217	5.859	1.17	5.606
OECYB	0.1E–04	0.856	0.9E–05	0.6	0.3E–04	1.977
DSSA	–0.202	–2.216	–0.121	–1.378	–0.206	–2.234
DEA	0.301	2.449	0.395	3.297	0.284	2.289
DLAC	0.195	2.159	0.268	3.059	0.147	1.641
CONSTANT	–0.43	–0.363	–0.41	–0.346	–1.943	–1.828
Adjusted R Squared	0.828		0.821		0.819	
R Squared	0.928		0.923		0.922	
P Value	0.033		0.045		0.85	
Number of Observations	120					
Number of Countries	60					
Period of Estimation	1984/85, 1989/90, 1994/95					

Notes:

XNTY	Ratio of Non-Traditional Exports to GDP (current US$/current US$)
RERMIS	Real Exchange Rate Misalignment: Log (RER) – Log (Equilibrium RER)
RERVAR	Real Exchange Rate Variability: Standard Deviation of Δ Log (RER)
MM	Imports of Machinery
TOT	Terms of Trade
TOTVAR	Terms of Trade Variability: Standard Deviation of Δ Log (TOT)
SCH	Index of Schooling: Average of Primary and Secondary Enrolment ratios
OECYB	OECD Countries GDP per worker (Constant 1987 US$)
DSSA	Dummy Variable for Sub-Saharan Africa
DEA	Dummy Variable for East Asia
DLAC	Dummy Variable for Latin American Countries
P Value	Refers to the Hausman test for Fixed vs. Random Effects Model

RERMIS (measured as undervaluation) has an elasticity of 0.55, while RER variability (the indicator of relevant macroeconomic instability) has a negative effect at –4.4. As expected, terms of trade variability has a deleterious effect on non-traditional exports at –2.5. A less clear effect, from a theoretical perspective, is the negative elasticity of the level of terms of trade at –1.6. However, since the terms of trade variable refers to aggregate exports, this effect may reflect the influence of the secularly declining terms of trade for traditional (rather than non-traditional) exports. Human capital (measured by the schooling ratio) has an elasticity of 1.2. Imports of machines (a proxy for capital goods imports or investment in capital goods) has an elasticity of 0.2.

Finally, and not surprisingly, other regional characteristics (proxied by dummies) matter. The results suggest that, *ceteris paribus*, the ratios of non-traditional exports to GDP tend to be higher in both East Asia (EA) and Latin America (LAC) than in Sub-Saharan Africa (SSA). The derived elasticities of the estimated coefficients of these dummies[16] suggest that, relative to average performance of the sample of sixty developing countries, other non-accounted-for region-specific characteristics expand the non-traditional exports/GDP ratio by 57 and 100 per cent in LAC and East Asia, respectively, while these factors reduce non-traditional exports by 40 per cent in SSA. To the extent that these dummies reflect supply constraints related to market imperfections, technological capabilities, etc., this finding can be taken as providing strong support for the analysis at the beginning of this chapter, which argued that beyond 'getting the prices right' the leading role of the state in addressing the endemic problems of market imperfection is indispensable for generating sustained and adequate export supply response to appropriate incentives.

Regressions 2 and 3 are designed indirectly to test the Rodrik model. First, the results of regression 2, which excludes imports of machinery, is marginally inferior to that of regression 1 in terms of the degree of fit and the strength of the Hausman specification tests (of the fixed versus the random effects model). This suggests that imports of machinery contribute significantly to explaining non-traditional export performance in developing countries. Second, regression 3, which excludes RERMIS (the measure of export profitability) does not pass the Hausman specification test (i.e. the fixed effects model is superior to the random effects model of regression 2). Comparing regression 1 of Table 5.4 with the fixed effects version of regression 3 suggests that regression 1 is vastly superior. This suggests that export profitability (as reflected by an appropriate real exchange rate) is indispensable for sustained expansion of non-traditional exports. Therefore, the comparison of the results of regression 1 to each of regressions 2 and 3 strengthens the finding about the existence of robust association between non-traditional exports and imports of machinery, on the one hand, and real exchange rate-based indicators on the other. These findings suggest very important policy implications. First, they lend support to the argument that basic capabilities, investment, and maybe some strategic interventions to resolve market failures are important for successful export-orientation. Second, however, the results also suggest that export promotion and export diversification require a supportive structure of incentives, especially appropriate and stable real exchange rates.

Conclusions

This chapter has analysed the impact of exchange rate competitiveness and exchange rate stability on non-traditional export performance for 60 developing countries.

The empirical framework used for the analysis of non-traditional export performance is a unification of two theoretical approaches. One model (motivated by the experiences of Korea and Taiwan) explains export expansion as driven by a sustained boom in investment (and import) demand (Rodrik, 1994). The other model, influenced by the Latin American experience, predicts a significant role for real exchange rate competitiveness (as a proxy for profitability of exporting) and real exchange rate stability in the determination of export supply (Paredes, 1988). The unifying empirical framework of this chapter attempted to account for: the profitability of the export sector (measured by the evolution of the RER and RER misalignment); macroeconomic stability relevant for export performance (RER variability); investment in capital goods; as well as the school enrolment ratio (as a proxy for human capital).

To generate the required exchange rate measures for the estimation of the export equation, this chapter estimated a real exchange rate model that accounts for both current account and capital account fundamentals for a panel of 63 developing countries over three periods (1980–5, 1986–9, 1990–5). The estimation results allowed the derivation of two key indicators of real exchange rate policy for all of the 63 countries. These are the equilibrium RER index (ERER) and the index of RER misalignment (RERMIS). In addition, an index of RER instability (RERVAR) was constructed. The novelty of this approach is that it provides a systematic and model-consistent method for disentangling the channels through which the RER affects exports. The estimation results of the RER model strongly corroborate the predictions of the theoretical model, in which current account and capital account fundamentals are found to be associated with the RER in the long run. In addition, the estimated equilibrium RER and RER misalignment indexes appear very plausible from the point of view of other stylized facts about macroeconomic adjustment in the countries.

The non-traditional export supply function was estimated using panel regressions of 60 countries (the same set used in the RER estimation except for three countries, excluded for lack of data) over two periods (1989/90 and 1994/5). The results strongly corroborate most of the main predictions of this chapter's theoretical framework. Two of the RER-based variables (RERMIS, RERVAR), terms of trade variability, the schooling variable, and imports of machinery are all very significantly and robustly associated with non-traditional export performance, and their effects are consistent with theoretical predictions. However, the levels of RER (as well as the equilibrium RER) were not significantly related to non-traditional export performance, when RERMIS was included in the same equation. The former result suggests that as long as real overvaluation is avoided, the level of the RER (or its equilibrium level) is irrelevant to export performance.

Moreover, the estimated effects of other regional characteristics (proxied by dummies) suggests that, *ceteris paribus*, the ratio of non-traditional exports to GDP will tend to be higher in both East Asia and Latin America relative to SSA. To the extent that these dummies reflect supply constraints related to market imperfection, technological capabilities, etc., this finding corroborates the argument that beyond 'getting the prices right', there may be an important role for the state in addressing the endemic problems of market imperfections in order to generate sustained and adequate export supply response to appropriate incentives. Finally, our results lend partial support to the Rodrik model in that basic capabilities including schooling, investment in machinery, and maybe governmental interventions to resolve market failures, are important for successful export orientation. However, our results also suggest that export promotion and export diversification require a supportive structure of incentives, especially appropriate and stable real exchange rates.

Data Appendix

Countries

Sub-Saharan African countries include Burkina Faso, Burundi, Cameroon, Central African Republic, Congo, Côte d'Ivoire, Gabon, Gambia, Ghana, Kenya, Madagascar, Malawi, Mauritania, Mauritius, Niger, Nigeria, Rwanda, Senegal, South Africa, Sudan, Tanzania, Togo, Uganda, Zambia, Zimbabwe.

North African countries include Algeria, Egypt, Morocco and Tunisia.

East Asian countries include China, Indonesia, Korea (Rep.), Malaysia, Singapore, Thailand.

Latin American countries include Bolivia, Brazil, Chile, Colombia, Costa Rica, Dominican Republic, Ecuador, El Salvador, Guatemala, Guyana, Honduras, Jamaica, Mexico, Nicaragua, Paraguay, Peru, Trinidad & Tobago, Uruguay, Venezuela.

Others include India, Iran, Pakistan, Papua New Guinea, Philippines, Sri Lanka, Syrian Arab Republic, Turkey.

Sources

All national accounts figures (including GDP, GNP, government consumption, public investment, capital inflows, international reserves, infrastructure) were obtained from the World Development Indicators database (World Bank, 1997).

All balances of payments and monetary figures (including nominal and real exchange rates, terms of trade) were obtained from the IMF database: IFS in CD-ROM.

Definitions

Net private capital inflows: Net capital inflows consist of private debt and non-debt flows. Private debt flows include commercial bank lending, bonds, and other private credits; non-debt private flows are foreign direct investment and portfolio equity investment.

Government consumption: General government consumption includes all current expenditures for purchases of goods and services by all levels of government, excluding most government enterprises. It also includes capital expenditure on national defence and security.

Net factor income from abroad: Net factor income includes the net labour income and net property and entrepreneurial income components of the Standard National Accounts. Labour income covers compensation of employees paid to non-resident workers. Property and entrepreneurial income covers investment income from the ownership of foreign financial claims (interest, dividends, rent, etc.) and non-financial property income (patents, copyrights, etc.). Data are in current US dollars.

Gross international reserves: Gross international reserves comprise holdings of monetary gold, special drawing rights, the reserve position of members in the IMF, and holdings of foreign exchange under the control of monetary authorities. The gold component of these reserves is valued at year end (31 December) London prices.

Gross domestic investment: Gross domestic investment consists of outlays on additions to the fixed assets of the economy plus net changes in the level of inventories. Fixed assets cover land improvements (fences, ditches, drains, etc.); plant, machinery, and equipment purchases; and the construction of roads, railways, and the like, including commercial and industrial buildings, offices, schools, hospitals, and private residential buildings.

Official development assistance and official aid: Official development assistance (ODA) consists of net disbursements of loans and grants made on concessional terms by official agencies of the members of the development assistance committee (DAC) of the OECD and certain Arab countries to promote economic development and welfare in recipient economies listed as developing by DAC. Loans with a grant element of more than 25 per cent are included in ODA. ODA also includes technical cooperation and assistance. Official aid refers to aid flows from official donors to the transition economies of Eastern Europe and the former Soviet Union and to certain advanced developing countries and territories as determined by DAC. Official aid is provided under terms and conditions similar to those for ODA.

Labour force (number of workers): Total labour force comprises people who meet the International Labour Organization's (ILO) definition of the economically active population: all people who supply labour for the production of goods and services during a specified period. It includes both the employed and unemployed. While national practices vary in the treatment of such groups as the armed forces and seasonal or part-time workers, in general the labour force includes the other unpaid caregivers and workers in the information sector.

Inflation: Inflation as measured by the consumer price index reflects the annual percentage change in the cost to the average consumer of acquiring a fixed basket of goods and services. In general, a Laspeyres index formula is used.

Roads: Paved roads that have been sealed with asphalt or similar road-building materials.

Telephone mainlines: Telephone mainlines refer to telephone lines connecting a customer's equipment (such as a telephone or facsimile machine) to the public switched telephone network. A mainline is normally identified by a unique number that is the one billed. Data are presented here as mainlines per 1000 people; this is a measure of telephone density or penetration.

Terms of trade: A ratio of the export to import price indexes (1987 = 100).

Real exchange rate: A multilateral index defined as a ratio of the nominal effective exchange rate index multiplied by the CPIs of major trading partners to the CPI of the country in question. This is the reciprocal of an index constructed by the IMF, normalized to equal 100 in 1980. No information about trade weights, however, is provided.

Imports of machinery goods: The total machinery exports by developed countries to the country in question. This is a proxy for imports of capital goods.

Non-traditional exports: Defined as all exports that are not classified as 'traditional', where the latter is defined as: the ten largest three-digit commodity groups in the country's exports in the base year (1983–4), unless these ten do not account for at least 75 per cent of those exports, in which case more three-digit groups are added until at least 75 per cent is reached (World Bank, 1997).

Acknowledgements

Helpful comments from Gerry Helleiner were greatly appreciated. I am also grateful to Azita Amjadi for providing the data on non-traditional exports. The author would also like to acknowledge the research assistance by Radha Ruparel and Rajal Upadhyaya. Methodological details may be found in Elbadawi, 1998.

Notes

1. A succinct list of policy measures normally prescribed in the context of structural adjustment programmes (SAPs) as compiled by John Williamson, which he dubbed the 'Washington Consensus'. Williamson describes the Washington

Consensus as offering 'a description of what is agreed about as the set of measures that are typically called for in the first stage of the policy reform' (Williamson, 1994a:17). A summary of the list of the elements of the Washington Consensus includes: fiscal discipline; redirection of public expenditure priorities towards health, education and infrastructure; tax reform, including the broadening of the tax base and cutting marginal tax rates; unified and competitive exchange rates; secure property rights; deregulation; trade liberalization; privatization; elimination of barriers to foreign direct investment (FDI); and financial liberalization.

2. On the other hand, the experience of East Asia suggests that these countries did not all fare well in terms of implementation of the latter set of reforms (Rodrik, 1996: Table 3).

3. However, the recent financial markets' crises and the subsequent weakening of currencies in several South East Asian countries – which are mainly attributed to an overborrowed and under-regulated private sector and not to fundamental macroeconomic disequilibria – suggest that exchange rate management is still a major challenge, even for these successful countries.

4. One of the most frequently used empirical measures of the RER is the multilateral index defined as the ratio of the nominal effective exchange rate index multiplied by the ratio of the weighted average of the CPIs of the trading partners to the CPI of the country in question. This is the measure of the RER adopted in this chapter, where a decline (increase) in the index implies an appreciation (depreciation) in the real value of the currency. The RER index used in this chapter is the reciprocal of an index constructed by the IMF, which prefers defining the RER as the relative price of non-tradables to tradables; unfortunately no information about trade weights is provided.

5. Also the literature abounds in empirical evidence linking export performance to the RER. For example, Diaz-Alejandro (1984) drew from the experience of Latin America to argue that RER misalignment and especially real currency overvaluation (with respect to the equilibrium RER) can be detrimental to an export-oriented development strategy, Caballero and Corbo (1989) emphasized the importance of RER stability for export promotion, while Paredes (1988) found both RER variability and uncertainty to have significant negative effects on export performance in Latin America.

6. See data appendix for a description of the data. While 63 countries are considered in the RER analysis, only 60 are used in the estimation of the export equation, because of the exclusion of the Republic of Congo, Malta and Honduras for lack of data.

7. This methodology was adopted in a country-specific time series context by Elbadawi (1997). Sekkat and Varoudakis (1998) also adopt a similar approach.

8. As indicated earlier, the Republic of Congo, Malta, and Honduras are not included in the export analysis because of lack of data.

9. Note that the model also predicts the long-run effects of Δresv and nki on RER to have equal, though opposing, coefficients.

10. Comparison of estimation results of the unrestricted model (not reported here) – which allows the size of the effect of the change in reserves to differ from that of net capital inflows – and that of the restricted model reveals that the latter is superior.

11. The derived long-run effects are obtained by setting the coefficient of MACRO to zero, setting $\text{Log } q_t = \text{Log } q_{t-1}$ and solving for the long-run equation of Log q as a function of the seven current and capital account fundamentals.

12. Using the case of Chile, Elbadawi (1994) and Elbadawi and Soto (1997a) compare the FEER method to an *ex post* approach for computing ERER indexes, where the ERER paths are based on the 'permanent' historical time series components of the fundamentals. No significant differences between the two approaches was found. However, the FEER approach is more amenable to policy simulations.
13. See Elbadawi and Soto (1997a) for a detailed discussion of the debate on the real exchange rate appreciation in Chile during the early 1980s.
14. Consistent data on non-traditional exports, obtained from the World Bank and employing its definition thereof, are available only for 1984/5, 1989/90 and 1994/5, where one lag was used as instrument.
15. Estimation was also undertaken using RER and ERER instead of, and in addition to, RERMIS; these results are not shown in Table 5.4 but are discussed in the text.
16. The elasticities are derived by subtracting one from the exponential of the estimated coefficients of the regional dummies of Table 5.4.

References

Caballero, R. and Corbo, V. (1989) 'How does Uncertainty About the Real Exchange Rate Affect Exports?', PPR WPS No. 221 (June), World Bank, Washington, DC.

Diaz-Alejandro, C. F. (1984) 'Exchange Rates and Terms of Trade in the Argentine Republic: 1913–76' in M. Syrquin and S. Teitel (eds), *Trade, Stability, Technology and Equity in Latin America*, Academic Press.

Edwards, S. (1986) 'The Order of Liberalization of the Current and Capital Accounts of the Balance of Payments' in A. Choksi and D. Papageorgio (eds), *Economic Liberalization in Developing Countries*, Oxford: Blackwell.

Edwards, S. (1987) 'Tariffs, Terms of Trade and Real Exchange Rate in an Intertemporal Model of the Current Account', NBER Working Paper.

Edwards, S. (1989) *Real Exchange Rates, Devaluation and Adjustment: Exchange Rate Policy in Developing Countries*, Cambridge, MA: MIT Press.

Edwards, S. (1992) 'Trade Orientation, Distortions and Growth in Developing Countries', *Journal of Development Economics*, 39: 31–57.

Edwards, S. (1997) 'Exchange Rate Issues in Developing and Transition Economies' in I. Elbadawi and R. Soto (eds), 'Foreign Exchange Markets and Exchange Rate Policies in Sub-Saharan Africa', *Journal of African Economies*, Supplement to 6, 3: 37–73.

Edwards, S. and van Wijnbergen, S. (1986) 'The Welfare Effects of Trade and Capital Market Liberalization', *International Economic Review* (February).

Edwards, S. and van Wijnbergen, S. (1987) 'Tariffs, Real Exchange Rates and the Terms of Trade: On Two Popular Propositions in International Economics', Oxford Economic Papers.

Elbadawi, I. (1994) 'Estimating Long Run Equilibrium Real Exchange Rates' in J. Williamson (ed.), *Estimating Equilibrium Exchange Rates*, Washington, DC: Institute for International Economics.

Elbadawi, I. (1997) 'Real Exchange Rate Policy and Export Competitiveness in Sub-Saharan Africa', presented at the UNU/WIDER project meeting on Growth, External Sector and the Role of Non-Traditional Exports in Sub-Saharan Africa, 16–18 June, Kampala, Uganda.

Elbadawi, I. (1998) 'Real Exchange Rate Policy and Non-Traditional Exports in Developing Countries', *Research for Action*, 46, Helsinki: WIDER.

Elbadawi, I. and Soto, R. (1997a) 'Capital Flows and Long-Term Equilibrium Real Exchange Rates in Chile', *Revista de Analisis Economico*, 12, 1 (June): 35–62.

Elbadawi, I. and Soto, R. (1997b) 'Real Exchange Rate and Macroeconomic Adjustment in Sub-Saharan Africa and Other Developing Countries' in I. Elbadawi and R. Soto (eds), 'Foreign Exchange Markets and Exchange Rate Policies in Sub-Saharan Africa', *Journal of African Economies*, Supplement to 6, 3: 74–120.

Faruqee, H. (1995) 'Long-Run Determinants of the Real Exchange Rate: A Stock-Flow Perspective', *IMF Staff Papers*, 42, 1 (March).

Helleiner, G. (1992) 'Trade Policy, Exchange Rates, and Relative Prices in Sub-Saharan Africa: Interpreting the 1980s', paper presented at Gothenburg Conference, Sweden, 6–8 September.

Helleiner, G. (1994) *Trade Policy and Industrialization in Turbulent Times*, Routledge: London and New York.

Mussa, M. L. (1974) 'Dynamic Adjustment in the Heckscher-Ohlin-Samuelson Model', *Journal of Political Economy*, 1191–203.

Paredes, C. (1988) 'Nominal Exchange Rate Regimes, The Real Exchange Rate and Export Performance in Latin America', unpublished mimeo, GRADE and the Brookings Institution.

Rodrik, D. (1992) 'Closing the Productivity Gap: Does Trade Liberalization really Help?', in G. Helleiner (ed.), *Trade Policy, Industrialization and Development: New Perspectives*, Oxford: Clarendon Press.

Rodrik, D. (1994) 'Getting Interventions Right: How South Korea and Taiwan Grew Rich', NBER Working Paper Series, No. 4964, December.

Rodrik, D. (1995) 'Trade Strategy, Exports and Investment: Another Look at East Asia', Institute of Policy Reform Discussion Paper, Washington, DC.

Rodrik, D. (1996) 'Understanding Economic Policy Reform', *Journal of Economic Literature*, 34 (March): 9–41.

Sekkat, K. and Varoudakis, A. (1998) 'Exchange Rate Management and Manufactured Exports in Sub-Saharan Africa', OECD Development Centre, Technical Paper No. 134, March.

Stiglitz, J. (1994) 'The Role of the State in Financial Markets', *Proceedings of the World Bank Conference of Development Economics, 1993*, Washington, DC: World Bank.

Stiglitz, J. and Weiss, A. (1981) 'Credit Rationing in Markets with Imperfect Information', *American Economic Review*, 71, 3 (June).

Valdés, A. (1985) 'Exchange Rates and Trade Policy: Help or Hindrance to Agricultural Growth', Proceedings of the XIX International Conference of Agricultural Economists in Malaga, Spain, September.

Williamson, J. (1994a) 'Latin American Reform and the Washington Consensus', paper presented to a Conference on 'Brazil and the New World Order', at UERJ in Rio de Janeiro.

Williamson, J. (1994b) 'Estimating the FEERs' in John Williamson (ed.), *Estimating Equilibrium Exchange Rates*, Washington, DC: Institute for International Economics, pp. 177–244.

Williamson, J. (1997) 'Exchange Rate Policy and Development Strategy' in I. Elbadawi and R. Soto (eds), 'Foreign Exchange Markets and Exchange Rate Policies in Sub-Saharan Africa', *Journal of African Economies*, Supplement to 6, 3: 17–36.

World Bank (1995) *A Continent in Transition: Sub-Saharan Africa in the Mid-1990s*, Washington, DC: World Bank.

World Bank (1997) *World Development Indicators, 1997*, Washington, DC: World Bank.

Part II

Five African Countries' Experience

6
Promotion of Non-Traditional Exports in Kenya, 1980–96

Francis M. Mwega

Introduction

Sub-Saharan Africa's importance in global trade has declined substantially over time. The region accounts for about 1.2 per cent of world exports, down from about 3 per cent in the 1960s. In the 1980s, exports expanded at a rate of only 1.8 per cent compared to a world average of 5.3 per cent (World Bank, 1996). This poor performance is postulated to reflect decreased demand for primary products and reduced competitiveness of the region. A related issue of concern is the slow responsiveness of exports to the substantial economic reforms that African countries have implemented in the 1980s and 1990s.

The performance of Kenya's export sector has been lacklustre and exports grew less than GDP in the first three decades of independence. While the real GDP grew at an average rate of 4.7 per cent in 1964–93, the trend growth in the volume of total and non-oil exports was only 1.6 per cent and 2.9 per cent, respectively (Mwega, 1995).

Table 6.1 shows that the share of exports in GDP decreased from 21.5 per cent in 1980 to 13.4 per cent in 1989 before increasing to 26.1 per cent in 1996. The absolute value of exports declined from US$1318 million in 1980 to US$925.8 million in 1989 before increasing to US$2071.2 million in 1996. Export growth averaged –2.6 per cent in the 1980s compared to a growth rate of 15 per cent in the 1990s. UNDP/World Bank (1993) attributes the overall poor export performance in the 1980s to domestic policies rather than external constraints, with incentives biased against exports, especially manufactured exports.

Table 6.2 shows merchandise exports are dominated by Food and Live Animals (SITC 0) which account for more than half of Kenya's merchandise exports. The next important primary export category is Mineral Fuels (SITC 3) which is dominated by refined petroleum exports. The share of this export has decreased over time from 26.9 per cent in 1980–4 to 9.6 per cent in 1995–6. The other primary exports in order of importance are Crude Materials (SITC 2), Beverages & Tobacco (SITC 1) and Animal & Vegetable Oils (SITC 4). Primary exports (including petroleum products) accounted for 88.4 per cent of total exports in the 1980s, this declining to 72 per cent in the 1990s.

Coffee, tea and petroleum remain by far the dominant commodity exports, although the contribution of the latter to forex earnings is small as the country mainly re-exports petroleum products after processing. While export volumes of coffee and tea expanded in this period (coffee from an average 86 994 metric tons in 1989–93 to an average 94 976 metric tons in 1994–6, and tea from an average 84 905 metric tons in 1979–83 to an average 218 336 metric tons in 1994–6), their prices have either generally declined or remained stagnant. The price of coffee, for example, averaged US$2.95 in 1979–83 and US$2.90 in 1994–5, while that of tea was US$1.81 and US$1.64 in the two periods respectively. The average price of petroleum exports also declined in this period (from US$0.23 to US$0.19 per litre) as did the volume exported (from an average 814 metric tons in 1979–83 to an average 444 metric tons in 1994–6).

Table 6.1   Total exports and exports as % of GDP, Kenya, 1980–96

Year	Exports as % of GDP	Exports US$ million[a]
1980	21.8	1,318.0
1981	19.8	1,388.8
1982	18.5	992.2
1983	19.1	994.8
1984	19.6	1,041.2
1985	17.9	957.4
1986	18.8	1,182.6
1987	13.3	913.2
1988	14.2	986.8
1989	13.4	925.8
1990	14.7	1,022.8
1991	16.1	1,091.6
1992	15.0	943.6
1993	25.6	1,063.2
1994	24.7	1,162.0
1995	24.2	1,674.8
1996	26.1	2,071.2

Note: [a] Converted to dollars at the exchange rates in Table 6.5.

Source: Kenya, *Economic Survey*, various issues.

Table 6.2   Composition of total Kenyan exports, 1980–96 (%)

SITC	Description	1980–4	1985–9	1990–4	1995–6
0	Food and Live Animals	52.7	64.0	51.0	51.2
1	Beverages and Tobacco	0.4	0.7	2.0	2.6
2	Crude Materials, inedible, except Fuels	7.4	9.6	9.1	9.6
3	Mineral Fuels, Lubricants & Related Materials	26.9	13.4	9.9	6.6
4	Animal and Vegetable Oils, Fats and Waxes	0.2	0.1	0.6	1.9
5	Chemicals and Related Products n.e.s.	3.1	3.2	4.2	6.5
6	Manufactured Goods classified by materials	6.7	6.2	11.4	15.0
7	Machinery and Transport Equipment	0.5	0.7	0.6	1.3
8	Miscellaneous Manufactured Articles	1.2	1.7	10.4	5.2
9	Other	0.0	0.3	0.8	0.2
	Total	100	100	100	100

Source: Kenya, *Economic Survey*, various issues.

Table 6.3 shows the principal destinations of Kenya's exports. There has been little market diversification of Kenya's exports. Except in 1994–6 when a significantly larger share of exports went to African countries due to political crises in the region, the European Union is still the largest single market, and has accounted for 32–50 per cent of Kenya's exports. The EU share increased steadily from 35.9 per cent in 1980 to 49.4 per cent in 1988 before declining to 32.7 per cent in 1994. The major importers in this region are United Kingdom, Germany, Italy, France and the Netherlands.

Table 6.3   Destinations of Kenya's exports, 1980–96 (%)

Year	EU	US and Canada	Africa	Far East & Australia
1980	35.9	4.5	28.9	13.9
1981	34.6	4.6	30.5	14.1
1982	36.1	7.3	29.3	9.9
1983	40.2	7.0	30.8	10.3
1984	46.1	5.9	26.8	11.7
1985	44.1	7.6	26.3	10.8
1986	46.0	9.9	22.1	10.3
1987	44.4	6.5	29.1	10.6
1988	49.4	6.0	26.5	8.4
1989	44.7	5.9	22.7	12.7
1990	44.7	4.3	21.9	12.6
1991	41.2	4.4	24.8	11.4
1992	40.5	4.4	27.5	13.8
1993	36.4	4.6	35.1	12.3
1994	32.7	4.2	45.8	11.6
1995	33.4	3.5	51.0	11.4
1996[a]	34.3	3.4	48.5	10.7

Note: [a] Provisional.

Source: Kenya, *Economic Survey*, various issues.

The next important destination for Kenya's exports is Africa. There was a rapid increase in the share of exports to this region in the 1990s (from 21.9 per cent in 1991 to 51 per cent in 1995 before it declined to 48 per cent in 1996), making exports to Africa for the first time exceed exports to the traditional European markets. A considerable proportion of the exports, however, goes to the former East African Community countries. Uganda and Tanzania for example accounted for 52.3 per cent of the total exports to African countries in 1994, while the Common Market for Eastern and Southern Africa (COMESA) region (of which the two countries are members) took 83.3 per cent of total exports to Africa. Major exports to Uganda are motor spirits (fuel), cement, wheat and sugar, while those to Tanzania are iron products, beer, sugar, soaps and medicaments (medicines).

The share of exports to Australia and the Far East (mainly Japan, India and China) has not changed much over time and accounted for about 14 per cent of total exports. The US and Canada, on the other hand, have accounted for less than 10 per cent of total exports. The Middle East and Eastern Europe have been unimportant destinations of Kenya's exports.

This chapter analyses the experience of Kenya in developing non-traditional exports (NTX) in the 1980s and 1990s. It looks at the key components of non-traditional exporting and the main constraints to diversifying the country's export basket. Diversification of exports is important because it reduces a country's vulnerability to external developments as well as commercial risks arising from relying on a few exports. Export diversification can be expected to reduce the instability of export earnings and to promote economic growth (Jebuni et al., 1992). The potential for learning-induced productivity improvements may also increase with the number and variety of export products. According to Mayer (1996), the primary objective of an export diversification policy should be to upgrade a country's production and export pattern by successfully moving up the technological and skill ladder of its products, consistent with the country's human and physical resource endowments, while taking into account dynamic demand potentials in the world markets.

The rest of the chapter is organized as follows. First, the initial conditions and national characteristics as well as the macroeconomic performance in the 1980s and 1990s relevant to export performance, are examined. Next, NTX is specified and categorized based on the government's usage of the term (NTX1), a World Bank definition (NTX2), and the project's own definition (NTX3). I then move on to discuss the performance of non-traditional exports; briefly describe the trade, exchange rate and other policies implemented in the 1980s and 1990s that were expected to enhance export performance; and then to explore the response of NTX to policies and the constraints to success. The chapter ends with some conclusions.

Initial conditions and macroeconomic performance in the 1980s and 1990s

Initial conditions (resource endowments and economic structure) have an important influence on export performance through their impact on national political institutions, forms of economic organization and economic policy. The principal features usually associated with differences in patterns of growth and structural change are size of country, natural resource endowments and more generally the extent of participation in international trade. In the 1960s and 1970s, Kenya was classified as an outward industry-oriented country as it had relatively high exports of manufactures. The share of manufactured exports has however declined over time, leading Syrquin (1992) to classify Kenya as a 'balanced' country as it did not fit easily into the 'outward-primary', 'outward-industry' or 'inward orientation' categories.

Kenya is a small poor economy. The country has a land area of 225 000 square miles, of which about 60 per cent can be described as semi-desert, and land use is very low. The country had a per capita income of about US$281 and a population of 28.3 million in 1996, up from 8.6 million at independence. The rate of population growth of more than 3 per cent has put tremendous pressure on the available resources. The labour force has grown faster than the capacity to absorb it, increasing unemployment and under-employment. The rate of unemployment in Kenya's urban areas was about 16 per cent in the 1980s, increasing to 17.8–23 per cent in the 1990s (Manda, 1997). The increase in unemployment reflected a decline in the level of economic activities and the public sector's restrictive employment policies, including civil service reforms.

Historically, Kenya was a colony of Britain between 1895 and 1963. During this period, agriculture received priority. European settlers had taken ownership of some of the best lands in the country (the White Highlands), creating a large-farm sector that produced for the domestic and overseas markets. Until the early 1970s, large-scale farms produced the bulk of Kenya's main cash crops – wheat, coffee, tea and maize.

After the Second World War, there were policy changes in three main areas (Mosley, 1991). First, driven by shortages during the war, British settlers established a small industrial base, mainly to produce import substitutes and to process agricultural products. Second was encouragement of African small-holders to grow cash crops under the so-called Swynnerton Plan (1954). Third was establishment of a system of boards to market these products. These changes had a major influence on economic management later, with the policy of import-substitution continued, smallholder agriculture expanded, and the role of the state substantially entrenched after independence. Kenya has mainly followed a 'mixed' development strategy, with a state ownership and control apparatus nurtured and extended after independence in such areas as price and wage controls, industrial protection and agricultural marketing. The 1960s and 1970s can be described as an era of state-led development characterized by pervasive controls in the various markets.

Until the early 1970s, the economy performed very well with an average growth rate of about 6 per cent while the rate of inflation remained at single digits. Then came the oil shocks of 1973 and 1979, compounded by bad policies (especially the mismanagement of the 1976–7 coffee boom), which led to balance of payments problems and acceleration of inflation. These forced the country to seek conditional finance from the Bretton Woods institutions. Substantial donor-driven reforms were implemented in the 1980s and 1990s that have covered nearly all sectors of the economy including the liberalization of the foreign exchange rate market, the trade and payments system, and domestic financial and capital markets; and privatization and commercialization of public corporations. These reforms, however, have not improved economic performance as shown in Table 6.4, where income growth has declined in virtually all the sectors.

Table 6.4   Average annual growth rates of real GDP, Kenya, 1964–95 (%)

	1964–73	*1974–9*	*1980–9*	*1990–5*
Agriculture	4.6	3.9	3.3	0.4
Manufacturing	9.1	10.0	4.8	3.0
Finance, Real Estate	9.8	12.4	6.8	6.6
Government Services	16.9	6.5	4.9	2.6
GDP	6.6	5.2	4.1	2.5

Source: Kenya, *National Development Plan, 1997–2001*.

The Kenyan economy is dominated by the agricultural sector in terms of raw materials production, food supplies, source of livelihood and generation of exports. In the mid-1990s, the sector accounted for 26.5 per cent of GDP, about three-quarters of Kenya's employment and a third of Kenya's non-oil export earnings. On the other hand, the country has a small manufacturing sector that employed about 205 000 people in the mid-1990s. The share of manufacturing increased from about 11 per cent in the early 1970s to 14 per cent of GDP in 1995 while the wage bill remained fairly constant at about a third of manufacturing value added. The country has become increasingly self-sufficient in the supply of manufactured goods.

Macroeconomic performance in the 1980s and 1990s

There now seems to be a consensus that achieving rapid economic growth on a sustainable basis requires good macroeconomic and financial management. Elbadawi and Schmidt-Hebbel (1996), for example, postulate that macroeconomic reforms may be more important than micro and sectoral policies in terms of their effects on economic performance in general and on whether countries can avoid development crises, especially following external shocks. Micro and sectoral policies constitute development strategy that could be implemented with varying degrees of intensity and policy mix, depending on the nature of institutions, macro policy and the external environment.

The first half of the 1980s was characterized by slow economic growth (averaging 3.2 per cent) that reflected the impact of the second (1979) oil price shock, a decline in the terms of trade (TOT), a military coup attempt in 1982 and a severe drought in 1983–4. Despite efforts to tighten fiscal and monetary policies in the context of a series of structural adjustment programmes (SAPs), inflation averaged 17.6 per cent per annum and was accompanied by a nominal depreciation in the currency (the Kenya shilling – Ksh) (see Table 6.5).

Table 6.5   Basic macroeconomic indicators, Kenya, 1980–96

Year	Inflation %	TOT 1987=100	Fiscal deficit /GDP %	External debt/GDP %	M2 growth %	Exchange rate Ksh/US$	Treasury bill rate %
1980	13.8	136	9.3	46.7	–1.2	7.4	5.2
1981	11.8	126	10.9	37.4	12.5	7.4	7.4
1982	21.0	125	15.0	52.4	15.4	11.0	12.4
1983	14.7	120	4.6	60.8	4.3	13.4	14.0
1984	9.1	126	4.4	56.9	12.1	14.5	13.3
1985	8.9	124	5.8	68.5	6.5	16.4	13.3
1986	8.4	125	4.2	65.2	28.2	16.2	13.8
1987	8.7	100	7.7	74.0	10.6	16.5	13.2
1988	12.3	98	4.1	69.3	10.6	18.6	12.9
1989	13.4	92	4.6	70.8	18.9	21.6	13.5
1990	18.6	90	6.4	114.5	14.4	24.1	13.9
1991	19.7	89	7.5	102.0	19.0	28.1	14.8
1992	27.1	81	3.6	97.3	29.0	36.2	16.6
1993	46.0	80	5.6	114.9	22.9	68.2	39.3
1994	28.8	80	3.6	87.5	26.5	44.8	17.9
1995	1.6	76	0.9	72.5	17.1	55.6	20.9
1996	9.1	74	1.4		23.8	55.0	21.6

Source: Kenya, *Economic Survey*, various issues.

In the second half of the 1980s, growth rebounded (averaging 5 per cent per annum). While the aggregate TOT continued to decline, this period is associated with a mini coffee boom in 1986, a decrease in oil prices, and good weather, while the government implemented a number of structural adjustment policies. Despite a further nominal depreciation of the shilling, the annual rate of inflation decelerated to an average of 10.3 per cent.

In the early 1990s, there was a worsening of the economic environment. There was a drought in 1991/2 and the price of oil increased due to the Gulf War, worsening the terms of trade. These exogenous shocks were accompanied by an increase in the budget deficit and money supply with the rate of inflation rising rapidly alongside large shilling depreciations. During this period, the exchange rate regime had changed to a dual system with an official exchange rate and a 'market' rate operated on the basis of Foreign Exchange Bearer Certificates (Forex-Cs). This foreign exchange liberalization was implemented during a period of severe macroeconomic imbalances reflected in historically large money supply increases, and a shortage of foreign exchange which was compounded by the aid embargo of 1991–3. At the same time prices were decontrolled in the presence of an inadequate supply of essential commodities and high consumer demand due to excess liquidity in the economy, as well as increased government spending in the run-up to the 1992 elections (Mwega and Ndung'u, 1996). As a result of efforts to mop up the excess liquidity after 1993, the Treasury Bill rate gradually came down and the rate of inflation started falling, leading to an improvement in macroeconomic stability in the 1994–6 period (ibid.). The rate of inflation declined from 46.0 per cent in 1993 to 13.2 per cent in 1994–6 due to a tightening of fiscal and monetary policies, stabilization of the exchange rate and favourable weather conditions that improved food harvests.

In summary, the good economic performance during the first decade of independence was not sustained subsequently and the country has been characterized by persistently low growth. This is despite a large measure of political stability and a fairly consistent development strategy. In addition to adverse exogenous factors, the poor economic performance is partly due to policy errors and structural rigidities. Since the early 1970s, the quality of economic management seems to have slackened. There was an increase in macroeconomic imbalances as the public sector expanded, creating inefficiencies and causing a decline in productivity.

Definitions of NTX

The government's usage of the term 'non-traditional exports' (NTX) is not well-articulated. Official publications do not explicitly define nor do they give special emphasis to NTX. *Sessional Paper No. 1 of 1986*, for example, argues that although it would be desirable to diversify from the five largest merchandise and service exports (coffee, tea, petroleum products, transport and tourism), which accounted for about three-quarters of total exports in the early 1980s, their concentration is not so large as to suggest neglect of their further development. The sessional paper proceeds to argue that the need for generating export growth is so great that the country should pursue 'the expansion of any existing export commodity or service that promises sufficient returns for its investment' (20–2). The *1989–93 Development Plan*, on the other hand, pledges that the government 'is determined to attain effective diversification of the export base through the promotion of non-traditional exports ... In this regard, the industrial and commercial sectors will, by increasing their export potential, contribute to this diversification' (143). According to *Sessional Paper No. 2 of 1996* (63), the main thrust of export promotion is 'production of non-traditional exports and increased value addition to primary products'. Although none of these documents define NTX, one could infer that they include all exports other than the five items listed above. The *Sessional Paper No. 1 of 1994* (63), for example, refers to 'horticulture and other non-traditional exports', hence including horticulture in this category.

The World Bank (*World Development Indicators, 1997*) defines traditional merchandise exports to include the top ten three-digit export items in the base year, unless they total less than 75 per cent of exports, in which case more items are added until 75 per cent is reached. According to this definition, the traditional exports (base year = 1980) are shown in Table 6.6, with the NTX (discussed below) defined to include the remaining products (NTX2). All these traditional exports are primary products except Lime, Cement & Fabricated Construction Materials (SITC 661) and perhaps Petroleum Products (SITC 334).

This chapter utilizes a broader definition (NTX3), where NTXs include merchandise exports accounting for less than 3 per cent of total exports in the base year (but excluding items not domestically produced unless there is significant domestic value added) plus gross non-factor services exports (including tourism).

Traditional merchandise exports are therefore comprised of Petroleum products (SITC 334), Coffee (SITC 071), Tea and Mate (SITC 074) and Crude Vegetable Materials n.e.s (SITC 292) which include cut flowers, hence leaving many of the horticultural products among NTX.

Table 6.6   Traditional exports in Kenya (World Bank definition), 1980

SITC	Export product	% of Total exports
334	Petroleum Products, refined	33.3
071	Coffee[a]	22.2
074	Tea and Mate	11.9
292	Crude Vegetable Materials n.e.s.	3.2
061	Sugar and Honey	2.7
278	Other Crude Minerals	2.3
058	Fruit, Preserved and Fruit Preparations	2.2
661	Lime, Cement & Fabricated Construction Materials	2.1
211	Hides and Skins (except furskins), raw	2.0
057	Fruit and Nuts (not oil nuts), fresh or dried	1.4
	Total	83.3

Note: [a] Whether or not roasted or caffeine-free as well as coffee husks and skins.

Source: Kenya, *Annual Trade Report*, various issues.

Table 6.7   Composition of Kenyan merchandise non-traditional exports, 1980

Export product		% share of total exports
1. Food & live animals (SITC 0)		7.8
Sugar and honey	2.7	
Preserved fruit & fruit preparations	2.2	
Fruit & nuts (not oil nuts), fresh or dried	1.4	
Vegetables – roots, tubers & others	1.3	
2. Manufactured goods classified by materials (SITC 6)		7.2
Lime, cement & fabricated construction	2.1	
Paper & paperboard	2.0	
Leather	0.9	
3. Crude materials (SITC 2)		7.0
'Other' minerals	2.3	
Raw hides & skins, except fur skins	2.0	
Vegetable textile fibres	1.2	
Cotton	0.6	
4. Chemicals & related products n.e.s (SITC 5)		3.1
Soap preparations	0.9	
Medicinal & pharmaceutical products	0.7	
5. Miscellaneous manufactured articles (SITC 8)		1.3
6. Machinery & transport equipment (SITC 7)		0.6
7. Beverages & tobacco (SITC 2)		0.5
8. Animal & vegetable oils, fats & waxes (SITC 4)		0.1
9. Mineral fuels, lubricants & related materials (SITC 3)		0.07

Source: Kenya, *Annual Trade Report*, 1980.

Table 6.7 shows the composition of merchandise NTXs in 1980. Primary NTX (SITC 0–4) comprised 16.5 per cent of total exports in 1980 and manufactures (SITC 5–8) 12.3 per cent of total exports.

Performance of NTXs

Merchandise NTXs

Table 6.8 shows the performance of these exports. The share of merchandise NTXs in GDP increased in the study period from 6.3 per cent (US$398.2 million) in 1980 to 13.4 per cent (US$1067 million) in 1996, increasing their share in total exports from 29.4 per cent in 1980 to 53.1 per cent in 1996, so that the export basket has become considerably more diversified. Merchandise NTXs hence grew much faster (20.1 per cent) than traditional exports (7.4 per cent). There are four clear episodes: 1980–5, when the share of NTX was 5.7 per cent of GDP; 1986–8, when it averaged 12.8 per cent; 1989–91, when it fell again to 5.8 per cent; and 1992–6, when it climbed back to 12.4 per cent. According to Landell-Mills and Katz (1991), the first half of the 1980s experienced a large decline in merchandise NTXs due to restrictive trade policies. The quantitative restrictions imposed in 1980 and 1982 resulted in an increase in effective rates of protection that protected inefficient activities and tended to discriminate against products in which Kenya had a comparative advantage such as food-based manufacturing. The system was also discretionary and non-transparent, making costs, competition in the domestic markets, and access to inputs difficult to predict. They also attribute the high share in 1986–8 to a massive increase in the volume of horticultural exports.

Table 6.8   Merchandise non-traditional exports – value, % of GDP and growth rates, Kenya, 1980–96[a]

Year	Value in US$ millions[b]	% of GDP	Growth %
1980	398.2	6.3	
1981	449.8	6.4	13.0
1982	283.0	5.3	–37.1
1983	298.2	6.0	5.4
1984	274.2	5.2	–8.0
1985	266.0	4.9	–3.1
1986	1,002.0	16.0	276.7
1987	735.4	10.7	–26.6
1988	819.6	11.8	11.4
1989[a]	464.7	6.8	–43.3
1990	379.8	5.5	–18.3
1991	460.2	6.8	21.2
1992	644.4	10.2	40.0
1993	529.8	12.7	–17.8
1994	967.0	12.8	82.5
1995	896.6	13.0	–7.3
1996	1,067.8	13.4	19.1
Average			20.1

Notes: [a] Data for 1989 were reported for the first nine months of the year and hence were adjusted by a factor of 1.33. The Kenya Bureau of Statistics switched to a new version of the SITC classification in 1990 and apparently failed to input data for the last three months of 1989.
[b] Converted to dollars at the exchange rates in Table 6.5.

Source: Kenya, *Annual Trade Report*, various issues.

In the 1980s, 70.5 per cent of merchandise NTXs were primary exports (SITC 0–4). Primary exports' share declined to 44.2 per cent in the 1990s as there was some diversification away from these exports towards manufactures.

Table 6.2 showed that exports of manufactures (SITC 5–8) comprised only 11.7 per cent of total exports in the 1980s (down from 40 per cent in the

1960s). The data in Table 6.10 show that, except for beverages and tobacco, the proportion of manufactured output exported by the various industries declined in the 1980s.

Table 6.9   Composition of non-traditional merchandise exports, Kenya, 1980–96[a]

Code	Description	1980–4	1985–9	1990–4	1995–6
0	Food and live animals	28.6	68.8	22.7	24.7
1	Beverages and tobacco	2.2	1.8	5.1	6.0
2	Crude materials, inedible except fuels	16.3	5.4	4.8	3.4
3	Mineral fuels, lubricants & related materials	0.6	0.5	0.8	1.0
4	Animal and vegetable oils, fats and waxes	1.0	0.3	1.4	4.5
	Total	48.7	76.8	34.7	39.6
5	Chemicals and related products n.e.s.	18.7	7.5	10.9	15.2
6	Manufactured goods classified by material	22.1	10.1	25.7	30.0
7	Machinery and transport equipment	3.0	1.4	1.6	2.9
8	Miscellaneous manufactured articles	7.3	3.8	24.9	12.0
	Total	51.0	22.8	63.1	60.0
9	Other	0.3	0.4	2.2	0.4
	Total	100.0	100.0	100.0	100.0

Note: [a] There was a large increase in the relative value of SITC 0 exports. As noted by Landell-Mills and Katz (1991), there was a massive increase in the volume of horticultural exports (including maize) in 1986–8, which also coincided with a mini coffee export boom.

The decline in the share of manufactured exports in total exports as well as in total output in the 1980s has been attributed to a decrease in exports to the neighbouring countries, especially Tanzania where the volume of imports from Kenya has not yet reached the levels attained before the break-up of the East African Community in 1977; growth in domestic demand for such products as paper; the anti-export bias of the trade policies; and supply constraints, especially the intermittent shortage of foreign exchange to purchase intermediate inputs (Sharpley and Lewis, 1988).

The growth of the manufacturing sector drastically slowed in the 1980s and early 1990s (to 4–5 per cent per annum) after a rapid growth in the 1960s and 1970s. One cause of the decline in economic growth was a reduction of investment and its productivity. Until the reforms of 1992–3, this was attributed to increased political instability, cumbersome bureaucracy, price controls, constraints on repatriation of dividends, and shortages of foreign exchange that made acquisition of imported inputs uncertain or irregular (Friedrich-Naumann-Stiftung, 1992). Another factor was the reduced opportunity for easy consumer goods import-substitution.

Manufactured exports have rebounded, however, in the 1990s and comprised 26.6 per cent and 28 per cent of total exports in 1990–4 and 1995–6, respectively. Nearly all manufactured exports increased their shares in the 1990s. The authorities attribute this to trade reforms and the depreciation of the Kenya shilling achieved in the period. Another important source of manufactured export growth was rescue activities arising from turmoil in neighbouring countries, particularly Somalia and Rwanda.

Table 6.10   Share of Kenyan manufacturing output exported in the 1980s

	1979–83	*1984–8*
Food manufacturing	5.7	2.7
Beverages and tobacco (excl. coffee and tea)	2.0	2.4
Chemicals (incl. petroleum)	7.3	4.6
Machinery and transport equipment	1.5	1.3
Other manufactures	7.5	5.7
Total manufacturing sector	5.9	3.8

Source: Compiled from World Bank (1990).

NTX and export concentration

Table 6.11 gives data on the Gini-Hirschman concentration index for total exports. This declined steadily from 0.43 in 1980 to 0.28 in 1996, so that as a result of the growth in NTXs, Kenya has experienced reduced export concentration.

Table 6.11   Evolution of the Gini-Hirschman (GH) concentration index, Kenya, 1980–96

Year	*GH*	*Year*	*GH*
1980	0.43	1989	0.38
1981	0.41	1990	0.36
1982	0.42	1991	0.34
1983	0.40	1992	0.35
1984	0.43	1993	0.33
1985	0.42	1994	0.29
1986	0.47	1995	0.28
1987	0.38	1996	0.28
1988	0.37		

In the 1980s, Kenya's annual trade reports listed 227 export items. Of these, 11 had zero entries in 1980, 22 in 1984, and 37 in 1989, reflecting the poor export performance in the 1980s. In 1990–6, the annual trade reports listed 249 export products. Of these, 23 had zero entries in 1990, 10 in 1994, and 15 in 1996, again reflecting the better export performance in the 1990s.

Table 6.12 shows the share of the top three exports in total exports. Their share declined from 66.9 per cent in the 1980s to 41.2 per cent in 1995–6, indicating again that the export basket has been diversified away from these exports.

Table 6.12   Top three exports as a proportion of total exports, Kenya, 1980–96 (%)

SITC	Item	1980–4	1985–9	1990–4	1995–6
71	Coffee	27.6	68.8	22.7	24.7
74	Tea and mate	2.2	1.8	5.1	6.0
334	Petroleum products	16.3	5.4	4.8	3.4

Source: Kenya, *Annual Trade Report*, various issues.

Non-factor service exports

Table 6.13 shows the evolution of gross non-factor service exports. The most important of these is foreign travel (tourism). Gross travel earnings generally increased to an average of 8.5 per cent of GDP in 1993–5. The country had a peak of 782 000 arrivals in 1993 accounting for 4.4 per cent of the African market, after Morocco (22.5 per cent), Tunisia (20.5 per cent), South Africa (18.5 per cent) and Algeria (6.3 per cent) (World Tourism Organization, 1995). Travel earnings declined substantially in 1996 to 5.9 per cent of GDP. The decline in 1996 (extending to 1997–8) has been attributed to the bad publicity that the country experienced over this period; rundown of infrastructure; a decline in security and safety in the country's coastal region and within parks; the recession in Europe, which is the main source of Kenya's tourists; the Gulf War; and an appreciation of the shilling, which has made Kenya a relatively expensive place compared to competing destinations.[1]

Export earnings from transportation declined in the 1980s, increased in the early 1990s and then declined again. Similarly, 'other' earnings in the private sector from goods, services and income declined in the 1980s but increased to about 1 per cent of GDP in the 1990s.[2]

Trade, export (and related) policies for promoting exports

Numerous trade, export and allied macroeconomic policies that had a bearing on exports were implemented in the 1980s and 1990s. The following is a brief discussion of the most important of these policies, not necessarily in the order of their importance.

Tariffs

In 1981, there were tariff reductions on about 20 items used mainly by export-oriented industries. These tariff reductions were gradually extended in the 1980s and 1990s to more import items, particularly under the second World Bank Structural Adjustment Loan in 1983–4 and the World Bank industrial sector adjustment credit in 1987–91. Over the 1987–92 period, the number of tariff categories was reduced from 25 to 11, while the maximum tariff rate was reduced from 170 per cent to 70 per cent. In 1994–6, the maximum rate was reduced to 35 per cent and the number of bands to five.

Table 6.13 Non-factor service exports (NFSX) and NTX3 as % of GDP, Kenya, 1980–96

Year	Transpor-tation	Foreign travel	Other: private	Total NFSX	NFSX plus merchandise NTX (NTX3)
1980	1.7	4.0	1.0	6.7	13.0
1981	5.7	3.7	0.9	10.3	16.7
1982	5.6	4.2	0.9	10.6	15.9
1983	3.8	3.9	0.7	10.2	16.2
1984	3.6	3.9	0.3	8.1	13.3
1985	3.2	4.7	0.3	8.6	13.5
1986	3.2	4.8	0.3	8.3	24.3
1987	3.3	5.2	0.3	8.7	19.4
1988	3.6	5.4	0.3	8.9	20.7
1989	4.6	5.8	0.2	9.7	14.8
1990	5.3	6.4	0.8	11.7	17.2
1991	4.9	6.2	1.0	12.5	19.3
1992	7.0	6.3	0.9	12.0	22.2
1993	4.9	8.6	1.5	17.1	29.8
1994	4.8	8.3	1.1	14.3	17.1
1995	4.7	8.5	1.1	12.5	25.5
1996	6.3	5.9	0.7	11.2	24.6

Source: Kenya, *Economic Survey*, various issues.

The average unweighted tariff rate declined from 41.3 per cent in 1989/90 to 34 per cent in 1992/3 (UNDP/World Bank, 1993).

Tariff reforms implemented in the 1980s and early 1990s had some impact in reducing the effective (i.e. actually collected) tariffs. The collected tariff rates increased to a peak in 1982 and then generally declined over the rest of the period (Mwega, 1995).

Quantitative restrictions

Since the balance of payments crisis of 1971, Kenya has extensively used administrative controls to manage the balance of payments and to provide protection to some industries. Until their abolition in 1993, quantitative import restrictions in Kenya were mainly administered through import licensing. The number of import products under licence increased from 228 in 1972 to 2737 in 1985, and in the mid-1980s the Import Management Committee was processing an average of 2000 applications for foreign exchange per week (Dlamini, 1987).

Some progress was made towards relaxation of quantitative restrictions, with an arbitrary mechanism such as the 'no objection' certificate eliminated in June 1980 while import items in the less restrictive categories were increased. The share of quota-free imports increased from about a quarter in

1980 to a half in 1987 (Mwega, 1995). The coverage of the restricted imports dropped from about 15 per cent in 1990/1 to 0.2 per cent in 1991/2 (UNDP/World Bank, 1993).

Reforms in the direct allocation of foreign exchange were continued in the 1990s. In August 1992, a 100 per cent retention scheme for exporters of 'non-traditional' products was introduced; foreign exchange retentions were subsequently extended (at 50 per cent) to coffee and tea (in November 1992) and tourism (in February 1993).[3] The policies on retention accounts and the inter-bank foreign exchange market were reversed in March 1993, however, to contain the inflationary spiral following the floating of the shilling. The government accused the retention account holders of hoarding foreign exchange for speculative purposes when the country faced a serious balance of payments problem.

In May 1993, these reforms were reintroduced with retention at a rate of 50 per cent (later increased to 100 per cent in February 1994) for exporters of both goods and services (so long as the proceeds were utilized or sold within three months, after which they would be sold to the Central Bank at the official rate, before it was unified with the inter-bank rate). Import licences were abolished except for a short list of items that require prior approval for security, environmental and health considerations. Importers were still required, however, to provide documentary evidence of shipments or of actual importation and the sellers' final invoice before commercial banks could make the appropriate payments. In addition, all imports worth over Ksh 100 000 (about US$1800 at the 1996 exchange rate) FOB were still subject to pre-shipment inspection and a clean report of finding issued by an inspection agency approved by the Central Bank. These reforms have been maintained to date.

Direct export promotion policies

By the late 1970s it was generally agreed that the impact of the manufactured export subsidy introduced in 1974 (at 10 per cent of the FOB value of goods manufactured in Kenya with a local value added of at least 30 per cent) was quite limited not least because payments were subject to much delay. In the 1980s, one-third to two-thirds of the total subsidy payments accrued to four firms while the payments comprised only about 5 per cent of manufactured exports; hence the subsidy had minimal incentive value (World Bank, 1990). In effect, the subsidy was treated as a windfall by those few firms that received it rather than an incentive for increased exportation.

A major shortcoming in the management of the manufactured export subsidy scheme was that it experienced numerous changes, making planning by exporters difficult. The rate, for example, was increased from 10 per cent to 20 per cent in 1980. Because of balance of payments problems, however, the entire scheme was suspended in June 1982. It was reintroduced in December 1982 at a rate of 10 per cent with a bonus (incremental) rate of 15 per cent for new exporters and those who increased their exports in the previous year. This bonus rate was abolished in 1985 and the basic rate raised to 20 per cent. In 1986 the items eligible for export compensation were reduced from 2000 to 700, but later they were increased again to 1260. In 1990, exporters were permitted to process their claims through commercial banks to speed up payments while export firms were given the option to claim import duty/VAT exemptions on imported inputs rather than export compensation. The subsidy was eventually abolished in September 1993, to be replaced by an import duty/VAT remission scheme for intermediate inputs.[4]

Other direct export promotion policies have included the following:

- Attempts to strengthen government departments for export promotion and to expedite the handling and processing of the relevant export documents. The 1997–2001 Development Plan argues that export promotion is a government-led activity, which it charges to the Export Promotion Council (EPC) established in 1992. The role of the EPC is to organize and participate in trade fairs and exhibitions, to sponsor contact promotion programmes and sales missions, and to carry out market opportunity surveys.
- Support for regional and multilateral trade arrangements including the Treaty for East African Cooperation (in 1993) and the Common Market for Eastern and Southern Africa (COMESA), the Lagos Plan of Action and the WTO.
- Manufacturing-under-bond (since 1989) whereby production is done exclusively for the export market, simplifying the export documentation processing and facilitating the importation of inputs.
- Establishing export processing zones (EPZs). EPZs were legislated in 1990, and since then 13 EPZs have been gazetted in Nairobi, Mombasa and in Nakuru (1997–2001 Development Plan). Of these, 12 are privately promoted while one at Athi River was developed by the government with World Bank support. Since establishment, 54 manufacturing projects have been approved but only 20 are operational. The EPZs have created 3000 jobs and exports from the zones were valued at US$22.3 million in 1994 and US$23.4 million in 1995. The Plan attributes the relatively poor performance to a shortage of industrial space for rent at the existing facilities.
- A pre-shipment export financing facility was introduced in 1992 but abolished thereafter following massive frauds.

The exchange rate

One objective of economic reforms in Kenya has been to reduce real exchange rate (RER) misalignment – defined as sustained deviations of the actual real exchange rate from the 'equilibrium' real exchange rate (Edwards, 1989).[5] Figure 6.1 shows the evolution of the RER, using both bilateral and multilateral measures thereof; it is fairly successful in representing the salient episodes in the macroeconomic history of Kenya.[6]

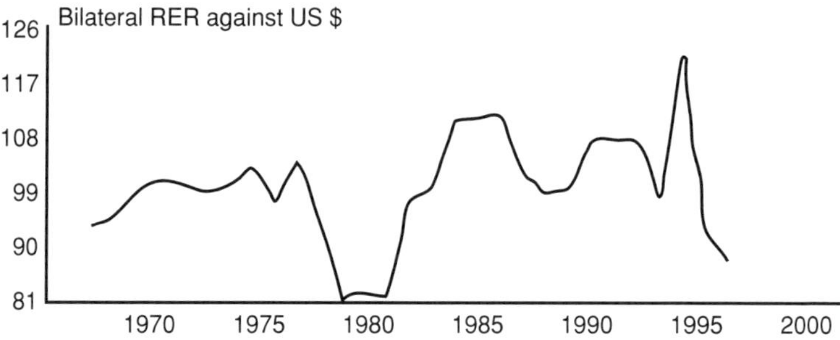

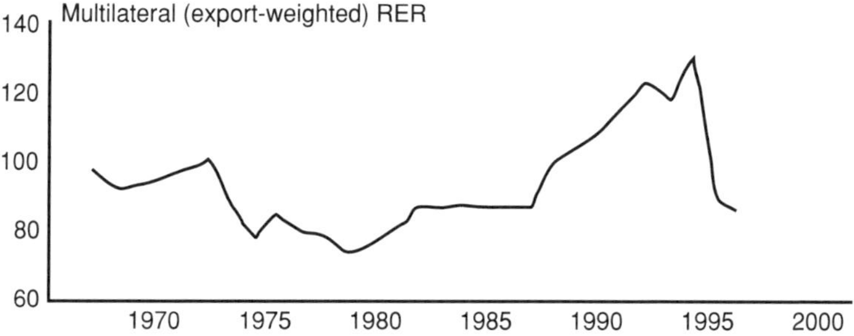

Figure 6.1   Evolution of the RER in Kenya, 1967–95

Between October 1975 and December 1982, the Kenya shilling was pegged to the SDR which, calculated from a basket of currencies, was considered to be relatively more stable than a single currency peg especially following the floating of the US dollar in 1973. During the period of the SDR peg, the shilling was subjected to a number of discretionary devaluations, resulting in relative instability in the RER in the 1977–82 period.

The country employed a crawling peg exchange rate regime in the 1983–91 period in which the exchange rate was adjusted on a daily basis against a composite basket of currencies of the country's main trading partners to reflect inflation differentials between Kenya and these countries. The abandoned SDR peg was considered inadequate to maintain competitiveness of the Kenya shilling because the SDR weights used did not reflect Kenya's trade pattern which is more diversified; the currencies included in the SDR accounted for only 40 per cent of the country's combined exports and imports.

Since 1991, the authorities have adopted a more market-based exchange rate regime (described earlier). It became government policy to make the shilling convertible by fully liberalizing both the current and the capital accounts, with a stable and 'realistic' rate to be maintained through prudent fiscal and monetary policies. On 30 June 1994, the government officially accepted the obligations of Article VIII of the IMF's Articles of Agreement, committing itself to full convertibility of the Kenya shilling at least for current account transactions.

The introduction of the interbank market in August 1992 was accompanied by a massive real depreciation of the shilling in 1993. The real value of the shilling subsequently appreciated in 1994–6.

In a study of the fundamental determinants of the bilateral RER, Mwega and Ndung'u (1996) found that the terms of trade, government expenditure and real economic growth are significantly negatively correlated (at least at the 10 per cent level) with the real value of the currency. Hence government expenditure appears to have been mainly spent on non-tradables while technological progress (proxied by real economic growth) mainly favoured tradables. Using annual data, they also found that the degree of openness and net capital inflows were insignificantly correlated with the RER, perhaps reflecting the fact that Kenya has not undertaken deep reforms. While the real value of the shilling has generally depreciated in the study period the trade ratio shows that the Kenyan economy became less open. The reduction in openness reflects poor export performance, particularly in the 1980s, leading to import compression. Net capital inflows as a proportion of GDP also have declined since the 1980s.[7]

Since the long-run equilibrium level of the RER (ERER) is not observable, it can only be proxied in various ways. One method suggested by Ghura and Grennes (1993) is to estimate the time path of ERER from a cointegration equation. By normalizing it so that it starts from a common base with the actual RER during a period when the economy was to a large extent in internal and external balance, it is possible to estimate the degree of real currency misalignment at different times.

Taking 1970 as a year when Kenya had both internal and external balances (Elbadawi and Soto, 1995), the results showed that the country registered average misalignment of 7.2 per cent in the 1970s, 6.8 per cent in the 1980s and 7.9 per cent in the first half of the 1990s, supporting the contention that Kenya has on average maintained a fairly good foreign exchange rate policy (Takahasi, 1997). (See also Elbadawi, this volume.)

Other policies relevant to export performance

Highly relevant to NTX performance is the limited availability and/or high cost of debt and equity finance. As will be seen below, survey evidence suggests that Kenyan enterprises experience major difficulties in acquiring the finance they require.

In the 1960s and 1970s, the government followed a policy of maintaining low fixed interest rates to promote investment. In the 1980s this policy was changed and the rates were frequently adjusted upwards in an effort to maintain them positive in real terms. They were fully liberalized in July 1991 to allow them to vary with the demand and availability of loanable funds. A major concern through the 1990s was the high level of interest rates, which were pegged to the Treasury Bill rate, which itself remained high as the authorities implemented a tight monetary policy at the same time as the government accumulated a large internal debt (US$2.7 billion in mid-1998). High rates also reflect the oligopolistic nature of the banking system, which is dominated by four banks which control four-fifths of total deposits.[8] These banks focus on short-term lending to finance commerce, mainly foreign trade. As argued by the 1997–2001 Development Plan, 'the short-term nature of their own corporate interests are in conflict with national interests which require longer term commitments and a better appreciation of the needs of the Kenyan economy. Their policies of concentrating on a small corporate clientele have implied indifference or even hostility to small savers and borrowers' (p. 38). The state itself has major interests in two of the major banks.

Development finance institutions (DFIs), on the other hand, have lacked effective statutory powers to raise funds independently and have been dependent on the state for funds. As the government budget has become squeezed, financing of DFIs has lost out. In any case, since they have mainly financed parastatals, they have had limited impact on export performance.[9]

The capital market is still in its infancy, with only 30 per cent of the shares quoted on the Nairobi Exchange. The market for short-term securities continues to be dominated by government paper. Business firms in Kenya rarely raise capital through public issues of equity and debt securities. The main sources of local equity for new investment continue to be retained earnings, savings of family groups, direct government investment and the development banks. For debt finance, parastatals and private firms rely to a large extent on direct borrowing, largely through bank overdrafts.

Another policy with potential adverse consequences for exports was until recently price controls. During their existence, affected producers complained about long delays between application and the grant of a price increase while the cost-plus method applied to determine prices did not fully incorporate differences and changes in input structures. The method also did not encourage firms to reduce their costs of production and to be efficient which is necessary if a firm is to venture into foreign markets. It was therefore argued that price controls impeded entrepreneurship, investment and growth which was likely to outweigh their positive impact on price stability. Price decontrol started in 1987 when 10 products were removed from the price control order. In 1988 another 20 products were price-decontrolled and the process continued so that only thirteen commodities were subject to controls by 1991. All price controls were eventually abolished in December 1993.

Since 1973 the government has also used wage guidelines and the Industrial Court to regulate wages. As a consequence of the pursuit of an active incomes policy, real wages declined drastically in the 1980s and 1990s. Private sector real wages declined at an average rate of 1.2 per cent per year in the 1980s and by 4.4 per cent per annum in 1991–5. Those of the public sector declined even more – by 1.9 per cent per year in the 1980s and by 7.7 per cent per year in 1991–5 (Manda, 1997). Figure 6.2 shows the evolution of average dollar wages in the primary sectors (agriculture, forestry and mining) and in the manufacturing sector. The massive decline in 1991–3 is due to a large nominal depreciation of the exchange rate, while the Kenya shilling wages were fairly constant.

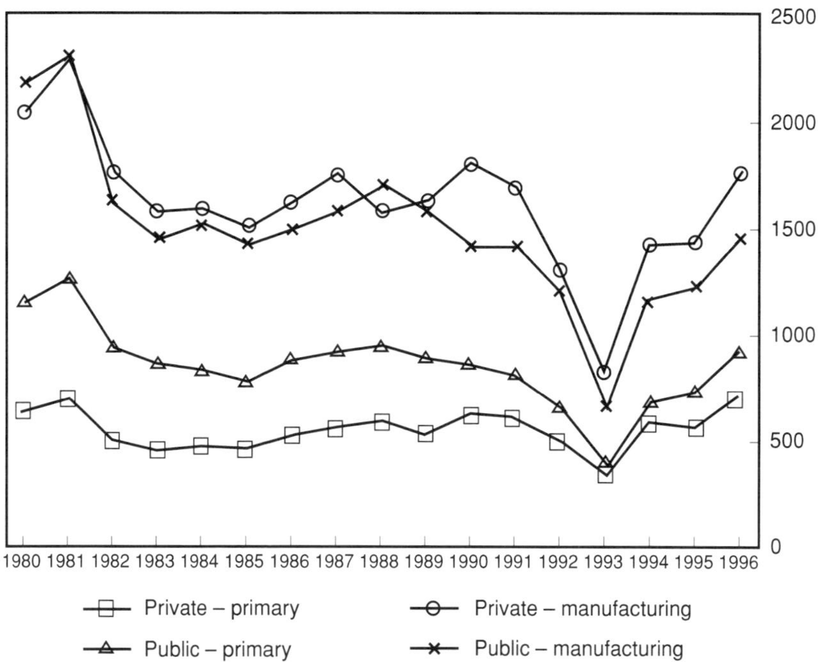

Figure 6.2   Average dollar wages in Kenya's private and public sectors, 1980–96

Merchandise NTX response to policies

NTX performance is likely to be influenced by a whole range of policies and factors. The 1997–2001 Development Plan (8), for example, calls for more outward-oriented policies in order to increase the volume of exports, particularly NTXs. Liberalization of the trade regime through a reduction of the levels and variance of tariffs as well as the tariffication of quantitative restrictions (QRs) is often expected to lead to a diversification of exports as new markets are discovered and new products become exportable. Dynamic effects during the liberalization process caused by resource flows into new exporting firms may increase creativity and innovation, which in turn can result in further diversification. The impact of trade liberalization, however, is likely to depend on the nature of the accompanying policies, particularly a high and stable real exchange rate, compatible fiscal and monetary policies, and low distortions in factor markets (Nogues and Gulati, 1994). It is therefore difficult to empirically verify the causal linkages between trade liberalization and export performance.

In standard analysis, the supply of exports is postulated to be a function of domestic capacity to produce (usually measured by real GDP) and the price of exports relative to other domestic prices (usually proxied by the real exchange rate). It is assumed that Kenya is 'small', hence demand considerations can be omitted from the analysis. To take into account constraints on the input side (particularly the supply of intermediate imports), we also include episodes of trade liberalization in the 1980s and through the 1990s. In an earlier study (Mwega, 1995) we found that a majority of estimated quantitative measures of trade liberalization showed that Kenya experienced trade liberalization in 1980–1, 1983, 1985, 1988–9 and 1993, probably later extending to 1994–6.[10]

To assess the extent to which NTXs have responded to the real exchange rate and trade liberalization policies, the following model was estimated for both primary (SITC 0–4) and manufacturing (SITC 5–8) NTX:

$$\text{RNTX}_t = f(\text{RGDP, RER, trade liberalization episodes, RNTX}_{t-1})$$

where RNTX_t is NTX volume, measured as nominal NTXs deflated by their one-digit SITC category's export price indices; RGDP is real GDP and RER is the bilateral RER. There are likely to be significant feedback effects from exports to RER and RGDP with exports included in the national income. The lagged dependent variable is also correlated with the equation's error terms. These variables were therefore replaced by instrumental variables. The instruments used were lagged values of the endogenous variables, a time trend and the trade liberalization dummies which were taken to be exogenous.

Using recursive least squares (Hendry, 1989), Mwega (1995) investigated for structural breaks in the volume of total primary exports from their trend in 1972–93 using the one-step Chow Test. The results showed there were *no* significant structural breaks from the trend in the exports of Food and Live Animals (SITC 0) and Crude Materials (SITC 2) as well as Mineral Fuels (SITC 1) in the 1980s and 1990s using the one-step Chow Test. There were, however, increased exports (from the trend) of Beverages and Tobacco (SITC 1) in 1983, 1985–6 and 1993; and Animal and Vegetable Oils (SITC 4) in 1993.

His results also suggested that the 1993 trade liberalization episode was particularly good for manufactured exports (SITC 5–8), although other extraneous factors were also important. In the field survey cited above, the increase was dramatic. Of the 19 firms that reported dollar exports over 1992–4, exports increased by 59.2 per cent in 1993 and 152 per cent in 1994. Ten of these firms were exporting for the first time in this period.

Tables 6.14 and 6.15 show the results from estimating the above model for primary and manufactured NTXs using panel data and assuming random effects (after removing a 1992 outlier). The random effects model assumes that there is an overall intercept and some component of the error term that is export-type specific.

First, in both cases, NTXs increase with capacity to produce, with the GDP coefficient positive and significant at least at the 5 per cent level. This however is not a robust result for primary exports as the second equation in Table 6.14 shows.

Table 6.14 Random effects estimate of Kenyan constant price NTX models: primary products (SITC 0–4)

Variable	Coefficient	t-value	Coefficient	t-value
Constant	−7.1778	−0.6869	6.2298	0.8318
Ln RGDP	1.2043	1.9509	0.2628	0.4817
Ln RER	0.2042	0.1313	−0.8919	−1.0500
D83	0.2892	0.9733		
D85	−0.4697	−1.5740		
D88–9	−0.8137	−3.9598		
D93	−0.0512	−0.1189		
D94–5	0.5332	1.6216		
D83–5–8–9			−0.4402	−2.7189
D93–4–5			0.4377	1.8611
$RNTX_{t-1}$	0.4848	12.8387	0.4839	12.7732
Adjusted R^2	0.56		0.55	
Std error	2.11		2.12	
Observations	845		845	

Second, RER coefficients are insignificant at the 5 per cent level. This suggests that RER has not played a significant role in the promotion of NTX in Kenya.[11] This may reflect the fact that RER misalignment in the country has not been large in the study period. Movements in the RER may also not adequately capture changes in the relative price incentives facing Kenyan exporters. Firm-level studies also find that sunk costs are important in determining firms' response to export incentives, implying that even if the exchange rate were to increase profitability the response may be limited unless profitability crosses the threshold at which firms are willing to invest in exporting (Bigsten et al., 1998).

Table 6.15   Random effects estimate of Kenyan constant price NTX models: manufactured products (SITC 5–8)

Variable	Coefficient	t-value	Coefficient	t-value
Constant	−1.9397	−0.3682	0.9424	0.2734
Ln Manuf. RGDP	1.1986	3.8308	0.6608	2.3705
Ln RER	−0.7913	−0.8787	−0.6943	−1.3259
D83	0.0170	0.0963		
D85	0.0938	0.5458		
D88–9	−0.7246	−6.1651		
D93	0.1108	0.4437		
D94–5	0.2001	1.1009		
D83–5–8–9			−0.3832	−4.0582
D93–4–5			0.2543	1.9219
$RNTX_{t-1}$	0.7698	35.4805	0.7719	35.5183
Adjusted R^2	0.59		0.58	
Std error	1.73		1.74	
Observations	1,841		1,841	

Third, the results show that NTXs significantly increased in the liberalization episode of 1993–5. However, both results show a significant decline of NTXs in 1988–9.[12] NTXs did not increase significantly in the trade liberalization episodes of 1983 and 1985 either. (Indeed, primary NTXs significantly fell in the latter year.)

Key constraints to growth of NTX

The results above show that the real exchange rate and trade liberalization (except for the 1993–5 episode) do not seem to have significantly influenced the growth of non-traditional exports. These results may reflect the fact that trade liberalization efforts in the 1980s were not credible and were characterized by reversals (Reinikka, 1994). Even though the trade liberalization episodes in the early and mid-1980s were implemented mainly as part of the policy conditionalities of the World Bank, they faced problems of macro-economic incompatibility and probably time inconsistency as a new government had just taken over (in 1978) when they were initiated in 1980. The 1988–9 episode was also perceived to be macro-incompatible as aid flows contracted and compensating devaluation was delayed. Tariffication of QRs and reduction of tariffs were also undermined by loopholes in the tariff law, import duty avoidance, and illegal importation.

In Kenya, foreign direct investment (FDI) has played only a limited role in strengthening export capabilities. As seen in Table 6.16, FDI and net long-term capital inflows as a proportion of GDP have declined in the study period. The FDI/GDP ratio declined from 1.37 per cent in 1980 to 0.03 per cent in 1993 before increasing to 0.35 per cent in 1995. FDI also has declined in absolute terms when compared to the levels obtaining in the late 1970s.

Table 6.16 Balance of Payments and Investment, Kenya, 1980–96 (%)

Year	Current account/ GDP	Net capital inflows/ GDP		Gross investment/ GDP	FDI/GDP
		Long-term	Short-term		
1980	−12.3	8.0	1.7	29.3	1.37
1981	−10.8	5.9	1.6	27.8	0.15
1982	−7.4	3.9	0.5	21.8	0.06
1983	−2.2	3.3	0.7	20.8	0.17
1984	−2.9	3.1	0.7	20.7	0.07
1985	−1.5	−0.8	0.4	25.5	0.22
1986	−0.6	1.4	0.4	21.8	0.39
1987	−6.2	4.0	0.7	24.3	0.51
1988	−5.4	3.9	0.7	25.0	−0.02
1989	−7.1	7.4	0.6	24.9	0.74
1990	−5.4	2.0	1.7	23.7	0.63
1991	−2.8	1.7	0.0	20.7	0.22
1992	−1.2	−2.0	−0.1	16.9	0.08
1993	1.7	0.8	5.4	17.6	0.03
1994	1.5	−3.7	3.5	19.3	0.05
1995	−4.5	−0.8	3.6	22.3	0.35
1996	−0.8	−0.7	7.2	21.1	

Source: Kenya, *Economic Survey*, various issues, and a World Bank database for the FDI/GDP data.

This is consistent with the argument by Collier (1996) that economic reforms implemented in African countries are only a necessary (but not sufficient) condition for a significant increase in FDI and export growth because Africa is viewed by investors (both foreign and domestic) as a high risk area, with the perceived high probability of policy reversals a major deterrent to investment. The high level of perceived risk partly reflects the long history of utilization of economic controls in the region. This is compounded by poor dissemination to potential investors of information on the conditions in individual African countries and the region in general.

According to Collier (1996), it should be a high priority of a reforming government to accelerate the reduction of the perceived risks by establishing and utilizing policy lock-in mechanisms or 'agents of restraint', both domestic (e.g. export lobby groups, an independent central bank, use of a cash budget, balanced budget constitutional amendments, etc.) and external (WTO, reciprocal trade arrangements, the Multilateral Investment Guarantee Agency (MIGA) and associated insurance agents, currency convertibility, etc.) to signal their determination to implement reforms, for example by extending and deepening them even when foreign aid is not forthcoming in order to establish reputation and credibility of their policies.

Table 6.16 also shows that net long-term capital inflows have declined from 8 per cent of GDP in 1980 to an average of negative net flows in the

1990s, so that they have not been able to cover the deficit in the current account. The rate of domestic investment has also declined from 29.3 per cent in 1980 to 16.9 per cent in 1992 before partially recovering to 21.1 per cent in 1996.

The ability of exporters to respond to exchange rate and trade liberalization policies will also depend on non-price variables. Jebuni et al. (1992) identify several of these. First is availability of finance. Producing for export requires access to finance for working capital, including pre-shipment activities, as well as to expand production to enhance export capabilities. Export credit insurance is also important since it helps exporters gain confidence in tapping new markets. Kenya does not provide either export credit or insurance guarantee facilities.

In Kenya's Regional Programme on Enterprise Development (RPED) survey, a large proportion of firms (80 per cent) mentioned lack or costs of financing their operations and expansion as a moderate to a major obstacle. Lack of credit, for example, was ranked ahead of lack of demand, infrastructure and business support services as a major constraint to firm expansion. An analysis of this survey concludes that collateral borrowing did not work well so that access to debt is restricted for nearly all groups of firms, particularly the very small ones (Departments of Economics, 1994). One of the recommendations is strengthening and expanding property rights such that owners can transfer real property without the permission of the Land Control Boards; these boards can veto the transfer of land to a bank after a borrower's failure to repay a loan, creating uncertainty in the loan recovery process.

The second constraint is infrastructural inadequacies with respect to transportation, water, electric power, waste disposal, security and telephones as well as availability of secure, reasonably priced storage and warehousing facilities at ports. In the RPED survey, only 31 per cent of the firms felt unaffected by infrastructural problems. In the face of poor delivery of these services, many firms take recourse to self-provision of some of these infrastructural services such as electricity, water and security arrangements, thereby reducing their competitiveness.

The third constraint is lack of access to external markets arising from ignorance, lack of agents abroad, the high cost of operating in foreign markets, lack of interest (and experience) to sell abroad given the availability of a fairly protected domestic market; and the poor quality of products.

The fourth constraint is an adverse regulatory environment with respect to ownership of firms, tax structures, investment, labour regulations, licensing and registration procedures, obstacles to exit as well as price controls (Departments of Economics, 1994). However, these have undergone rapid liberalization through the 1990s.

These constraints would need to be addressed to make NTX more successful, besides maintaining appropriate trade, macroeconomic and exchange rate policies.

Performance of manufactured exports: results of a 1995 industrial survey

Some indication as to the characteristics and constraints of non-traditional exporters may be gleaned from our 1995 survey of Kenyan manufacturers (all in Nairobi) which devoted particular attention to export activity.[13] (Recall that over 60 per cent of Kenyan merchandise NTXs in the 1990s are manufactured products.)

About one-fifth (17.4 per cent) of the firms were foreign-owned. Ethnically, 63 per cent were owned by Asians, 17.4 per cent by Africans, 17.4 per cent by Europeans and 2.2 per cent by Middle Easterners. Kenya was the country of origin of 69.6 per cent of the owners. Exporters of manufactured products were therefore mainly Asians with already established firms. Firms in the sample were all established between 1920 and 1991, before the major reforms of the 1990s.

By the design of the survey, about one-third of the firms had zero export orientation, i.e. they sold their output exclusively in the domestic market. The rest exported 2–80 per cent of their output. On average, about one-fifth (21.7 per cent) of these firms' output was exported. Exporting firms were larger in size (average 173 workers and sales of Ksh 265 million) than non-exporting firms (average 60 workers and sales of Ksh 47 million).

These findings are consistent with the results from a survey undertaken for the RPED over 1991–4. The export orientation of exporting firms (26 per cent of the total sample) in the first round was 28 per cent. This varied from 28 to 29 per cent for large and medium firms to 12 per cent for micro firms so that most of the exporting appeared to be done by large and medium-sized firms. Bigsten et al. (1998) find that most (71 per cent) of the large firms in the RPED survey export; hence the problem is not enabling them to *enter* the external markets but understanding why they export relatively so little – on average, less than 30 per cent of their output.[14] The export orientation of exporting firms in Kenya varied from 54 per cent in the food sector, to 27 per cent in furniture, 30 per cent in garments, 17 per cent in metals, 18 per cent in textiles and 15 per cent in wood.

An important issue discussed earlier is the sources of NTX growth and whether there is evidence of new investment. The share of firms reporting new investments in the 1995 survey increased from 40.6 per cent in 1990 to 55 per cent in 1994. Real gross fixed capital formation (GFCF) (nominal GFCF deflated by the CPI) by these firms increased by 3.5 per cent in 1991, 37.1 per cent in 1992, 96.8 per cent in 1993 and 22 per cent in 1994, perhaps reflecting the oversampling of exporting firms.

Apart from new investments, increased exports were also made possible by utilizing the firms' excess capacity.[15] Of the reporting firms, exporting firms had substantially less excess capacity (44.8 per cent) on a one-shift basis than non-exporting firms (61.1 per cent). Overall, 85 per cent of the firms were operating below capacity, and cited, as explanations, lack of demand (71.7

per cent), high cost of credit (34.2 per cent), machinery that was too old (18.4 per cent), shortages of raw materials (18.4 per cent), lack of credit facilities (15.8 per cent), expensive labour (13.2 per cent), shortage of foreign exchange (7.9 per cent) and other factors such as 'dumping' (58.3 per cent). Of the firms, 82.2 per cent were operating one shift, 10.9 per cent two shifts and 6.5 per cent three shifts.

On expectations about the future, about three-quarters of the non-exporting firms hoped to export in the future and the same proportion expected the number of their full-time employees to increase by about half in three years. The majority either had no clear expectations or did not expect adverse developments in the main policy variables. Of those who expected changes, only in the case of expected reductions in regional trade barriers did more than 10 per cent of the respondents expect adverse effects on their output or the number of full-time employees within one to three years.

More than 90 per cent of Kenya's manufactured exports are sold in Africa and the Middle East. Our survey was therefore also concerned about trade barriers within the regional (COMESA) market. All exporting firms sold in the region. The trade was imbalanced, however, with only about one-fifth of the reporting firms sourcing raw material imports from the region, either partially (20 per cent) or fully (2.5 per cent). Only about one-third reported increased competition from imports from within the region compared to about two-thirds from outside the region. They also reported less competition in export trade from within the region (53.3 per cent) than from outside (70 per cent).

Only about one-third of the reporting respondents said there were barriers to exporting to the region and about one-quarter to importing from within the region. More (60.9 per cent) said that it was easy to establish links within the region and that they were competitive with other firms with respect to labour costs (93.5 per cent), availability of capital (78.3 per cent) and production costs (86.2 per cent). The main barriers to exports were seen as high tariffs (53.3 per cent), export licensing arrangements (50 per cent), and 'others' such as government bureaucracy, breakages during transportation, pre-shipment inspection, re-export restrictions, infrastructure and political problems (72.7 per cent). A majority reported as 'important' or 'very important': reductions in regional tariffs, general tariffs and changes in investment rules and licensing. One major reason for the little intra-PTA (Preferential Trade Agreement)/COMESA trade is the limited diversity of the products that members produce.

Conclusions

This chapter has analysed the experience of Kenya in developing NTXs in the 1980s and 1990s. It has looked at the key components of NTXs and the main constraints to diversifying the country's export basket.

The chapter first examined the initial conditions and national characteristics relevant for export performance as well as macroeconomic performance in the 1980s and 1990s and then defined and categorized NTXs. It utilized a broad definition of non-traditional exports to include merchandise exports accounting for less than 3 per cent of total exports in the base year (1980) plus non-factor service exports (including tourism). Non-traditional merchandise exports are therefore defined as those exports other than petroleum products, coffee, tea and crude vegetable materials.

The chapter has shown that merchandise NTXs increased faster than traditional exports in the 1980s and 1990s so that the export basket has become more diversified. Both the Gini-Hirschman concentration index and the share of the top three products in total exports declined steadily over time. The share of manufactured exports also increased faster than primary NTXs, especially in the 1990s.

The most important service export is tourism. Gross earnings from foreign travel generally increased to a peak in 1993–5 and declined in 1996–8 for a variety of reasons, mainly internal to Kenya.

The chapter then described some trade, exchange rate and other policies relevant for export performance that have been implemented in the country in the 1980s and 1990s. These include tariffs, which generally declined in the study period; QRs, which were eventually abolished in May 1993; introduction of an export retention scheme since August 1992; direct export promotion policies (the manufactured exports subsidy, institutional reforms, EPZs and manufacturing under bond); exchange rate management; availability of debt and equity finance; and price and wage controls.

The chapter then explored the response of merchandise NTXs to policies and the constraints to their success. Panel data random effects regression results show, first, that NTXs increase with capacity to produce, with the GDP coefficient positive and significant at least for manufactured exports. Second, RER coefficients are non-significant so that the RER has not played much of a role in the promotion of merchandise NTXs in Kenya. This may reflect the fact that RER misalignment has not been large in the study period or that movements in the RER may not adequately capture changes in the relative price incentives facing Kenya exporters. Third, the results show that NTXs only increased significantly in the liberalization episode of 1993–5, perhaps because the liberalization episodes of the 1980s were not credible and were characterized by reversals.

FDI, net capital inflows and domestic investment as a proportion of GDP have declined in the study period. FDI declined from 1.37 per cent in 1980 to 0.03 per cent in 1993 before increasing to 0.35 per cent in 1995, and net capital inflows fell from 8 per cent of GDP in 1980 to an average of negative net flows in the 1990s. Domestic investment declined from 29.3 per cent in 1980 to 16.9 per cent in 1992 before partially recovering to 21.1 per cent in 1996. The surge in exports through the 1990s may therefore be unsustainable.

The ability of exporters to respond to exchange rate and trade liberalization policies will also depend on non-price variables. Four constraints were identified: (i) availability of debt and equity finance; (ii) infrastructural inadequacies with respect to transportation, water, electric power, waste disposal, security and telephones as well as availability of secure, reasonably priced storage and warehousing facilities at ports; (iii) lack of access to external markets arising from ignorance, lack of agents abroad, the high cost of operating in foreign markets, lack of interest (and experience) to sell abroad given the availability of a fairly protected domestic market; as well as the poor quality of products; and (iv) an adverse regulatory environment which, however, has undergone rapid liberalization through the 1990s. These constraints would need to be addressed for improved NTX performance besides the maintenance of appropriate trade, macroeconomic and exchange rate policies.

Notes

1. The government in 1996 set up a Kenya Tourist Board to market the country abroad with strong financial support from the European Union. The objective of the Board is to assist the country to reverse the decline in the tourism industry. However, it only became operational in mid-1998 when it received an allocation of funds from the government budget.
2. Figures for the public sector are not reported because they involve transactions of foreign governments and their interests abroad with residents of Kenya. The item therefore arises from diplomatic service and is largely non-commercial.
3. The statement issued by the government on this, however, did not define 'traditional' exports. One is left to infer that these exports included coffee, tea, (petroleum) and tourism to which the retention scheme was extended later.
4. The elimination of the scheme came after a massive fraud in which Goldenberg International was paid a subsidy of about US$100 million for the exportation of gold and diamonds in which Kenya has no significant deposits. The subsidy was given at a rate of 35 per cent, above the statutory rate of 20 per cent.
5. The equilibrium RER is defined as the rate at which the economy would be at internal and external balance for given sustainable levels of the other variables such as taxes, international prices and technology. The equilibrium RER therefore varies continuously in response to changes in actual and expected economic fundamentals.
6. The RER is estimated as the product of the nominal exchange rate (NER) and foreign wholesale price indices (WPI) divided by the domestic consumer price index (CPI). The NER is measured in shillings per unit of foreign currency. Real currency appreciation is thus measured as a decline in the RER.
7. Kenya experienced substantial short-term net capital inflows after 1992 in response to an increase in interest rate differentials and currency depreciation in the context of liberalized financial and foreign exchange markets (Asea and Reinhart, 1996). The impact of such net capital inflows on the real exchange rate is not adequately captured by the Mwega and Ndung'u model which uses low-frequency (annual) data and a long time-horizon (1967–95). The short-term net

capital inflows were also substantially offset by a decline in long-term net capital inflows following the aid embargo of 1992–3.

8. In 1996, Kenya's financial system included 51 commercial banks, 23 non-bank financial institutions (NBFIs), 5 building societies, 39 insurance companies, 3 reinsurance companies, 10 development finance institutions (DFIs), 1 Capital Markets Authority, 20 securities and brokerage firms, 1 stock market, 12 investment advisory firms, 57 hire purchase companies, 13 forex bureaus and 2670 Saving and Credit Cooperative Societies (1997–2001 Development Plan: 36).

9. Kenya has five state-owned DFIs that were expected to provide medium and long-term finance to industry, commerce and agriculture. These are: the Industrial Development Bank established in 1973; the Development Finance Company of Kenya (1963); its subsidiary, the Small Enterprises Finance Company of Kenya (1983); Kenya Industrial Estates; and the Industrial and Commercial Development Corporation (1954) and Agricultural Finance Corporation.

10. Trade liberalization dummies are likely to underestimate the impact on exports due to lags in adjustment. A continuous variable was not used as a whole range of diagnostics which did not move in the same direction were utilized to identify these episodes. These diagnostics included six measures of the implicit tariff index estimated by the domestic producer price of importables divided by their counterpart import price index; three measures of openness (exports, imports and their sum as a proportion of GDP); two measures of import compression, one comparing actual and predicted imports from an import demand equation and another comparing the demand for importables from estimated coefficients *vis-à-vis a priori* more plausible coefficients; and two measures of the real exchange rate, one based on purchasing power parity and the other on the price of tradables divided by the price of non-tradables.

11. Bigsten et al. find a similar result utilizing firm-level data from the RPED survey, and emphasize the need to distinguish responses by firm size, with large firms likely to respond positively and significantly to changes in the real exchange rate.

12. This partly reflects data shortcomings as 1989 export data were available only for the first nine months of the year.

13. The survey covered 46 firms in Nairobi. The sampling frame of the survey was provided by Kenya Industrial Research and Development Institute (KIRDI) *Directory of Kenya's Manufacturing Industries* (1993) and the Ministry of Commerce and Industry *Kenya Export Directory* (1993). Exporting and non-exporting firms were selected in proportion to the overall firm size distribution in the KIRDI directory. Exporting firms were deliberately oversampled and constituted 65.2 per cent of the sample. Among the characteristics of the sample firms: about three-quarters were unlisted companies, with the rest distributed among listed companies and partnerships (17.4 per cent), sole proprietorship (4.3 per cent) and public and private joint companies (4.3 per cent).

14. Bigsten et al. (1998) found that the probability that a firm would be an exporter significantly increased with firm size, location in Nairobi and foreign ownership. Capital intensity, firm age, state ownership and type of industry were not significant influences. The propensity to export was not significantly different between the first and the next two rounds of the survey.

    Their model was less successful in explaining the degree of export orientation among exporting firms. None of the above variables were significant in explaining the percentage of output exported by these firms. The results showed, however,

that the food sector is significantly more likely to export a higher proportion of its output.
15. Information on 'excess capacity' was derived from responses by firms to the question, 'How much more compared to now could you produce with the existing equipment?'

References

Asea, P. K. and Reinhart, C. M. (1996) 'Le Prix de l'Argent: How (Not) to Deal with Capital Inflows', *Journal of African Economies*, Supplement, 5, 3.

Bigsten, A. et al. (1998) 'Exports of African Manufactures: Macro Policy and Firm Behaviour', Centre for the Study of African Economies, mimeo.

Collier, P. (1996) 'The Role of the State in Economic Development: Cross-Regional Experiences', paper presented at the African Economic Research Consortium (AERC) Plenary of December 1996.

Departments of Economics (1994) 'Limitations and Rewards in Kenya's Manufacturing: A Study of Enterprise', Gothenburg University, Sweden, and University of Nairobi, Kenya.

Dlamini, A. T. (1987) 'Management of Foreign Exchange Reserves through Quantitative Controls: the Kenyan Experience', MBA Research Paper, University of Nairobi.

Friedrich-Naumann-Stiftung (1992) *Blueprint for a New Kenya: Post Election Programme*, Nairobi.

Edwards, S. (1989) *Real Exchange Rates, Devaluation and Adjustment*, Cambridge, MA: MIT Press.

Elbadawi, I. A. and Soto, R. (1995) 'Real Exchange Rate and Macroeconomic Adjustment in Sub-Saharan Africa and other Developing Countries', paper presented at an AERC Workshop, Johannesburg, December 1995.

Elbadawi, I. and Schmidt-Hebbel, K. (1996) 'Macroeconomic Policies, Instability and Growth in the World', paper presented at the AERC Plenary of December 1996.

Ghura, D. and Grennes, T. J. (1993) 'The Real Exchange Rate and Macroeconomic Performance in Sub-Saharan Africa', *Journal of Development Economics*, 42: 155–74.

Hendry, D. F. (1989) 'PC-GIVE: An Interactive Econometric Modelling System', Institute of Economics and Statistics and Nuffield College, University of Oxford.

Jebuni, C. D., Oduro, A., Asante, Y. and Tsikata, G. K. (1992) 'Diversifying Exports: The Supply Response of Non-Traditional Exports to Ghana's Economic Recovery Programme', ODI Research Reports, Overseas Development Institute.

Landell-Mills, J. and Katz, M. (1991) 'Kenya – The Evolution of the External Competitiveness of the Tradables Goods Sector Since 1972', mimeo.

Manda, D. M. (1997) 'Labour Supply, Returns to Education, and the Effect of Firm Size on Wages: The Case of Kenya', Ekonomiska Studier Utgivna av Nationalekonomiska Institutionen Handlshögskolan vid Göteborg Universitet 75.

Mayer, J. (1996) 'Implications of the New Trade and Endogenous Growth Theories for Diversification Policies of Commodity-Dependent Countries', UNCTAD/OSG/DP/122, December.

Mosley, P. (1991) 'Kenya', in P. Mosley et al. (eds), *Aid and Power: The World Bank and Policy-Based Lending*, London: Routledge.

Mwega, F. M. (1995) 'Trade Liberalization, Credibility and Impact: The Case of Kenya, 1972–94', report prepared for the AERC Collaborative Project on 'Trade Liberalization and Regional Integration in Sub-Saharan Africa', mimeo.

Mwega, F. M. and Ndung'u, N. S. (1996) 'Macroeconomic Policies and Exchange Rate Management: the Kenya Case', mimeo.

Nogues, J. and Gulati, S. (1994) 'Economic Policies and Performance Under Alternative Trade Regimes: Latin America During the 1980s', mimeo.

Reinikka, R. (1994) 'How to Identify Trade Liberalization Episodes: an Empirical Study on Kenya', Working Paper Series/94.10, Centre for the Study of African Economies.

Syrquin, M. (1992) 'Growth and Industrialization since 1965', in G. K. Helleiner (ed.), *Trade Policy and Industrialization in Turbulent Times*, London: Routledge.

Sharpley, J. and Lewis, S. R. (1988) 'Kenya's Industrialization, 1964–84', Discussion Paper No. 242, Institute of Development Studies, Sussex.

Takahasi, M. (1997) 'Changing Rules of the Game in a Multi-Ethnic Sub-Saharan African Country: Economic Resource Mechanism in Kenya', paper presented at a Workshop on Political Economy of Rural Development Strategy at the World Bank, 5–6 May 1997.

UNDP/World Bank (1993) *Kenya: The Challenge of Promoting Exports*, Washington, DC: World Bank.

World Bank (1990) *Kenya: Stabilization and Adjustment: Towards Accelerated Growth*, Washington, DC: World Bank.

World Bank (1996) *World Development Report*, Washington, DC: World Bank.

World Tourism Organization (1995) *International Tourism Overview: A Special Report*.

7

The Role of Non-Traditional Exports in Mauritius

Beealasingh Dabee

Introduction

Mauritius is a very small and remote island[1] with no exploitable resources. It depended, up to the 1960s, almost entirely on one agricultural commodity – sugar – for all its export earnings and also for the bulk of its employment and income. The economy in fact stagnated during the 1960s, incapable of generating employment opportunities for about 20 per cent of its labour force which was estimated to be unemployed. This seemed to give credence to Meade's view that Mauritius would find it difficult to deal with its Malthusian problem (Meade, 1961, 1967). As from the 1970s, however, the economy started to undergo significant structural transformation following the establishment of an export processing zone producing labour-intensive manufactured goods. The Mauritian export processing zone (MEPZ) expanded rapidly and was largely responsible for the attainment of full employment in the late 1980s. In 1997, it accounted for 12.3 per cent of the GDP, 70 per cent of commodity exports and about 20 per cent of employment. The tourist industry, which also emerged in the 1970s, has equally expanded significantly over the past three decades. Although its contribution to GDP (about 4.5 per cent in 1997) is relatively more modest than that of the MEPZ, the industry has considerably strengthened the export orientation of the economy. As from 1994, its gross foreign exchange earnings have consistently exceeded those of the sugar industry. Furthermore, as from 1992, the establishment of an offshore banking and business centre and of a free port has given a boost to earnings from exports of services.

The Mauritian economy has maintained an average real growth rate of 5.8 per cent over the period 1970–97, transforming itself from a monocrop economy to an industrializing economy. Its GDP per capita has risen from US$270 in 1970 to US$3640 in 1997. This performance has been commended by international institutions (see, for example, World Bank, 1989, 1992) and has been analysed by various studies which have tried to explain why the development strategy adopted by Mauritius has been successful (Kearney, 1990; Romer, 1993). Other studies have looked more specifically at the performance of the MEPZ and the special factors behind its success (Hein, 1989; Alter, 1990). This chapter is more in line with the latter studies. It tries to evaluate the performance of non-traditional exports, including MEPZ exports, using the framework agreed by the African authors in this volume. The rest of the chapter is organized as follows. I start with some background information on the difficulties faced by the Mauritian economy in the 1960s and on its take-off in the 1970s, triggered by the establishment and rapid expansion of the MEPZ. There follows a review of the significant changes which have taken place in the Mauritian economy over the period 1980–97, the period of interest for this volume. These changes include structural changes, the attainment of full employment and the maintenance of macroeconomic balance. I then introduce the three definitions of non-traditional exports used in this chapter, the most important of which is a broad definition which includes MEPZ exports and exports of non-factor services. This is followed by an analysis of overall export performance and, more importantly, by an analysis of non-traditional exports. I then discuss the various policies which have favoured the expansion of the latter exports. Finally, the chapter concludes with a discussion of the major constraints facing the growth of non-traditional exports and the implications of these constraints.

Initial conditions

The Mauritian economy stagnated during the 1960s. Although the GDP at current factor cost grew at an average of 4.1 per cent per annum, the relatively high population growth rate of 2.4 per cent coupled with an inflation rate of 1.7 per cent turned the 1960s into a decade of zero economic growth. Per capita income remained unchanged at about US$200 throughout the 1960s. There were, of course, special reasons for this poor record. The island was visited by a very destructive cyclone in 1960 – the sugar crop was drastically reduced, the physical infrastructure was seriously damaged and thousands were left homeless. Moreover, the latter part of the 1960s witnessed racial riots over the independence issue. Business confidence plunged very low amid the prevailing political uncertainty. Private investment fell gradually as from 1964 and started to pick up only in 1971.

Prospects for future growth and development looked fairly bleak towards the end of the 1960s. The population had doubled to about 850 000 in a record period of 25 years. The increasing labour force could not be absorbed in agriculture as all the arable land had already come under cultivation. About 20 per cent of the labour force was estimated to be unemployed and there were very few new employment opportunities available. Import-substitution industries, which had been actively encouraged during the 1960s, could not significantly contribute to employment creation given the limited size of the domestic market to which their production was geared. To alleviate the rising level of poverty, the government introduced a public works programme whereby four days of work per week were provided to the unemployed so that they would have a source of income; 16 000 persons were absorbed by the programme out of a pool of about 40 000 unemployed. More daunting for policymakers was the task of devising an appropriate long-term strategy for the creation of 130 000 productive jobs by 1980 for the rapidly increasing labour force. The main long-term solution to the unemployment problem was seen to be the establishment of labour-intensive industries geared to the export market. It is in this context that the government, with the collaboration of the private sector, put forward a strategy for the establishment of an export processing zone which was set up in 1970.

The 1970s marked the first decade of sustained economic growth in Mauritius; the economy started to pick up through a combination of favourable exogenous circumstances and growth-enhancing policies. The early years of the decade witnessed a boom in the world sugar market. Favourable climatic conditions at home led to record levels in production and exports. As a result of the windfall gains in export revenues, there was a significant rise in real wages in both the agricultural and non-agricultural sectors, ensuring a steady increase in living standards. The higher profits of the sugar industry allowed Mauritian businessmen to invest in the recently set up MEPZ and also in the emerging tourist sector.

The establishment of the MEPZ is in fact a good example of growth-enhancing policies adopted by the government. Given the limited potential for employment creation in the import-substitution sector, the government actively promoted the creation of an export processing zone which would give priority to labour-intensive manufacturing activities. There was therefore a clear commitment taken by the government to encourage manufactured exports, and a generous package of incentives was proposed to investors in the EPZ Act of 1970. These included complete exemption from payment of import duties on raw materials and equipment, exemption from payment of corporate tax, free repatriation of profits as well as concessionary finance and infrastructure facilities.

The MEPZ made a timid start, with 19 firms operating in the second year of its existence and providing about 2500 jobs. Initially, the firms in the MEPZ were mainly foreign firms, concentrating on diamond polishing, assembly of electronic components and textiles. It is precisely in textiles that businessmen from the sugar industry invested their windfall profits from the boom years. As a result, the MEPZ expanded quite fast over the period 1973–6, with the number of firms increasing from 32 to 85, and employment rising from 5721 to 17 403. MEPZ exports provided 17 per cent of gross foreign exchange earnings in 1976.

The higher export earnings from the sugar boom years led to a very important rise in consumer as well as government expenditures which both, ironically, led to a foreign exchange crisis. As real wages increased in all sectors of the economy, there was a significant upsurge in the demand for imported goods. The government also stepped up its recurrent and capital expenditures as it obtained higher tax revenues and found it relatively easy to borrow from the domestic money market. It also borrowed heavily from overseas as from the early 1970s. Total expenditures in the economy in fact consistently exceeded GDP in spite of a decline in investment. The level of foreign exchange reserves declined very quickly, they were almost completely depleted by August 1979. At the same time, the expansion of the MEPZ slowed down as a result of increasing labour costs. The number of firms increased only by nine from 1976 to 1979. The tourist industry also experienced a setback with the unprecedented increase in fuel costs worldwide in the late 1970s.

Although the 1970s were a decade of relatively high growth, the failure of the government to maintain sound macroeconomic conditions led to a balance of payments crisis in 1979. The assistance of the IMF had to be sought. One of the first measures adopted was the devaluation of the rupee by 23 per cent. To make matters worse, exceptionally unfavourable climatic conditions in 1979 caused a reduction of about 20 per cent in the sugar harvest, leading to a record negative growth rate of –10.1 per cent in 1980.

Recent macroeconomic performance

Even if the main targets of the first two-year stabilization programme could not be achieved because of exceptionally adverse climatic conditions and a new programme had to be agreed upon in 1980, the economy began to recover as from 1983. This was again due to a combination of favourable exogenous conditions and of growth-enhancing policies pursued by the government. The latter policies were in fact adopted as part of the stabilization and adjustment programme which covered the 1979–86 period.[2] Among the exogenous conditions were the improving demand conditions in Europe and the US, to which almost all Mauritian exports were directed. The tourist industry, which depends heavily on European visitors, also began to pick up its momentum. Foreign direct investment (FDI) in the MEPZ rose to a record level following a successful investment promotion campaign in South East Asia. The uncertainty about Hong Kong's political future encouraged some investors to relocate their textile factories in Mauritius. Furthermore, their exports from Mauritius to Europe were allowed duty-free access, under the terms of the Lomé Convention, and were not subject to the restrictions of the Multifibre Agreement (MFA).

The policies adopted by the government during the adjustment period gradually helped to restore a relatively sound macroeconomic balance which has been maintained up to now. The main features of the country's recent macroeconomic performance are summarized in Table 7.1 and are briefly discussed below.

Table 7.1   Selected indicators, Mauritius, 1970–97

	1970–9	1980–4	1985–9	1990–4	1995–7[c]
GNP per Capita at Current Prices (Rs)[a]	7,396	14,055	31,418	56,321	74,827
Growth Rate of Real GDP (%)	6.7	1.4	7.0	5.7	5.7
Population Size (thousands)[a]	935	983	1,023	1,113	1,148
Inflation Rate (%)	10.9	16.2	6.2	8.6	6.4
Savings Rate (%)	23.5	19.5	23.2	24.6	23.8
Investment Rate (%)	26.8	23.4	27.6	29.3	25.9
Real Interest Rate on Deposits (%)	–5.9	–5.8	3.68	2.28	4.09
Value Added in Agriculture (%)	29.3	14.2	13.9	10.6	9.4
Value Added in Manufacturing (%)	8.5	19.1	23.2	23.2	24.1
Exports (Rs million)[a]	2,433	5,179	15,049	24,097	32,890
Tourism Earnings (Rs million)[a]	260	630	2,796	6,415	10,068
Imports (Rs million)[a]	3,634	6,494	20,217	34,548	41,600
Foreign Direct Investment (millions of US$)	3[b]	2	18	22	36
Current Account Deficit/GDP (%)	–2.0	–6.8	–0.1	–2.9	–0.9
Foreign Exchange Reserves (Rs million)[a]	214	557	8,049	14,283	21,443
Import Equivalent (weeks)	3	5	21	22	27
Exchange Rate of US$ (Rs)[a]	6.31	13.80	15.25	17.96	20.56

Notes:
[a] End of period.
[b] Average for 1976–9.
[c] Figures for 1997 are provisional.

Sources: CSO, *Annual Digest of Statistics*, various issues; IMF, *International Financial Statistics Yearbook*, 1998.

Steady increases in real GDP

The real GDP, which had started to rise in the 1970s, continued its upward trend over the 1981–97 period. The annual average growth rate over the latter period was 5.2 per cent. As growth rates were generally positive and sustained over the 1970–97 period, their cumulative effect means that real per capita GDP increased roughly threefold. The GNP per capita, at current prices, rose from a low figure of US$230 in 1970 to US$3640 in 1997.

High saving and investment rates

Capital accumulation has been an important determinant of sustained economic growth in Mauritius since the 1970s. This has been made possible by relatively high saving and investment rates. Over the period 1981–97, the savings rate was 22.9 per cent per annum whereas the investment rate was 25.6 per cent. The higher investment rate was financed by overseas borrowing.

Full employment

Given the high rate of unemployment in the 1960s (estimated at about 20 per cent), a full employment strategy for the year 1980 was adopted as early as 1970, based on the premise that the labour-intensive industries to be established in the MEPZ would mop up all the excess labour in the economy. After a decline in the 1970s, the unemployment rate in fact increased again to about 20 per cent in the early 1980s. It was only in 1983 that employment opportunities began to expand significantly. Full employment (with 2 per cent unemployment) was achieved in the late 1980s and was maintained until around 1995 when unemployment started to rise again, although it was still relatively low at about 5 per cent.

Structural changes

The Mauritian economy was basically a monocrop economy based on sugar up to the 1960s. With the setting up of the MEPZ in 1970, a gradual transformation of the economic structure began to take place. It was accelerated during the 1980s when the value added in manufacturing rose to 23 per cent of GDP, a level at which it has stabilized up to now. The share of agriculture, which was 29.3 per cent in the 1970s, continued to decline over the 1981–97 period, reaching 8.9 per cent in 1997. There was also a concomitant change in the structure of exports. Sugar exports made up only 22 per cent of total exports in 1997, with the share of EPZ exports rising to 70 per cent.

Sustainable current account deficits

The current account typically shows deficits since the 1970s. However, in sharp contrast with the adjustment period of 1979–86, the more recent years show sustainable deficits of less than 1 per cent of GDP. The relatively higher deficit of 2.9 per cent shown for the period 1990–4 was in fact due to the relatively high expenditures incurred in the purchase of one ship and one aircraft. Payment was spread over the financial years 1989/90 to 1994/5. The current account deficits are completely offset by private and official capital flows, leading to an increase in foreign exchange reserves. It may be noted that current and capital transactions have been fully liberalized since the early 1990s.

Increasing foreign exchange reserves

The level of foreign exchange reserves, which had fallen to US$15 million (equivalent to two weeks of imports) in 1979, started to rise steadily during the 1979–86 adjustment period. They reached US$1043 million (equivalent to six months of imports) at the end of 1997. This was achieved in spite of the persistent deficit in the trade balance over the 1970–97 period.

Export performance

Three definitions of non-traditional exports are used in this chapter – a national definition, the World Bank definition and the project definition (NTX1, NTX2, NTX3, respectively; see Chapter 1). There is no official definition of non-traditional exports in Mauritius, but given that the country's exports consisted almost exclusively of three goods – sugar, molasses (a byproduct of sugar) and tea – before the adoption of an industrialization strategy based on manufactured exports in the early 1970s, it seems appropriate to identify all exports other than sugar, molasses and tea as non-traditional exports. These are denoted as NTX1 and refer essentially to MEPZ exports. The second (World Bank) definition excludes the top (ten or more) three-digit SITC exports accounting for 75 per cent of total exports in 1980 and considers the remaining three-digit exports as non-traditional exports. In the case of Mauritius, however, the top two export items (SITC 061 – Sugar, molasses and honey; and SITC 845 – Outer garments, other) accounted respectively for 68 per cent and 11.3 per cent of total exports; so that non-traditional exports, according to the World Bank usage, can refer to all three-digit export items other than SITC 061 and SITC 845. These are denoted as NTX2. The number of export commodities included in NTX2 rises significantly from 122 in 1980 to 172 in 1997. Finally, the project definition of non-traditional exports, NTX3, includes two components: (a) all three-digit export items accounting each for less than 3 per cent of total exports in 1980, and (b) exports of non-factor services. The first component is in fact NTX2 in the case of Mauritius so that the project definition simply adds exports of non-factor services to NTX2.

The relationship between NTX1, NTX2 and NTX3 is easy to understand in the case of Mauritius. NTX1 refers to all three-digit exports other than SITC 061 and SITC 074 (Tea and mate). NTX2 covers all exports other than SITC 061 and SITC 845. As exports of tea have declined significantly from 1.3 per cent of total exports in 1980 to only 0.04 per cent in 1997, we may ignore SITC 074 and simply think of NTX1 as including SITC 845 and of NTX2 as excluding SITC 845, a dynamic export item whose share of total exports has risen steadily from 11.3 per cent in 1980 to 29.2 per cent in 1997; thus, NTX1 = NTX2 + SITC 845. And, as we have already indicated above, NTX3 = NTX2 + exports of non-factor services.

Export trends and growth rates

Table 7.2 shows 1980–97 data on total exports (X), NTX1, NTX2 and NTX3, expressed in millions of US dollars. As expected, NTX2 is the smallest series for non-traditional exports given that it excludes exports of garments (SITC

845 – Outer garments, other) which were non-existent before 1970 and which today have attained 29.2 per cent of total commodity exports. NTX3 turns out to be the largest series as it includes earnings from the tourist sector which has expanded significantly since the 1980s. Table 7.2 also shows various ratios of exports to GDP which all confirm the increasing importance of trade for the Mauritian economy. They are also an indication of the increasing openness of the economy as from the 1980s.

Table 7.2 GDP, total exports, non-traditional exports and export ratios, Mauritius, 1980–97

	GDP and exports (millions of US$)					*Export ratios (%)*			
Year	*GDP*	*X*	*NTX1*	*NTX2*	*NTX3*	*X/GDP*	*NTX1/GDP*	*NTX2/GDP*	*NTX3/GDP*
1980	1,132	435	134	90	236	38	12	8	21
1981	1,142	336	136	80	255	29	12	7	22
1982	1,078	367	128	84	226	34	12	8	21
1983	1,090	368	126	86	223	34	12	8	21
1984	1,028	375	170	125	254	37	17	12	25
1985	1,076	430	227	158	304	40	21	15	28
1986	1,458	673	395	286	499	46	27	20	34
1987	1,884	893	543	381	703	47	29	20	37
1988	2,136	1,002	656	447	828	47	31	21	39
1989	2,185	987	652	438	845	45	30	20	39
1990	2,642	1,184	821	530	1,053	45	31	20	40
1991	2,832	1,195	845	533	1,099	42	30	19	39
1992	3,193	1,301	913	588	1,198	41	29	18	38
1993	3,200	1,303	965	625	1,191	41	30	20	37
1994	3,503	1,342	1,011	669	1,302	38	29	19	37
1995	3,967	1,539	1,164	754	1,564	39	29	19	39
1996	4,299	1,765	1,291	804	1,765	41	30	19	41
1997	4,173	1,606	1,246	783	1,701	38	30	19	41

Sources: CSO, *Annual Digest of Statistics*, various issues; IMF, *International Financial Statistics Yearbook*, 1998.

Table 7.3 shows two sets of growth rates for total exports and for non-traditional exports. The first set is based on the value of exports expressed in millions of US dollars already shown in Table 7.2. A better picture is obtained by considering the growth rates of real exports. These are shown as the second set of figures in Table 7.3. It is very clear that non-traditional exports expanded most significantly over the period 1984–90. This period in fact witnessed an exceptionally high rate of expansion of the MEPZ and it also saw a rapid development of the tourist sector. This explains the relatively higher growth rates of NTX1 and NTX2 over the period 1984–90. For the period 1981–97 as a whole, NTX1 and NTX2 expanded much faster on average at annual rates of 12.4 per cent and 12.2 per cent respectively compared to NTX3 which grew at 10.3 per cent. And NTX1, NTX2 as well as NTX3 grew much faster than total exports, which rose by an average of 6.2 per cent per annum.

Table 7.3   Growth rates of current exports and of real exports, Mauritius, 1981–97

	Current exports[a]				Real exports[b]			
Year	*X*	*NTX1*	*NTX2*	*NTX3*	*X*	*NTX1*	*NTX2*	*NTX3*
1981	−22.8	1.7	−11.7	8.2	−19.1	6.6	−7.4	13.4
1982	9.3	−5.8	5.9	−11.2	22.3	5.4	18.4	−0.7
1983	0.4	−1.8	2.2	−1.3	−0.4	−2.5	1.5	−2.0
1984	1.9	35.2	44.9	13.9	11.8	48.4	59.1	25.0
1985	14.6	33.7	26.6	19.5	18.4	38.1	30.8	23.5
1986	56.4	73.7	81.1	64.0	26.3	40.2	46.2	32.4
1987	32.6	37.7	33.1	40.9	13.6	17.9	14.0	20.7
1988	12.2	20.8	17.4	17.7	5.7	13.7	10.5	10.8
1989	−1.5	−0.6	−2.0	2.1	0.7	1.7	0.2	4.4
1990	20.0	25.8	21.0	24.6	6.2	11.3	7.0	10.3
1991	0.9	2.9	0.5	4.4	−1.1	0.9	−1.5	2.4
1992	8.9	8.1	10.4	9.0	2.2	1.5	3.6	2.3
1993	0.2	5.6	6.3	−0.5	5.1	10.8	11.5	4.3
1994	3.0	4.8	7.0	9.3	−2.1	−0.4	1.7	3.8
1995	14.7	15.2	12.8	17.7	5.8	6.3	4.0	8.6
1996	14.7	10.9	6.6	15.2	11.5	7.8	3.7	12.0
1997	−9.0	−3.5	−2.7	−3.6	−2.5	3.4	4.3	3.3
Average for 1981–97	9.2	15.6	15.3	11.3	6.2	12.4	12.2	10.3

Notes:
[a] Growth rates calculated from exports expressed in millions of US dollars.
[b] Calculated from exports (in millions of rupees) deflated by GDP deflator with base year 1990.

Sources: CSO, *Annual Digest of Statistics*, various issues; IMF, *International Financial Statistics Yearbook*, 1998.

Composition of exports

As we have already indicated, the exports of Mauritius consisted essentially of exports of sugar, tea and molasses up to the 1960s. For the decade as a whole, sugar accounted for 92.1 per cent of total exports, with molasses and tea contributing 2.6 per cent and 1.9 per cent respectively. Following the setting up of the MEPZ in 1970 and the rapid expansion of manufactured exports, the contribution of sugar to total exports declined steadily to 22.1 per cent in 1997. MEPZ exports currently provide a little over three times as much gross foreign exchange earnings as sugar exports.

The composition of non-traditional exports is shown in Table 7.4. NTX1 and NTX2 refer essentially to MEPZ exports. As shown in the table, throughout the period 1980–97 there is a heavy concentration of clothing and textile exports which made up about 75 per cent of MEPZ exports. An additional 10 per cent of MEPZ exports is provided by a limited number of products – optical goods, toys, games, jewellery, fish and fish preparations. NTX3 is dominated by exports of tourist services. As the tourist sector has maintained a steady rate of growth over recent years, unlike the MEPZ, NTX3 is likely to become the most important aggregate for non-traditional exports.

Direction of exports

Up to the 1960s, about 75 per cent of total exports were directed to the UK alone. With the setting up of the MEPZ in 1970, manufactured exports began to be shipped to other European countries – mainly France, Germany and Italy – as well as to the US from the 1980s. A high level of concentration on these markets still persists today. In 1980, 91.2 per cent of total exports were directed to Europe and 4.9 per cent to the US. While the share of exports going to Europe declined to 76.4 per cent and that of the US increased to 13.7 per cent in 1996, the combined share of exports to Europe and the US declined marginally from 96.2 per cent in 1980 to 90 per cent in 1996.

Exports are heavily concentrated on Europe because of various trade preferences obtained by Mauritius. Sugar exports are sold at a guaranteed price under the terms of the Sugar Protocol and all other exports have duty-free access under the Lomé Convention. This latter preference has allowed the MEPZ to expand significantly over the past three decades. And, as from the 1980s, the MEPZ began to take advantage of preferential access to the US under the general system of preferences (GSP). It is therefore easy to understand why exports to Africa have been negligible. Up to the end of the 1980s, exports to African countries accounted for less than 1 per cent of total exports. However, as from the mid-1990s, exports to the COMESA/SADC (Southern African Development Community) countries began to increase, rising to about 2 per cent of total exports in 1997.

Performance of the Mauritian export processing zone

As we have already seen, the non-traditional exports included in NTX1 refer essentially to MEPZ exports. The latter in fact accounted for an average of 95 per cent of NTX1 over the period 1980–97, and their share of NTX2 was 90 per cent on average over the same period. Of course, as NTX3 includes MEPZ exports as well as exports of non-factor services which are becoming almost as important as MEPZ exports, the ratio of MEPZ exports to NTX3 was much lower at 55 per cent. But MEPZ exports still predominate in all three definitions of non-traditional exports. It would be useful to discuss MEPZ exports separately as they have dramatically transformed the Mauritian economy in the 1970s and 1980s. An analysis of the more recent

Table 7.4   Composition of non-traditional exports, Mauritius, 1980–97 (percentages)

Selected components		NTX1					NTX2					NTX3				
Commodities	SITC codes	1980	1985	1990	1995	1997	1980	1985	1990	1995	1997	1980	1985	1990	1995	1997
1a Clothing	841–4, 846–8	18.5	36.5	22.1	35.1	34.6	27.5	52.4	34.2	54.1	55.1	10.5	27.3	17.2	26.7	25.3
1b Clothing	845	36.6	35.7	34.4	35.3	37.2	n/a	n/a	n/a	n/a	n/a	n/a	n/a	n/a	n/a	n/a
2 Textiles	651–659	5.5	2.5	3.7	5.6	6.4	8.2	3.5	5.7	8.7	10.2	3.1	1.8	2.8	4.3	4.7
3 Optical Goods, Watches and Clocks	884, 885	3.6	6.5	6.1	3.5	2.6	5.3	9.4	9.5	5.3	4.2	2.0	4.9	4.8	2.6	1.9
4 Toys, Games	894	1.6	1.3	1.0	1.0	0.6	2.3	1.8	1.6	1.6	1.0	0.9	1.0	0.8	0.8	0.5
5 Jewellery	897	1.9	1.7	1.2	1.1	1.4	2.8	2.4	1.8	1.8	2.2	1.1	1.3	0.9	0.9	1.0
6 Fish & Fish preparations	034–7	4.0	4.1	1.3	3.2	3.6	5.9	5.8	2.0	4.9	5.7	2.2	3.0	1.0	2.4	2.6
7 Tourism Earnings	n/a	n/a	n/a	n/a	n/a	n/a	n/a	n/a	n/a	n/a	n/a	18.0	20.0	23.2	24.1	28.8
8 Transportation	n/a	n/a	n/a	n/a	n/a	n/a	n/a	n/a	n/a	n/a	n/a	24.8	20.9	18.7	13.9	13.0

Source: Computed from data provided by the CSO.

performance of the MEPZ can be contrasted with its past performance which has been evaluated by various studies. What follows is a brief review of the performance of the MEPZ over the period 1980–97, followed by a discussion of the contribution of exports of non-factor services. The analysis of the latter exports will be less comprehensive given that the data available are relatively more limited. For the MEPZ, however, a comprehensive range of data is available, summarized in Table 7.5.

The stabilization and adjustment period, which lasted from 1979 to 1986, provided an important stimulus to the expansion of the MEPZ. The number of firms as well as employment increased roughly threefold over a short period of six years (1983–8). This period also saw the highest growth rates of real value added and real exports which the MEPZ experienced over the period 1980–97. The rapid increase in employment, real value added and real exports were accompanied by a marked rise in real investment. As the level of unused capacity tends to be low or negligible in the MEPZ, and as production is meant for export, it can be argued that the main source of growth of MEPZ exports, on the supply side, was the additional investment undertaken.

The performance of the MEPZ in the 1990s is in very sharp contrast with its performance in the 1980s, especially with the 1983–8 period. The number of enterprises declined steadily from 564 in 1992 to stabilize around 480 over the 1995–7 period. This decline is mainly due to the fall in the number of enterprises in the clothing sector. With the increasing liberalization of world trade in textiles and clothing, some firms in the MEPZ are unable to withstand the international competition and have to close down. The declining level of employment from 87 317 in 1992 to 79 447 in 1996 is mainly due to the closure of clothing firms in the MEPZ. However, many firms are adapting to the competition by upgrading their technology and moving to higher value added products. Their efforts are showing positive results as employment has started to rise in the clothing sector. The increase in employment in 1997 by about 4000 was due mainly to increasing employment in the clothing sector. This increase occurred in spite of some relocation of labour-intensive production processes to Madagascar, where labour costs are much lower.

In spite of the recent decline in the number of enterprises and employment, real value added and real exports continued to rise. However, value added stabilized at around 12 per cent of GDP since 1990. This contrasts with the threefold increase which took place over the 1980–9 period when value added increased from 4.3 per cent to 12.3 per cent. The implication is that whereas the MEPZ was growing three times faster than the rest of the economy over the period 1980–9, thereafter grew at the same rate as the rest of the economy. Value added in the MEPZ in fact grew only at 6 per cent since 1990. Real MEPZ exports kept on increasing steadily from 1980. However, the ratio of MEPZ exports to total exports stabilized at

Table 7.5   Selected indicators for the Mauritian EPZ, 1980–97

Year	No. of enterprises (September)	Employment (September)	Growth of employment (%)	Value added/GDP (%)	Real value added[a] (Rs million)	Growth of real value added (%)	Real value added per worker (Rs)	Real exports[a] (Rs million)	Growth of real exports (%)	Real exports per worker (Rs)	Real net exports[a] (Rs million)	Real investments[a] (Rs million)	Growth of real investment (%)
1980	112	21,113	–	4.3	799	–	37,821	2,225	–	105,391	588	*	*
1981	112	22,406	6.1	4.8	944	18.2	42,129	2,437	9.5	108,785	909	*	*
1982	122	22,526	0.5	4.5	926	–1.9	41,098	2,547	4.5	113,088	1,017	78	–
1983	129	23,424	4.0	5.2	1,042	12.5	44,477	2,485	–2.5	106,071	875	137	74.7
1984	179	33,751	44.1	7.3	1,531	47.0	45,361	3,807	53.2	112,783	885	372	171.5
1985	244	47,842	41.7	9.6	2,178	42.3	45,527	5,346	40.5	112,599	1,212	556	49.5
1986	365	67,938	42.0	11.6	2,874	32.0	42,310	7,490	40.1	101,250	1,646	847	52.5
1987	469	82,554	21.5	12.7	3,503	21.9	42,429	8,898	18.8	107,789	2,393	888	4.8
1988	559	87,392	5.9	13.0	3,820	9.1	43,714	9,999	12.4	114,413	2,797	1064	19.8
1989	571	87,085	–0.4	12.3	3,800	–0.5	43,630	9,976	–0.2	114,552	1,714	991	–6.8
1990	528	84,285	–3.2	12.0	3,975	4.6	47,161	11,474	15.0	136,133	4,126	690	–30.4
1991	539	86,391	2.5	11.7	4,097	3.1	47,422	11,300	–1.5	130,799	4,719	603	–12.6
1992	564	87,313	1.1	11.8	4,403	7.5	50,432	11,495	1.7	131,650	5,228	492	–18.4
1993	543	85,254	–2.4	11.9	4,636	5.3	54,376	12,863	11.9	150,874	5,280	732	48.7
1994	502	83,382	–2.2	11.7	4,839	4.4	58,034	12,563	–2.3	150,664	4,875	683	–6.6
1995	477	80,698	–3.2	11.7	5,135	6.1	63,627	13,218	5.2	163,793	5,363	590	–13.7
1996	477	79,447	–1.6	12.0	5,564	8.4	70,039	14,316	8.3	180,191	6,061	665	12.7
1997	480[b]	83,391[b]	5.0	12.3	5,849	5.1	70,145	14,700	2.7	176,273	5,837	916[c]	37.9

Notes:
* Not available.
[a] At constant 1990 prices.
[b] As at December 1997.
[c] Excluding investment in buildings.

Sources: CSO, *Annual Digest of Statistics*, various issues and *Digest of Industrial Statistics*, various issues.

around 67 per cent over the period 1990–7. As MEPZ exports accounted for the largest share of total exports, as well as of NTX1, NTX2 and NTX3 over the period 1980–97, the implication is that there was a slowing down of the growth of MEPZ exports over the 1990–7 period. Table 7.5 in fact confirms that real MEPZ exports grew at an annual average rate of 5.1 per cent per annum over the period 1990–7 whereas the average growth rate was 17.6 per cent over the period 1981–9.

The general conclusion which emerges is that the 1990s marked a turning point in the performance of the MEPZ. Its contribution to economic growth and exports slowed down considerably. In fact, the MEPZ was no longer the driving force behind the country's economic growth and export growth.

Exports of non-factor services

With the establishment of the MEPZ in 1970 and its rapid expansion in the 1970s and especially in the 1980s, the share of manufacturing in GDP increased from 6.5 per cent in the early 1970s to 24 per cent in the late 1990s. At the same time, the relative share of agriculture was declining rapidly from 34 per cent in the early 1970s to 14 per cent in the early 1980s and to 9 per cent in the late 1990s. This decline was partly offset by the services sector whose contribution increased from 62 per cent to stabilize at around 66 per cent since the early 1980s. The production of services, therefore, consistently outweighed the production of goods in the economy as from the 1970s. However, when it comes to trade, exports of goods by far outweigh exports of services. During the 1980–97 period, exports of goods were a little more than double the exports of services. And exports of non-factor services accounted for about 75 per cent of exports of services.

Table 7.6 shows the exports and imports of non-factor services over the period 1980–97. Transportation services refer mainly to the transportation of tourists and travel refers to the expenditures made by tourists on items other than transportation. The receipts from transportation and travel can therefore be considered as the foreign exchange contribution of tourism services. As some additional data are available for the tourist sector, it will be possible to attempt some analysis of the contribution of this sector. The third non-factor service in Table 7.6 is a miscellaneous category of services, referring mainly to private business services. Unfortunately, we do not have any detailed breakdown of these services and it is therefore not easy to assess the contribution of this component of non-factor services. However, we will briefly look at the contribution of offshore services and of services provided by the free port since 1992.

Like the MEPZ, the tourist industry emerged in the early 1970s and expanded during the sugar boom years, benefiting from an upsurge in investment coming from the windfall gains of the sugar industry. With favourable demand conditions in Europe, the number of tourists increased almost fourfold, from 27 650 in 1970 to 128 360 in 1979. The worldwide recession in the early 1980s led to a decline in the number of tourists over the period 1980–3 but, as from 1984, the tourist industry – like the MEPZ – witnessed a very high rate of growth which generated a fourfold increase in the number of tourists for the period 1979–97. The number of tourists increased to 536 125 in 1997. In absolute terms, the contribution of the tourist industry is less significant than that of the MEPZ. For example, in 1997 employment in hotels and restaurants totalled 15 425 compared to 83 391 in the MEPZ. The value added in the tourist sector was estimated at 4.5 per cent of GDP in 1997, whereas it was 12.3 per cent for the MEPZ. And exports of tourist services (including transportation) accounted for an average of 39 per cent of NTX3 over the period 1980–97. The corresponding figure for the MEPZ was 55 per cent. Table 7.7 shows that the growth rate of real exports of tourism services has also been lower at 10 per cent over the period 1981–97 compared to 12.8 per cent for real exports from the MEPZ. However, as from 1990, real earnings from tourism in fact grew consistently much faster than MEPZ exports, indicating the increasing importance which tourism services will have for NTX3 in the near future.

Table 7.6   Exports and imports of non-factor services, Mauritius, 1980–97 (US$ millions)

Year	Transportation Exports	Transportation Imports	Travel Exports	Travel Imports	Other services Exports	Other services Imports	Total exports	Total imports
1980	58	129	42	23	45	28	145	179
1981	57	108	48	20	70	24	175	153
1982	62	95	41	20	39	27	142	142
1983	61	81	43	20	33	25	137	127
1984	56	83	46	18	28	25	130	126
1985	64	97	55	19	28	24	146	139
1986	85	108	88	26	39	38	213	172
1987	126	168	139	51	58	48	322	267
1988	138	193	177	64	65	68	380	324
1989	155	203	183	79	68	73	406	355
1990	197	258	244	94	81	95	522	447
1991	216	254	252	110	99	104	567	468
1992	187	234	299	142	91	147	578	523
1993	156	237	304	128	107	157	566	522
1994	205	275	357	143	104	143	666	561
1995	233	300	430	159	147	197	810	656
1996	218	250	504	179	239	244	961	673
1997	221	252	490	177	208	255	919	684

Source: Bank of Mauritius, *Annual Report*, various issues.

Table 7.7   Growth rates of real exports of non-factor services, Mauritius[a], 1981–97

Year	Tourism-related earnings[b]	Other services
1981	9.5	64.3
1982	9.5	–37.7
1983	0.1	–15.0
1984	7.9	–9.8
1985	20.0	3.5
1986	18.0	15.2
1987	30.7	25.4
1988	12.4	5.8
1989	9.5	8.1
1990	15.6	4.6
1991	4.0	19.5
1992	–2.5	–13.3
1993	–0.9	22.8
1994	16.4	–7.7
1995	8.7	31.4
1996	5.9	57.6
1997	5.5	–6.7
Average for 1981–97	10.0	9.9

Notes:
[a] Calculated from real earnings (in rupees), using GDP deflator with base year 1990.
[b] Earnings from travel and transportation.
Sources: Bank of Mauritius, *Annual Report*, various issues; IMF, *International Financial Statistics Yearbook*, 1998.

The data for exports of other non-factor services are limited to the total earnings from other services shown in Table 7.7. These services would normally include the contribution of the offshore business and banking centre and of the free port which were established in 1992. These two institutions have incentive schemes which are similar to the incentives for the MEPZ and they are expected to contribute increasingly to the exports of services – just as the MEPZ has contributed to the exports of goods over the past three decades. Here again, the data available at present are extremely limited for any meaningful analysis. It is estimated that the offshore businesses and banking contributed 0.85 per cent of the GDP in 1997 and provided 500 jobs. The free port, which started its import and export operations in 1994, has witnessed a rapid growth. Exports shipped in 1995 amounted to US$24.7 million and increased sharply to US$99.5 million in 1997.

Export policy analysis

The significant transformation of the Mauritian economy from a monocrop economy to an industrializing economy over the past three decades is to a large extent due to the emergence and rapid expansion of non-traditional exports. This section discusses the policies which have favoured the growth of these exports. It will lay emphasis on the role of the MEPZ for two reasons: first, MEPZ exports have largely contributed to the structural transformation of the economy over the past three decades; second, policies for exports were mainly designed for the MEPZ and were extended to other sectors, with appropriate adjustments.

The role of incentives

The MEPZ was accorded a free trade status since its establishment in 1970. The original package of incentives (Ministry of Economic Planning and Development, 1971) included exemption from payment of import taxes on raw materials and equipment, free repatriation of capital and profits, corporate tax holiday for a minimum of ten years, and permanent residence permits. Other incentives included subsidies on inputs: bank loans at preferential rates of interest determined by the central bank, government contributions towards export market surveys, trade fairs, and provision of industrial buildings by the government. Over the years, the attractiveness of the package has been improved marginally by some additional incentives which include a zero corporate tax rate for the life of the firm.

The MEPZ incentive scheme was clearly designed to attract foreign investment, which was considered crucial, given the very limited experience of Mauritian entrepreneurs with the production and export of manufactured goods. Investment promotion campaigns in Europe and South East Asia publicized the advantages of setting up business in the MEPZ. These included a large pool of literate unemployed young persons who could easily be trained for manufacturing operations, relatively low minimum wages (the daily wage for a female worker was US$0.57 in 1970 and US$1.60 in 1980), competitive rates for electricity, telecommunications and freight charges, and duty-free access of Mauritian goods to the European Market under the Yaoundé Convention (subsequently the Lomé Convention).

The investment promotion campaign gave positive results as foreign investment started to flow in as from the very first year of operation of the MEPZ. The most important investments came from Hong Kong, Taiwan and Britain. Business links already existed with these countries and the presence of a multicultural society having its origins in France, China, India and Africa provided an additional incentive to foreign investors who later also came from South Africa, India and Singapore.[3] A complete set of published FDI data is unfortunately not available. As shown in Table 7.1, FDI has never been significant in Mauritius, but its role in the MEPZ was crucial at the very outset because of the learning-by-doing process it generated among Mauritian businessmen (Romer, 1993). The latter not only gradually came to master the production techniques in the textile and clothing industries, they also learned how to market goods in overseas markets. According to a recent study (Lall and Wignaraja, 1998), only US$77 million was invested by foreigners in the MEPZ over the period 1990–7. This contrasts sharply with the rapid surge in FDI which took place in the wake of the highly successful 1979–86 stabilization and adjustment programme. Table 7.8 shows FDI flows in the MEPZ from the top five investing countries for the period 1985–90.

Table 7.8   Top five foreign investors in the MEPZ, 1985–90 (US$ millions)

Year	Total investment	France	Germany	Hong Kong	Taiwan	United Kingdom
1985	7.4	0.6	0.03	5.9	0.02	0.1
		(8.7)	(0.4)	(79.7)	(0.2)	(2.0)
1986	5.4	0.3	0.3	1.8	0.1	0.2
		(5.9)	(4.7)	(32.6)	(1.9)	(4.3)
1987	14.7	0.6	0.04	0.8	1.0	0.5
		(4.0)	(0.3)	(5.4)	(6.6)	(3.4)
1988	17.6	1.0	0.1	8.9	0.1	0.9
		(5.6)	(0.8)	(50.9)	(0.8)	(5.3)
1989	19.6	2.1	3.3	1.3	0.9	1.9
		(10.7)	(16.6)	(6.5)	(4.5)	(9.6)
1990	18.2	3.9	0.3	3.7	4.2	0.5
		(21.4)	(1.4)	(20.2)	(23.2)	(2.7)

Note: Figures between brackets refer to percentages.

Source: Adapted from Yin et al. (1992: Table 1.2).

Incentives for the tourism sector, which were first introduced in 1974, were relatively less pervasive than those granted to the MEPZ. Corporate tax relief was limited to five years and imports for capital development were only partly exempted, but free repatriation of profits was allowed. A more comprehensive package was introduced in 1982 for hotels. These included a reduction in the corporate tax from 30 per cent to 15 per cent, exemption of dividends from income tax for ten years, exemption from customs duty for capital equipment, and loans at preferential rates. Partly as a result of these incentives, the number of hotels increased from 22 in 1971 to 75 in 1990, and to 89 in 1998. Unlike the MEPZ, which had to rely on the inflow of FDI for its initial start up and expansion, the tourist sector benefited from the substantial increase of domestic investment triggered by the windfall gains of the sugar boom years in the early 1970s. Hotels and other tourism-related businesses are mostly owned by Mauritians. This is partly explained by the higher limits on investment imposed on foreign hotels and by restrictions imposed on foreign participation in some businesses like car hire, yacht charter and the operation of duty-free shops.

Although the government does not invest directly either in the MEPZ or in the tourist sector, it has tried to provide these sectors with a reasonable range of institutional support, with a relatively higher level of assistance going to the MEPZ. The institutions which have been set up are largely financed by the government but they are managed jointly by the private sector and the public sector. We discuss here three types of support – the provision of credit at preferential rates, investment and export promotion, and technological and training schemes.

Short-term and long-term loans are provided at preferential rates by the Development Bank of Mauritius (DBM), especially to small and medium enterprises in almost all lines of production. The DBM was in fact set up in 1964 to support the sugar sector and especially the import-substitution industries which the government actively encouraged during the 1960s. When the MEPZ was established, small- and medium-sized firms in that sector found a readily available source of finance. Similarly, small- and medium-sized hotels are provided with soft loans for upgrading the quality of their services so as to meet the exigencies of upmarket tourism which the government supports.

Overseas marketing support for MEPZ exporters and for the tourist industry was initially undertaken by government ministries with the help of overseas agencies. However, in the context of the 1979–86 adjustment programme, a new agency – the Mauritius Export Development and Investment Agency (MEDIA) – was created in 1984 for the promotion of MEPZ investments and exports. MEDIA, which currently has fourteen overseas offices, not only facilitates the participation of Mauritian exports in international trade fairs and exhibitions but also carries out market surveys which are readily made available to investors. It has succeeded in encouraging firms producing for the domestic market to tap the regional markets. As for the promotion of the tourist industry, it had to continue relying on a government department up to 1996 when an autonomous agency, the Mauritius Tourism Promotion Agency (MTPA), was created. The MTPA's main objective is the promotion of Mauritius as a tourist destination through participation in tourism fairs and promotional campaigns.

As for technological support, this is more crucial for the MEPZ which has to maintain and enhance its competitiveness in the context of an increasing liberalization of world trade and the entry of cheaper producers of textile and clothing products on the world market. The Export Processing Zone Development Authority (EPZDA) was in fact created in 1992 to look at the bottlenecks facing the expansion of the MEPZ and to prepare practical solutions. Apart from the dissemination of information and the organization of training sessions by international specialists for improving design capability in the textile and clothing sector, an important component of EPZDA's strategy is to help firms, mostly but not exclusively MEPZ firms, to enhance their competitiveness through technological improvements. A grant covering half the costs incurred by any eligible firm is advanced by the EPZDA. Out of 339 firms interviewed at the end of July 1996, 129 applications were approved. This scheme has been quite successful as each dollar spent has generated an increase in exports ranging from US$9 to US$22, instead of the increase of US$2 which is normally expected elsewhere (Lall and Wignaraja, 1998).

The demand for training by firms in the MEPZ has been fairly limited. This may be due to the low level of skills required by firms which can easily provide the necessary training on the job. The tourist industry, however, requires higher skill levels, given the emphasis on upmarket tourism. Over the period 1992–5, 1044 persons were trained for kitchen, restaurant and front-of-house work in a specialized school – a relatively high figure, considering that hotels and restaurants employed 15 425 persons in 1997. In addition, a newly set up training school provides post-secondary-level training in hotel management, although the intake is still relatively low at about 50 per annum.

Exchange rate policy

To maintain the competitiveness of the MEPZ and the tourist sector, the rupee was devalued by 23 per cent in 1979 and again by 17 per cent in 1981 as part of the stabilization and adjustment programme. The rupee has in fact depreciated against most major currencies. Over the period 1981–98, the average annual rates of depreciation against the French franc, the UK pound, the US dollar, the German mark and the Japanese yen were 3.8 per cent, 4.2 per cent, 5.7 per cent, 5.7 per cent and 7.9 per cent, respectively. Given the heavy reliance of the tourist industry on the European market and the high concentration ratio of MEPZ exports on Europe and the US, it can be argued that an implicit policy of depreciation has been pursued up to now to maintain the competitiveness of non-traditional exports. The real effective exchange rate of the rupee has in fact remained unchanged throughout the period 1981–97.[4] The high rates of growth of real exports, including NTX1, NTX2 and NTX3 (shown in Table 7.3) tend to confirm the high sensitivity of these exports to depreciation.

Reduction in anti-export bias

Although the MEPZ has been operating very closely to free trade conditions since it was set up in 1970, it must be noted that it has always evolved within a trade policy regime with a high degree of anti-export bias. Import substitution industries were in fact promoted in the early 1960s through a Development Certificate (DC) scheme. This scheme offered a package of incentives which included a corporate tax holiday, loans at preferential rates and exemptions from import duties on imports of equipment and raw materials. The DC firms were also given protection through very high tariffs and quota restrictions on imports. In the early 1980s, there were 150 DC firms employing close to 8000 workers. Greenaway and Milner (1989) estimate that the effective rates of Protection (ERPs) exceeded 100 per cent in 11 out of 19 industry groups to which these firms belonged. Beverages and tobacco, the most important industry group in terms of value added and employment, had an ERP of 123 per cent. After a first episode of trade liberalization in the early 1980s, there was a significant reduction in the ERPs for all industry groups. For beverages and tobacco there was a 50 per cent reduction in the ERP.[5]

The tariff regime was harmonized in 1994 with 10 basic rates instead of 60. The rates of taxation were reduced significantly, the maximum being 100 per cent compared to an overall combined average of 250 per cent. These changes may have led to a reduction in ERPs, although it is suspected that they would still be relatively high even by developing country standards.

It may be argued that the dichotomy in the trade regime facing the MEPZ and the import-substitution industries may have hampered the growth of the latter firms. As they could not buy inputs from MEPZ firms until very recently, and as they could not supply inputs competitively to the MEPZ, forward and backward linkages failed to develop between MEPZ and non-MEPZ firms. These firms contributed 7.8 per cent of value added in 1998 and provided 27 360 jobs. The corresponding figures for the MEPZ were 12.3 per cent and 83 391, respectively, for 1997.

Increasing liberalization

Non-traditional exports have expanded significantly in recent years because of the strengthening of the export orientation of the economy and its increasing liberalization. Not only have there been improvements in the incentives granted to the MEPZ and to the tourist sector, but new complementary sectors have been set up. These include an offshore banking and business centre and a free port. It is now possible for foreign firms in the MEPZ to borrow from offshore banks, which charge lower interest rates. There has also been a gradual liberalization of the money market and the emergence of various institutions on the capital market, most notably a stock exchange which is a major source of term finance for the larger hotels. The foreign exchange market has also been completely liberalized and there are no restrictions on capital outflows. Finally, it can be argued that the maintenance of a sound macroeconomic stance in recent years has provided a favourable climate for the growth of non-traditional exports.

Constraints on the growth of non-traditional exports and implications

Here, we look at the constraints on the growth of non-traditional exports and the implications of these constraints. Given the importance of MEPZ exports for NTX1, NTX2 and NTX3, there is a continued emphasis on the MEPZ.

One constraint facing the growth of MEPZ exports, which has been evident since the establishment of the MEPZ, is the heavy concentration of production in one sector – the textile and clothing sector. This concentration has been accentuated over the years, in 1997, textile and clothing exports accounted for 78 per cent of NTX1. With the increasing liberalization of world trade in textiles and clothing and the impending dismantling of the MFA, Mauritian exports of textiles and clothing will face tougher competition in Europe and the US where they currently have preferential access. The survival of firms producing basic textile and clothing products is likely to be threatened. A survey of MEPZ firms included in a study of trade liberalization in Mauritius (Dabee and Milner, 1996) indicated that some firms were already facing tougher competition overseas and had to curtail production and employment. This trend was later confirmed by the employment figures published for the MEPZ. Employment in the clothing sector declined from 69 037 in December 1994 to 65 809 in December 1996. However, it seems that the more productive units in the MEPZ have been able to increase production and employment by moving to higher quality and higher value added products. Total employment in the clothing sector in fact began to rise again in 1997 when it reached 69 322.

One way to reduce the concentration on textiles and clothing is to diversify into new areas. Whereas in the 1970s and in the 1980s the government had not interfered to influence the type of industries set up in the MEPZ, in the 1990s it reacted to the high concentration in textiles and clothing by announcing the new areas it would encourage – jewellery, printing and publishing, and light electronics. These areas were emphasized during investment promotion campaigns. Training programmes for workers in these areas were also provided to strengthen the skill base. However, there has not yet been any significant increase in employment in these new areas. It seems that the rationale has been to build on areas where some skills already existed, expecting that investment would flow into these areas. But the initial size of these new sectors was very small and the level of skills was not adequately developed to attract foreign investments. It would be useful to consider alternative strategies whereby one or two leading international companies in a particular sector may be approached directly and induced to set up business in the MEPZ. The choice of the sector need not be limited to the sectors already identified by the government; it could be extended to new sectors and should certainly include services, given the government's policy of increased trade in services.

However, a major obstacle in attracting a diversified range of industries is the low level of skills in the MEPZ. In the 1970s Mauritius had a large pool of unemployed persons who were considered suitable for routine production operations which could be learnt fairly quickly on the job. The predominance of the textile and clothing sector has perpetuated the low-skill base of the MEPZ workforce. In fact, according to a recent study (Lall and Wignaraja, 1998), only 5 per cent of the manufactured exports from Mauritius could be regarded as constituting high-skill production. Low-skill jobs in the textile and clothing sector are quite vulnerable and may be seriously affected by the increasing competition from countries with lower wages. Already, some large Mauritian firms in the MEPZ have relocated their labour-intensive processes in Madagascar. A rising trend in this direction will imply a gradual deindustrialization of the Mauritian economy unless it is offset by new industries which have a higher skill base. Here again, investment promotion should be more proactive and could be geared to the search for targeted industrial groups. It should also include a search for service-based industries in which Mauritius may have a competitive advantage. This could include remote services, including back-office work for large firms, which are transmitted by satellite or on the internet. An alliance with Indian investors who have already made some headway with remote services may be fruitful, given that Mauritius may currently have an edge over India in the quality of its telecommunications.

It becomes very clear that FDI should in fact increase in Mauritius. In the textile and clothing sector, FDI has performed a useful role. It has helped Mauritian businessmen to master production, marketing and management operations in export industries. This kind of knowledge has unfortunately not helped the economy to move to higher skill industries. There is an urgent need to reverse the declining trend in FDI which has been noticed in recent years by attracting investments in new export industries, including service industries.

Finally, it would be useful to add that the growth of non-traditional exports in Mauritius will be strongly influenced by the emerging world trading system in three important respects. First, the increasing liberalization of trade in industrial goods in general, and the phasing-out of the MFA by the end of 2004 in particular, implies a gradual loss of preferential access currently obtained on the EU and US markets. Mauritian exporters will soon be facing tougher competition in these markets. Second, some WTO rules may pose a threat to Mauritian exporters of manufactured goods. For example, following the trade policy review of Mauritius in 1995, clarifications were sought on the incentives granted to MEPZ industries. Although, at the level of the WTO, Mauritius has maintained that it does not grant any export subsidy, some WTO members may argue that some incentives granted to the MEPZ (for example, the complete exemption from import duties granted to the MEPZ only on all raw materials and machinery) may constitute implicit export subsidies. To avoid countervailing action by importing countries, it is necessary to ensure that all MEPZ incentives are in fact compatible with the WTO. Third, it is also true that the new trading system offers new opportunities to Mauritius. The opening up of markets, not only in industrialized countries but also in large developing countries like India and China, may be an incentive for the production of a more diversified range of products for a larger number of importing countries. New opportunities also exist for an increase in trade in services, especially in telecommunications, offshore business, and free port activities where Mauritius may have some comparative advantage in the Southern African region.

In dealing with the constraints facing non-traditional exports, we have concentrated on issues of strategic importance which are likely to change the long-term commodity composition, skill base and technology of export industries. We have avoided a discussion of day-to-day or short-term problems which negatively impact on the performance of non-traditional exports. These include a high level of absenteeism, complaints about red tape, fluctuations in the voltage of electricity supplied and other similar problems. These problems will also have to be addressed. However, they may only require minor adjustments on the part of workers, managers and the government. The constraints we have raised here are more crucial for the long-term performance of non-traditional exports.

Notes

1. The territory of Mauritius, located in the Indian Ocean, comprises the main island of Mauritius which has an area of 1860 square kilometres and the island of Rodrigues (about 550 kilometres away) which has an area of 100 square kilometres. It also includes some much smaller islands where some fishing activity takes place.
2. See Gulhati and Nallari (1990) for an analysis of the factors leading to the balance of payments crisis of 1979 and for a detailed discussion of the stabilization and structural adjustment programmes adopted during the 1979–86 period.
3. See Lamusse (1985) for a discussion of the ownership pattern of MEPZ firms.
4. Various real effective exchange rate (REER) indices estimated by the author show the REER was almost stable over the period 1980–96. For example, the CPI-based REER showed a low of 98.1 and a high of 101.2 over that period.
5. The latter figures for 1990 come from a Maxwell Stamp study and are quoted from the study by Milner and McKay (1996).

References

Alter, R. (1990) 'Export Processing Zones for Growth and Development: The Mauritian Example', IMF Working Paper WP/90/122, Washington, DC: International Monetary Fund.

Dabee, B. and Milner, C. (1996) 'Evaluating Trade Liberalization in Mauritius', paper presented to AERC Collaborative Research Project. Forthcoming in A. Oyejide et al. (eds), *Regional Integration and Trade Liberalization in Sub-Saharan Africa*, Vol. 2, London: Macmillan.

Greenaway, D. and Milner, C. (1989) 'Nominal and Effective Tariffs in a Small Industrializing Economy: The Case of Mauritius', *Applied Economics*, 21: 995–1009.

Gulhati, R. and Nallari, R. (1990) 'Successful Stabilization and Recovery in Mauritius', Economic Development Institute of the World Bank, Washington, DC.

Hein, P. (1989) 'Structural Transformation in an Island Economy: The Mauritius Export Processing Zone (1971 to 1988)', *UNCTAD Review*, 1, 2: 41–57.

Kearney, R. C. (1990) 'Mauritius and the NIC Model Redux: Or, How Many Cases Make a Model?', *Journal of Developing Areas*, 24: 195–216.

Lall, S. and Wignaraja, G. (1998) 'Mauritius: Dynamising Export Competitiveness', Commonwealth Secretariat, London.

Lamusse, R. (1985) 'The Breakthrough in Export Processing Industrialization in Mauritius', Discussion Paper 13, African-American Issues Centre, Boston, MA.

Meade, J. E. (1961) 'Mauritius: A Case Study of Malthusian Economics', *Economic Journal*, 71: 521–34.

Meade, J. E. (1967) 'Population Explosion, the Standard of Living and Social Conflict', *Economic Journal*, 77: 233–55.

Milner, C. and McKay, A. (1996) 'Real Exchange Rate Measures and Trade Liberalization: Some Evidence for Mauritius', *Journal of African Economies*, 5: 61–91.

Ministry of Economic Planning and Development (1971) *Four-Year Plan for Social and Economic Development 1971–75*, Mauritius: Ministry of Economic Planning and Development.

Romer, P. M. (1993) 'Two Strategies for Economic Development: Using Ideas and Producing Ideas', Proceedings of the 1992 World Bank Annual Conference on Development Economics, 63–91.

World Bank (1989) *Mauritius: Managing Success*, Washington, DC: World Bank.

World Bank (1992) *Mauritius: Expanding Horizons*, Washington, DC: World Bank.

Yin, P. et al. (1992) *L'Ile Maurice et sa Zone Franche*, T-printers: Mauritius.

8
Growing Without Gold?
South Africa's Non-Traditional Exports Since 1980

Anthony Black and Brian Kahn

Introduction

Several years after the advent of democracy, South Africa continues to face long-standing problems of low growth and exceptionally high rates of unemployment. While a number of factors have led to this situation the shock resulting from the fall in the price and output of South Africa's major traditional export, gold, has been key. Revenues earned from gold exports averaged US$11.3 billion for the years 1980–1 and accounted for no less than 52 per cent of total merchandise exports. In 1997 gold export revenues had declined to US$5.6 billion and comprised only 18 per cent of merchandise exports. Partly as a result of this, the economy has, since the early 1980s, been forced into a deep and protracted period of adjustment. This process has been made more difficult by inappropriate policies, structural problems in the manufacturing sector and, of course, by the political turmoil of the apartheid era.

South Africa's dependence on gold and to a certain extent other minerals has long been a preoccupation of policymakers. Early efforts to promote import substitution were motivated partly by the desire to diversify the economy away from dependence on gold. Since the 1970s, policy became more concerned with diversifying exports even though the rising price of gold during that decade both blunted the imperative for this as well as producing a strong currency unfavourable to manufactured exports. Related to this has been a concern with the beneficiation of South African raw materials and, more recently, efforts to promote downstream processing of products such as steel, aluminium, industrial chemicals and wood pulp which are exported in large quantities. This has been driven by desire to export products in a more processed form as well as to encourage production in more labour-intensive subsectors. In the South African context, therefore, non-traditional exports have essentially meant the export of manufactures, particularly higher value added products. The following analysis accordingly places considerable emphasis on manufactured exports which have been divided into traditional and non-traditional categories with the former category including steel, non-ferrous metals and industrial chemicals. More recently, growing importance in policy discussions has been attached to manufacturing firms 'moving up the value chain'.[1] Adherents to this perspective argue that South Africa cannot compete in low end, labour-intensive manufactures and needs to produce higher value products (for example more upmarket clothing where competitive advantage is based partly on design and not simply on cheap labour). This notion has yet to find concrete formulation in significant policy initiatives.

The decline of gold revenues together with limited growth in some other commodity exports has seriously constrained the growth of the South African economy. Much will now depend on the performance of non-traditional exports, especially manufactures. Export of manufactures has required a further adjustment, within the manufacturing sector, in the form of a reorientation from the domestic market to a more export-oriented approach. This chapter shows that non-traditional exports including manufactures have been growing quite rapidly, especially since the late 1980s. While the trends are only recently established, the expansion of non-traditional manufactured exports augurs well for employment creation over the medium term.

We begin with an outline of the macroeconomic performance of the South African economy since 1980. Next, the dimensions of South Africa's export performance are set out, focusing on overall growth rates, composition and the direction of trade. Trade policy and support measures for non-traditional exports are then analysed, followed by an assessment of the supply response of exporters in the turbulent economic environment of the last decade.

Macro performance

The period 1980–97 was a highly volatile one for the South African economy. This phase was characterized by a high degree of gold price volatility and numerous political crises, and both of these factors had significant impacts on the exchange rate and its management. This in turn impacted on the export potential of the country. In addition financial and trade sanctions were intensified during the 1980s which culminated in the debt crisis of 1985. Trade sanctions retarded the expansion of exports although they did not prevent exports from increasing since the mid-1980s. Financial sanctions, on the other hand, imposed a severe constraint on growth and complicated macroeconomic management (see Kahn, 1991; Leape, 1991). The major macroeconomic indicators are set out in Table 8.1.

The South African economy has been characterized by declining rates of economic growth since the mid-1960s when real growth rates averaging 6 per cent were recorded. Since then growth has been on a downward trend albeit with some marked fluctuations. The most severe and sustained recession was experienced between 1989 and 1993. Real growth averaged 2.3 per cent from 1980–5 and 1.7 per cent from 1986–90. This decade included five years of negative or zero growth. In the 1990s, growth was negative in 1991 and 1992, due in part to the severe drought, and became positive again in 1993–6 with an average growth rate of 2.7 per cent and peaking at 3.4 per cent in 1995. Per capita GDP growth rates were even less impressive, given a population growth rate of 2.6 per cent. Per capita GDP declined by an average 0.6 per cent per year over the entire period but growth has been positive since 1994.

Table 8.1   Historical macroeconomic indicators, South Africa, 1980–97

Indicators	*1980–5*	*1986–90*	*1991–5*	*1996*	*1997*
1. Real GDP growth (%)	2.3	1.6	0.8	3.2	1.7
2. Growth of real GDP per capita (%)	–2.6	–0.7	–1.4	1.1	–0.4
3. Gross Domestic Investment/GDP (%)	26.1	19.7	16.6	17.2	17.4
4. Gross Domestic Savings/GDP (%)	25.8	22.2	17.4	16.9	15.2
5. Consumption expenditure/GDP					
Private	54.1	56.1	60.5	61.0	61.6
Government	15.3	18.3	20.4	20.4	21.3
6. Fiscal deficit (% of GDP)	–2.7	–3.9	–5.6	–6.1	–5.2
7. Labour productivity (% change)	0.8	–0.1	1.7	4.5	7.1
8. Unit labour costs (% change),					
constant prices	0.9	0.0	0.8	–4.2	–6.2
9. Inflation (%)	14.0	15.3	11.3	7.4	8.6
10. Export growth, volume (%)					
Including gold	0.8	2.3	3.5	7.4	5.2
Excluding gold	1.6	4.9	6.4	14.9	5.3
11. Import growth, volume (%)	0.8	3.5	10.3	11.5	4.9
12. Nominal effective exchange rate,					
change in %	–49.6	–34.1	–7.0	–13.0	–5.4
13. Real effective exchange rate, change in %	–25.0	19.5	–0.5	–8.3	0.7
14. Terms of trade (merchandise) (%)					
Including gold	–17.7	–4.9	0.3	2.4	–1.3
Excluding gold	–9.4	2.6	0.3	0.4	1.0
15. Current Account as % of GDP	–0.8	2.7	0.5	–1.3	–1.5
16. Capital Account as % of GDP	0.4	–2.3	–0.2	0.7	3.4
17. Gross Official Reserves					
(in weeks of current imports)	9.7	6.8	6.4	5.4	8.2
18. Debt Service (% of exports)	7.1	8.7	6.4	7.2	n.a.
19. External Debt (% of GDP)	30.1	25.7	22.4	26.1	n.a.
20. Real interest rates					
Short term (3 month Treasury Bill)	1.1	–2.1	2.0	7.7	6.6
Long term (15 year Government stock)	0.4	0.5	3.8	8.8	5.6

Source: South African Reserve Bank.

Economic stagnation has resulted in rising rates of unemployment, with less than 10 per cent of new labour market entrants being absorbed into formal sector employment. There are differing estimates of total unemployment, although it is generally accepted to be above 30 per cent. These figures exclude informal sector employment which has grown in recent years, although in many cases such employment is of a subsistence nature.

There are various reasons for the poor recent performance of the economy. Political instability and uncertainty have contributed to fairly low levels of private sector investment. The ratio of gross domestic fixed investment to GDP declined from 26.2 per cent in 1980 to a low of 15.5 per cent in 1993. This dramatic decline in investment was, in part, caused by the intensification of financial sanctions against South Africa. The adjustment to the debt crisis required current account surpluses which were achieved primarily through declining levels of investment. The precipitous decline in investment enabled the economy to maintain positive savings-investment balances between 1985 and 1994, despite the fact that the savings ratio declined from 34.5 per cent in 1980 to 15.2 per cent in 1996. Part of the decline in the savings ratio was attributable to increased government dissaving. Following the 1994 elections, investment rose somewhat to average 17.2 per cent of GDP for the period 1995–7.

Structural factors in the economy are also to blame for the secular decline in growth rates (Gelb, 1991). Import-substitution policies had made the manufacturing sector inwardly-oriented, although recently, as seen below, there have been attempts to promote an export orientation in this sector and overcome the anti-export bias that the system of protection had fostered. A feature of the manufacturing sector has been steadily declining multifactor productivity (Fallon and Pereira da Silva, 1994), rising capital intensity of production and rising unit labour costs in an economy with excess supplies of labour. Unit labour costs increased by 10 per cent from 1990–4 but declined by almost 15 per cent between the end of 1994 and the end of 1997.

At the same time the parlous state of the education system for blacks has resulted in a large unskilled black labour force and shortages of skilled labour. The terms of trade during this period were strongly influenced by the gold price, particularly in the first half of the 1980s. Since 1985 the merchandise terms of trade have been relatively stable, although the terms of trade including gold showed a greater decline over the period.

Balance of payments and exchange rate developments

The movement of the real and nominal effective[2] exchange rates are shown in Figure 8.1. The nominal value of the currency has followed a depreciating trend, indicated by an increase in the exchange rate index, with sharp variations that were associated with gold price movements and political shocks. The effective nominal index rose from 30.5 (index 1990 = 100) in 1980, to average 174.7 in 1997. The real exchange rate on the other hand displayed a fairly high degree of variability until 1988,[3] whereafter it exhibited a high degree of stability apart from the 1996 currency crisis.

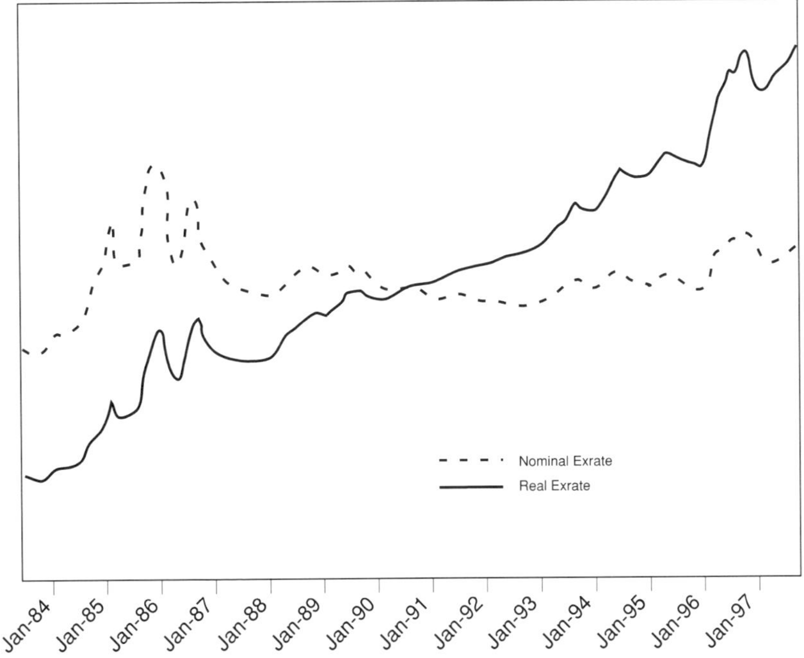

Figure 8.1 Real and nominal effective exchange rates in South Africa, 1984–97[*] (1990 = 100)

[*] Increase denotes devaluation.

On the balance of payments and exchange rate front, three distinct periods can be distinguished. The period 1980–5 represented a period of high gold price volatility with the gold price fluctuating between US$850 in January 1980 and US$300 in February 1985. During this period exchange controls were relaxed with the abolition of the financial rand in 1983 and the exchange rate became more market determined. Exchange rate volatility, both real and nominal, also increased during this period. Changes in the monetary policy regime also saw real interest rates fluctuating between –10 per cent and +10 per cent. As a result of the record high dollar gold price in 1980, a current account surplus of 4.2 per cent of GDP was recorded in that year and a capital account deficit of 3.1 per cent. Thereafter between 1981–4 current account deficits averaged 3.3 per cent of GDP financed by capital inflows of 2.68 per cent of GDP.

During the second period, from September 1985, following the 1985 debt crisis, until the 1994 elections, South Africa was cut off from international capital following the 1985 debt crisis. This effectively meant that the economy was constrained to running current account surpluses in order to meet capital repayment commitments. From the onset of the debt crisis, current account surpluses averaged 2.5 per cent of GDP in the period 1985–93 and this financed capital outflows of similar magnitudes. This implied high interest rates, particularly from 1988 when monetary policy became directed to balance of payments considerations. At the same time, monetary policy also became more concerned with combating the inertial inflation of around 15 per cent during the 1980s. The inflation rate began to subside significantly in 1992 and by 1998 was below 8 per cent. The adjustment to the debt crisis did, however, mean that by the end of 1993 the foreign debt to GDP ratio had declined from 42 per cent in 1985 to 22 per cent. By the end of 1996 this had risen to 26 per cent.

The advent of democracy in 1994 marked a new period with the resumption of capital inflows and the lifting of trade sanctions. Between 1993 and 1996 current account deficits averaged 1.3 per cent of GDP while capital account surpluses averaged 1.9 per cent of GDP, including 4 per cent in 1995. Increased liberalization of the capital account and higher volumes of reversible portfolio capital flows meant that the exchange rate and the balance of payments were now vulnerable to a new source of shocks (Kahn, 1997). The vulnerability of the economy to capital outflows was illustrated in 1996 when there was a sudden change in sentiment towards South Africa and the rand faced its first major crisis since the new government came into power. Again in 1998 the rand came under severe pressure in the wake of the Asian crisis.

The Reserve Bank has had no explicit targets for either the real or the nominal exchange rate. According to the Reserve Bank, a major objective was the maintenance of orderly foreign exchange market conditions, and intervention was directed at supporting the market, rather than a particular exchange rate. However, exchange rate policy in the past does appear to have been driven by different considerations at times, with intervention to achieve changing objectives.

During the 1980s, the exchange rate moved in such a way as to stabilize the real rand gold price, and it is argued by Kahn (1992) that concern for the gold mining industry was one of the objectives of exchange rate policy. This resulted in a highly variable real exchange rate which cushioned the gold mining industry from terms of trade fluctuations, but this variability had a negative impact on the manufacturing export sector. Since 1988 the Reserve Bank has appeared to be more active in stabilizing the real effective exchange rate, in particular to prevent excessive real and nominal appreciations. This indicates some concern (at times explicit) for the impact of the real exchange rate on the international competitiveness of South Africa's manufacturing exports. The result has been a far more stable real exchange rate measured on a trade weighted basis.

In 1996 the GEAR[4] framework committed the Reserve Bank to maintaining a fairly stable real exchange rate to provide some certainty to manufacturing exporters. However, there was no indication of how this was to be achieved, whether through direct intervention or through acting on the exchange rate fundamentals. Nor was there any indication as to the range of fluctuations or deviations that would be allowed.

Since the lifting of financial sanctions against South Africa and the liberalization of the capital account, volatile capital movement has become the main cause of real and nominal exchange rate volatility. The continued low level of foreign exchange reserves has limited the Bank's ability to intervene to protect the currency during periods of outflow. These capital flows have, therefore, resulted in problems for macroeconomic management (Kahn, 1997). On the one hand, portfolio flows are the main form of foreign capital inflow and the Reserve Bank has been loath to place restrictions on them. On the other hand, these flows are becoming a source of real exchange rate instability which could impact negatively on the foreign trade climate. During 1996 the rand depreciated by over 8 per cent in real terms and in May 1998 the rand lost over 20 per cent of its value. The reliance on portfolio capital inflows has also resulted in a bias towards high real interest rates, which in conjunction with the Reserve Bank's anti–inflation objectives, has tended to have a negative effect on economic growth.

Export performance

There are different ways of classifying non-traditional exports. For the purposes of this chapter, we consider three alternative definitions; namely, the national definition (NTX1), the World Bank definition (NTX2) and the project definition (NTX3) (see Chapter 1).

National definition, NTX1

Disaggregating exports into merchandise, gold and non-factor services (Tables 8.2 and 8.3), it is clear that South Africa's overall export performance has been significantly affected by the decline in gold exports which in 1980 accounted for over 45 per cent of total exports. By 1996 this had declined to 18 per cent, down from 17 per cent to 5 per cent of GDP. Although rand receipts for gold have remained stable, output has been falling since the early 1980s as a result of falling ore grades and poor productivity performance in the industry. Table 8.2 also shows that merchandise export volumes have generally shown positive increases, with substantial increases in 1995 and 1996. Table 8.3 shows the breakdown of non-factor service exports, with a doubling of tourism (categorized as 'travel') receipts between 1991 and 1996.

Table 8.2   Merchandise, gold and non-factor service exports/GDP, South Africa, 1980–96

	Goods/ GDP	Gold/ GDP	NFS/ GDP	% change merchandise volume	% change gold volume
1980	15.6	16.5	3.8	2.4	–3.2
1981	13.8	11.7	3.6	–6.2	–2.9
1982	12.6	10.7	3.9	–3.2	0.7
1983	11.0	10.9	3.3	–1.9	0.0
1984	11.9	10.9	3.3	0.7	6.5
1985	16.0	12.6	3.7	19.8	–2.1
1986	16.7	11.7	3.4	1.8	–9.0
1987	15.3	10.7	3.1	–0.1	–3.3
1988	16.0	9.8	3.1	14.8	3.3
1989	16.0	8.0	3.6	6.7	–4.6
1990	15.5	6.6	3.6	4.0	–0.8
1991	14.4	6.3	3.3	1.7	1.9
1992	14.3	5.7	3.2	3.4	2.0
1993	14.8	5.9	3.2	6.6	–0.6
1994	15.1	5.5	3.4	3.0	–8.1
1995	16.8	4.7	3.5	17.5	–8.2
1996	18.2	4.8	3.5	13.9	–4.3

Source: SARB Statistics.

Although, strictly speaking, South Africa does not have an official definition of 'non-traditional exports', given the predominance of gold and other mining, manufactured exports are generally regarded as the non-traditional exports. Within the manufacturing sector, iron and steel, non-ferrous metals and industrial chemicals are regarded as the main traditional categories.

According to the narrow definition of manufactured exports in Table 8.4, manufactures increased their share of exports from 5 per cent in 1988 to 20 per cent in 1997. Using a broader definition (including beneficiated primary products and material-intensive products) the share of non-primary exports increased from 35 per cent to 55 per cent over the period. The major manufactured exports are material-intensive products such as beneficiated iron and steel, processed chemicals, processed foods and non-ferrous metals. Fast-growing export sectors include the larger export industries (e.g. iron and steel) but also 'non-traditional' manufactured exports such as motor vehicles and components, and plastic products (Appendix Tables 8.A1–3). (Appendix Table 8.A3 takes the data back to 1980; however, because of a change in reporting conventions and coverage the pre-1988 data are not strictly comparable.) After 1993, manufactured exports increased by two-thirds, from approximately US$9 billion to approximately US$15 billion in 1997.

Table 8.3   Breakdown of South African exports, 1980–96 (US$ millions)

	Net gold exports	Merchandise exports	Service receipts	of which: Freight and insurance	Transportation: passenger fares	Other transportation	Travel	Non-merch. insurance	Receipts for other services
1980	13,021	12,293	3,529	280	232	713	619	227	912
1981	9,504	11,150	3,466	255	240	577	655	300	926
1982	7,945	9,352	3,310	202	234	732	577	263	860
1983	8,912	9,067	3,310	160	192	592	639	128	974
1984	7,918	8,663	3,121	154	194	510	599	138	836
1985	6,940	8,863	3,011	193	182	417	426	149	671
1986	7,322	10,476	3,320	230	166	389	416	177	777
1987	8,755	12,579	3,908	207	204	419	599	178	974
1988	8,669	14,136	3,909	255	213	443	691	119	976
1989	7,299	14,638	4,402	349	243	539	811	118	1,211
1990	7,024	16,515	4,385	295	330	596	956	324	1,334
1991	7,094	16,194	4,486	246	305	658	1,103	155	1,245
1992	6,800	17,187	4,668	364	363	662	1,182	199	1,059
1993	6,872	17,299	4,446	353	316	701	1,327	161	872
1994	6,668	18,298	5,062	381	361	659	1,569	244	958
1995	6,214	22,412	5,547	335	528	477	1,917	406	1,001
1996	6,120	23,613	6,147	253	520	417	2,293	378	865

Table 8.4   Composition of SACU's total export basket by stage of manufacturing, 1988–97

| | Percentage of total exports | | | |
Category	1988	1991	1994	1997
Gold	44	34	30	21
Primary Products	21	23	22	23
Beneficiated Primary Products	25	27	27	29
Material Intensive Products	5	6	6	7
Manufactured Products	5	10	15	20

Source: *Trade for Growth*, Industrial Development Corporation, May 1998.

It can be seen in Appendix Table 8.A1 that iron and steel, non-ferrous metals, chemicals, paper and paper products, and processed foods are the main traditional export items, and together they made up 76 per cent of manufactured exports in 1988. In 1996 this had declined to 62 per cent of the total. Most of these traditional categories displayed lower-than-average annual growth rates. Significant increases in the share of manufactured exports were recorded by mechanical machinery (from 4.7 per cent to 8 per cent and an annual growth rate of 18.6 per cent in US$ terms), motor vehicles (2.2 per cent to 4.9 per cent with an annual growth rate of 23 per cent); electrical machinery (1.4 per cent to 3.2 per cent) and transport equipment (0.7 per cent to 1.7 per cent and a growth rate of 34.4 per cent). Beverages (particularly wine, which had been affected by trade sanctions) increased its share to 2.4 per cent from 0.6 per cent at a growth rate of 35.5 per cent. Wood and glass were the only non-traditional categories that did not increase their shares of total manufactured exports.

World Bank definition, NTX2

Figure 8.2 shows the evolution of the role of non-traditional exports. It uses the World Bank definition – NTX2 (all three-digit export items other than the top ten or those accounting for 75 per cent of exports in the base year, in this case 1983) excluding gold.(Appendix Table 8.A4 shows that when gold is excluded, the top ten three-digit items make up 56 per cent of exports. It also shows all the categories that fall into the top 75 per cent. When gold is included, the top ten items make up 75 per cent of exports.) The figures show that in terms of this definition, non-traditional exports increased from 24 per cent of exports in 1983 to 44 per cent in 1996, whereas when we exclude gold, we have an increase from 24 per cent to 40 per cent. When we only consider the 300 level manufacturing sector categories, and we assume that the five top categories make up the traditional export sector, the non-traditional categories, so defined, increased from 33 per cent in 1980 to 40 per cent in 1996.

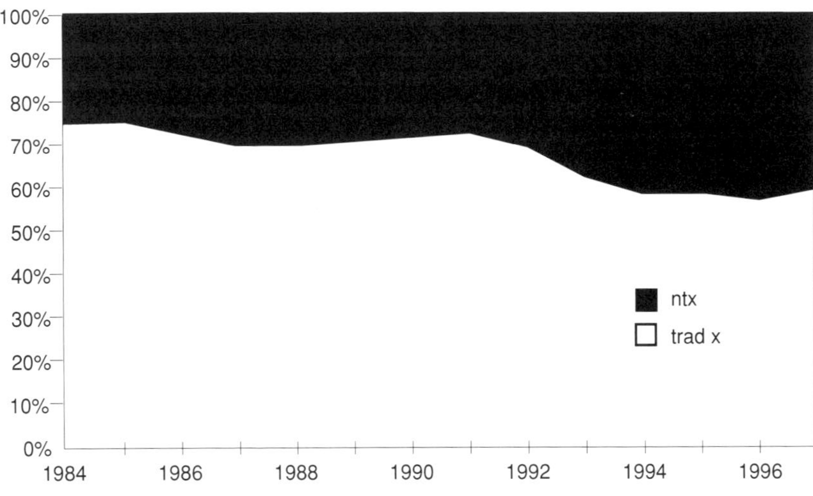

Figure 8.2   Traditional and non-traditional exports (World Bank definition NTX2), South Africa, 1984–97

Project definition, NTX3

The project definition of non-traditional exports (NTX3) allows for non-factor services exports (including tourism) plus merchandise exports accounting for less than 3 per cent of total exports in the base year. Given that non-factor services have been a significant proportion of exports it means that the size of NTX3 is relatively large compared to the other two measures. In Table 8.5 the ratios of NTX3 are shown, excluding and including gold in total exports. In terms of this definition, there are only four export categories that comprised more than 3 per cent of exports in 1983 (three-digit SIC) when gold is included. These were gold, coal, silver/platinum and non-ferrous base metals. If we exclude gold, the traditional categories include the latter three as well as works of art/gold coin, precious and semi-precious stones, pig iron, radioactive materials and wool and wool products.

Measures of export concentration

Table 8.6 applies the Gini-Hirschman index to measure the degree of diversification or concentration of South Africa's exports, using different data sets including the three-digit classification from the World Bank data base. What emerges from the data is that there has been a trend towards greater diversification of South Africa's exports. Not surprisingly, this trend is strongest when gold is included in the index; when gold is excluded, the trend towards diversification is strongest when only the manufacturing sector categories are considered.

Table 8.5   Non-traditional exports (NTX3), South Africa, 1983–96

	Including gold (NTX3a)			Excluding gold (NTX3b)		
	NTX3a /Total X	NTX3a /GDP	Total X /GDP	NTX3b /Total X	NTX3b /GDP	Total X /GDP
1983	47.8	12.1	25.2	62.5	9.0	14.3
1984	37.7	13.6	27.5	57.8	9.6	16.6
1985	39.5	17.2	34.2	57.3	12.4	21.7
1986	40.4	16.5	32.5	59.7	12.4	20.8
1987	35.6	12.6	26.6	62.3	9.9	15.9
1988	39.6	13.7	26.9	59.5	10.2	17.1
1989	42.8	14.5	25.7	60.4	10.7	17.8
1990	39.7	12.6	22.8	60.6	9.8	16.1
1991	39.7	11.8	21.6	62.4	9.5	15.2
1992	42.6	12.1	21.0	67.4	10.3	15.3
1993	43.6	12.5	21.3	69.6	10.7	15.4
1994	46.2	13.5	21.8	70.7	11.6	16.4
1995	49.5	14.8	22.5	70.0	12.5	17.9
1996	49.8	16.8	24.8	70.1	14.1	20.0

Note: Total exports and non-traditional exports include non-factor service receipts.

Source: World Bank and South African Reserve Bank.

Table 8.6   Export concentration Gini-Hirschman measures, South Africa, 1983–96

	WB 3–digit excl. gold	WB 3–digit incl. gold	ISIC 300
1983	0.208	0.504	n/a
1984	0.222	0.465	n/a
1985	0.232	0.431	n/a
1986	0.224	0.422	n/a
1987	0.229	0.470	n/a
1988	0.228	0.433	0.354
1989	0.228	0.387	0.362
1990	0.247	0.379	0.347
1991	0.241	0.377	0.324
1992	0.225	0.352	0.313
1993	0.210	0.354	0.337
1994	0.202	0.329	0.318
1995	0.200	0.288	0.282
1996	0.197	0.281	0.281

Direction of trade

As with most South African trade data during the 1980s, the reliability of
South Africa's direction of trade statistics during the sanctions period can be
questioned. Nevertheless certain trends are clear. If gold exports and other

unidentified exports (mainly oil, arms and platinum, for which destinations are not reported) are excluded, 50 per cent of Southern African Customs Union (SACU) exports went to Western Europe in 1988 (Table 8.7). By 1996 this proportion had declined to 41 per cent. Most other areas remained fairly stable except for Africa which showed the largest relative increase as an export destination, from 8.1 per cent in 1988 to 18 per cent in 1996. Within Africa, Zimbabwe has been the largest export destination, accounting for about one-third of SACU exports (Table 8.8). The share of exports going to Mozambique rose to 15 per cent, whilst the relative importance of Zambia, Malawi, Zaire and Mauritius declined significantly. These top six countries

Table 8.7   Destination of exports, South Africa, 1988–96 (% of total)[*]

Destination	1988	1989	1990	1991	1992	1993	1994	1995	1996
Western Europe	50.0	45.1	45.1	46.3	48.3	47.7	45.0	42.7	40.8
Eastern Europe	0.2	0.2	0.5	0.7	0.8	0.7	0.7	1.0	0.5
North America	8.1	7.7	6.4	6.0	7.3	7.8	8.5	9.4	8.0
South, Central America	2.5	2.5	2.8	2.9	2.9	3.0	4.1	3.2	4.0
Africa	9.1	10.4	11.7	13.1	13.5	13.3	14.6	16.5	17.9
Mideast	3.0	3.4	3.7	3.7	3.7	5.3	3.3	3.0	3.3
Asia	26.6	30.0	28.9	26.7	23.1	21.6	23.1	22.8	24.1
Oceania	0.5	0.7	0.7	0.5	0.4	0.7	0.7	1.3	1.4

[*] Excluding Unidentified and Gold.

Table 8.8   Major SACU export destinations in Africa, 1988–96 (% of total SACU exports)

Country	1988	1989	1990	1991	1992	1993	1994	1995	1996
Zimbabwe	33.0	31.0	31.0	33.7	27.0	26.0	29.0	34.0	32.0
Mozambique	12.0	11.0	12.0	14.4	11.0	14.0	16.0	14.0	15.0
Zambia	12.0	14.0	14.0	13.8	19.0	19.0	13.0	10.0	10.0
Malawi	11.0	13.0	11.0	12.1	12.0	9.0	7.0	5.0	6.0
Zaire	11.0	11.0	12.0	6.4	5.1	4.0	4.0	5.0	5.0
Mauritius	9.0	8.0	8.0	7.9	6.9	7.0	6.0	5.0	5.0
Kenya	0.0	0.0	0.0	0.6	2.7	3.0	7.0	6.0	5.0
Angola	0.0	0.0	1.0	2.9	6.4	4.0	3.0	3.0	4.0
Tanzania	0.0	0.0	0.0	0.2	0.5	0.0	2.0	4.0	3.0
Ghana	0.0	0.0	0.0	0.1	0.4	0.0	1.0	1.0	1.0
Madagascar	0.0	0.0	1.0	0.9	0.9	0.0	0.0	1.0	1.0
Egypt	0.0	1.0	1.0	0.7	0.6	0.0	0.0	0.0	1.0
Nigeria	0.0	0.0	0.0	0.1	0.1	0.0	0.0	1.0	1.0
Seychelles	1.0	1.0	1.0	1.0	1.1	1.0	1.0	1.0	1.0
Uganda	0.0	0.0	0.0	0.0	0.1	0.0	0.0	0.0	0.0
Côte d'Ivoire	1.0	1.0	1.0	1.4	1.5	1.0	0.0	0.0	0.0
Rest	3.0	3.0	3.0	3.6	3.7	3.0	3.0	3.0	3.0
Total Exports	1.02	1.22	1.47	1.74	1.99	2.00	2.35	3.44	3.83

accounted for just over three-quarters of South Africa's non-gold exports to Africa. South Africa's total trade with Africa increased from US$1.02 billion in 1988 to US$3.83 billion in 1996.

The major change in South Africa's export destinations (excluding gold) has been that of Zimbabwe which in 1988 accounted for 3 per cent of South Africa's exports. By 1996 it was the fourth-largest export destination at 5.7 per cent of South African exports, after the UK (13.7 per cent), Japan (7.2 per cent) and the US (7.1 per cent).

Tourism and other services

International trade in services has been growing more rapidly than merchandise trade over the past two decades and the main components of this have been producer services and tourism. South African service exports grew only slowly in comparison to world services during the 1980s. Trade in services was particularly affected by sanctions because it is more difficult to disguise the country of origin of services than is the case with goods (Hodge, 1996). The expansion of tourism was particularly constrained and political change has led to massive expansion with tourism-related receipts totalling US$2.8 billion in 1996, equivalent to 11.9 per cent of non-gold merchandise exports (Table 8.9). In spite of this expansion, receipts from international tourism as a share of GDP remain low relative to comparator countries and the sector is widely seen as having high growth and employment creation potential. Producer services (communication, transport, finance and other business services) are also an area with high growth potential, especially in developing country markets, because of the low cost of professional staff in South Africa and experience in adapting products to the requirements of a developing country (ibid.).

Table 8.9   Receipts from international tourism, South Africa, 1988–96

	Travel expenditure and passenger fares (US$ million)	*Travel expenditure receipts and passenger fares as % of non-gold merchandise exports*
1988	904	6.4
1989	1,054	7.2
1990	1,286	7.8
1991	1,408	8.7
1992	1,545	9.0
1993	1,643	9.5
1994	1,930	10.5
1995	2,445	10.9
1996	2,813	11.9

Note: Travel expenditure and passenger fares are used as a proxy for receipts from international tourism.

Source: South African Reserve Bank Quarterly Bulletins.

The impact of policy on exports

South African trade policy in general and export policy as it impacts on exports of manufactures and other non-traditional exports can be divided into four phases (Table 8.10). Import-substitution policies pursued since the 1920s encouraged the development of a large and diversified manufacturing base. This was accompanied by a steady decline in overall import penetration although the import propensity remained high in the two major import sectors, capital goods and transport equipment (Kahn, 1987). The underlying philosophy during this import-substitution phase which lasted for 50 years was for industrialization behind protective barriers with foreign exchange requirements met by natural resource exports. Over this period, there developed in South Africa a protective regime which, while offering only average levels of protection compared to other developing countries, was characterized by an extraordinarily high degree of complexity and variability (Belli et al., 1993).

The beginnings of trade liberalization can be dated back to the early 1970s as some of the classic problems of import substitution became apparent. Trade reform has been characterized by a gradual strengthening of export promotion policy combined with an equally gradual reduction of protection, interrupted at times by political and economic crises. Early efforts to promote exports were motivated more by an attempt to diversify away from dependence on gold than to promote manufactured exports. These were ineffective partly because of the limited nature of export assistance (mainly in the form of marketing assistance) and also because the rising gold price in the late 1970s led to a strengthening of the rand as well as temporarily removing the need to promote non-traditional exports.

Trade reforms in the late 1980s and early 1990s involved the removal of quantitative controls and the introduction of a series of 'Structural Adjustment Programmes' (not conventional SAPs) in sectors such as clothing and textiles, automobiles and electronics. The structural adjustment programmes were, however, seen as too complicated and in 1990 the General Export Incentive Scheme was introduced which provided large export subsidies of up to 20 per cent for manufactured exports.

In assessing South Africa's trade policy and export performance during this period it needs to be remembered that as international isolation deepened, strategic considerations became a key imperative. This blunted the shift to trade liberalization and led the state to prioritize self-sufficiency in certain key sectors. These included major investments in a large oil-from-coal industry (Sasol), a refinery based on uneconomic offshore gas reserves (Mossgas) and a diesel engine facility (Atlantis Diesel Engines). While it is difficult to quantify the impact of sanctions imposed during the apartheid era, they certainly slowed export expansion especially in non-traditional exports where Africa would have been the major market. One indicator of this is the massive growth of exports (mainly manufactures) into African markets since sanction pressures started to ease in the early 1990s. Also, foreign direct investment dried up in the 1980s and there was significant disinvestment, especially by US firms. Commodity-type products were less affected by sanctions because the source country was more difficult to identify and sanctions were not strongly applied by the developed countries which were the major markets for these products.

Table 8.10   The chronology of trade liberalization and export orientation, South Africa, 1925–98

Year(s)	Policy change, event
1925–72	**Phase of Import Substituting Industrialization (ISI)**
1925	Implementation of ISI; Customs Tariff and Excise Duty Amendment Act
1948	Introduction of QRs
1972–83	**First Trade Liberalization Episode**
1972	Reynders Commission recommends export promotion
1972	Mild export incentives introduced
1972–6	Relaxation of QRs
1975–9	Devaluation of rand
1978	Van Huyssteen Committee – further assistance to exporters
1979–80	Rising gold price – rand appreciates sharply
1983–91	**Second Trade Liberalization Episode**
1983	Kleu Study Group recommends shift away from ISI to greater export promotion
1983–5	Continuing reduction of QRs
1984–5	Sharp fall in value of the rand
1985	Debt crisis; import surcharges introduced
1989	Structural adjustment programmes; export incentives for clothing, textiles and automotive sectors
1990	Introduction of GEIS
1990	Partial phasing out of import surcharge
1994–	**Third Trade Liberalization Episode**
1994–7	Conversion of QRs to tariffs
1994	Elimination of import surcharges
1995–	Beginning of tariff reduction in line with WTO requirements
1995	Abolition of dual exchange rate (financial rand)
1995–8	Negotiations with EU over free trade agreement
1995	Introduction of Motor Industry Development Programme
1995	Decision taken to phase out GEIS ahead of schedule
1995–8	Introduction of supply-side incentives
1996	Introduction of GEAR with further commitment to tariff phase-down
1996	Signing of SADC free trade protocol
1997	Continuing liberalization of exchange controls
1998	Sharp depreciation of the rand

Source: Adapted from Jenkins and Siwisa (1997: 50).

The third trade liberalization phase can be dated from 1994. Although this was the year of South Africa's first democratic election, there was no major shift in policy which continued to liberalize trade, reducing tariffs in line with and sometimes beyond GATT commitments. Reacceptance into the world trading community, if anything, accelerated moves towards trade liberalization and also opened the way for the negotiation of trade agreements as well as the phased dismantling of exchange controls. A wide range of supply-side assistance measures and incentives have also been introduced (see Table 8.12).

Incentives and support measures for exporting

The shift to policies which are more promotive of manufactured exports has had two main elements apart from exchange rate policy: first, a range of support measures for exports have been introduced; and, second, protection has been reduced over time.

As indicated earlier the export incentives introduced as far back as the 1970s comprised mainly marketing assistance and were not very effective. This changed with the introduction of the General Export Incentive Scheme (GEIS) in 1990. GEIS was introduced in 1990 and provided (an initially tax-free) subsidy to exporters which was based on the local content value of exports and the level of processing. There were four levels of incentive. Primary products (e.g. mineral products) attracted no incentive while fully manufactured products attracted subsidies of up to 20 per cent. In the first five years of its operation (1990–4), GEIS payments averaged R1.205 billion per year ranging from 6–8 per cent of the value of exports in sectors which qualified. In its earlier tax-free version, this benefit was effectively enhanced and GEIS payments in 1993 accounted for over 20 per cent of net profits of receiving firms in 5 out of 25 industrial sectors.

GEIS suffered from a number of problems (see Hirsch and House, 1994), not least that the highly visible annual outlay made it a quick target for a cash-strapped finance ministry. The major beneficiaries of GEIS were large firms in capital-intensive sectors. Because GEIS payments only covered the local content portion of exports, highly labour-intensive firms with imported components derived relatively little benefit. Also, the level of GEIS subsidy was not related to the rate of protection of inputs. The result was that although in the aggregate GEIS produced a situation of reasonable neutrality between production for domestic and foreign markets, there was an extreme level of variability in the degree of anti-export bias between sectors and subsectors. As Table 8.11 indicates, even with GEIS (based on inputs at domestic prices) the anti-export bias coefficient ranged from 1.64 for textiles and apparel (a strong anti-export bias) to 0.70 in the case of paper and paper products (a pro-export bias). At the subsectoral level, Belli et al. (1993) found that in the textiles sector, the anti-export bias coefficient (after GEIS) indicated a pro-export bias in two subsectors, an anti-export bias in five cases and an extreme anti-export bias[5] in two sectors. The GEIS export subsidy, illegal in terms of WTO rules and considered problematic for the reasons stated above, has been phased out ahead of schedule and is being replaced by a revamped duty drawback system.

Table 8.11   Anti-export bias coefficient (with and without GEIS), South Africa

	With GEIS Anti-Export Bias		Without GEIS Anti-Export Bias	
	(lw)[a]	*(ld)[b]*	*(lw)[a]*	*(ld)[b]*
Food, Beverages and Tobacco	0.71	1.03	0.71	2.05
Textiles, Apparel and Leather	0.94	1.64	0.94	16.65
Wood and Wood Products	0.78	0.97	0.78	2.14
Paper and Paper Products	0.62	0.70	0.62	1.57
Chemicals	1.08	1.27	1.08	1.90
Non-Metallic Minerals	1.15	1.20	1.15	1.42
Basic Metal	1.06	1.14	1.06	1.35
Metal Products and Equipment	0.66	0.82	0.66	1.88
Other Manufacturing	0.46	0.49	0.46	1.99
All Manufacturing	0.82	1.03	0.82	1.89

Notes:
[a] lw indicates that value added was calculated based on inputs purchased at world prices.
[b] ld indicates that value added was calculated based on inputs at domestic prices.

Source: Adapted from Belli et al. (1993: 75).

By the early 1990s, the level of protection had been reduced to some extent. According to a major World Bank study (Belli et al., 1993), South Africa's average statutory tariff (weighted by the value of imports) of 27.5 per cent was the thirteenth highest of the developing countries for which the Bank had comparable data. For agriculture, mining and capital goods its tariffs were below the average of the developing country sample. Furthermore, the Bank's estimates were probably on the high side because of the method by which formula duties were calculated (Bell, 1997: 75).[6] They also included import surcharges which were abolished during 1994 and 1995. According to the Industrial Development Corporation (IDC), the average rate of duty on manufactured goods was 15 per cent for 1994 (ibid.).

The current phase of trade policy reform involves a number of elements, the most important of which is the reduction of tariffs. This process began before the advent of democratic government in 1994 but the African National Congress (ANC) and its alliance partner, the Confederation of South African Trade Unions (COSATU), were heavily involved in the discussions leading up to the 1993 GATT offer. The new government has continued to pursue trade liberalization and in many sectors is reducing tariffs to below the terms of its agreement under the Uruguay Round. Nevertheless, the programme of tariff cuts now in place is moderate rather than drastic. The average percentage rate of tariff duty (on a weighted basis according to 1994 imports) is declining from 34 per cent to 18 per cent in 2002 for consumption goods and from 15 per cent to 8 per cent for industry as a whole (ibid.: 76). However, it is possible that the tariff phase-down will be accelerated as stipulated in terms of the GEAR strategy introduced in 1996. GEAR comprises a fairly orthodox package of fiscal restraint and privatization measures and re-emphasizes the role of manufactured exports as a key pillar of South Africa's growth strategy.

Apart from phasing-down tariff protection, policy since 1994 has also been directed at putting in place a range of supply-side incentives to boost competitiveness in domestic and foreign markets. These measures involve support for new investment, training, small firms, innovation and exports (Department of Trade and Industry, 1997). Those which are partly or wholly aimed at supporting exports are listed in Table 8.12.

The support measures listed in Table 8.12 are directed at a range of firm types and mainly offer fairly limited levels of assistance. For most exporters, it is unlikely that they would compensate for the cash subsidy that was available under GEIS. The Rebate Provision (duty drawback) was not available for GEIS beneficiaries and more use is being made of it now that GEIS has been abolished. For new investments, the most important incentive is the recently introduced tax holiday. Under this scheme, which is designed to kick-start investment, including foreign investment, new industrial projects can qualify for a tax holiday of up to six years depending on factory location, industrial sector and the ratio of wages to value added. However, this scheme is not aimed specifically at exports. It is too early to draw firm conclusions as to the effectiveness of the package of supply-side measures which have been introduced over the past few years as some of the incentives are not yet being widely used. It is possible that there are too many incentive schemes which have led to administrative problems and delays in accessing the support measures. Certainly they need to be marketed more effectively by government and industry federations. A considerable amount of support is directed to smaller firms and medium-sized and larger exporters would in almost all cases receive less support than was the case under GEIS. Exceptions would include firms which operate under sector-specific programmes such as the Motor Industry Development Programme (automotive industry) and the Duty Credit Scheme (textiles and clothing) and can earn rebates on import duties by exporting.

Estimates by the IDC (Table 8.13) show that in spite of ongoing tariff reductions the phasing-out of GEIS has meant that anti-export bias increased from 1.19 to 1.32 for the total economy between 1993 and 1996 and remained static from 1996–9.

The physical, financial and social infrastructure to support non-traditional exports is highly variable and reflects the priorities of the previous government. For example, the road infrastructure is excellent in most parts

Table 8.12   Incentive schemes available for the promotion of exports, South Africa

Name of scheme	Objective and description
Competitiveness Fund	Aimed at encouraging competitiveness particularly by small, medium and micro enterprises (SMMEs); 60% of funds are allocated to SMMEs which also receive advisory support.
Short Term Export Finance Guarantee Facility	Aimed at SMME exporters. Provides guarantees to providers of export finance.
Export Marketing and Investment Assistance Schemes	Assists exporters with export market research and trade missions.
Life Scheme	Low interest financing to export-oriented projects through the Industrial Development Corporation.
World Player Scheme	IDC provides low-interest loans to firms in sectors which are most affected by tariff reductions (textiles, clothing, footwear and automotive).
Finance for Export of Capital Goods and Services	Special credit facilities for the export of goods and services.
Duty Credit Certificate Scheme for exporters of textiles and clothing	Temporary measure to promote exports by offering import rebate certificates to exporters.
Motor Industry Development Programme	To encourage specialization and competitiveness by enabling exporters of vehicles and components to rebate import duties.
Tax Holidays	Aimed at encouraging investment by offering tax holidays for new investments which meet certain qualifying criteria.
Rebate Provisions	Provides drawbacks of duties on imported raw materials and components used in manufacturing for export.
Low Interest Rate Scheme for the Promotion of Exports	To encourage new investment for export by providing low interest rate finance for investment aimed at exports.

Source: Department of Trade and Industry (1997).

of the country but huge backlogs exist in education for blacks. The apartheid heritage of very poor levels of general education and training is a serious deficiency. Strenuous efforts are now being made to address this, including the introduction of a training levy on all employers. The workforce is strongly unionized and there have been major advances in the rights of workers since 1994 to the extent that labour market regulation is increasingly being seen as an obstacle to investment and employment creation. While labour costs are not low compared to countries with similar per capita incomes, this is partly compensated for by excellent infrastructure, extremely low electricity prices and low industrial rents. In a new 27-country index of business costs compiled by the Economist Intelligence Unit, South Africa emerged as the least expensive place to do business, coming in lower than India, China and Malaysia.[7]

Table 8.13   Anti-export bias (with and without export incentives), South Africa, 1993–9

	1993	*1996*	*1999*
No export incentives			
Total economy	1.63	1.49	1.42
Total manufacturing	1.98	1.69	1.59
Including export incentives			
Total economy	1.19	1.32	1.32
Total manufacturing	1.27	1.45	1.44

Source: Industrial Development Corporation (1997).

South Africa has a well-developed financial system and its stock market ranks in the top twelve in the world by market capitalization. Capital to fund large projects is available but real interest rates are high. With the exception of the support given to mega-projects there has been relatively little concessionary financing for industrial investment and while a number of funds are available for smaller firms these are generally difficult to access. A recent high profile policy to promote investment is the introduction of Spatial Development Initiatives (SDIs) which are aimed at kick-starting investment in specified regions through the development of infrastructure and the packaging of incentives to attract key anchor projects. The SDIs are, however, not specifically aimed at exporting industries. South Africa has no export processing zones although these are under discussion.

The system of scientific and technological research is relatively well developed in South Africa with the main problem being weak linkages between research institutions (universities, technikons and science councils) and firms (Blankley and Kaplan, 1997). Another problem is the lack of manufacturing technology extension services and export marketing assistance, especially for smaller firms. These problems are being addressed through new initiatives such as SPII,[8] THRIP,[9] and the introduction of manufacturing technology extension centres. It is, however, too early to assess the effectiveness of these new forms of support.

There is a high level of cooperation between government and the private sector in shaping economic policy and in a variety of related development initiatives. The National Economic Development and Labour Council (NEDLAC) provides statutory representation for business and unions in the economic policymaking process. The government has also initiated a range of 'clusters' which are aimed at developing greater cooperation between firms and institutions on a sectoral basis with the objective of promoting competitiveness.

The supply response of exports

As discussed earlier, it is clear that there has been a strong export supply response to the changed economic environment of the late 1980s and 1990s across a range of non-traditional export sectors. Total exports of manufactures doubled from US$8 billion to US$16.4 billion in 1996 (Appendix Table 8.A1). For many non-traditional manufactured exports, the growth rate was even more rapid and exports of 17 out of 24 manufacturing sectors trebled in dollar terms. Some of the most spectacular increases over this period have been in high value added products such as machinery (385 per cent) and motor vehicles and components (455 per cent).

The strong supply response to a more supportive trade regime for exports has replicated the experience of a range of other middle income countries. As indicated above, a number of positive factors have coincided in producing this export boom. Falling export receipts for gold resulting both from a weaker gold price since 1980 and falling production (see Table 8.2) has produced quite pronounced 'reverse Dutch disease' effects leading to an expansion of non-traditional exports. The weaker currency since 1984 and a range of policies aiming at reducing the anti-export bias through increasing export incentives and phasing-down protection have played an important role. Levels of protection have never been inordinately high except in some sectors and the strong currency until the mid-1980s ameliorated some of the worst effects of high protection. Added to this has been the rapid opening-up to South African exporters of international markets since 1990 with full trade relations since 1994. This has benefited non-traditional exports far more than traditional exports such as gold and other primary resources. Non-traditional exports frequently require significant marketing efforts and this together with the greater importance of branding and tie-ups with foreign firms previously hindered exports.

Nearly two-thirds of fully manufactured exports go to Africa and the opening-up of these markets with the demise of apartheid has provided a massive boost to South African exports of manufactured goods. Many African countries did not trade with South Africa at all during the apartheid years. This boom in exports has been assisted in some cases by structural adjustment inspired import liberalization in some of South Africa's neighbours. The result has been a rapidly expanding trade surplus with neighbouring countries which is causing considerable concern. The Southern African Customs Union runs huge trade surpluses with its SADC neighbours. The total surplus in 1996 was R11.3 billion based on exports of R13.9 billion and imports of only R2.6 billion. SACU has a trade imbalance of nearly five to one with its largest African export market, Zimbabwe. Exports to

Mozambique climbed to nearly R3 billion in 1996 although imports from that country were negligible. Neighbouring countries are justifiably irritated that South Africa has been slow to open up to trade from the north with very damaging results for the Zimbabwean clothing industry, for example. Intensive efforts are underway to establish a common market for the SADC region which could eventually provide a building block for a larger African common market.

However, it is clear that the rapid expansion of exports to Africa can be traced back to the mid-1980s. South Africa's two largest African export markets (Zimbabwe and Mozambique) were always open to South African exports although more active trade promotion can now take place. Full trade relations have created significant opportunities for South African firms which can now adopt a much higher profile and are also investing heavily in the region. This process will be accelerated by moves towards a free trade region within the 12-nation Southern African Development Community. South Africa is also engaged in negotiations with the European Union regarding a free trade agreement which could prove particularly significant in improving market access in a range of agricultural and related products. The dropping of sanctions has also played a major role in opening access to a number of other important emerging markets such as India. It has also allowed firms to establish major marketing campaigns to export products which are well established in the domestic market. One of the best examples is the wine industry which was the subject of a successful boycott in key European markets but increased exports twelvefold from 1990 to 1996.

The major exporters have been large and medium-sized indigenous firms. Although weak domestic demand has undoubtedly played a role in pushing firms to seek foreign markets,[10] it would appear that the tendency for South African firms to view international markets as short-term expedients during domestic recession has changed quite fundamentally. Since the mid-1980s, South African firms have gradually become much more oriented to international markets. While larger firms have been the leading exporters, a number of export-oriented medium-sized firms with proprietary technology have emerged. Firms of this type include Bell Equipment which manufactures earthmoving, mining and forestry equipment and achieved exports of R320 million (39 per cent of turnover) during its 1996/97 financial year (Bell Equipment Ltd, *Annual Report*, 1997).

An important recent development has been the 'unbundling' of large diversified conglomerates. These firms were frequently established by the large mining or financial groups which, in an environment of controls on capital outflows and protection in the domestic market, had become exceptionally diversified into the industrial sector. The industrial conglomerates were frequently characterized by a lack of specialization, dependence on foreign licensed technology and an inward focus. This was the result of exchange controls which placed limits on foreign investment and comfortable levels of protection. Some of these groups have unbundled their industrial interests and others have been selling off non-core interests. Remaining core interests will be developed and may reach the critical mass required to become world players in their particular market segments. Some, such as Boart, the mining equipment producer within the Amic group, or the pulp and paper producer, Sappi, formerly owned by Gencor, have already achieved this.

Foreign investment has been less of a factor with some important exceptions. Foreign direct investment into South Africa from 1995 to 1997 totalled R30 billion. By far the largest source of investment has been the US. US investment has included reinvestments by US firms which disinvested as a result of sanction pressures, political turmoil and low growth in the 1980s. The large foreign investments in the telecommunications sector have been as a result of the partial privatization of Telkom. Besides telecommunications, the largest recipients of foreign investment have been food and beverages, automotive, chemicals, energy and tourism sectors. Most inward investment has been aimed at the domestic market, but South Africa frequently acts as the regional or continental headquarters for multinational firms so regional exports will be generated.

Recent investments in automotive components are generally highly oriented to exports. The buying out of local firms, and the establishment of joint ventures can create export opportunities as the domestic plant becomes integrated into the international network. For example, in the automotive industry since 1994, Ford, Nissan, Toyota and General Motors have all taken equity stakes in licensed domestic firms, increasing access to foreign markets and allowing them to make full use of the import complementation arrangements under the Motor Industry Development Programme (MIDP). Deals of this type in other sectors have included the purchase of South Africa's third-largest chemical firm, Sentrachem, by Dow Chemical.

As stated above, the growth in manufactured exports reflects a much greater export orientation among South African firms resulting from a range of factors including the weaker currency since 1984, weak domestic demand, improved incentives for exports, reduced protection in the domestic market and the opening up of international markets as a result of the demise of apartheid. However, the specific factors driving export growth of manufactures vary significantly from sector to sector.

Growth in non-traditional exports has taken place in sectors which have not been heavily protected in the past but have now become increasingly export-oriented as well as formerly highly protected import-substitution industries. The machinery sector has traditionally received little protection and has a huge negative trade balance. However, exports grew from US$378 million in 1988 to US$1454 million in 1996. The most protected industry historically has been the automotive industry. Exports of automotive components have expanded massively to R4.77 billion in 1997 up from only

R200 million in 1988. Vehicle exports have taken longer to materialize but jumped 69 per cent to 19 569 units in 1997. BMW(SA) plans to export 30 000 cars per year by the year 2002, an 80 per cent increase on their total 1997 production for both the domestic and export markets. Volkswagen (South Africa) announced that they planned to export 60 000 vehicles to the UK in 1999. The massive expansion of automotive exports has been partly driven by the import complementation arrangements of the MIDP, but lower protection in the domestic market has also been a major factor. While a large share of component exports could be described as peripheral components with relatively light investments, virtually all categories have expanded (Table 8.14).

Table 8.14   Exports of components, South Africa, 1995–7 (FOB values, R millions)

	1995	*1996*	*1997*	*% of 1997 total*
Stitched leather covers	1,019	1,259	1,396	29.4
Catalytic converters	388	485	686	14.5
Tyres	219	296	327	6.9
Automotive tooling	259	279	326	6.9
Road wheels/parts	175	227	301	6.3
Silencers/exhaust pipes	76	170	228	4.8
Engine parts	112	137	163	3.4
Glass	49	71	106	2.2
Batteries	53	60	90	1.9
Engines	10	86	62	1.3
Filters	13	42	50	1.1
Brake parts	23	29	39	0.8
Body parts/panels	18	39	37	0.8
Shock absorbers	38	53	35	0.7
Gauges/instruments/parts	18	28	33	0.7
Clutches/shaft couplings	16	21	33	0.7
Car radios	7	4	28	0.6
Jacks	13	21	24	0.5
Springs	16	19	21	0.4
Other components	797	727	762	16.1
Total	3,318	4,051	4,747	100.0

Source: Department of Trade and Industry.

While automotive exports have to some extent been driven by import-export complementation arrangements under the MIDP, other sectors which were recipients of GEIS but no longer receive incentives also show massive export growth, albeit not to the same extent. Large South African groups which were mainly oriented to the domestic market have shifted to a greater export focus. The country's largest indigenous electronics and telecommunications firm, Altron, exported telecommunications equipment, cabling and batteries to the value of R540 million in 1998 up from virtually zero five years previously. A number of firms which were nurtured under government support for strategic reasons have become major exporters as their privileged position in the domestic market has been stripped away. Most prominent is the formerly state-owned oil-from-coal producer, Sasol, which is now a diversified producer and exporter of a range of chemical products. The state-owned diesel engine producer, Atlantis Diesel Engines, is transforming itself into a producer of engine components for the export market following the ending of its virtual monopoly in the domestic truck engine market. It has also secured niche export markets including a R400 million contract to supply engines for the refurbishment of the Cuban sugar industry. Export expansion in armaments and certain categories of electronics has been based on capabilities acquired during the development of a large arms industry during the apartheid era. The state-owned defence firm, Denel, is now a major exporter of a range of sophisticated weaponry.

South Africa's manufactured exports remain dominated by processed primary products and products such as steel have been classified as 'traditional' for the purposes of this analysis. In certain sectors (steel, ferro alloys, pulp and paper, industrial chemicals), competitive advantage is based on domestic raw material supply and cheap electricity, sometimes reinforced by privileged access to purpose-built infrastructure and both loan and equity capital via the state-owned IDC. Government policy supported this through a range of direct and indirect forms of assistance. This assistance included special accelerated depreciation allowances which facilitated a number of investments in mega-plants such as the Columbus stainless steel facility and the large new Hillside aluminium smelter. Firms in this category benefited disproportionately from GEIS as well. The largest single recipient of benefits from the inception of GEIS until March 1995 was Iscor, the country's major steel producer. The top ten recipients included three steel producers and two paper and pulp producers. Three other firms were large-scale producers of processed fruit.

Although there is no comprehensive information on the size of exporting firms, small firms are not generally major exporters.[11] For instance, in the relatively weakly developed electronics sector, a recent survey of 36 small firms found that the average export propensity was only 7 per cent of output compared to an average export propensity of 15 per cent for the sector as a whole (Kaplan, 1997). Although 61 per cent of these small firms were doing some exporting, only 22 per cent were exporting 10 per cent or more of output. The majority were therefore marginal exporters with Africa being the major market. Major electronics exporters on the other hand cited Europe as the major market. Marketing was seen to be the major retarding factor and firms felt there was little government support for exporting activity with the exception of GEIS which has now been phased out (Kaplan, 1997).

The trade regime, exports and employment

There is general consensus that unemployment is the key problem facing South Africa. Alleviating unemployment requires more rapid growth but also a more labour-demanding pattern of growth. The employment impact of the emerging trade regime is, therefore, a key element as is the capacity of export growth to generate employment.

As Table 8.15 indicates, there was no growth in manufacturing employment from 1993 to 1997 and employment declined during the first half of 1998. While there are a number of factors which can account for whether employment grows in manufacturing (see, for example, Kaplinsky, 1995), changes in the trade regime are potentially very significant. Many of South Africa's traditional manufactured exports are very capital-intensive (steel, aluminium, industrial chemicals, paper and pulp, etc.). Labour-intensive activities such as clothing and electronics assembly which could rapidly generate employment have not been a significant component of the expansion of non-traditional exports. Heavily subsidized labour-intensive firms in backward regions which received government largesse under the previous homeland policy[12] are facing declining incentives. Labour-intensive sectors such as textiles and footwear have been hit hard by tariff reductions although textile exports are now expanding rapidly, supported by new investment into this sector. Clothing exports have not grown significantly until very recently and the major market, paradoxically, is Mozambique, one of the poorest countries in the world.

The fact that manufactured exports are less labour-intensive than import-competing industries has led Bell and Cattaneo (1997) to argue that trade liberalization will have a negative impact on employment. However, it could be argued that the expansion in beneficiated metal exports has in part been driven not simply by comparative advantage but by direct and indirect subsidies for mega-projects. In this case a more rational policy structure would presumably lead to the emergence of export sectors which are more labour-demanding. During the 1980s, the most rapid export expansion was recorded by the category of beneficiated products. However, the more recent expansion of higher value added manufactures indicates that a more predictable trend is indeed now emerging which augurs well for employment creation.

The main factor explaining the lack of employment growth has simply been weak domestic demand. Lower protection has led to falling employment in certain sectors but there is little evidence that this has been dramatic. Interestingly, sectors which have faced quite substantial declines in tariff protection such as the clothing and motor sectors have shown increases in employment. Export growth has been dominated by the bigger firms within the subsector which tend to be more capital-intensive. Export production is also likely to be more capital-intensive than import-competing production within a particular sector.

Table 8.15   Manufacturing employment, South Africa, 1993–7 (000s)

	1993	1994	1995	1996	1997[*]
Total	1,407.0	1,406.3	1,414.1	1,438.1	1,407.7
Food	190.8	179.3	176.0	177.3	172.5
Beverages	35.6	34.3	32.6	31.2	30.0
Tobacco	3.4	3.1	2.9	2.8	2.7
Textiles	81.3	83.4	60.5	96.8	75.9
Clothing	111.2	110.9	120.5	130.5	140.7
Leather	9.5	9.1	9.1	7.3	7.8
Footwear	25.6	26.9	27.8	25.2	23.7
Wood	59.6	65.1	62.9	59.9	60.2
Furniture	41.1	42.3	42.0	44.3	45.9
Paper	49.6	48.9	50.4	48.3	37.6
Printing	53.6	52.9	53.4	52.6	51.8
Industrial Chemicals	55.9	55.1	52.7	51.5	n.a.
Chemicals	65.9	61.9	61.5	60.8	n.a.
Rubber	16.1	16.3	17.3	17.7	16.2
Plastics	46.4	42.3	47.5	45.8	47.4
Glass	9.7	10.2	9.9	9.8	9.6
Non-Metallic Basic	73.3	67.0	64.9	65.9	63.7
Basic Iron and Steel	67.3	61.8	60.6	59.3	55.9
Non-Ferrous Metals	16.9	16.2	15.8	14.2	13.2
Metal Products	122.3	124.7	123.4	126.5	122.9
Machinery	66.5	67.5	73.3	77.0	74.9
Electrical	91.7	111.0	108.9	102.2	98.6
Motors	70.9	73.8	79.9	82.1	77.6
Transport	13.1	11.8	11.0	12.1	n.a.
Professional	7.5	7.6	7.5	7.6	6.5
Other Manufacturing	23.5	22.4	21.7	25.2	23.7

[*] Average for first three quarters.

Source: Industrial Development Corporation.

The rate and sequencing of import liberalization

Tariff reductions have already had a major effect on the clothing and textile sectors and are starting to bite in sectors such as the strongly unionized automotive industry. This raises the issue of the effectiveness of import liberalization versus direct export support in promoting exports as well as issues of sequencing.

The issue also arises as to the sequencing of exchange rate policy changes and tariff reductions. The experience of trade liberalizations internationally has shown that those that are accompanied by currency devaluations are more likely to be successful and sustained (Papageorgiou et al., 1991). On the other hand, the literature on compensated devaluations argues that the inflationary impact of devaluations or depreciations can be offset by appropriate tariff reductions. The liberalization of the trade regime was initially not coordinated with exchange rate policy developments. This tended to put pressure on the liberalizing industries at a time when the currency was appreciating in real terms as a result of the strong capital inflows. As noted in the GEAR, 'many firms have been under intense pressure, compounded by the real appreciation of the exchange rate in 1995. Nevertheless, exports and employment in manufacturing have increased, taking advantage of the international cyclical upswing' (GEAR, 1996: 12).

The GEAR explicitly called for a greater coordination of trade and exchange rate policies. However, the real depreciation of the rand in 1996 was not seen as a compensation for firms that had experienced rapid tariff reductions; rather the depreciation was seen as a means to speed up the pace of tariff reform, and the depreciation was seen as a means to compensate firms for the accelerated pace of reform. According to GEAR, as a result of the real depreciation,

> a compensating lowering of tariffs is desirable, within the context of an orderly implementation of agreed tariff realignments. The mid-1996 real effective exchange rate is some 12 per cent below the January value, which should permit a significant acceleration of the tariff reductions to which South Africa is committed in terms of the World Trade Organisation agreements. These reforms will be structured to lower prices for industrial inputs and low-income households, to avoid job losses in sensitive sectors, and to remove price distortions in domestic markets. The overall effect will be to minimise the negative effects of the depreciation on consumer prices and maximise the positive effects on industrial production. (ibid.: 12)

Conclusion

The sustainability of export growth

As this paper has shown, the supply response to a changing pattern of emphasis in government policy and the open trade environment of the 1990s has been reasonably strong. Many firms have become more export-oriented and a culture of exporting is becoming established. Exports of many categories of manufactures have grown strongly, in many instances building on capabilities developed during the long import-substitution phase. A recent World Bank study (Tsikata, 1998) argues that for a number of reasons this momentum may not be maintained. The first concern is that the increase in anti-export bias resulting from the phasing-out of GEIS more than offsets the decline in protection at least until 1996. However, this factor is now effectively out of the system and with continuing tariff reductions coupled with the improved effectiveness of supply-side support measures, anti-export bias should continue to decline. Much will also depend on the behaviour of the exchange rate.

A second concern raised by the Bank is that many of the export gains have been in African markets where trade opportunities have opened up as a result of the demise of apartheid. It is argued that the absorptive capacity of these countries may be limited, a factor exacerbated by the large trade surplus that South Africa is running with most of its African trading partners. However, growth prospects for Africa are better than they have been for two decades and large potential markets such as West Africa have hardly been tapped by South African exporters. Also, in the medium term, the establishment of a free trade area in SADC will improve South African market access.

A third concern raised by the Bank is the limited employment creation that has arisen from export expansion thus far. Tsikata (ibid.) points to the capital-intensive nature of many South African manufactured exports[13] and the weak growth of labour-intensive manufactures. However, as this chapter indicates, there are clear indications of a shift in the sectoral composition of exports away from the very capital-intensive sectors which have dominated export expansion of manufactures over the past two decades. The limited expansion in very labour-intensive exports, however, remains a concern.

Appendix

Table 8.A1   Value of exports (3-digit ISIC manufacturing categories), South Africa, 1988–96 (US$ millions)

Rank in 1988	% of total excl. other in 1988	Category	1988	1989	1990	1991	1992	1993	1994	1995	1996	% of Total in 1996	% growth p.a.
1	28.7	Iron and steel	1,806	2,182	2,210	2,139	2,186	2,050	2,302	2,769	2,608	20.1	5.2
2	18.3	Non–ferrous metals	1,154	1,271	1,130	1,225	1,302	871	759	1,617	987	7.6	5.2
3	13.5	Chem. (ind. and other)	850	892	862	1,055	1,361	1,189	1,559	2,652	2,936	22.6	19.0
4	8.8	Paper and paper products	557	614	597	562	647	570	705	1,180	748	5.8	7.4
5	7.1	Processed foods	449	560	608	714	661	633	656	808	853	6.6	8.9
6	5.2	Textiles	328	320	341	386	380	318	329	375	383	3.0	2.4
7	4.7	Machinery (excl. elec.)	293	291	366	427	543	601	642	1,048	1,041	8.0	18.6
8	4.0	Metal products	252	334	413	409	340	327	496	754	816	6.3	18.3
9	2.2	Motor vehicles	140	176	259	332	517	582	481	590	637	4.9	22.8
10	1.4	Electrical machinery	85	100	148	150	183	246	255	395	413	3.2	23.3
11	0.9	Wood and wood products	59	67	83	78	74	95	113	93	76	0.6	4.7
12	0.7	Glass	42	49	49	47	51	54	47	39	46	0.4	1.9
13	0.7	Transport equipment	41	38	109	98	184	178	187	189	217	1.7	34.4
14	0.6	Furniture	37	39	46	65	76	78	80	109	119	0.9	16.5
15	0.6	Leather and leather products	36	46	61	60	73	90	136	153	164	1.3	21.8
16	0.6	Beverages	35	45	75	125	137	144	273	236	310	2.4	35.5
17	0.5	Clothing	33	33	51	82	126	148	91	105	100	0.8	19.8
18	0.4	Rubber and rubber products	28	28	28	43	50	60	66	102	113	0.9	20.6
19	0.4	Plastic	24	28	33	38	53	63	69	101	95	0.7	19.7
20	0.4	Other metal products	24	31	54	72	87	87	105	132	127	1.0	25.0
21	0.2	Printing and publishing	24	10	16	16	17	21	44	49	122	0.9	42.9
22	0.1	Footwear	6	6	6	8	15	16	22	22	23	0.2	21.2
23	0.0	Tobacco	2	2	3	7	19	15	16	27	34	0.3	54.4
24	0.0	Ceramic	2	3	4	6	7	5	6	8	10	0.1	25.0
		Total–excl. Other	6,296	7,165	7,553	8,144	9,088	8,442	9,438	13,552	12,977		10.3
25		Other	1,749	2,123	2,335	2,233	2,348	3,264	3,095	2,845	3,388		9.6
		Total–incl. Other	8,045	9,288	9,887	10,377	11,437	11,706	12,533	16,397	16,365		9.6

Source: Industrial Development Corporation.

Table 8.A2 300-level manufacturing exports (as % of total 300 level), South Africa, 1980–96

Exports	ISIC	1980	1981	1982	1983	1984	1985	1986	1987	1988	1989	1990	1991	1992	1993	1994	1995	1996
Food	311–312	21.4	18.5	19.9	19.4	17.0	16.8	14.8	12.8	7.2	7.9	8.2	8.9	7.4	7.7	7.1	6.0	6.6
Beverages	313	1.1	1.1	1.1	1.1	1.0	1.3	1.4	1.3	0.6	0.6	1.0	1.6	1.5	1.7	3.0	1.8	2.4
Tobacco products	314	0.1	0.2	0.2	0.3	0.3	0.3	0.4	0.4	0.0	0.0	0.0	0.1	0.2	0.2	0.2	0.2	0.3
Textiles	321	7.3	7.6	7.3	7.0	6.4	6.7	6.9	6.5	5.2	4.5	4.6	4.8	4.3	3.8	3.6	2.8	3.0
Clothing	322	3.7	3.8	4.2	4.2	4.2	3.7	2.8	2.4	0.5	0.5	0.7	1.0	1.4	1.8	1.0	0.8	0.8
Leather and leather products	323	0.8	1.1	1.2	1.3	1.4	1.2	1.0	0.9	0.6	0.6	0.8	0.8	0.8	1.1	1.5	1.1	1.3
Footwear	324	0.4	0.4	0.4	0.4	0.4	0.4	0.4	0.4	0.1	0.1	0.1	0.1	0.2	0.2	0.2	0.2	0.2
Wood and wood products	331	1.9	1.7	1.5	1.3	1.2	1.6	2.0	1.9	0.9	0.9	1.1	1.0	0.8	1.2	1.2	0.7	0.6
Furniture	332	0.4	0.5	0.4	0.4	0.3	0.4	0.5	0.5	0.6	0.5	0.6	0.8	0.8	0.9	0.9	0.8	0.9
Paper and paper products	341	3.7	3.7	4.7	5.5	6.3	6.3	5.8	4.9	8.9	8.6	8.0	7.0	7.3	6.9	7.6	8.8	5.8
Printing and publishing	342	0.4	0.4	0.4	0.4	0.4	0.4	0.3	0.3	0.2	0.1	0.2	0.2	0.2	0.3	0.5	0.4	1.0
Chemical products	351–354	13.6	14.4	14.3	15.8	17.0	13.7	16.2	18.1	13.6	12.5	11.6	13.1	15.3	14.4	16.9	19.8	22.9
Rubber products	355	0.4	0.4	0.4	0.4	0.3	0.4	0.4	0.5	0.5	0.4	0.4	0.5	0.6	0.7	0.7	0.8	0.9
Plastic products	356	0.1	0.1	0.1	0.1	0.1	0.2	0.2	0.2	0.4	0.4	0.4	0.5	0.6	0.8	0.7	0.8	0.7
Pottery, china and earthenware	361	0.0	0.0	0.0	0.0	0.0	0.0	0.0	0.0	0.0	0.0	0.1	0.1	0.1	0.1	0.1	0.1	0.1
Glass and glass products	362	0.6	0.5	0.5	0.4	0.4	0.5	0.5	0.6	0.7	0.7	0.7	0.6	0.6	0.7	0.5	0.3	0.4
Other non–metallic mineral products	369	2.6	0.4	1.6	1.0	0.6	0.8	0.9	1.0	0.4	0.4	0.7	0.9	1.0	1.1	1.1	1.0	1.0
Iron and steel basic industries	371	16.1	18.3	15.8	16.6	18.0	21.1	22.1	24.4	28.9	30.6	29.7	26.6	24.6	24.8	24.9	20.7	20.3
Non–ferrous metal basic industries	372	8.1	10.0	10.9	10.8	12.0	11.7	10.5	9.8	18.4	17.8	15.2	15.2	14.6	10.5	8.2	12.1	8.2
Metal products	381	5.3	4.8	4.1	3.3	2.8	3.1	3.1	3.0	4.0	4.7	5.5	5.1	3.8	4.0	5.4	5.6	6.4
Mechanical machinery and equipment	382	6.1	7.1	5.3	5.1	3.9	4.3	4.6	4.7	4.7	4.1	4.9	5.3	6.1	7.3	6.9	7.8	8.1
Electrical machinery	383	1.6	1.8	1.6	1.6	1.3	1.5	1.5	1.7	1.4	1.4	2.0	1.9	2.1	3.0	2.8	3.0	3.2
Motor vehicles	384	2.7	2.6	2.5	2.4	2.3	2.5	2.4	2.5	2.2	2.5	3.5	4.1	5.8	7.0	5.2	4.4	5.0
Other transport equipment	385	1.7	1.5	1.4	1.3	1.2	1.2	1.2	1.1	0.6	0.5	1.5	1.2	2.1	2.2	2.0	1.4	1.7

Notes: The data have been obtained by combining two different IDC data bases on exports. The data from 1980–7 are not strictly comparable with the 1988–96 data series.

Source: Industrial Development Corporation.

Table 8.A3 South Africa: merchandise exports by product category, 1980–95 (US$ millions)

	1980	1981	1982	1983	1984	1985	1986	1987	1988	1989	1990	1991	1992	1993	1994	1995
Food and livestock	2,108	1,870	1,569	1,124	799	832	1,058	1,206	905	1,592	1,401	1,431	1,314	1,262	1,868	1,513
Beverages and tobacco	53	37	28	33	21	21	28	37	36	51	76	140	139	130	190	295
Inedible raw materials, including fuels	2,864	3,136	2,723	2,605	2,870	2,958	3,007	2,796	3,746	4,601	4,049	3,854	3,457	3,566	3,345	3,859
Hides and skins	154	92	96	89	100	91	98	107	98	112	90	63	64	73	75	82
Coal	933	1,230	1,118	1,092	1,189	1,422	1,391	1,142	1,002	1,199	1,315	1,370	1,233	1,480	1,263	1,359
Metal ores	761	764	644	502	636	593	613	576	1,142	1,526	1,328	1,217	1,181	1,085	908	1,169
Other	1,017	1,051	865	922	945	852	905	971	1,504	1,764	1,316	1,204	978	928	1,098	1,249
Animal and vegetable oils and fats	46	71	37	30	25	33	31	41	37	50	37	42	37	37	37	45
Chemicals	570	469	443	439	504	455	581	624	663	859	789	947	1,139	1,080	1,545	1,663
Manufactured goods	3,954	2,913	2,715	3,050	2,782	3,086	3,824	4,562	3,964	6,036	6,701	7,325	5,387	6,008	6,590	6,203
Textiles	71	58	52	67	65	108	122	115	87	114	160	161	159	148	160	200
Metal & metal products	1,995	1,662	1,508	1,638	1,575	1,740	2,027	2,200	2,436	3,669	4,107	4,503	3,659	3,400	3,013	3,238
Other	1,888	1,193	1,155	1,345	1,142	1,239	1,674	2,247	1,441	2,252	2,433	2,661	1,569	2,459	3,416	2,765
Machinery and transport equipment	514	497	462	377	331	406	516	475	511	671	909	1,101	1,372	1,546	1,663	2,131
Miscellaneous manufactured articles	174	136	119	101	121	149	175	187	175	231	301	381	414	514	655	844
Clothing	53	40	36	39	54	53	53	48	41	53	79	127	150	190	123	132
Other	121	96	83	62	67	96	121	139	135	178	222	254	264	324	533	712
Unclassified	2,269	2,118	1,725	1,868	2,404	1,584	2,200	2,565	1,332	1,155	1,265	460	2,008	1,914	2,680	2,160
Grand Total	12,551	11,246	9,822	9,626	9,856	9,524	11,419	12,493	11,369	15,246	15,528	15,681	15,267	16,058	18,572	18,712

Source: World Bank.

Table 8.A4   South Africa: traditional exports, World Bank definition (NTX2): top 10 and top 75% of exports in base year (1983), excluding gold

SIC code	Exports (excluding gold)	Ranking	Value of exports (US$ 000s)	Percentage of total exports (excl. gold)	Cumulative share of total exports
321	Coal, coke, briquettes	1	1,097,637.0	12.1	12.1
681	Silver, platinum, etc.	2	774,608.2	8.6	20.7
283	Non-ferrous base metal ore	3	564,754.2	6.2	26.9
896	Works of art	4	456,436.8	5.1	32.0
667	Pearls, precious and semi-precious stones	5	415,121.5	4.6	36.6
671	Pig iron	6	386,701.4	4.2	40.8
515	Radioactive material	7	362,876.9	3.9	44.7
262	Wool and animal hair	8	356,597.8	3.9	48.6
051	Fruit, fresh nuts, fresh drinks	9	345,718.1	3.7	52.3
682	Copper	10	331,285.7	3.6	55.9
281	Iron ore, concentrates	11	253,017.1	2.7	58.6
285	Silver and platinum ore	12	241,922.6	2.6	61.2
044	Maize, unmilled	13	241,230.1	2.6	63.8
674	Iron, steel universal plate sheets	14	214,056.0	2.3	66.1
276	Other crude minerals	15	197,292.2	2.1	68.2
053	Fruit, preserved, prepared	16	171,920.2	1.8	70.0
251	Pulp and waste paper	17	168,470.0	1.8	71.8
061	Sugar and honey	18	143,005.3	1.5	73.3
684	Aluminium	19	132,509.4	1.4	74.7

Note: The World Bank definition of non–traditional exports (NTX2) excludes the top 10 categories or the top 75%.

Source: World Bank Data Base.

Notes

1. See, for example, Joffe et al. (1995).
2. The effective exchange rate is the weighted average exchange rate of the rand. The currencies in the basket and their weights (in brackets) are: US dollar (51.7), British pound (20.2), Deutschmark (17.2), Japanese yen (10.9).
3. For a detailed analysis of the real and monetary determinants of the real exchange rate, see Aron et al. 1997.
4. The Growth, Employment and Redistribution macroeconomic framework published in June 1996.
5. An extreme anti-export bias was recorded where, in spite of protection for output, the level of protection of inputs was so heavy that export sales were unprofitable to the extent of value added in exports being negative.

6. According to Bell, the World Bank study developed its average tariff estimates using the highest formula duties. The later calculations by the IDC were based on average formula duties.
7. The index was drawn up before the recent collapse of South East Asian currencies and is based on wage data, costs for expatriate staff, air travel, subsistence, corporate taxes, perceived corruption levels, office and industrial rents and road transport. See 'SA the cheapest place to do business', *Business Day*, 3 February 1998.
8. Support Programme for Industrial Innovation. SPII provides small grants for pre-competitive development activity.
9. Technology and Human Resources for Industry Programme. THRIP provides support for partnerships between industry and research and educational institutions.
10. Historically, there has been a strong inverse correlation between domestic demand and exports of products such as steel.
11. This is in line with international experience particularly for Latin American firms (Schwartz, 1995). One important exception is that of Taiwan.
12. See Wellings and Black (1986) for an account of industrial decentralization policy.
13. Bell and Cattaneo (1997) make a similar point although in their case as part of a critique of import liberalization.

References

Aron, J., Elbadawi, I. and Kahn, B. (1997) *Determinants of the Real Exchange Rate in South Africa*, Working Paper Series WPS/97–16, Centre for the Study of Africa Economies, Oxford University.

Bell, T. (1997) 'Trade Policy', in J. Michie and V. Padayachee (eds), *The Political Economy of South Africa's Transition: Policy Perspectives in the Late 1990s*, London: Dryden Press.

Bell, T. and Cattaneo, N. (1997) *Foreign Trade and Employment in South African Manufacturing Industry*, Geneva: International Labour Office.

Belli, P., Finger, M. and Ballivian, A. (1993) *South Africa: A Review of Trade Policies*, Informal Discussion Papers on the Economy of South Africa, Discussion Paper No. 4, Washington, DC: World Bank.

Blankley, W. and Kaplan, D. (1997) 'Innovation Patterns in South African Manufacturing Firms', Foundation for Research Development and the Industrial Strategy Project, University of Cape Town.

Department of Trade and Industry (1997) *Incentive Schemes*, Republic of South Africa, Department of Trade and Industry, Pretoria.

Fallon, P. and Pereira da Silva, L. A. (1994) *South Africa: Economic Performance and Policies*, Informal Discussion Papers on Aspects of the Economy of South Africa, Discussion Paper No. 7, Washington, DC: World Bank.

GEAR (1996) *Growth, Employment and Redistribution*, Republic of South Africa, Department of Finance, Cape Town.

Gelb, S. (ed.) (1991) *South Africa's Economic Crisis*, Cape Town: David Philip.

Hirsch, A. and House, B. (1994) 'The Continuing GEIS Tango', *Trade Monitor*, 6.

Hodge, J. (1996) 'Trade in Services', *Trade Monitor*, 12.

Industrial Development Corporation (1997) 'The Effective Protection Rate and Anti-Export Bias', *IDC Research Paper Series*, Johannesburg: Industrial Development Corporation.

Jenkins, C. and Siwisa, N. (1997) 'Overview of Trade Policy in South Africa', paper presented to the Trade and Industrial Policy Secretariat Annual Forum, Johannesburg.

Joffe, A., Kaplan, D., Kaplinsky, R. and Lewis, D. (1995) *Improving Manufacturing Performance in South Africa: Report of the Industrial Strategy Project*, Cape Town: UCT Press.

Kahn, B. (1987) 'Import Penetration and Import Demand in the South African Economy', *South African Journal of Economics*, 55, 3.

Kahn, B. (1991) 'The Crisis and South Africa's Balance of Payments', in S. Gelb (ed.), *South Africa's Economic Crisis*, Cape Town: David Philip.

Kahn, B. (1992) 'Exchange Rate Policy in South Africa, 1979–1991', Research Paper No. 7, Centre for the Study of the South African Economy and International Finance, London School of Economics.

Kahn, B. (1997) 'Capital Flows and Policy Responses in South Africa in the 1990s', paper presented to the WIDER Project on Short-term Capital Movements and Balance of Payments Crises.

Kaplan, D. (1997) 'Small and Medium Firms in the Electronic Sector with Special Reference to Technology and Export Development', unpublished mimeo.

Kaplinsky, R. (1995) 'Capital Intensity in South African Manufacturing and Unemployment, 1972–90', *World Development*, 23.

Leape, J. I. (1991), 'South Africa's Foreign Debt and the Standstill, 1985–1990', Research Paper No. 1, Centre for the Study of the South African Economy and International Finance, London School of Economics.

Papageorgiou, D. et al. (1991) *Liberalising Foreign Trade in Developing Countries. Lessons from Experience*, 7 vols, Oxford: Basil Blackwell.

Schwartz, H. (1995) 'Factors Affecting the Supply of Manufacturing Exports: An Overview', in H. Schwartz (ed.), *Supply and Marketing Constraints on Latin American Manufacturing Exports*.

Tsikata, Y. M. (1998) 'Liberalization and Trade Performance', World Bank, mimeo.

Wellings, P. and Black, A. (1986) 'Industrial Decentralization under Apartheid: the Relocation of Industry to the South African Periphery', *World Development*, 14, 1.

9
Promoting Non-Traditional Exports in Tanzania

Benno Ndulu, Joseph Semboja and Ammon Mbelle

The policy environment and incentives for non-traditional export performance (1980–97)

The initial conditions at the beginning of the 1980s

Focus on promoting the expansion of non-traditional exports was motivated by the government's concerns with inadequacy and instability of foreign exchange earnings relative to Tanzania's requirements for sustained growth and improved welfare of its population. These concerns arose from three main realities that Tanzania faced by the beginning of the 1980s.

Tanzania's export of the principal agricultural commodities faltered badly during the 1970s without being made good by emergence or growth of other export products. In fact some of the minor agricultural export commodities of the 1960s disappeared from the list. By the end of the 1970s four out of the principal agricultural export commodities had either stagnated or declined sharply.[1] The output of coffee, the most important of these, stagnated. Cotton production registered a declining trend throughout the 1970s. The export of sisal, previously the leading product, fell by more than half making Tanzania lose its leadership on the world market. Cashew nut production declined disastrously to 29 per cent of its 1973 peak. Only tobacco and tea maintained a positive growth trend (Bank of Tanzania (BOT), 1982). The resultant shortage of foreign exchange led to severe import strangulation particularly considering that Tanzania had embarked on an ambitious and highly import-dependent basic industrialization strategy under the Third Five Year Plan (1976–81) (see United Republic of Tanzania (URT), 1976). Much as the bulk of the financing for this initiative was from foreign aid, it generated a large expansion of requirements for intermediate imports to add to the increasing demand for the imports of consumer goods.

For these, the country had to rely primarily on own foreign exchange generation and therefore the need to expand exports.

Second, it became evident in policy circles that sole reliance on primary agricultural exports exposed the country both to the long-term weakening of the world demand for these and to the instability of world market prices. This was not a new concern and it found support in the earlier arguments expressed by Prebisch (1950) and Singer (1950), who advocated the need to diversify away from dependence on primary commodities on account of declining long-term trends of their prices in the world market. More recent evidence by Reinhart and Wickham (1994) confirms both the declining trend and the higher amplitude of world market price fluctuations around this trend during the 1980s.[2] Tanzania had also just faced a collapse of prices of its major primary products during 1978–9 after the coffee boom of 1975–7 and hence the effects of instability were fresh in the minds of policymakers. Broadening the range of export products was considered absolutely necessary to reduce risk from concentration and tap new potentials for overall expansion of exports. Although by African countries' standards Tanzania's export concentration index in 1980 was relatively low, the top three export items during 1981–2 accounted for a hefty 54 per cent.[3] The government aimed at exploiting the rich natural resource endowment and developing the export capabilities of the manufacturing sector to achieve its goals of expanding and diversifying the export basket. Therefore the target was to focus on promoting what were then termed as minor agricultural exports, mineral-based exports, as well as manufactures. These officially make up non-traditional exports. They include those commodities other than the six principal agricultural exports identified earlier.

The third concern was that exports of primary products in their raw forms prevented the country from capturing a higher proportion of their final value through processing. Although processed primary products faced higher tariff and non-tariff barriers in the markets for these, adding value to primary products prior to exporting was considered both viable and desirable. The principal immediate targets for processing in this respect were sisal products, cashew nuts, cotton fibre products and leather (URT, 1981; BOT 1982).

The policy environment which characterized this period strongly militated against exportation. This partly explains the short life of the National Economic Survival Programme (NESP). We highlight here the key features of this environment and provide links to the explanation of export performance later in the chapter. Trade barriers had been erected to provide protection to infant industries under the Import Substitution Industrialization (ISI) policies adopted since independence. High and complex tariff walls, import controls, 'no objection' certificates, and trade confinement to public entities to ensure control of importation were some of the explicit import barriers erected for the purpose. Import barriers are a penalty on exports as they raise the domestic resource cost to exporters. Rodrik (1997) confirms empirically the negative effect of import barriers on exports in the case of Sub-Saharan Africa, as did de Rosa (1990).

The foreign exchange crunch of this 'crisis' period (roughly 1979–85) also prompted more stringent application of exchange controls to protect reserves. These controls were also marginally applied for protection of local industry through the foreign exchange allocation system. Irrespective of the objective of such controls, when they are tightened they typically lead to a rise in the parallel market premium for foreign exchange. Given the mandatory surrender requirement of foreign exchange earnings at the official exchange rate, the implicit tax on exporters rose with the premium (Pinto, 1989).

A more or less fixed exchange rate regime was being pursued even when domestic inflation took off on a sharp rise from the late 1970s onwards. Although there were periods of significant overvaluation of the local currency prior to the 1980s, both the extent of deviation from parity and the longevity of such episodes were relatively not serious. Inability to control budget deficits and recourse to monetization of these deficits now quickly widened the inflation differential *vis-à-vis* trading partners without commensurate adjustment in the nominal exchange rate. The resultant unwarranted sharp rise in the real value of the local currency reduced both the profitability of exports and their competitiveness.

As we will show later, some measures during the early 1980s were taken to ameliorate the negative consequences of this policy environment on exports. These were in the form of compensatory arrangements for exporters. They included export subsidy schemes, tax rebates and other promotional measures. This compensation for exporters typically fell far short of the damages caused by the inimical policy environment to export performance. In any case it highlighted the ambivalence in the minds of the policymakers towards the policy stance/environment in place.

The changing policy environment (1986–97)

Since 1986, Tanzania has been engaged in substantial macroeconomic and structural reforms with significant success towards re-establishing internal and external balances as well as realigning the incentive structure broadly in favour of exports. Since the mid-1990s the focus has turned to maintaining conditions which are favourable to sustained growth and reducing poverty. These measures include sustaining macroeconomic stability with emphasis on entrenching fiscal discipline via cash budgeting; intensifying efforts at reducing inflation with a target of establishing a low-inflation economy; and preserving both the real value and the stability of the local currency. On the structural side, measures to free up both domestic and external trade have been complemented by eliminating exchange controls and freeing up the foreign exchange market. This has been an uphill task as the changes have so far yielded only modest results, confirming that the process of reform must be a long and sustained one if it is to be successful.

Table 9.1   Selected macroeconomic indicators, Tanzania, 1980–97

	1980	1981	1982	1983	1984	1985	1986	1987	1988	1989	1990	1991	1992	1993	1994	1995	1996	1997
GDP growth, real (%)	3.00	–1.00	1.00	–2.00	3.00	5.00	2.00	5.00	4.43	2.60	6.20	2.80	1.80	0.40	1.40	3.60	4.20	3.30
Inflation (%)	30.30	25.70	28.90	27.10	36.10	33.30	32.40	30.00	31.20	30.40	35.90	28.80	21.90	25.20	33.10	28.40	21.00	16.10
Govt rev/GDP, excl. grants	19.29	18.31	17.75	19.04	18.82	18.12	17.31	12.69	12.59	14.18	15.25	15.70	13.23	12.64	13.50	13.94	14.78	15.54
Govt exp/GDP (%)	34.07	32.73	29.37	28.75	28.64	26.88	28.67	21.24	19.38	21.21	22.90	23.66	21.84	22.06	20.06	15.42	14.54	14.99
External Curr.Ac. Def/GDP, excl. official transfers (%)	–12.23	–8.66	–9.25	–6.33	–8.16	–7.82	–12.09	–15.17	–16.23	–20.62	–21.12	–16.76	–18.27	–35.40	–21.54	–17.56	–10.65	–11.83
Gross Domestic Savings /GDP (%)	19.86	22.50	16.39	10.22	9.79	13.92	13.44	10.70	5.00	4.30	17.00	19.90	19.70	1.30	6.30	4.70	8.00	n.a.
Investment/GDP (%)	29.52	27.12	23.61	17.37	17.64	16.90	23.82	23.84	22.40	21.70	27.60	30.00	28.90	25.50	25.50	20.90	19.60	n.a.

Sources: Official publications by Government of Tanzania; World Bank/IMF publications; author's computation from above sources.

Table 9.1 presents the developments of key macroeconomic fundamentals over the recent past. There is one important caution to the reader regarding the trends of the various ratios presented in this table. GDP figures for the period 1987 to date have been revised substantially upwards rendering trend analysis comparing pre-1987 and the subsequent period highly inaccurate. Since previous data were not revised to be consistent with the more recent ones, longer-term trends of ratios to GDP are biased downwards in the post-1987 period.

Nevertheless, we can draw the following basic conclusions from the data with some caveats. Real growth has shown a relatively strong recovery from the crisis period of the first half of the 1980s. Since the data for real GDP during the period up to 1987 were not revised and the data for 1987–97 are on the same scale of revision, save for the transitional year of 1986–7, we can discern with reasonable accuracy the pattern of real growth. Average annual growth rates have increased from 1.3 per cent during 1980–5 to an average of slightly more than 3.3 per cent thereafter.[4] Since Tanzania's population growth rate averaged 2.8 per cent, real per capita income grew at an annual rate of about 0.5 per cent in the post-1985 period in contrast to negative 1.5 per cent during the 'crisis' period. This revival still fell far short of the 5 per cent real growth target and remains well below the 6–7 per cent required for reducing the pervasive and deep poverty in the country. Various estimates still put the head count ratios for poverty in the range between 40 and 50 per cent.

More success has been achieved in arresting the rising inflation of the past and in reducing fiscal deficits. Inflation has been brought down from its 36 per cent peak, reached in 1984, to 16 per cent in 1997. The more recent success is attributed partly to fiscal controls and partly to successful controls on monetary expansion. During fiscal year 1996–7, the budget achieved an overall surplus (after grants) and a deficit in the range of 1–2 per cent of GDP excluding grants. Stringent application of cash budgets was the main factor behind this success. The main factor in monetary policy was the concerted action of the monetary authority to reduce expansion of high-powered money. Relatively greater autonomy was granted to the central bank through revision of the Bank of Tanzania Act in 1995, which made its primary mission that of controlling inflation.

The trade environment has gradually and significantly been liberalized since 1984, reducing external and internal barriers to trade. The past decade has seen a dismantling of trade monopolies and exchange controls. Tariff levels have been scaled down from upper limit ranges in excess of 200 per cent to a current maximum of 40 per cent. Tariff categories have also been compressed to about five categories, providing more transparency to traders. The current tariff structure is escalated, with capital goods in the range of 0–10 per cent, intermediates 20–25 per cent, and consumer goods in the range of 30–40 per cent. The corresponding collection rates (or tariff revenue/imports) are 5 per cent for capital goods, 6–12 per cent for intermediates and 12.8 per cent for consumer goods. The trade weighted average tariff rate for Tanzania's imports in 1996 was 22 per cent while the actual collection rate was approximately 9.3 per cent. The difference is accounted for by large exemptions for various categories of imports for government or donor-funded projects. In the past two years these exemptions have been dominated by measures to attract private investment. Exemptions to investors, private companies and individuals currently account for 50 per cent of total collectable revenue (import duty revenue plus the value of exempted tax revenue) (Tanzania Revenue Authority (TRA), 1998). Mandatory surrender of export earnings to the central bank has been scrapped and an open foreign exchange market has been established.

Despite these measures, the responses of private investment and savings have been modest at best. This is a result of a combination of continuing risk aversion in the banking sector with respect to lending activities and lack of bank competition. Lending rates have remained stubbornly high while deposit rates have fallen rapidly with inflation. The interest rate spread has therefore widened over time and deposit rates have turned negative in real terms. Notwithstanding the fact that the banking system has been opened up to the private sector, competition in the banking industry is still inadequate. Banks have tended to direct most of their lending to the government by holding high-return Treasury Bills (for a long period) with minimum lending for private investment. Two major types of risk have been singled out to explain this state of affairs. One is that the private sector is still viewed as too risky for lending as institutional mechanisms for enforcing contracts are too weak. Second, the perceptions of both investors and banks may be that the policy changes in place will not be sustained and that the potential for reversals is real. One key signal contributing to this fear is the very high indebtedness of the government both in terms of external and domestic debt. It would be reasonable to fear that the pressures from the rising debt-servicing burden could trigger such reversals.

Later in this chapter, we attempt to provide a closer link between these policy changes and export performance. But before embarking on this analysis, we review trade and export performance in greater detail below, after which we focus more specifically on characterizing the performance of non-traditional exports. We conclude with a brief overview of the prospects for expansion of non-traditional exports as affected by the policy environment and external constraints.

Trade and export performance

Although the focus of the chapter is on non-traditional exports their performance can best be understood if placed within the context of total exports. Therefore we focus here on the analysis of total exports – trends, composition and concentration since independence, i.e. 1961–97.

The problem of data reliability was raised earlier. The data on exports are not spared from this problem. However, although interpretations of the data on absolute export values need to be made with caution, those on export trends can be made with greater confidence. Except for exports of tourism, information for which was obtained from the Ministry of Natural Resources and Tourism, data for this entire section were taken from Bank of Tanzania publications.

Table 9.2 presents some important indicators of merchandise trade in Tanzania for the period 1981–97. The country's level of openness rose considerably during this period. The ratio of exports to GDP rose from 4.9 per cent in 1981–5 to 7.1 per cent in 1985–91 and to 12 per cent in 1991–7. Similarly, that of imports to GDP also increased during these periods. The performance of non-traditional merchandise exports was equally good; its percentage in GDP rose from 1.7 per cent to 2.5 and 5.2 per cent, respectively, during these periods.

Table 9.2   Selected merchandise trade indicators, Tanzania, 1981–97 (%)

	1981–5	*1985–91*	*1991–7*
Exports/GDP	4.9	7.1	12.0
Non-Traditional Exports/GDP	1.7	2.5	5.2
Imports/GDP	11.0	23.8	31.0
Exports/Imports	44.3	30.7	40.9

However, judging from merchandise trade, the country's capacity to import has been quite low. The ratio of exports to imports, which was 44.3 per cent during 1981–5, declined to 30.7 per cent during 1985–91 before it rose again to 40.9 per cent during 1991–7.

Export trends

Five phases can be identified from the export data for 1961–97. Table 9.3 provides a summary): 1961–71, 1971–80, 1980–5, 1985–91 and 1991–7 (see also Appendix Table 9.A1).

The first phase (1961–71) was characterized by a moderate increase of exports from US$139 million to US$316 million, equivalent to annual growth of 6 per cent. Merchandise exports grew from US$120 million to US$211 million or at an annual rate of 6 per cent, compared to services whose exports rose from US$19 million to US$106 million, a growth of 19 per cent per annum. Exports of non-traditional products grew from US$53 million to US$200 million, or 14 per cent per annum, compared to traditional exports which increased from US$86 million to US$117 million, or 3 per cent per annum.

Table 9.3   Compound growth rates of US$ export values, Tanzania, 1961–97 (%)

	1961–71	*1971–80*	*1980–5*	*1985–91*	*1991–7*
Total Exports	6	12	–18	7	17
of which					
Merchandise	6	12	–18	7	13
Services	19	6	–10	5	23
Traditional Exports[a]	3	14	–16	2	12
Non-Traditional					
Exports (NTX)[a]	14	7	–15	10	19
of which					
Merchandise	11	8	–21	18	15
Services	19	6	–10	5	23

Note: [a] The definitions of traditional and non-traditional exports (NTX) are given later in this chapter (pp. 262–3). NTX in this table is NTX1 in the terminology of Chapter 1 of this volume.

The second phase (1971–80) was characterized by a fast growth of exports from US$316 million to US$764 million, equivalent to a growth rate of 12 per cent per annum. Merchandise exports grew from US$211 million to US$585 million, or 12 per cent per annum, compared to services whose exports rose from US$106 million to US$179 million, a growth of 6 per cent per annum. During this phase, exports from traditional products grew faster, from US$117 million to US$396 million, or 14 per cent per annum, compared to non-traditional exports whose value rose from US$200 million to US$368 million, or 7 per cent per annum.

The third phase (1980–5) experienced a dramatic decline of exports from US$764 million to US$330 million, equivalent to –18 per cent per annum. Merchandise exports declined from US$585 million to US$222 million or at an annual rate of –18 per cent, compared to services whose exports fell from US$179 million to US$108 million, an annual decline of 10 per cent. Both the non-traditional and traditional exports declined significantly from US$368 million to US$168 million, or –15 per cent per annum, and from US$396 million to US$163 million, or –16 per cent per annum, respectively.

The fourth phase (1985–91) was characterized by a modest increase of exports from US$330 million to US$481 million, equivalent to 7 per cent per annum. Merchandise exports grew from US$222 million to US$338 million, or at an annual rate of 7 per cent, compared to services whose exports rose from US$108 million to US$143 million, an annual growth of 5 per cent. The non-traditional exports grew from US$168 million to US$301 million, or 10 per cent per annum, compared to a much slower recovery of the traditional exports which grew from US$163 million to US$179 million, or 2 per cent per annum.

The fifth phase (1991–7) experienced the fastest growth of exports since independence in 1961, from US$481 to US$1213 million, equivalent to 17 per cent per annum. Merchandise exports grew from US$338 million to US$717 million, or at an annual rate of 13 per cent, compared to services whose exports rose from US$143 million to US$495 million, an annual growth of 23 per cent. Both traditional and non-traditional exports grew fast, from US$179 to US$359 million, or 12 per cent per annum, and from US$301 to US$854 million, or 19 per cent per annum, respectively.

Composition

Four phases of trade composition can be identified during 1961–97: 1961–71, 1971–7, 1979–86 and 1986–97. The years 1978 and 1979 can be considered to behave exceptionally to this categorization. With slight differences, these phases coincide with the trends of exports identified above.

The first phase (1961–71) was characterized by a declining contribution of traditional exports from 62 per cent of total exports in 1961 to 37 per cent in 1971; the average contribution for the period was 56 per cent and the range 37 per cent to 68 per cent. The declining contribution of traditional exports during the period was mainly explained by a rapid decline of sisal exports from US$63 million in 1963 to US$19 million in 1971, equivalent to –14 per cent per annum. As a result, the contribution of sisal in total exports declined to 6 per cent in 1971 from 35 per cent in 1963. Exports of services, which rose fast during the period, and of petroleum, a new product which came into production and the export market in 1966, added to the change. Merchandise exports, which accounted for 86 per cent of total exports in 1961, contributed 67 per cent in 1971.

The second phase (1971–7) was characterized by an increasing contribution of traditional exports from 37 per cent of total exports in 1971 to 64 per cent in 1977. The explanation for the increased contribution of traditional exports is the dramatic increase in exports of coffee from US$32 million in 1971 to US$224 million in 1977 or 38 per cent per annum. This period coincides with the coffee boom periods of 1975 and 1977. Its share in total exports rose from 10 per cent to 37 per cent. In 1978 and 1979 the share of traditional exports fell to 55 per cent and to 47 per cent, respectively, from 64 per cent in 1977, following the decline of coffee prices and therefore exports. The contribution of merchandise exports rose from 67 per cent in 1971 to 80 per cent in 1977; it declined to 74 per cent in 1978.

The third phase (1979–86) was characterized by fluctuating contributions of both traditional and non-traditional exports. The former's contribution fluctuated between 46 per cent and 62 per cent of total exports during the period. As noted earlier, during this period both traditional and non-traditional exports declined more or less at the same rate. Both merchandise and services exports behaved similarly.

The fourth and final phase (1986–97) was characterized by a declining contribution of traditional exports from 62 per cent of total exports in 1986 to only 30 per cent in 1997. Both traditional and non-traditional exports grew fast during the period. However, non-traditional exports grew faster mainly due to a dramatic growth of service exports.

Concentration

Four items have dominated the export sector since independence in 1961, as shown in Table 9.4 (see also Appendix Table 9.A1): coffee, cotton, manufacturing and services. Sisal exports, which dominated during the early 1960s, declined rapidly starting in the mid-1960s.

Table 9.4 Composition of major exports, Tanzania, 1961–97 (%)

	1961–6	1967–75	1976–80	1981–5	1986–9	1990–7
Coffee, Cotton and Sisal	57	38	45	38	41	26
Services	14	28	24	29	30	38
Coffee, Cotton, Manufacturing and Services	53	64	75	72	81	71

During 1961–6, sisal, cotton and coffee exports accounted for 57 per cent of total exports: the range was 53–62 per cent. Sisal dominated by contributing 26 per cent; its range was 14–35 per cent. The serious decline of sisal exports, which became more vivid in 1965, contributed to the decrease in the share of the three traditional export crops to 38 per cent during the second phase (1967–75); the range was 27–52 per cent. Cotton and coffee accounted for 14 per cent each and took over the leadership from sisal whose contribution fell to 9 per cent. Exports from sisal continued to decline and have never recovered.

During the remaining phases the contribution of four items rose continuously from 64 per cent during 1967–75 to 81 per cent during 1986–9; it fell to 71 per cent during 1990–7. This is still a high level of concentration; underlying it were declining sisal and mining contributions and the increasing contribution of services (and, to a lesser extent, manufactures).

Non-traditional exports

Non-traditional exports defined

There is no official definition of non-traditional exports in the country. A senior official from the Ministry of Industry and Trade (MIT) referred the authors of this paper to the Board of External Trade and the Customs Department for the definition. However, all the relevant institutions defined non-traditional exports as a residual, obtained after accounting for traditional exports. Therefore, the definition of traditional exports has first to be made.

According to the Customs Department, seven items belong to traditional exports. They are coffee, cotton, sisal, tea, tobacco, cashew nuts and cloves. This definition of traditional exports by specific products coincides with the Board of External Trade (BET) and the Bank of Tanzania definition which considers products whose exports are handled by government established/owned institutions, i.e. parastatals, to be traditional. By this definition, the seven crops mentioned above qualify as traditional exports. And, by implication, all products whose exports are handled entirely by the private sector are classified as non-traditional.

For practical purposes this definition is adopted in this paper, with a minor modification – namely that cloves are not considered as part of traditional exports. The justification for this exclusion is that Mainland Tanzania produces and exports hardly any cloves and the focus of the paper is Mainland Tanzania. To all intents and purposes, the data refer to what this volume refers to as NTX1 (see Chapter 1).

The structure of non-traditional exports

Detailed data on non-traditional exports (NTX) are hard to find. The Customs Department, the source of these data, has not published them as regularly as is required or in the detail that researchers of our type would wish to see. The Bank of Tanzania is the only institution that has published the data regularly. However, the level of detail has remained low. Only aggregate information on petroleum products, minerals, manufactured goods and services are available. The rest of the merchandise NTX is lumped under 'other' exports. And, as expected, in recent years, more specifically since 1990, this item has become the largest non-traditional merchandise export item. This study's requests for data may have facilitated the disaggregation of this item; an exercise that both the Bank of Tanzania and Tanzania Revenue Authority (TRA) have already begun, but a bit too late for the current study to benefit from.

The structure of non-traditional exports has changed significantly during the 1961–97 period. Table 9.5 provides an indication of this change.

The share of merchandise non-traditional exports declined from 60 per cent during 1961–6 to around 40 per cent starting in the mid-1980s. The structure of merchandise NTX also changed significantly during 1961–97. The contribution of exports from mineral and manufactured products declined from 56 per cent of NTX during 1961–6 to 21 per cent during 1990–7.

The dominance of minerals and manufacturing in the merchandise NTX declined partly due to the commissioning of the new petroleum refinery in 1966 and mainly due to the increasing share of 'other' NTX as new products entered the export market.

The contribution of services rose quickly from 40 per cent during 1961–6 and reached 60 per cent during the second half of the 1980s. Tourism, which contributed an insignificant 5 per cent of NTX during 1976–85, rose sharply to reach 38 per cent during the 1990s.

Table 9.5   The structure of non-traditional exports (NTX1), Tanzania, 1961–97 (%)

	1961–6	*1967–75*	*1976–85*	*1986–9*	*1990–7*
Merchandise	60	47	45	40	42
of which					
Petroleum Products	0	11	7	3	2
Minerals	32	19	13	6	8
Manufactured Products	24	16	19	20	13
Others	4	2	6	12	18
Services	40	53	55	60	58
of which					
Tourism	n.a.	9[a]	5	19	38

Note: [a] Only for 1970–5.

Sources: Bank of Tanzania; for data on Tourism, Ministry of Natural Resources and Tourism, Tourism Division.

Performance of non-traditional exports

Trends in non-traditional exports suggest that their performance can be divided into four phases: 1961–76, 1976–81, 1981–6 and 1986–97 (see Table 9.6). During the first phase, non-traditional exports grew reasonably fast, at an annual rate of 10 per cent. The impetus to this growth came from services, whose exports grew at 15 per cent per annum. Merchandise exports, which grew at 7 per cent per annum, were mainly driven by manufacturing and minerals, which grew at 8 per cent and 6 per cent, respectively.

During the second phase (1976–81) NTX also grew at a reasonably fast rate of 10 per cent per annum. Merchandise exports grew faster at 18 per cent per annum compared to services which experienced a growth of 5 per cent per annum. Exports of both minerals and manufacturing grew fast. However, exports of the other non-traditional merchandise products grew faster at 71 per cent per annum. During this period the tourist industry also began to pick up.

The performance of the third phase (1981–6) was very poor. Exports of non-traditional products fell dramatically at –18 per cent per annum as a result of the poor performance in all export products and services. Merchandise exports grew at –29 per cent per annum and exports from minerals and the manufacturing sectors accounted for most of the decline. Exports from the service sector also declined by recording a growth of –11 per cent per annum.

A dramatic recovery was recorded during the fourth phase (1986–97). Non-traditional exports grew at 17 per cent per annum. During this period, the impetus came from manufacturing and 'other' non-traditional exports; exports from minerals also recovered. Exports from services also picked up, most of the growth coming from tourism.

Table 9.6 Compound growth rates of non-traditional exports (NTX1), Tanzania, 1961–97 (%)

	1961–76	*1976–81*	*1981–6*	*1986–97*
Non-Traditional Exports	11	10	–18	17
of which				
Merchandise	7	18	–29	24
of which				
Petroleum Products	1	–5	–3	68
Minerals	6	21	–70	21
Manufactured Products	8	9	–42	39
Others	2	71	–19	18
Services	15	5	–11	15
of which				
Tourism	–2	10	–1	31

Note: For petroleum products, minerals and tourism, the periods are 1967–76, 1961–75 and 1970–6, respectively.

Source: Appendix Table 9.A1.

Growth, composition and diversification of merchandise non-traditional exports

As stated earlier, the item called 'other' merchandise non-traditional exports has now become the main export. In 1995 it accounted for 55 per cent of merchandise non-traditional exports. Its performance is of great significance to the sector. As indicated above, detailed information on merchandise non-traditional exports is lacking from official publications. The authors of this chapter were able to get access to the most disaggregated data (up to six-digit SITC classification) from the Customs Department.

Below we use the preliminary results from the analysis of data from customs files to observe detailed trends of growth, orientation and diversification of non-traditional exports. We do this by focusing on new entries into and exits from the export sector. In order to manage the data and the discussion we include only those items that have made significant export contribution during any of the years under consideration. All two-digit SITC export items which contributed at least 3 per cent of total merchandise exports in *any* year are considered to have made significant export contribution. Only data for 1981–90 and 1996 and 1997 can be analysed for this purpose; data for 1991–5 are unreliable. Table 9.7 provides some indication of growth (by number of items), composition and diversification of non-traditional items during the period. Two observations can be made. First, 13 out of 55 two-digit SITC exportable items have contributed significantly in any one year. Furthermore, out of the 13 significant export items only 5 sustained their performance for at least 6 out of the 11 years – fruit and vegetables; manufactures of coffee, cocoa, tea and spices; petroleum and products; textiles yarn and products; and non-metallic mineral manufactures. Exports of crude fertilizers and minerals, which performed well during 1981–4, declined almost to zero after 1984; and fish and fish preparations have recently emerged to be an important export. The remaining items basically appeared once and then disappeared. This result indicates that the level of concentration within merchandise NTX is still high.

Secondly, in spite of this high level of concentration, a tendency for increased diversification emerged after 1984. This is shown by the rising contribution of 'other' non-traditional merchandise exports. The number of export items rose after 1984. However, there are signs of increasing concentration during the second half of the 1990s. This also coincided with the declining share of merchandise NTX in total exports.

Table 9.7   Composition of non-traditional exports (NTX), Tanzania, 1981–90, 1996 and 1997 (% of total exports)

SITC[a]	1981	1982	1983	1984	1985	1986	1987	1988	1990	1996	1997
03	–[b]	0.1	0.3	0.3	0.4	0.8	1.5	2.1	1.7	6.8	10.1
04	1.3	–	–	–	–	0.1	1.6	0.5	2.5	3.5	1.0
05	2.4	2.8	1.3	0.6	0.9	2.7	3.7	3.3	4.6	2.9	1.1
07	9.1	10.4	3.7	3.8	15.1	5.5	3.7	7.9	2.0	1.0	2.0
22	0.6	0.4	0.2	0.3	0.2	0.1	0.3	1.1	1.1	3.2	1.8
26	5.5	–	–	–	–	–	0.1	–	–	0.1	–
27	4.4	5.0	8.2	4.0	0.2	0.1	0.1	0.3	0.2	1.3	1.3
33	2.6	3.1	3.5	5.5	8.6	1.3	2.9	3.2	2.4	1.3	0.4
62	0.1	–	–	–	–	–	6.2	–	0.1	–	0.1
63	0.1	0.1	0.1	–	0.1	0.1	2.8	0.1	0.1	0.1	1.1
65	2.3	3.0	2.9	3.6	2.8	2.8	0.7	5.5	6.4	2.4	1.8
66	5.3	4.7	4.1	4.9	6.8	3.8	0.1	3.9	2.9	2.1	3.8
99	–	–	–	–	–	–	–	–	3.4	–	–
Subtotal	32.7	29.6	24.3	23.0	35.1	17.5	23.5	27.9	27.4	24.7	24.5
'Other' NTX	7.0	6.9	8.4	7.3	7.4	11.6	10.2	14.5	14.7	12.0	11.7
Total NTX	39.7	36.5	32.7	30.3	42.5	29.1	33.7	42.4	42.1	36.7	36.2

Notes: [a] 03, Fish and fish preparations; 04, Cereals and cereal preparations; 05, Fruit and vegetables; 07, Manufactures of coffee, tea, cocoa and spices; 22, Oil seeds, oil nuts and oil kernels; 26, Textile fibre (excluding yarn, thread and fabrics); 27, Crude fertilizers and minerals; 33, Petroleum and products; 62, Rubber manufactures; 63, Wood and cork manufactures (excluding furniture); 65, Textile yarn and products; 66, Non-metallic mineral manufactures; 99, Gold coins and bullion.
[b] – implies insignificant.

Source: Customs files.

Direction of exports by region, 1981–97

Table 9.8 contains information on the direction of exports. Unfortunately data by export item do not exist at all. An attempt by the authors of this chapter to construct a meaningful data set on the direction of trade by export item was not successful.

The major export markets have remained basically the same over the 1981–97 period. Tanzania's exports have gone mainly to Western Europe and 'Asia and Oceanic'. The 1981–5 period was dominated by Western Europe which imported 56 per cent of Tanzania's exports; its share also increased from 51 per cent in 1981 to 61 per cent in 1984 before it started to decline in 1985. The increase in the share of traditional markets (dominated by the UK, the former West Germany and the Netherlands) during this period occurred at the expense of Eastern Europe and Africa (excluding PTA) whose share declined from 5 per cent to 1 per cent and 8 per cent to 3 per cent, respectively. The share of Asia and Oceania also declined from 23 per cent in 1981 to 18 per cent in 1984 before it rose to 24 per cent in 1985. Therefore, 1981–5 was a period of relative market concentration.

The 1985–97 period experienced some market diversification. The share of Western Europe fell from 58 to 30 per cent. Even within Western Europe, exports to Belgium, Finland, Italy, Portugal and Spain increased substantially. At the same time, the share of Asia and Oceanic increased to 31 per cent. The share of PTA also rose to 9 per cent in 1992 before it fell to 5 per cent by 1996. Within PTA Kenya and Uganda accounted for a significant part of the increase. The problems relating to uncaptured border trade are indicated by the absence of Uganda in 1990 from the data obtained from customs files, even though Uganda trade appears in Bank of Tanzania publications (cf. BOT, 1997). Concern about border information was also raised by Bol et al. (1997).

Explaining the performance of non-traditional exports in Tanzania

The time pattern of non-traditional export performance (1983–96)

The share of non-traditional exports, as defined above, stagnated at around 24.5 per cent during the period 1966–80. Their average share for 1981–2 rose to 30.25 per cent (Ndulu and Semboja, 1995). The significant increase of this share in these two years compared to the past is largely attributed to the efforts made under the NESP of 1981–4 which, in effect, was a response to the foreign exchange crisis by way of exhortation to producers of exportables to raise the share of exports in output. The main target of the NESP was to improve the extent to which domestic exports should finance Tanzania's imports. The ratio of exports to imports had declined from slightly above 100 per cent in the mid-1960s to only 40 per cent in 1980 (BOT, 1982: 65).

Table 9.8   Direction of exports by region, Tanzania, 1981–97[a]

	1981	1982	1983	1984	1985	1986	1987	1988	1989	1990	1991	1992	1993	1994	1995	1996	1997
Western Europe	51	54	56	61	58	57	42	55		50	54	47	40	35	32	30	30
Eastern Europe	5	5	5	2	1	2	2	1		2	–[b]	–	–	–	–	–	–
North America	4	5	3	4	2	11	11	3		4	5	3	3	3	4	3	3
Asia and Oceania	23	23	18	18	24	18	25	27		29	28	34	27	30	31	31	31
South & Central America	–	–	–	–	–	2	2	–		–	–	–	–	–	–	–	–
Middle East	2	2	4	1	3	2	1	1		2	–	–	–	–	–	–	–
Africa (excl. PTA)	8	8	9	6	3	2	7	2		5	1	1	1	1	1	1	1
PTA	5	3	4	4	3	3	5	7		8	5	9	7	5	6	5	5

Notes:

[a] Perhaps as a result of increased diversification, data from the Bureau of Statistics and the Bank of Tanzania during 1991–7 have lumped many countries and regions into the category of 'others'. Therefore the percentages do not add up to 100%. There appears to be a 'break' in these data between 1992 and 1993, for which we have been unable to find an explanation.

[b] – implies insignificant.

Source: Data for 1981–90 from Customs files; for 1991–7, from Bureau of Statistics and the Bank of Tanzania.

Based on data from the 26 major importing countries worldwide and three-digit SITC classification, Tanzania exported 96 non-traditional products in 1983. This count uses the classification of non-traditional exports by the official definition which excludes the six primary agricultural commodities. It coincidentally matches the project definition of cut-off at 3 per cent or less of total exports (NTX3). This data set is also broadly consistent with Tanzania Customs' data which were used in the analysis earlier in the chapter. We use it here for analysis due to the fact that it presents an unbroken and detailed series, while that of Tanzania Customs has accuracy problems between 1991 and 1995; it requires cleaning up. Table 9.9 presents a summary of the evolution of this count over the period 1983–94. It shows a relatively sharp and brief rise during 1984–5, most probably in response to the export promotion measures instituted between 1981 and 1983 in the forms of a virtual abolition of explicit export taxes, commodity exchange programmes (commodity export in exchange for inputs and technical assistance), and an export rebate scheme with rebates ranging between 5 per cent and 25 per cent of the FOB value of exports. Other measures included duty drawback and export subsidies.[5] Since most of these measures were targeted at promoting export of manufactures, they tended to promote an increase in the number of non-traditional export items. A more rapid and persistent rise in the number of the items occurred, however, after 1987 following a more comprehensive and intensive redressing of anti-export bias by way of more attractive exchange rates to exporters, dismantling of exchange controls, and application of a generalized foreign exchange retention scheme. These measures later on also included the abolition of mandatory surrender to the central bank of foreign exchange earned from exports. We return to this link later below.

This time pattern of change in export performance is also reflected in the shares and growth of non-traditional exports in the total based on the same data set. Table 9.9 presents the time pattern of shares and Table 9.11 the time pattern of the growth of non-traditional exports from the base period of the early 1980s. After a sharp rise in the share of non-traditional exports between 1984 and 1985 on account of the measures pointed out earlier, it declined and then rose again sharply between 1986 and 1990. The later climb was from 29 per cent in 1986 persistently to 49 per cent in 1990. This share stabilized subsequently at a lower average of about 42 per cent, mainly as a result of improved performance in traditional exports but also due to a slackening in the growth performance of non-traditional exports. This performance pattern is mirrored by the growth performance of earnings from non-traditional exports measured in US dollars. The highest growth rate was achieved during 1987–91 at an annual rate of 5.3 per cent. This compares very favourably with the annual rates of 1.2 per cent during 1983–6 and 1.7 per cent for 1992–4.

Table 9.9   The number, share and growth of non-traditional export products versus time pattern of export incentives, Tanzania, 1983–94

Year	No. of items	Share of exports %	Growth %	RER2[a]	CI (index)[b]	EBIAS1[c]	EBIAS2[d]	REER[e]
1983	96	30.55	–	171.59	113.6	1.10	3.66	188.29
1984	101	29.32	2.72	176.57	122.0	1.10	3.76	193.37
1985	103	43.21	28.63	204.97	137.9	1.09	5.83	222.60
1986	98	29.46	–20.76	141.87	138.0	1.08	5.14	153.38
1987	98	34.21	3.88	69.81	100.0	1.07	2.87	74.35
1988	107	37.53	13.81	54.96	70.1	1.06	2.17	58.21
1989	109	46.25	45.53	48.13	68.0	1.06	1.84	51.02
1990	112	49.00	–1.47	36.83	61.7	1.06	1.72	38.85
1991	103	41.98	–22.47	39.40	57.4	1.06	1.50	41.65
1992	107	41.43	6.42	36.23	53.5	1.05	1.41	38.12
1993	103	43.42	11.82	38.83	25.3	1.04	1.09	40.42
1994	105	41.26	–6.11	38.70	24.9	1.10	1.15	42.45

Notes:
[a] RER2 from *World Development Indicators*.
[b] Competitiveness Index, Elbadawi (1997).
[c] Anti-Export Bias computed as $\dfrac{1 + tm}{1 - tx}$

[d] Anti-Export Bias computed as $\dfrac{1 + tm + premium}{(1 - tx)}$

[e] Real Effective Exchange Rate (REER) computed as $\dfrac{(1 + tm)}{(1 - tx)}$ RER, where tm and tx are average import duty and export tax rates.

Source: Computed based on World Bank data and Table 9.10.

Based on official Tanzanian data sources and at a more aggregated level, the time performance of this category of exports retains the same pattern as above. The share of non-traditional exports in total exports registered the fastest rise during 1986–90, from 29 per cent in 1986 to nearly 50 per cent in 1990. Between 1980 and 1986 it registered a persistent sharp decline and during 1991–6 it averaged 41 per cent, below the average of nearly 45 per cent during the peak growth performance of 1987–91.

Table 9.10   Real exchange rate, competitiveness index and real effective exchange rate in Tanzania, 1970–95

Year	RER2 (1980 = 100)	CI (1987 = 100)	REER
1970	97.48	66.0	112.93
1971	96.14	78.9	108.61
1972	93.26	78.0	108.06
1973	93.94	73.0	111.18
1974	94.38	79.6	111.18
1975	84.86	93.3	97.26

Table 9.10   continued

Year	RER2 (1980 = 100)	CI (1987 = 100)	REER
1976	94.50	107.5	113.07
1977	88.93	107.0	112.36
1978	83.67	97.8	102.30
1979	88.82	105.8	107.74
1980	100.0	117.7	114.06
1981	129.69	117.7	141.21
1982	153.59	120.9	164.70
1983	171.59	113.6	188.29
1984	176.57	122.0	193.37
1985	204.97	137.9	222.60
1986	141.87	138.0	153.38
1987	69.81	100.0	74.35
1988	54.96	70.1	58.21
1989	48.13	68.0	51.02
1990	36.83	61.7	38.85
1991	39.40	57.4	41.65
1992	36.23	53.5	38.12
1993	38.83	25.3	40.42
1994	38.70	24.9	42.45
1995	40.17	n.a.	44.59

Source: see Table 9.9.

Table 9.11   Growth rates of non-traditional exports by SITC classification, Tanzania (1983–94) using the World Bank Data set

SITC	Description	Annual growth %
0	Food and Live Animals	2.44
1	Beverages and Tobacco	−8.33
2	Crude Materials, Inedible, except Fuels	16.70
3	Mineral Fuels, Lubricants and Related Materials	−7.89
4	Animal and Vegetable Oils, Fats and Waxes	6.55
5	Chemical and Related Products	170.17
6	Manufactured Goods Classified Chiefly by Material	5.04
7	Machinery and Transport Equipment	6.75
8	Miscellaneous Manufactured Articles	168.31
9	Commodities and Transactions n.e.c.	12.56

Source: Computed based on World Bank data.

The role of policy environment and incentives

Declining export performance in the first half of the 1980s

One can distinguish three major sources of growth deceleration for total exports in Tanzania during the first half of the 1980s. One source is the decline of the export base as reflected by the deceleration of the growth of output. Even if the share of exports in total output remains unchanged, output decline would lead to the decline of exports. Decrease in the expansion of productive capacity through lower investment or a reduction in the utilization of installed capacity would lead to a decline in the rate of output expansion.

The rate of investment and capacity utilization in Tanzania declined during the first half of the 1980s. Correspondingly output growth decelerated and in fact turned negative during 1982–3. This deceleration was much more severe for the import-dependent industrial sector. This fact is consistent with observations by Khan and Knight (1990), Helleiner (1986, 1990) and Ndulu (1986) that import compression resulting from declining export earnings curtails output growth and exports with the possible consequence of a vicious circle. Import compression negatively affected growth and exports through another channel. Importation of basic consumer goods was also curtailed during this period. As a result, incentives for agricultural production were also dampened with a negative effect on the export base. Commodity shortage mirrored by forced savings is, therefore, another reason for the overall deterioration of export performance during the first half of the 1980s.

The second source of export decline was the fact that the share of exports in output also registered a sharp decline during this period. This is reflected by the significantly lower ratio of exports to GDP during the period compared to the earlier ones. The ratio of exports to GDP declined from an average of 17 per cent during 1966–80 to 8.8 per cent in the first half of the 1980s (see Ndulu et al., 1997, and Table 2.1 using revised national accounts data). This happened in spite of the strong exhortation to export under the NESP. Two major reasons can be advanced to explain this situation. They are both related to the deterioration of incentives to export despite the export promotion measures implemented during this period. The most critical of these was the sharp rise in the implicit taxation of exports. The evidence for this is shown by four measures which reflect decline in the profitability of exports and erosion of export competitiveness.

Table 9.10 presents the trends of the real exchange rate, export competitiveness index, the real effective exchange rate and measures of the anti-export bias. They all depict a quantum leap in the implicit taxation of exporters during 1981–6. The real exchange rate (RER2) measures the extent to which the higher domestic price level relative to that of major trading partners is left uncompensated by required changes in the nominal exchange rate. On the one hand, exporters had to purchase their requirements from the home market at considerably higher prices than their competitors abroad. On the other, they faced declining profitability as they used imports at increasing domestic prices while their earnings were cashed in at an exchange rate which did not depreciate commensurately. The competitiveness index (CI) has a similar interpretation, measuring the degree to which the authorities did not appropriately react to changes in the fundamentals which influence movements in the real equilibrium exchange rate.

The real effective exchange rate (REER) incorporates the additional effects (to RER2) of import taxes and explicit export taxes, both driving a wedge between domestic and border prices, against exporters. The anti-export bias index, EBIAS1, includes the effects of the import and explicit export taxes, while EBIAS2 in addition includes the parallel market exchange rate premium (see notes to Table 9.9). The premium is in effect an implicit tax on exporters (Pinto, 1989). It measures the transfer of income from exporters to the government and those receiving import licences at an overvalued exchange rate. This transfer is enforced by the mandatory surrender requirements.

The effect of the decline in profitability and erosion of competitiveness is for exporters either to switch to the domestic market (market substitution effect) or to switch their resources away from production of exportables to non-traded goods or importables. In any event, the final result is a decline in export orientation or the ratio of exports to output. This effect holds for both traditional and non-traditional exports.

The second reason for export decline was the declining share of the world market price reaching producers even at the ruling exchange rates. This was a result of the state monopolistic marketing arrangements and official pricing structures which relegated prices to producers of exportables as residuals after exacting marketing costs and margins. Attempts at switching to make these margins the residual ran up against budget constraints for subsidizing state marketing arrangements, and hence low price shares to producers were maintained (Lipumba et al., 1988). Combined with the rapid inflation experienced during this period, real agricultural producer prices declined and so did supplies for export. This phenomenon also affected minor agricultural exports marketed under the National Milling Corporation (NMC) in the mainland and the Zanzibar Export Agency for cloves and other spices on the island.

The third source of decline was underground trade to evade taxation of exports particularly via mandatory surrender of foreign exchange earnings. The increase of illegal trade meant that officially recorded exports declined more sharply than the actual volume of exports. As long as the parallel market premium was significantly higher than the expected costs of detection and confiscation in the event of being caught, incentives for illegal trade existed.[6] The parallel market premium reached its peak in 1985 at 476 per cent and officially recorded exports reached their trough in the same period. This would tend to suggest that, in addition to the overall disincentive effects of implicit export taxation, larger effects of illegal trade might have been operative at the same time. We have pointed out this third source of decline so as to take it into account in explaining the rapid recovery of exports, particularly for non-traditional exports, in the late 1980s.

Recovery of exports, 1987 onwards

There was a fairly rapid recovery of exports, particularly of non-traditional products, between 1987 and 1990. This recovery was described earlier in terms of value growth and the number of products. The recovery was accompanied by the revival of output growth and a rise in export orientation especially for manufacturers (Ndulu and Semboja, 1995). We explain two aspects of this recovery: that of overall exports and a steeper rise in non-traditional exports as shown in the sharp rise in the share of non-traditional exports in total.

Table 9.9 depicts the trends of export value/growth against the various measures of incentives to export. It confirms the positive effects of reducing export taxation. Both the profitability of exports and competitiveness of Tanzanian exports sharply increased as the local currency depreciated steeply. During 1985–90, the local currency was depreciated in nominal terms more than tenfold (Tshs/US$). In real terms the currency depreciated by 83 per cent. In addition, import liberalization which began in July 1984 improved the availability of basic commodities, very significantly boosting the incentive for agricultural production. Furthermore, an import support scheme and balance of payments support under the Structural Adjustment Programme and the IMF's Structural Adjustment Facility (SAF) significantly reduced import compression and led to a rise in capacity utilization.

The fact that merchandise non-traditional exports responded relatively more strongly than total exports finds possible explanation in three factors. First, this response was overwhelmingly led by the export of manufactures, directly benefiting from the balance of payment support programmes mentioned earlier. Higher capacity utilization combined with a rise in the share of exports in total output to spur a rapid expansion in exports. Increased profitability and export competitiveness explain increased export shares in output from 5.8 per cent in 1986 to 30.2 per cent in 1990 (ibid.). Higher capacity utilization led to a strong revival of output of the manufacturing sector, growing at an annual rate of 23.7 per cent. Export of manufactures grew at an annual rate of nearly 20 per cent during this period, raising its share in total exports from 12.6 per cent in 1986 to 26.7 per cent in 1990 (ibid.: Tables 6.1 and 6.2).

The second reason was related to the differential application of the General Retention Scheme for foreign exchange earned, in favour of non-traditional exports. The scheme allowed exporters to retain a specified percentage of their foreign currency earnings for importation of essential inputs, incentive goods for resale, or for servicing their foreign debt. This scheme was instituted in 1986 and *de facto* considerably reduced the surrender requirement for exporters of non-traditional products. The applicable retention rate for non-traditional exports was 50 per cent while that of traditional exports was a low 10 per cent until 1989. The surrender requirement was subsequently abolished in 1992 for all products; but this interim provision very likely initially prompted a much larger response from exporters of non-traditional products. The scheme implied a much higher profitability of non-traditional exports as a large share of earnings from these fetched local currency at close to the parallel market rate. The parallel market premia during the period averaged 109 per cent, translating into at least 55 per cent higher earnings in local currency.

Finally, it is most likely that illegal trade in non-traditional exports was reduced much more than in traditional exports given the much lower effective premium exacted from exporters of these products. In any case, since export of traditional products was handled solely by public agencies, there is greater likelihood that most of the underground trade involved non-traditional export products.

The rate of expansion of non-traditional exports slackened considerably in the post-1990 period but it remained above that of the first half of the 1980s. After the sharp rise of export profitability and competitiveness over 1987–90, this trend showed a slight turn in the opposite direction in 1991 and 1992 as shown by appreciation of the real value of the currency (Table 9.9). This erosion strengthened following the adoption of the market-determined exchange rate system, first through auctions and open market operations of forex bureaux and then through the inter-bank market. Elbadawi (1998) provides part of the explanation for this reaction of the open market. Based on estimations of the real equilibrium exchange rate, the steep official depreciation pursued between 1986 and 1990 appears to have overshot the level necessary for seeking parity with long-run equilibrium conditions. The other reason for real appreciation pressure was a significant increase in capital inflows, the bulk of them in the form of reverse capital flight as exchange controls were dismantled and foreign currency denominated deposits were permitted. During 1994–7, this trend continued and, adjusting for the inflation differential with Tanzania's trading partners, the local currency was estimated by 1997 to be overvalued by nearly 20 per cent relative to its level in 1992 (BOT, 1998). The policy stance adopted by the authorities is not to intervene in the operation of the foreign exchange market and instead focus on trying to reduce domestic inflation to parity levels through monetary control. We return to this issue below in assessing the appropriateness of the policy environment for encouraging expansion of non-traditional exports.

Drawing together the effects of various components of the policy environment on non-traditional export performance

Previous studies have applied multivariate statistical analysis in attempts to determine the relative significance of various policy factors in influencing export performance. Here we will focus on those which explicitly influenced non-traditional exports and overall export competitiveness. We will supplement these with additional statistical evidence from the current study.

In a study on exports of manufactures from Tanzania, Ndulu and Semboja (1995) analysed the determinants of export supply response and export orientation for the manufacturing sector. Three important conclusions emerged from that study concerning this single largest contributor to non-traditional exports as a group. The responsiveness of manufactured exports to changes in the profitability of exports relative to domestic sales is indeed very high. The study obtained an elasticity slightly greater than 1.6 for export orientation in response to real exchange rate changes. Second, the supply of exports of manufactures is responsive to both incentive to export as measured by the real exchange rate and to the export base, i.e. output of the manufacturing sector. An elasticity of the volume of exports from the manufacturing sector to real exchange rate changes is close to 1. The speed of adjustment to changes in policy environment was also quite high, with the mean period being a year. Third, among the policy instruments of consequence to export response, the macroeconomic policy environment dominated the explanation of export performance. An exchange rate policy stance favourable to exports and the presence or absence of exchange controls are the most important determinants within the set of macroeconomic policies pursued in the country. A simulation of the relative impacts of the key determinants of export supply responsiveness confirmed this result (ibid.). Measures for controlling inflation and explicit trade policies (e.g. tariffs) turned out to be less significant.

These results are in part corroborated by those obtained in the Elbadawi (1998) study of seven African countries. Using a panel regression the study finds that a reduction in real currency overvaluation (level) as well as its predicted and unpredictable variability have a positive influence on export orientation. In the study, Tanzania was ranked second after Ghana in terms of export competitiveness in the 1990s, influenced by its stance on the exchange rate policy. Furthermore, the study also identified nominal exchange rate devaluation as the single most important factor behind the movement of the real exchange rate in the recent past.

In the context of the current study, we also carried out a statistical analysis to determine the most important driver of supply response for non-traditional exports as a group. We adopted the official definition for which a sufficiently long data series exists. The factors included were the various measures of export incentives from the macroeconomic point of view, export base as approximated by real GDP growth, and the time incidence of promotional measures which largely focused on non-traditional exports. Four measures of incentives were tried: RER, REER, competitiveness index from Elbadawi (ibid.) and anti-export bias – all as previously defined.

The results presented in Table 9.12 confirm the following. Irrespective of the incentive measure included, incentives turned out to be the single most important determinant of supply response for non-traditional exports. However, the most robust of them is the anti-export bias which takes into account the size of the parallel market premium and trade barriers. The supply elasticities of non-traditional exports with respect to the four measures range from 0.62 to 1.2. The time incidence of the promotional measures, included as a dummy variable for the relevant years they were applied, has the correct sign but is rather weak in terms of statistical significance. GDP growth as a proxy for changes in the export base for non-traditional exports turned out problematic (wrong sign and mainly insignificant) pointing to the likelihood that it is not a good proxy. The main reason is probably the fact that it represented total output and not the output of non-traditional export products.

Table 9.12 Regression results of non-traditional exports with respect to incentive measures, Tanzania (1970–95)

	(1)		(2)		(3)	
Constant	8.6	(19.7)	7.96	(17.09)	9.2	(26.07)
Competitiveness Index			0.25	(0.84)		
Real Exchange Rate	–0.15	(–0.56)	–1.71	(–3.44)		
Real Effective Exchange Rate					–0.63	(–3.36)
Anti-Export Bias	–0.80	(–2.69)				
Growth of GDP	–0.29	(–1.80)	–0.29	(–1.76)	–0.32	(–1.64)
Dummy for Promotional Measures	0.20	(1.88)	0.19	(1.96)	0.14	(1.24)
R square	0.62		0.63		0.44	
Adjusted R square	0.54		0.55		0.35	
F statistic	7.78		8.04		5.2	

Notes: Bracketed figures are t values. All variables in logs. Dummy for promotional measures is equal to 1 in years when these were applied. Real Exchange Rate, Real Effective Exchange Rate, Competitiveness Index, and Anti-Export Bias are measures such that a rise implies an increase in the taxation of exports and erosion of export competitiveness. When export competitiveness index is included on its own with output and dummy variables, it has a correct negative sign and is statistically significant.

A focus on export promotion measures

Measures towards promoting exports go hand in hand with policies relating to importing, as the primary aim of exporting is to increase capacity to import. Despite the realization that impediments to exporting mirror perfectly on importation, control measures on exporting were mainly instituted as a monitoring mechanism of foreign exchange proceeds rather than a restriction *per se* (except for restricted items like animal trophies).

A detailed review of the export promotion measures is provided in Ndulu and Semboja (1995) and Ndulu et al. (1997). Below, the measures are mentioned in passing in order to provide room for a focus on the reporting of results from other studies.

Two broad phases relating to controls on exports and imports in Tanzania can be categorized: before 1984 and after 1984.

Export promotional measures before 1984

The economic crisis which Tanzania faced from the late 1970s was mainly caused by lack of capacity to import. A number of measures were designed in order to improve on the foreign exchange position. The first package of such measures was contained in the NESP launched in 1981 with the primary aim of reviving exports. Subsequent packages were to address the deficiencies of NESP strategies.

(a) *Granting of export licences*
    Though in effect licensing is a control measure (and hence restrictive to exporting), during the early 1980s, in the environment of controls, the granting of an export licence, especially to private sector agents, was an incentive, since the policy of confinement had designated export business to parastatals.
(b) *Foreign exchange allocation*
    Among the criteria used in the allocation of foreign exchange was that an activity had to export or had a high potential to export. This was done in the hope of achieving a net foreign exchange earning capacity.
(c) *Export subsidies*
    These were mainly intended to offset costs of exporters in order to maintain competitiveness in the export market. Explicitly the subsidies were negligible and only featured implicitly in the form of general subsidies to exporting parastatals, since export business was mainly confined to the public sector.
(d) *Export guarantee and foreign exchange entitlement certificates*
    These schemes in practice remained only as intentions since the government could not honour its commitment due to the severe foreign exchange shortage persisting in the economy by then. The schemes were, in effect, not functioning.
(e) *Retention of export proceeds to targeted products*
    This was designed in order to ease pressure from the foreign exchange allocation mechanism as well as promote the export of certain products (high value products). The retention was targeted mainly to exports other than the principal agricultural export crops. There was no uniform retention rate; highest rates were granted to high priority exports.
(f) *Seed capital revolving scheme*
    This involved granting initial capital, in foreign exchange, to potential exporters. Once the exporter realized proceeds the advanced foreign exchange was recovered and this was advanced to another potential exporter.

(g) *Non-monetary promotional incentives*
These mainly involved opportunities granted to exporters and potential exporters to advertise their products. Such opportunities included participation in trade fairs domestically or abroad under the auspices of the sole parastatal dealing with the promotion of external trade, the Board of External Trade. Though it may not look like an incentive, the fact was that BET had to approve the participation. Related to this was the Presidential Export Award, a certificate usually issued in person by the President, as a recognition to outstanding exporters.

General assessment of the pre-1984 incentives   Though some of the incentives led to increased exports, their effect was limited given the multitude of other controls in place and the limited number of institutions dealing with export promotion. Restrictions on the importing sides which were exerted with great pressures discouraged exportation through official channels as importers were required to explain in detail their sources of imports. Imports, once they had entered the country, were closely monitored. Possession of foreign currencies and undeclared imports, however small in value, was criminal. These and other restrictive arrangements clouded the prospects of private sector export growth, whether official or non-official.

Export promotional measures after 1984

(a) In July 1984 the first liberalization measure with regard to external trade was declared: that Tanzanians who possessed foreign exchange holdings abroad were allowed to bring freely into the country 'incentive' goods without questions being asked as to the source of the foreign exchange holdings. This measure, known as the introduction of the 'Own Funds' scheme, has lasted 'stubbornly' over the years.

The result of this limited liberalization was an upsurge in Own Funded imports to become one of the two most important sources of imports. By implication this meant increased efforts to export (legally or illegally).

(b) *Continuation of pre-1984 export incentive schemes*
All the pre-1984 incentive schemes were retained, though their use was limited given the administrative procedures and the fact that more market-oriented procedures were now in place. Such schemes as export retentions, forex entitlement certificates, export guarantees are still in operation. Other schemes were little heard of, e.g. the Presidential Export Award.

(c) *Introduction of the duty drawback scheme managed by the Board of External Trade*
In 1986 the government established this scheme in order to provide 'qualifying exporters with a rebate on duties, sales and excise taxes paid on imported inputs contained in the exported product' (URT, 1995). The scheme initially benefited parastatals and by 1995 only about 11

importers utilized it. Underutilization was a result of inadequate budgetary provision resulting in long queues of around one year, thus eroding exporters' confidence in the scheme. Administrative bottlenecks further limited use of this facility rendering the facility inadequate and poorly implemented.

(d) *Expanded range of import funding possibilities*

As pointed out earlier, importing can be done in order to increase export capacity. This is true for cases of capital and intermediate inputs. The most notable measure in this regard was the introduction of the Open General Licence (OGL) in 1988 opening the floodgates to foreign exchange accessibility on the basis of 'first come, first served'. This was complemented by the introduction of foreign exchange bureaus in 1992.

(e) *Simplification of administrative procedures regarding exporting*

An important landmark has been the abolition of export licences. Exporting was *de facto* deconfined and export procedures were greatly streamlined. The marketing and processing of traditional export crops was opened to the private sector in 1994. Surrender requirements on traditional exports including coffee were abolished in June 1994.

With regard to non-traditional exports, the retention policy was reviewed in 1993 leading to the abolition of the surrender requirement. Retention of 100 per cent was allowed for all non-traditional exports.

(f) *Enhanced promotional measures*

Apart from participation in trade fairs, etc. other measures included the establishment of export processing zones (EPZs), endorsing the Cross-Border Initiative in 1995, and membership in regional groupings with export promotion ranking high on the agenda.

The licensing of EPZs in particular marked a significant move in expanding the range of incentives. Following reports of EPZ successes elsewhere, e.g. Mauritius, the government commissioned a study in 1995 to look into the feasibility of establishing EPZs in Tanzania. The following year, two EPZs were in operation, dealing mainly in garments. There has been little success given the continuing existence of other bottlenecks to exporting (see below) and frequent labour disputes in the EPZs.

(g) *Increased number of institutions dealing with export promotion*

In addition to the Board of External Trade, institutions catering to both public and private interests have been formed. One of the main purposes is to promote exports. Such institutions include the Tanzania Chamber of Commerce, Industry and Agriculture (TCCIA), the Tanzania Confederation of Industries (TCI), the Textile Manufacturers Association of Tanzania (TEXTMAT), the Tanzania Exporters Association (TANEXA), the Association of Horticultural Products Exporters, etc.

(h) *Investment promotion measures*

The establishment of the Investment Promotion Centre (IPC) in 1990 and subsequently the Tanzania Investment Centre (TIC) in 1997 has led to increased foreign investments doing export business.

Overall assessment of the post-1984 export promotion measures   There is no doubt that Tanzania went full length to institute measures to create a benign environment for exporting, especially of non-traditional products. The measures, falling largely under two groups, namely macro policy incentives and specific policies, led to an initial swift response and general upswing in non-traditional exports. The momentum, however, was not sustained in terms of consistency in the range of products after the initial upswing. This requires an explanation of entry and exist 'procedures', which we attempt below.

Constraints to exporting, entry and exit dynamics in the liberalization era

Here, we attempt to identify constraints to exporting non-traditional exports, in order to assess the potency of the promotional measures in operation.

(a) *Constraints inhibiting growth of enterprises in general*
Exporting is closely related to the growth of the enterprise. Despite the improved macro environment for enterprise development certain limitations still exist. The most binding constraint in the post-1984 era is capital (start-up and working capital). Wangwe et al. (1997) found this to be severe, affecting 76 per cent of enterprises surveyed. Capital cost was prohibitive, forcing the majority of entrepreneurs to rely on own savings and retained earnings as the main source of start-up capital (for new investments) and working capital (over 60 per cent of enterprises).

The above observation points to one contradiction: that despite the liberalization in the financial sector (financial markets) the facilities of the many commercial banks which sprang up have been inaccessible to many potential beneficiaries. Restrictive operations and expensive credit are among the ills (Mbelle, 1997). In the foreign exchange market, accessibility is mainly limited by effective demand.

Apart from capital considerations, other factors which inhibit growth are production constraints that are generally experienced in the economy – erratic supplies of production utilities (water and electricity), transportation bottlenecks and inferior communication networks, etc. These impinge heavily on the quality, quantity and delivery schedules (so sensitive in export markets, especially when firm orders have already been secured) (Bagachwa and Mbelle, 1995).

(b) *Constraints to non-traditional exporting*
In addition to production-related constraints other inhibitive factors include:

(i) Limited knowledge of foreign markets: despite improved 'literacy' on exporting some potential exporters are still not knowledgeable about export possibilities and have had no interaction with export promotion institutions. This, coupled with high price and low quality, is the main reason inhibiting penetration of the foreign market. Of the firms surveyed in Bol's (1995) study, 80 per cent failed to export due to limited knowledge of export possibilities!

   (ii) Unawareness of export incentives in operation: even the best known and utilized incentive scheme – export retention – did not benefit all potential exporters, 10 per cent of whom were not aware of the scheme (ibid.). Of the respondents, 40 per cent were not aware of the duty drawback scheme, while 20 per cent were unaware of the OGL scheme.

  (iii) Lack of export credit facilities and inadequate supporting infrastructure, especially packaging.

  (iv) Incentive schemes in place not working. The duty drawback scheme, for example, is in arrears as far back as ten years. This definitely acts as a disincentive to potential and existing exporters.

  (v) Limited accessibility to start-up and working capital. Formal credit to exporters accounted for only 10 per cent of start-up funds and only 20 per cent of working capital (ibid.).

Ranking of constraints to exporting   Table 9.13 summarizes the results of three studies on the relative importance of constraints to non-traditional exporting. The five most constraining factors are identified.

The ranking of constraints to exporting as summarized in Table 9.13 points to one fact: that the sector is not targeted. The first two highly-ranked constraints in the three studies reflect just this. As Bol (1995) emphasizes, general policy influences played a more important role in export promotion than specific policies.

Table 9.13   Constraints to non-traditional exporting in the liberalization era in Tanzania

Study		Ranking: 1 = most severe
Bol (1995)	1	Credit (limited)
	2	Bureaucracy
	3	Competition
	4	Power interruptions
	5	Transport bottlenecks
Bagachwa and	1	Bureaucracy
Mbelle (1995)	2	Limited access to credit
	3	Inadequate supportive infrastructure (e.g. power)
	4	Competition
	5	Weak institutional support
Ndulu, Semboja	1	Lack of credit facilities
and Mbelle (1997)	2	Inadequate supporting infrastructure (e.g. packaging)
	3	Production constraints (power, etc.)
	4	Competition
	5	No information on opportunities (markets)

The role of new investments in the development of non-traditional exports in Tanzania

New developments in export incentives   The range of export promotion measures in Tanzania has recently been widened by the Tanzania Investment Act of 1997, to include the granting of Certificates of Incentives. By this Act, the former Investment Promotion Centre metamorphosed into the Tanzania Investment Centre. Eligibility for the Certificate is confined to investments of at least US$100 000 for investments with majority shareholding by Tanzanian nationals and at least US$300 000 for majority foreign share-holding. The investments have to be in 'Lead Sectors', e.g. EPZs, and in 'Priority Sectors' like export processing.

The pattern of new investments in Tanzania   Tracking of investments has been made easier in recent years through improved record keeping in the two main centres of monitoring: the Tanzania Investment Centre (TIC) and the (Presidential) Parastatal Sector Reform Commission (PSRC). While in the past new applicants did not have to show full commitment to actually undertaking the investment, TIC now requires some form of commitment before granting approval, even though the success rate is still low, between 40 per cent and 50 per cent.

Between September 1990 and March 1999 a total of 1,250 projects had been approved. Out of these, 934 were new projects and 316 were expansions and/or rehabilitations. The extent of export orientation of the approved projects is difficult to determine. Our judgement is based on our experience of export-oriented sectors in Tanzania. A quick look at Table 9.14 suggests that investments in agriculture, manufacturing, tourism, and petroleum and mining are more likely to produce 'exportables'. However, since much of agriculture's exports fall under traditional exports, only manufacturing, tourism, and petroleum and mining are of relevance to our analysis.

Table 9.14 shows that the three sectors account for 69 per cent of the approved projects during the period September 1990 to March 1999. Manufacturing accounts for 50 per cent, tourism for 15 per cent, and petroleum and mining for 4 per cent. Therefore, recent investments have tended to favour non-traditional exporting activities. The three sectors also account for 65 per cent of the projected employment and 22 per cent of the projected investment cost, suggesting that non-traditional export activities may be more labour-intensive than non-tradables.

A prospective assessment of policy environment for non-traditional exports

By way of concluding, we wish to highlight three key issues with respect to the maintenance of an appropriate policy environment for sustained expansion of non-traditional exports in Tanzania. First, the liberalization of the trade and exchange regimes has obviated the need for compensatory

Table 9.14   Sectoral distribution of registered projects in Tanzania between September 1990 and March 1999

Sector	Total projects approved	New projects	Exp/reh. projects	Local projects	Foreign projects	Joint ventures	Total employees	Total investment (Tshs, million)
Agriculture and Livestock								
Development	93	51	42	24	25	44	28,442	94,379
Natural Resources	80	62	18	34	18	28	22,779	314,238
Tourism	182	140	42	84	35	63	17,941	241,385
Manufacturing	627	471	156	349	107	171	97,345	129,725
Petroleum and Mining	50	45	5	17	11	22	6,828	246,602
Construction	56	49	7	29	13	14	5,133	996,644
Transport	71	46	25	28	13	30	5,486	91,607
Services	47	34	13	20	12	15	8,716	99,094
Computers	3	2	1	1	2	–	20	281
Telecommunications	10	9	1	3	2	5	646	94,211
Human Resources								
Development	8	2	6	6	1	1	50	37,440
Financial	22	22	–	3	9	8	990	97,800
Energy	1	1	–	–	–	1	80	336,256
Grand Total	1,250	934	316	598	249	403	194,466	2,779,662

Source: Tanzania Investment Centre.

measures such as the retention scheme. However, export rebate schemes should be maintained as a corrective device against import tariff levies which will remain positive in the future so as to ensure a level playing field for exporters and domestic producers who sell in the protected domestic market at considerably higher prices. Other promotional measures which strengthen export competence in marketing and production will remain necessary for breaking into new markets and helping the entry of new exporters.

Second, and probably more contentious, is the choice of an appropriate exchange rate regime in relation to sustained profitability and competitiveness of Tanzanian exports. Tanzania has adopted a policy stance of minimal intervention in the foreign exchange market. The system which is currently maintained is that of a 'dirty float' with occasional interventions by the central bank to stabilize the value of the local currency through open market operations. This stabilization target runs against two major constraints. One is that given the large amplitude of the movements in fundamentals, particularly capital flows, the available foreign exchange reserves are not adequate for ensuring such stability. Two, the monetary authority has adopted the approach of reducing inflation to the level of that of trading partners but Tanzania's inflation remains significantly high. Part of the reason is the downward stickiness of domestic prices and wages for a variety of structural reasons and inertial inflation. The gap with world inflation remains wide, eroding the competitiveness and profitability of Tanzania's exports.

Exporters have increased pressure against the recent real appreciation of the local currency associated mainly with capital flows and the authorities' policy stance of maintaining a stable local currency in nominal terms. Exporters wish to maintain a stable real value of the currency by applying a crawling peg to protect profitability and competitiveness of exports. The authorities have recently considered maintaining the exchange rate within acceptable bands through the active intervention of the central bank in the foreign exchange market aimed at ensuring that the real value of the currency stays within it. However, as long as the inflation differential with trading partners remains wide, the likelihood of success in keeping the real value of the local currency within the band will be very low indeed.

Finally, there is the issue of a proactive export promotion in the context of the new world trading arrangements under the WTO. The recent changes in the world trading system have eroded preferences accorded to Tanzania. Although this erosion will potentially affect mainly traditional exports, for which supply-side constraints are more important, some non-traditional exports such as textiles will also be affected. Addressing barriers to exports of processed and manufactured products as well as fresh fruits and vegetables is more important for expansion of non-traditional exports. In both developed and developing importing countries, tariffs tend to be higher for processed than primary commodities, resulting in tariff escalation. Products in which LDCs (including Tanzania) tend to face relatively high applied tariffs include wood products, textiles and clothing, fish and fish products, and leather and leather products. These are particularly relevant in efforts to diversify the export base and sustain export growth. Application of quantitative restrictions in the principal export markets is likewise relatively loaded against non-traditional exports. Applications of these restrictions correlate closely with high tariff levies, compounding the problem pointed out earlier. In light of the foregoing, it is important that Tanzania, along with other developing countries, seeks to address these constraints through active involvement in future negotiations under the WTO.

Notes

1. The six principal agricultural export commodities include coffee, cotton, sisal, tea, tobacco and cashew nuts. Including cloves, these accounted on average for 63 per cent of Tanzania's total domestic exports during the 1970s.
2. In a study of trends and amplitudes of primary commodity prices, Reinhart and Wickham (1994) confirmed the long-run declining trend of most primary commodity prices. What was more disturbing in the findings is that over the two decades (the 1970s and 1980s), the study confirmed a worsening of instability of price movements in the later decade. The amplitudes of price movements along the declining trend were larger, exposing the countries most dependent on them to both falling earnings and greater uncertainties.
3. Tanzania's export concentration index, as calculated in the 1997 UNCTAD *Handbook of International Trade Statistics*, estimated at 0.286, was far below the African average. The three products which accounted for 54 per cent of total exports in 1980 were coffee, spices and cotton.
4. The average growth rate for the post-1985 period uses the old GDP services growth rates prior to 1988 so as to avoid inclusion of an unrealistic magnitude for 1987 due to the series break between 1986 and 1987.
5. Ndulu et al. (1997) present a comprehensive review of these promotional measures and the extent of their application and utilization. The main conclusion from this review, including the gleanings from a firm-level survey, is that both awareness of these measures and actual utilization were quite low. In any case they did not compensate for the draconian implicit taxation they faced on account of a grossly overvalued local currency and the mandatory surrender requirements at the overvalued rate.
6. Let p be the probability of detection if an exporter engages in illegal trade, μ the expected return from it and Z be the penalty if caught. It is trivial to show that as long as $(1 - p)\,\mu > p.Z$ there is reason to trade illegally. Expected return to such engagement is obtained by multiplying the probability of successful evasion $(1 - p)$ times the exchange rate premium. (See Kaufmann and O'Connell, 1991, for motivational analysis of illegal trade in Tanzania.)

References

Bagachwa, M. S. D. and Mbelle, A. V. Y. (1995) 'Tanzania' in S. M. Wangwe (ed.), *Exporting Africa: Technology, Trade and Industrialization in Sub-Saharan Africa*, London: Routledge.
Bank of Tanzania (BOT) (1982) *Twenty Years After Independence*, Dar es Salaam.
Bank of Tanzania (BOT) (1997) *Economic Bulletin*, Vol. 27, No. 1, Dar es Salaam.
Bank of Tanzania (BOT) (1998) *Economic Bulletin*, Vol. 28, No. 1, Dar es Salaam.

Bol, D. (1995) 'Winners and Losers of Trade Liberalization? Tanzania's Non-Traditional Exports' in M. S. D. Bagachwa and F. Limbu (eds) *Policy Reform and the Environment in Tanzania*, Dar es Salaam: DUP.

Bol, D. and Luvanga, N. (1997) 'Export Diversification' in D. Bol, N. Luvanga and J. Shitundu (eds), *Economic Management in Tanzania*, Dar es Salaam: TEMA Publishers.

De Rosa, D. (1990) 'Protection and Export Performance in Sub-Saharan Africa', *Weltwirtschaftliches Archiv* 128, 1: 88–124.

Elbadawi, I. (1998) 'Real Exchange Rate Policy and Non-Traditional Exports in Developing Countries', *Research for Action*, 46, Helsinki: WIDER.

Helleiner, G. K. (1986) 'Outward Orientation, Import Instability and African Economic Growth: An Empirical Investigation' in S. Lall and F. Stewart (eds), *Theory and Reality in Development: Essays in Honour of Paul Streeten*, New York: St Martin's Press.

Helleiner, G. K. (1990) 'Trade Strategy in Medium-Term Adjustment', *World Development* 18, 6: 879–97.

Kaufmann, D. and O'Connell, S. (1991) 'The Macroeconomics of the Unofficial Foreign Exchange Market in Tanzania' in A. Chhibber and S. Fischer (eds), *Economic Reforms in Sub-Saharan Africa*, Washington, DC: World Bank.

Khan, M. and Knight, M. (1990) 'Import Compression and Export Performance in Developing Countries', *The Review of Economics and Statistics*, 70, 2.

Lipumba, N., Ndulu, B., Horton, S. and Plourde, A. (1988) 'A Supply-Constrained Macroeconometric Model for Tanzania', *Economic Modelling*, vol. 5: 354–76.

Mbelle, A. V. Y. (1997) 'The Impact of Liberalization of the Foreign Exchange and Financial Markets in Tanzania', paper presented at the UNU/WIDER meeting on the Impact of Liberalization on Key Markets in Sub-Saharan Africa, Kampala, Uganda, June 1997.

Ndulu, B. (1986) 'Investment, Output Growth and Capacity Utilization in an African Economy: The Case of the Manufacturing Sector in Tanzania', *East African Economic Review* (New Series) 2, 1.

Ndulu, B. and Semboja, J. (1995) 'The Development of Manufacturing for Export in Tanzania' in G. Helleiner (ed.), *Manufacturing for Export in the Developing World: Problems and Possibilities*, London: Routledge.

Ndulu, B., Semboja, J. and Mbelle, A. (1997) 'Trade Liberalization in Tanzania: Episodes and Impacts' in A. Oyejide, B. Ndulu and J. Gunning (eds), *Regional Integration and Trade Liberalization in Sub-Saharan Africa, Vol. 2: Country Case Studies*, London: Macmillan.

Pinto, B. (1989), 'Black Market Premia, Exchange Rate Unification, and Inflation in Sub-Saharan Africa', *World Bank Economic Review* 3, 3: 321–38.

Prebisch, R. (1950) *The Economic Development of Latin America and Its Principal Problems*, New York: United Nations.

Reinhart, C. and Wickham, P. (1994) 'Commodity Prices: Cyclical Weaknesses or Secular Decline?', *IMF Working Paper WP/94/7*, Washington, DC: International Monetary Fund.

Rodrik, D. (1997) 'Trade Policy and Economic Performance in Sub-Saharan Africa', paper prepared for Swedish Ministry of Foreign Affairs.

Singer, H. (1950) 'The Distribution of Gains Between Investing and Borrowing Countries', *American Economic Review* 40, 2 (May): 473–85.

United Republic of Tanzania (URT) (1976) *The Third Five Year Plan*, Vol. 1, Dar es Salaam: Government Printers.

United Republic of Tanzania (URT) (1981) *National Economic Survival Plan* (NESP), Dar es Salaam: Government Printers.

United Republic of Tanzania (URT) (1995) *Tanzania Export Development Strategy and Action Plan (1995–2000). A Dynamic Strategy to Forge Strategic Alliances to Develop Exports: Policies, Institutions, Infrastructure and Capacity*, Dar es Salaam: Government Printers.

Wangwe, S. M. et al. (1997) 'Multi-Country Comparative Study on Private Enterprises Development in Africa' (MCC.PED), a report for Tanzania.

Appendix

Table 9.A1   Total Tanzanian exports, 1961–97 (US$ millions)

	Coffee	Cotton	Sisal	Tea	Tobacco	Cashew nuts	Subtotal (trad.)	Petrol. products	Minerals	Manufac. products	Other	Services Total w/o Tourism	Subtotal merchandise non-trad.	Subtotal non-trad.	Total export merchandise	Grand total exports
1961	18.93	19.04	39.28	3.74	0.22	5.05	86.27	0.00	17.08	13.24	3.12	19.32	n.a.	33.44	52.76	119.71	139.03
1962	18.41	20.71	44.06	4.51	0.22	6.54	94.44	0.00	15.36	14.28	3.11	20.16	n.a.	32.75	52.91	127.19	147.35
1963	19.15	30.00	63.48	4.34	0.20	5.67	122.84	0.00	15.27	14.55	4.07	24.08	n.a.	33.89	57.97	156.73	180.81
1964	30.94	27.66	61.22	4.37	0.10	9.21	133.50	0.00	23.51	18.06	0.49	27.44	n.a.	47.06	69.50	175.56	203.00
1965	24.05	34.19	39.98	4.23	1.36	11.55	115.36	0.00	25.03	13.80	1.30	30.80	n.a.	40.13	70.93	155.49	186.29
1966	42.38	48.89	32.86	6.31	2.25	14.00	146.69	0.66	29.47	18.83	1.01	38.36	n.a.	49.97	88.33	196.66	235.02
1967	33.43	35.20	28.13	6.05	4.70	12.91	120.41	18.68	34.66	19.82	2.48	42.52	n.a.	75.64	118.16	196.05	238.57
1968	37.11	39.61	22.22	6.29	5.54	14.22	124.99	22.74	20.89	17.65	0.18	53.59	n.a.	61.46	115.05	186.45	240.04
1969	36.73	33.53	22.80	6.90	5.04	16.99	121.99	15.01	27.27	19.76	0.77	60.38	n.a.	62.81	123.19	184.80	245.18
1970	44.60	35.31	25.54	6.03	6.40	16.46	134.34	15.93	24.79	17.50	0.37	91.10	13.39	58.59	149.69	197.93	284.03
1971	32.49	34.97	19.11	6.99	6.16	17.09	116.80	20.49	31.37	31.20	10.83	105.67	13.65	93.89	199.56	210.69	316.36
1972	41.14	48.06	20.69	7.69	7.00	21.47	146.04	3.07	28.40	24.49	4.84	111.14	27.66	60.80	171.94	206.84	317.98
1973	70.73	76.16	31.66	7.74	7.93	20.17	214.39	12.43	28.24	27.47	2.90	106.72	20.50	71.04	177.76	285.43	392.15
1974	53.59	67.51	66.20	9.89	12.53	28.03	237.74	18.54	30.60	41.09	1.34	102.68	12.81	91.57	194.25	329.31	431.99
1975	69.26	42.56	43.33	11.61	12.49	25.27	204.51	19.87	38.71	33.13	4.31	138.31	9.89	96.02	234.33	300.53	438.84
1976	133.12	73.24	28.76	16.06	22.43	15.65	309.25	20.65	24.78	39.08	3.56	154.82	10.52	88.07	242.89	397.37	552.14
1977	224.06	65.23	27.65	21.45	25.47	22.64	386.50	17.47	26.76	45.18	10.68	121.69	9.00	100.09	221.78	486.59	608.28
1978	169.00	54.53	28.68	21.82	28.72	20.86	323.61	10.75	32.99	55.30	14.73	151.52	12.73	113.77	265.29	437.38	588.90
1979	147.93	59.88	31.65	19.96	18.10	17.68	295.19	16.62	44.19	99.70	18.68	151.61	16.94	179.19	330.80	474.38	625.99
1980	280.07	43.83	30.05	22.24	12.05	7.34	395.58	24.34	49.01	92.79	23.25	178.92	19.70	189.39	368.31	584.97	763.89
1981	165.06	78.10	33.89	19.57	18.24	34.49	349.35	16.14	64.94	59.87	59.30	195.70	21.61	200.25	395.95	549.60	745.30
1982	133.51	56.35	24.11	18.64	19.29	9.89	261.79	13.55	43.74	42.88	37.36	117.25	15.22	137.53	254.78	399.32	516.57
1983	129.27	61.83	13.09	21.81	11.40	6.50	243.90	13.00	43.60	44.50	19.17	108.08	12.81	120.27	228.35	364.17	472.25
1984	125.66	14.99	7.82	23.48	9.03	22.33	203.30	19.02	16.51	30.48	3.34	172.78	9.38	69.35	242.13	272.65	445.43

1985	93.01	25.95	4.43	16.20	13.57	9.76	162.92	14.34	20.44	20.11	4.52	108.09	10.30	59.41	167.50	222.33	330.42
1986	164.07	30.85	5.22	13.91	13.73	12.94	240.72	0.04	11.15	3.54	19.99	110.24	20.00	34.72	144.96	275.44	385.68
1987	90.14	37.07	5.10	12.93	11.73	11.09	168.07	8.34	9.38	58.15	4.27	111.28	31.05	80.14	191.42	248.21	359.49
1988	71.12	64.75	3.79	14.83	12.78	2.28	169.54	4.39	11.74	51.86	25.04	120.57	40.40	93.03	213.60	262.57	383.14
1989	97.95	77.36	3.51	17.31	13.11	3.22	212.47	13.92	6.37	66.64	33.96	122.69	60.00	120.89	243.58	333.36	456.05
1990	82.15	75.82	16.99	37.56	12.87	5.27	230.67	5.15	18.56	16.28	61.40	134.89	65.00	101.39	236.28	333.06	466.95
1991	75.53	62.20	2.19	21.68	1.65	16.07	179.32	6.25	38.69	56.67	56.68	143.11	94.73	158.29	301.40	337.61	480.72
1992	58.11	95.29	1.31	24.10	2.20	21.79	202.81	8.35	43.40	61.94	94.64	147.02	120.04	208.33	355.35	411.14	558.16
1993	97.29	78.21	3.55	38.03	1.64	22.54	241.26	13.90	69.27	53.36	64.58	317.91	146.84	201.11	519.02	442.37	760.28
1994	123.04	111.86	5.53	39.52	1.70	55.50	337.16	5.84	32.22	82.00	98.00	418.30	192.10	218.06	636.36	555.22	973.52
1995	141.24	120.48	6.15	23.36	1.10	62.78	355.11	10.81	44.45	74.89	159.21	582.61	259.44[a]	289.36	871.97	644.47	1,227.08
1996	133.50	125.30	3.10	25.70	33.80	86.40	407.80	8.10	36.30	116.80	127.50	537.30	322.37 [a]	288.70	826.00	696.50	1,233.80
1997	117.43	116.46	8.54	30.06	12.91	73.40	358.81	12.35	92.81	131.88	121.30	495.43	392.41[a]	358.34	853.77	717.15	1,212.58

Note: [a] Projections.

Sources: Bank of Tanzania; for data on Tourism, Ministry of Natural Resources and Tourism, Tourism Division.

10
Economic Reforms and Non-Traditional Exports in Zimbabwe: Is Anything Taking Shape?

Jesimen Chipika and Rob Davies

Introduction

For much of the time since the Second World War, Zimbabwe's trade regime has been relatively restrictive. As a member of the Sterling area, the immediate post-war period was characterized by capital account restrictions. This was followed by the Federation of Rhodesia and Nyasaland (1953–62) in which, although trade amongst federal partners was free, there were substantial tariff barriers with the rest of the world. This was followed by the UDI period (1966–80), in which the illegal settler regime faced international sanctions, to which it responded by imposing its own system of exchange controls and import licensing. Of course, trade regulations went hand in hand with other regulations: price controls, labour market interventions, investment controls. This regulatory system was kept in place after independence in 1980. Although some aspects of the regulations started to break down in the late 1980s, it was only in 1990 that a formally announced regime shift was inaugurated, as trade liberalization (and removal of other regulatory devices) was introduced as part of a structural adjustment package. It could thus be argued that it was only in 1990 that the economy embraced a liberalized trade policy for the first time in almost 50 years.

This chapter is concerned with the effect this profound change in trade regime has had on the pattern of exports in Zimbabwe. Such a long period of 'distortions' should have shifted exports away from what they would have been under a freer regime. Will removal of the distortions lead to comparative advantage reasserting itself and a growth of traditional exports? Or did the trade restrictions inhibit the development of new exports, so that their removal will see a flourishing of non-traditional exports?

In what follows we begin by outlining the macroeconomic circumstances in which liberalization was undertaken. We then examine some of the institutional changes which have occurred. We present the results of a statistical examination of the commodity composition of Zimbabwe's exports, followed by an examination of the country composition. Since we do not undertake a rigorous analysis of the causes of perceived changes in export composition, in our conclusion we speculate about possible causation.

Background: from controls to liberalization

Zimbabwe is a land-locked country sharing borders with South Africa, Botswana, Mozambique and Zambia. It has a total population of around 12 million people (98.8 per cent Blacks, and 1.2 per cent European, Asian and other races). Population growth rate has averaged 3 per cent per annum since 1980.

The country's 90 years of minority settler–colonial rule up to 1980 explains its economic structure – a typical dualistic, agricultural-based economy, with highly unequal distributions of wealth and incomes. About 70 per cent of the population derive their livelihood from small-scale communal area farming or as large-scale commercial farm labourers, making agriculture the largest employer. Agriculture accounts for about 30 per cent of formal employment, followed by manufacturing at 16 per cent. Manufacturing output contributed 21 per cent to GDP during 1985–90; its share declined steadily to 18 per cent in 1994 and to 16 per cent in 1996. Agriculture contributed an average of 15 per cent during the entire period 1985–96, with tourism (represented by Distribution, Hotels and Restaurants) accounting for 14 per cent in the 1980s, rising to 16 per cent in the 1990s (Central Statistical Office (CSO), 1997).

There is a strong interdependence between agriculture and manufacturing sectors. A recently published input-output table (Thomas et al., 1999) shows that the manufacturing sector absorbed an average of 48 per cent of the total supply of the agricultural sector as intermediate inputs, while agriculture absorbed 20 per cent of manufacturing supply. Whenever agricultural growth is negative, usually because of drought, manufacturing sector growth is also negative or weak. This interdependence means that Zimbabwe is an agricultural-dependent economy, even though agriculture is not itself the dominant sector in terms of contribution to GDP.

Zimbabwe's economy, like most other developing countries, is highly dependent on imports. Imports averaged 23 per cent of GDP through the 1980s, about 84 per cent of which are capital goods and critical inputs (Davies, 1991). Ability to expand export earnings is a major determinant of growth performance.

The major exports are primary commodities: agricultural – tobacco, sugar, maize, cotton and beef – and mineral. The fact that declining real prices are forecast for most traditional primary exports for the next decade (World Bank, 1995), generally builds a bleak picture for traditional exports.

Before independence, Zimbabwe pursued a *de facto* import substitution industrialization strategy. A wide range of international trade and financial sanctions were imposed on the settler regime after 1965. Coupled with domestic direct controls and regulations implemented for macroeconomic management purposes, these gave rise to a highly protected economy. Foreign exchange controls and import quotas and licensing were used for balance of payments purposes, while investment, price and agricultural marketing controls were used to ensure macroeconomic stability domestically. A wide range of parastatals grew up, dominating key sectors of the economy. Although the foreign sector became relatively more open with the lifting of sanctions after independence, Zimbabwe continued to use the inherited regime of controls to manage the economy, since this *dirigisme* accorded with the socialist programme of the new government. In addition to the UDI controls, labour market controls were introduced in the form of national minimum wages coupled with restrictions on firing workers.

Table 10.1 provides period averages for various performance indicators since independence. During the 1980s there was relative macroeconomic stability and positive per capita growth. Despite high budget deficits, the current account balance was reasonable. This was managed through the import controls and other regulatory mechanisms, which forced the private sector to maintain a high excess of savings over investment, thereby accommodating the public sector deficit. Investment was constrained, with gross fixed capital formation growing at less than 1 per cent annually and falling to 15.9 per cent of GDP in the period 1985–9.

Table 10.1   Economic performance indicators, Zimbabwe, 1980–97

	Real Growth	Investment Share	Growth	Inflation	Budget deficit	Government debt Total	Domestic	Balance on Current account	Capital account
	% pa	% GDP	% pa	% pa	% GDP	% GDP	% Total	% GDP	% GDP
1980–4	3.9	20.1	5.9	14.3	–8.3	43.9	69.2	–2.3	1.3
1985–9	4.0	14.5	0.8	10.8	–9.6	59.1	61.4	0.2	0.9
1990–4	2.3	21.0	11.7	26.2	–8.9	62.3	44.8	–10.3	11.3
1995–7	2.6	19.0	–6.7	21.0	–10.2	75.5	54.2	–4.1	n.a.

As early as 1982, government recognized the importance of export growth. An export revolving fund targeted at exports in the manufacturing sector was established in that year, via a World Bank loan. However, it was only after the middle of the decade that concern began to mount about the long-run growth implications of low investment. Trade policy started to shift. Initially, government pursued a two-pronged policy, continuing direct import rationing but coupling it with a range of export promoting measures. These measures included various export subsidies and the establishment of the Zimbabwe Export Promotion Council. The most significant influence was an export incentive scheme which allowed exporters to retain a portion of their foreign exchange earnings to buy intermediate imports. Many firms producing for the domestic market used this as an opportunity to ease the tight rationing they faced. It was rational, given the overvaluation of the exchange rate, to export at a loss, import the inputs to which this entitled one and sell the resultant output on the more profitable domestic market. The export diversification it succeeded in creating was therefore fragile, and in large measure disappeared once access to foreign exchange was liberalized.

The Economic Structural Adjustment Programme and the 1990s: the overall package

The primary motive behind the adoption of the Economic Structural Adjustment Programme (ESAP) in 1990 was to encourage growth by encouraging new investment, thereby overcoming the problems of unemployment and manufacturing stagnation. Implementation of the ESAP programme did not begin seriously until 1991. The programme encompassed domestic wage, price and financial deregulation; trade liberalization; public sector reform; macroeconomic stabilization; and a 'social dimensions' programme to provide a safety net for vulnerable groups.

As Table 10.1 shows, macroeconomic performance since then has been mixed. Although investment growth picked up significantly and the investment share returned to its early 1980s level, real growth fell, while inflation, government debt and the current account deficit all rose. The remaining macroeconomic weakness is generally attributed to a combination of the effects of severe droughts of 1991/2 and 1994/5, and the failure to reduce the budget deficit.

In general, droughts not only affect agricultural production but also result in water shortages and unreliable electricity supply in the urban areas, both of which have a direct negative impact on the manufacturing sector. They also depress domestic demand for both agricultural and non-agricultural goods.

The budget deficit has been a persistent worry since the reforms were introduced. It has been fuelled by drought relief payments; weak revenue collection as qualified but poorly paid civil servants opted for retrenchment packages; slow progress in public enterprise reform; high interest payments on past borrowing; failure to reduce the number of civil servants; and, in more recent years, large off-budget expenditures related to social discontent.

Inflation was fuelled by the domestic borrowing related to the fiscal deficit, the impact of drought on food and agricultural raw material prices and the sharp devaluation of the currency accompanying trade liberalization. The decontrol of prices and removal of food subsidies created a climate in which previously suppressed inflation was able to manifest itself. To counter inflation, the Reserve Bank attempted to maintain a tight monetary policy, which, coupled with the deficit-related domestic borrowing, resulted in high nominal interest rates.

Central government debt, which grew by about 10 percentage points in the 1980s, grew more rapidly after liberalization. The share of foreign debt in this total rose over the whole period, but this was mainly due to the devaluation of the Zimbabwe dollar, not to extra borrowing. The foreign debt-service ratio rose shortly after ESAP, peaking at 30 per cent in 1992, but has since fallen to 16 per cent in 1997. Zimbabwe's principal debt problems are domestic, not foreign.

Trade, investment and exchange rate policies in the 1990s

Trade liberalization and exchange rate policies

According to a study carried out in 1983, Zimbabwe had high effective rates of protection, provided mainly by the import quota system. World Bank studies in 1988 revealed that Zimbabwe industry was much more efficient than expected on the basis of protection afforded under the foreign currency allocation system. The argument for trade liberalization in the case of Zimbabwe became that industry could prosper from more export-orientation rather than to induce competition and efficiency first.

The trade policy reforms began in 1990 by placing some raw materials on Open General Import Licence (OGIL), to be followed in subsequent years by intermediate inputs and then other imports. Foreign exchange allocation was phased out, leaving tariffs as the only direct protection to local industry. The currency was allowed to depreciate in real terms in order to encourage a shift of resources to the export sector and sustain export competitiveness. In addition, a number of new export incentives were introduced, among them, an export retention scheme (ERS), allowing productive sectors to retain a proportion of their export earnings for the purchase of machinery and raw materials needed to boost output. The proportion of these retentions was increased over time until 1994 when all exporters were allowed 100 per cent retention.

In October 1991, duties became payable on imported intermediates but these could be claimed back under a duty-drawback mechanism for export production only. In 1992 an Inward Processing Scheme was introduced, allowing large exporters to establish bonded warehouses and import raw materials and other inputs duty-free provided these were used for export production. This was intended to avoid long delays associated with the duty-drawback scheme.

With the removal of quotas, tariffs became the main instrument for protecting local industries. The major tariff rates introduced in 1992 were 10 per cent for raw materials, 20 per cent for intermediate goods and 30 per cent for finished products. This afforded relatively low protection by developing country standards, but the addition of a 20 per cent surtax on all imports raised levels of protection. This resulted in effective protection levels for the manufacturing sector ranging from 20 per cent to 260 per cent, with an average rate of 70 per cent.

Subsequent review of tariff policy culminated, in February 1997, in a simplified tariff schedule with capital goods attracting zero nominal tariffs, raw materials 5 per cent, spares and partly processed inputs 15 per cent, intermediate goods and consumables 20 per cent to 30 per cent and finished goods 40 per cent to 85 per cent. The intention was to lower the cost of production and make Zimbabwe's manufacturing sector products more competitive, while still providing some level of protection on the local market. The new structure reduced effective protection levels generally, but raised them for firms producing fabricated metal products, cars assembled from kits, plastics and clothing.

Although most imported goods are imported under an open general import licence, the Department of Customs still ranks high as a hindrance to exporters because of the delays involved in processing necessary imports and duty rebates. The time taken for import clearance is unduly long compared to other countries. Lall and Wignaraja found that in 1997 customs clearance at the border took 14–28 days in Zimbabwe compared to 3–4 days in Mauritius, Sri Lanka and Indonesia (Lall et al., 1997). At the airport it took 7–14 days in Zimbabwe, compared to 2 days in the other countries. Refund of duties on imported inputs takes 12–36 weeks in Zimbabwe compared to 4–24 weeks in Mauritius, 2 weeks in Sri Lanka and 2–6 weeks in Indonesia.

Table 10.2 shows Zimbabwe's merchandise export and import performance in the various periods. Both exports and imports have risen sharply as a percentage of GDP since ESAP. The current account deficit, after being reduced in the late 1980s by tight import controls, which had serious effects on the economic performance of the economy, creating a trade-off between capacity utilization and growth (Davies and Rattsø, 1993), returned to the levels of the early 1980s. By the end of the ESAP period, exports were around 30 per cent of national income and imports 37 per cent.

Table 10.2   Exports, imports and the current account, Zimbabwe, 1980–97

Period	Exports		Imports		CAB
	% GDP	*Growth rate*	*% GDP*	*Growth rate*	*% GDP*
1980–4	17.5	−5.4	16.7	−7.3	−5.5
1985–9	20.9	6.0	16.7	10.8	0.1
1990–4	23.4	5.1	29.0	6.5	−4.2
1995–7	30.9	6.8	37.3	9.1	−4.4

Notes: The growth rate is the average annual growth rate of the US$ values. CAB: current account balance.

In the immediate post-independence period, the currency appreciated in real terms, despite depreciating nominally by over 4 per cent per year (Table 10.3). However, after 1985, real depreciation averaged over 5 per cent annually. Until January 1994, the Reserve Bank of Zimbabwe continued to manage the exchange rate by operating a two-tier system, with a Reserve Bank rate and a market-determined rate. Since July 1994, a unified exchange rate determined by an inter-bank market has operated. The underlying exchange rate policy was to devalue the currency at the start of ESAP to encourage exports and then keep the real exchange rate constant. Inflation, high interest rates and capital inflow pressures have kept the real value of the currency varying with a depreciating trend since mid-1994. The real depreciation after the reforms was no faster than in the late 1980s, although the nominal depreciation was more than twice as fast.

Table 10.3   Exchange and interest rates, Zimbabwe, period averages, 1980–97

		Exchange rate						Interest rates			
		Nominal[a]	Real[a]		Depreciation			Commercial Bank overdraft rate			
	US$	MER[b]	RER[c]	US$	MER[b]	RER[c]		Nominal		Real	
		(1990 = 100)		%pa	%pa	%pa		avg	max	avg	max
1980–4	0.98	54.4	72.5	24.5	4.1	–0.9		11.3	11.9	–8.7	0.8
1985–9	1.84	75.5	82.5	8.9	7.9	5.2		13.0	13.0	–4.3	5.6
1990–4	5.68	153.7	113.8	32.7	18.9	5.7		25.9	33.0	–3.0	7.8
1995–7	12.92	242.5	111.5	33.0	16.4	5.2		34.1	39.0	13.1	21.7

Notes:
[a] Increase denotes devaluation.
[b] MER = multilateral exchange rate.
[c] RER = real multilateral (effective) exchange rate.

Despite this real depreciation, imports have grown much faster than exports since 1990. There was a sharp jump in imports immediately after liberalization began, partly fuelled by the release of pent-up demand from the rationing period and by doubts as to the credibility and sustainability of liberalization. Importers of the first goods placed on OGIL took the opportunity to stockpile, both as a hedge against the potential reversal of the policy and as a speculative move against the likely devaluation of the Zimbabwe dollar.

Trade liberalization resulted in considerable improvement in product quality and production efficiency in the manufacturing sector, with some firms complaining about the strong competition. The liberalization appears to have resulted in deindustrialization, with the manufacturing sector's contribution to GDP falling from a high of 29 per cent in 1992 (reflecting mainly the decline in agricultural output due to the drought) to 18 per cent in 1997. On the other hand, the response of exports to export incentives is constrained by short-run supply and production constraints.

Investment policies

Expansion of investment was a central intended consequence of the reform programme. While it was hoped that macroeconomic stability would stimulate domestic investment, most explicit investment policies were directed towards foreign direct investment (FDI). This was seen as the principal source of technology transfer, export growth, job creation in the manufacturing sector and as an important contributor to the development of small and medium-sized enterprises (SMEs).

The capital account was liberalized early in the reform process. A wide range of incentives to attract foreign capital into mining and manufacturing was introduced, including easier access to foreign exchange for essential imports by export-oriented ventures and relaxed local borrowing rules for foreigners. Dividend remittance rules were relaxed so that by 1995 companies could remit 100 per cent of their after-tax profits.

Other measures included institutional changes, epitomized by the establishment of the Zimbabwe Investment Centre and the Export Processing Zones Authority (EPZA).

The Zimbabwe Investment Centre (ZIC) was established in November 1993 as an autonomous organization, to promote, facilitate, and coordinate domestic and foreign private investment. It was intended to bring together in a 'one-stop shop' all aspects of government's controls over FDI, thereby reducing the bureaucracy involved. It was envisaged that the importance of this function would diminish over time until, in a fully liberalized economy, it would retain only promotional functions. In practice, ZIC was not as successful in reducing bureaucracy as was hoped, since it proved impossible to bring together *all* regulations affecting FDI, particularly those that did so only indirectly (e.g. zoning laws). Foreign investors are still required to seek approval and, if they are in 'non-specialized' services, will be required to find a local partner.

Although the EPZA of Zimbabwe was formally established in 1995, it has been in operation only since the beginning of 1997, so its impact on investment and trade flows has been minimal.

To be allowed to operate in an EPZ, a project should be new, export 80 per cent of sales, create employment, develop human resources and result in transfer of technology and technical know-how. The company should also be operating in manufacturing, processing, assembly and services (EPZA, 1998).

The package offered specifically to firms investing in an EPZ include:

- Duty-free importation of capital equipment, raw materials and intermediate goods associated with EPZ operations;
- A corporate tax holiday of five years, a low flat tax rate of 15 per cent thereafter (compared to the current 37.5 per cent corporate tax rate outside EPZs), and exemption from capital gains tax.

By 1998, although seven EPZ industrial parks had been approved by the EPZA, only four were being developed: two near the Harare International Airport and two along the Harare–Beira railway. The absence of an incentive package for the developers was highlighted as a major constraint by the EPZA. Industrial parks provide zone investors with ready infrastructure and other facilities required for projects to take off. EPZ status companies wishing to locate outside the EPZ industrial parks for special reasons are still given consideration (ibid.).

By June 1998, the EPZA had received more than 150 applications to operate in an EPZ since the start of EPZ operations in early 1997. Of these, 74 had been approved, with a total value of Z\$5 billion; 38 projects were operational by June 1998 and had generated over Z\$500 million in export earnings and more than 6000 new jobs (ibid.).

Even though the EPZ companies produce mainly for export, they are allowed to sell a maximum of 20 per cent of their output on the domestic market. In the first one and a half years of operation, the EPZ companies 'imported' Z\$90 million worth of raw materials from the domestic market and generated Z\$19 million in sales to the same market (ibid.).

The EPZA identified dried, canned and frozen vegetables and fruits, fruit juices, grey and black granite and marble, and furniture in the form of knocked-down units as non-traditional exports from EPZs, even though these may not be noticed yet in national statistics (ibid.).

Although the EPZA was pleased with the take-off of the EPZ project and its potential in Zimbabwe, it has argued that much more investment could have been attracted had the overall economic environment been more supportive. The current economic environment characterized by high nominal interest rates was stifling investment as investors preferred to put their money in money markets where the returns were higher.

In addition, the inability of government systems and institutions to respond quickly and adapt to the changing economic environment was a major impediment. The failure by government to amend the Customs Act to allow the duty-free importation of capital goods was cited as a particular cause for concern. One of the major incentives for EPZ companies, as noted earlier on, was that they could bring in equipment free of duty and although this was clearly stated in the EPZ Act other ancillary legislation had not been amended in line with the new regulations. The EPZA and EPZ companies, which so far import 100 per cent of their capital equipment (ibid.), are caught between the 'promised' EPZ environment and reality which is very discouraging and retrogressive.

Table 10.1 has already shown how gross fixed capital formation grew relative to GDP after the reforms. Most of this growth was concentrated in the early years of the reforms. In constant 1990 prices, gross fixed capital formation (GFCF) fell by 1.5 per cent in 1989. It then grew by 34.7 per cent in 1990 and 23.0 per cent in 1991. This burst represented a combination of catch up and pre-emptive effects. After years of import constraints there was a high pent-up demand for new investment; there was also incredulity about the sustainability of the reforms and thus an urgency to get what was necessary done as quickly as possible.

GFCF fell in 1992 (possibly as an adjustment to overshooting in the previous years) and then grew slowly – less than 4 per cent on average – until 1995. In 1996 and 1997, new determinants were coming into play: increased macroeconomic uncertainty, high nominal interest rates, an unstable and depreciating domestic currency. All of these led to investment falling by 8.8 per cent and then 13.5 per cent in real terms.

The data on private foreign capital flows are weak. Table 10.4 shows data from two sources. Despite disagreement between them, they both suggest that there was a collapse of inflows in the late 1980s which was reversed in the 1990s.

Table 10.4 Net private capital inflows as % of gross fixed capital formation, Zimbabwe, 1980–96

	1980–4	*1985–9*	*1990–4*	*1995–6*
Private Long Term Capital	0.6	0.1	3.2	9.3
Net Private Long Term Capital including Statistical Discrepancy	9.9	–0.1	9.1	27.4[a]

Note: [a] 1995 only.

Sources: Row 1: Reserve Bank of Zimbabwe, *Quarterly Statistical and Economic Review*, various dates. Row 2: CSO, *Quarterly Digest of Statistics*, various dates.

The figures in Table 10.4 show *net* flows relative to GFCF. They therefore underestimate the share of FDI in overall investment. The balance of payments figures suggest that this grew from around 5 per cent in the late 1980s to 35 per cent by 1995. These figures also include the 'statistical discrepancy' so they are very crude. The inflows in the 1990s were higher than those in some other reforming African countries, such as Kenya, Mauritius and South Africa, but are considerably lower than in South and East Asian and some Latin American countries.

In this chapter, we are not concerned with overall investment as much as with investment in non-traditional as opposed to traditional exports. Although we have little data on this, some idea can be gleaned from the operation of ZIC and EPZs.

The bulk of FDI approvals by ZIC have been in traditional activities like mining, agriculture and tourism rather than in high-skill manufacturing. In 1994 manufacturing FDI approvals were 18.7 per cent of all approvals, in 1995, 41.8 per cent and in 1996, 7.5 per cent. Of the cumulative manufacturing sector approvals during 1994–6, 37.5 per cent (US$357.2 million) was in food, drinks and tobacco, 23.1 per cent in chemicals and petroleum, 12.5 per cent in metals and metal products and 9.4 per cent in non-metallic minerals. High-skill activities accounted for 38.5 per cent, while low-skill activities accounted for 61.5 per cent (Zimbabwe Investment Centre, personal contact, 1997).

Even though the ZIC promotes investment in general, it has noticed new investments geared towards non-traditional exports, although the outcomes may still be too small to feature in national data trends. Such projects include horticulture, ostrich farming, poultry products and new minerals (particularly platinum). Investment in tourism has increased with the setting-up of the Zimbabwe Tourism Authority.

Generally, FDI in export-oriented manufacturing is low. For example, by February 1997, only thirteen of the thirty-two projects approved to operate in EPZs were foreign (EPZA, personal communication, 1997). The bulk of FDI approvals in the manufacturing sector during ESAP came from South Africa, Germany, UK and China. The FDI contribution by Asian countries to Zimbabwe is still very low.

Comparison between FDI patterns in Zimbabwe and those in Malaysia and Thailand shows that the major investors are generally the same but FDI in the Asian countries has been concentrated in export-oriented manufacturing. In Malaysia FDI is clustered in transport equipment, basic metal products, non-metallic and electronics while in Thailand it is more diversified. Nearly 75 per cent of industrial FDI in Sri Lanka, another latecomer like Zimbabwe, is in textiles and garments, a sector which has faced serious investment shortage in Zimbabwe.

Although the evidence is scant, there does not seem to have been a particular investment boom in non-traditional exports.

Export support institutions and other infrastructure

Apart from reforms to the general trading environment, a number of institutional reforms were made, to try to boost exports.

Before the reforms, the main institutional support for exporters was supplied through the Ministry of Industry and Commerce and the commercial attachés in Zimbabwe's foreign missions abroad. In 1988 the Zimbabwe Export Promotion Programme was launched with EU support. It was aimed at creating an export promotion organization outside government but with sufficient influence within government to secure changes in economic policy needed to ensure an export-oriented environment. This resulted in ZimTrade, which became operational in January 1992. Its main function is to provide information and to assist firms in finding new markets, specifically for new exports.

Institutional support for R&D in Zimbabwe is still in its infancy. Current linkages between industry and technology institutions are weak or non-existent and firms themselves do little in terms of R&D. Only 23 manufacturing firms in Zimbabwe have been certified with the ISO 9000 quality management standards.

The general assessment is that Zimbabwe comes second only to South Africa in terms of its physical infrastructure for exporting firms in Sub-Saharan Africa. However, the residual bureaucratic mind-set from the pre-reform days reduces its effective use. For example, there are long delays – which many Zimbabwean companies still regard as part of the natural order – in installing water, electricity and telecommunication utilities for new companies and in meeting official bureaucratic requirements. Some of these problems may be overcome in EPZs, where office park development is being undertaken on a private basis.

The supply and cost of human resources are important factors determining export performance. Investment in this area was one of Zimbabwe's top priorities at independence in 1980. Its achievements in primary health and education, particularly during the first decade of independence, are among some the country's notable independence gains. Primary, secondary and tertiary enrolments in the mid-1990s as percentage of age group (115 per cent, 44 per cent and 6 per cent, respectively) compare favourably to the rates for Sub-Saharan Africa (SSA) (72 per cent, 24 per cent and 2 per cent respectively). The only SSA country ahead of Zimbabwe is South Africa. However, Zimbabwe lags behind East Asian countries (Singapore, Korea and Taiwan) in post-primary level enrolment (UNESCO, 1996).

Despite this success in general education, the picture regarding technical skills is more bleak. In 1990, before the launch of ESAP, it was estimated that Zimbabwe's manufacturing sector faced a shortage of up to 60 000 skilled artisans and the gap in engineering skills was estimated at 37 per cent of needs (Biggs et al., 1995). While the inflow of expatriate skills confirms the shortage of these skills in the country, it is ironic that the few engineering graduates from the University of Zimbabwe are failing to secure employment (Ministry of Labour and Social Welfare Services, personal contact 1998). The technical skills gap may increase with increased liberalization and competition.

Zimbabwe could exploit its advantage of having a broadly literate and trainable workforce compared to other countries in the region. However, vocational education is generally held in low esteem in Zimbabwe, attracting low-quality applicants going into mostly agriculture, commerce, accounting, fashion and areas not directly relevant to industrial skill needs. By 1994 Zimbabwe had 8 technical colleges, 14 youth training centres, more than 100 private colleges, 5 correspondence schools, and many training opportunities offered by NGOs and the donor community. Most of these are understaffed and their technology lags behind the needs of industry (Knight, 1996).

On-the-job training provided by firms in Zimbabwe is generally aimed simply at giving new employees basic operational skills. There is little effort to provide continuous retraining to update skills and improve the workers' ability to cope with new technologies and changing organizational techniques. The most important government initiative in the field of worker training in Zimbabwe is the Zimbabwe Manpower Development Fund which is based on a 1 per cent levy on the payroll of formal sector firms. Firms are compensated depending on how many workers they train. Large firms benefit most from the fund while the informal sector is excluded from it.

Average real wages in the manufacturing sector declined from US$3241 per annum in 1985 to US$2239 per annum in 1994. By 1994 Zimbabwe's real wages were only 15 per cent of real wages in the mature Asian tigers and approximately 50 per cent of real wages in Malaysia and Thailand (UNIDO, 1996). Other studies have suggested that, while unskilled and skilled labour in Zimbabwe is relatively cheap, managerial and supervisory levels are relatively expensive (World Bank, 1994; Knight, 1996). This could be a reflection of the relative scarcity of skills and qualifications at the higher levels as well as the entrenched racial inequalities in firm ownership and management.

One way of considering labour costs is to look at hourly costs in a common industry. A 1995 study made such comparisons for the Garment and Apparel industry. With hourly labour costs less than US$0.45, Zimbabwe was classified as a low labour cost location, along with China (US$0.25), Vietnam, Pakistan, India (all US$0.29) and Indonesia (US$0.33). The remaining countries (both Asian and developed countries) who are successful exporters of garments, maintain their competitiveness through a combination of high productivity, high product quality, greater supply reliability, design capabilities, etc. It is clear that if Zimbabwe is to continue to export competitively it will have to improve in these areas. This will in turn require greater training and skills development (Lall et al., 1997).

Assessment

The foregoing suggests that Zimbabwe has made some progress in creating an 'export friendly' environment. The reforms in the 1990s have covered both the incentive structure – particularly through exchange rate depreciation and removal of import quotas – and institutional reforms. Most of the latter have, however, only occurred late in the reform process and have as yet had little effect on exports.

Although it is likely that the reforms outlined above will have had a positive effect on the level of exports, it is not clear whether they would work in favour of or against non-traditional exports *vis-à-vis* exports in general. Few are targeted specifically at non-traditional exports. Those that are – the EPZs, the tax cuts – will not show up yet in the data available. It is possible that some general developments in the economy may have a differential impact on new exports. For example, high interest rates probably inhibit new firms more than old. Insofar as new exports arise from new firms, they would be inhibited.

The characteristics of exporting firms

A survey carried out in 1996 allows us to identify some features of exporting firms which distinguish them from non-exporting firms (SAPES, 1996). The survey covered a total of 51 manufacturing sector firms just after the completion of Phase I of the economic reform programme – 36 were from the textiles and garments subsector, while 15 were from the food processing subsector. Of the firms, 3 with less than 10 employees, were classified as 'small'; 20 were 'medium' (11–100 employees); 13 firms were 'large' (101–250 employees); and 15 firms, with more than 250 employees, were classified as 'very large'.

The researchers classified firms exporting more than half of their total output as 'large exporters', those exporting less than half as 'small/medium exporters' and those with no exports as 'non-exporters'. Table 10.5 cross-tabulates firms by size and export category.

Table 10.5   Firm size and export performance, Zimbabwe

| | Firm size | | | | | | | | | |
| Firm class | Small | | Medium | | Large | | Very large | | Total | |
	N	%	N	%	N	%	N	%	N	%
Large Exporters	0	0.0	0	0.0	0	0.0	3	20.0	3	6.0
Small–Medium Exporters	0	0.0	4	20.0	7	53.8	8	53.3	19	37.0
Non-Exporters	3	100.0	16	80.0	6	46.2	4	26.7	29	57.0

Source: SAPES Manufacturing Sector Survey, 1996, in Chipika et al. 1998.

Only very large firms were large exporters while small/medium exporters came from all sizes except small; large/very large firms dominated this exporting category. The small and medium-sized firms largely supplied the domestic market even though there is some move by medium firms (20 per cent of them) who supplied the export market.

The survey allows some simple comparisons between the behaviour of exporting and non-exporting firms. To compare management practices, firms were asked whether they keep accounts. As might be expected, all the exporting firms kept accounts, while as many as 22 per cent (28 firms) of the non-exporters did not. The survey interpreted this as demonstrating that exporting firms follow better management practices. Clearly it reflects the importance of small (informal) enterprises amongst the non-exporters. It could as easily be interpreted as a sign that non-formal firms do not engage in exporting.

Of exporting firms, 95 per cent had trained at least some of their work force since 1991, while only 33 per cent of non-exporters had. Although this difference is significant, the direction of causality is not clear. Do firms that train workers succeed better in exporting? Do exporting firms have greater incentive or capacity to train?

Table 10.6 shows that a significantly larger proportion of exporters relied on bank loans for financing investment projects, while the domestic-oriented firms made greater use of retained earnings. This difference, which is statistically significant, could reflect a number of alternative factors. The larger size of exporting firms could mean that they have no choice other than to borrow for expansion. Alternatively, it could reflect the preferential access that exporters have, under the foreign currency regulations, to offshore borrowing. Finally it could simply reflect the credit rationing that the banking sector in Zimbabwe continues to operate. Small firms often have difficulty in raising bank loans – often rationalized by the banks as being because they have no collateral. Table 10.6 could simply reflect the higher proportion of these firms in the non-exporting category.

Table 10.6   Sources of finance, exporting and non-exporting firms, Zimbabwe

| | Exporters | | Non-exporters | |
	N	*%*	*N*	*%*
Bank Loan	9	45	6	26
Retained Earnings	6	30	15	65
Other	5	25	2	9
Total	20	100	23	100

Source: As Table 10.5.

Both categories of firms showed similar patterns of responses when asked whether capacity utilization and profits had changed since ESAP. Interestingly, more of the domestic-oriented firms reported increases in both: for example, 54 per cent of non-exporters as opposed to 40 per cent of exporters said profits had risen. However, these differences were not statistically significant.

Exporting firms encountered problems first and foremost with the Customs Department whose reform, as already noted, lagged behind during economic reform. Non-exporting firms faced more problems with the Tax Department than with the Customs Department. The most pressing problems faced by exporters are high interest rates, cost of raw materials and insufficient demand while those faced by non-exporters are taxes, high interest rates, insufficient demand and cost of raw materials.

Problems with timely delivery of goods, product quality, cost of finance, raw materials and utilities were cited by all firms as important obstacles to expansion. Most firms faced cash flow problems during ESAP. Electricity and water supplies were too expensive and supply unstable while telephone services were unstable for most firms. A number of firms found ZimTrade and price decontrols as helpful moves from government.

While the results of this previous study do give us some insights into problems faced by exporters and into differences between exporting and domestic firms, it does not allow us to say anything about the basis for growth of non-traditional exports.

Zimbabwe's commodity exports, 1981–97[1]

A major objective of the reform programme was to reduce the foreign exchange bottleneck by promoting exports. While this objective was targeted at exports in general, liberalization should change both the level and the composition of exports. Since an overvalued currency keeps the export earnings below what they might otherwise be, liberalization, with appropriate exchange rate adjustment, should raise them. Our discussion of Table 10.2 has indicated that the export response was slow, but there is some indication that export growth was faster after the reforms than before, particularly if the latest years are taken into account. While total exports in US$ value rose by 6 per cent annually on average over the period immediately preceding ESAP, they rose by only 5 per cent annually over 1990–4. Since 1995, the rate has picked up to nearly 7 per cent per annum.

The impact of the reforms on export composition is less certain, *a priori*. 'Distortions' inherent in the regulated regime will have affected resource allocation, but the exact way in which export composition responds to their removal will depend on the nature of those distortions, the structure of the economy, and the underlying process of trade determination.

Below, we use a statistical-descriptive approach to measure whether Zimbabwean exports have diversified since trade liberalization in the 1990s or not. It is obvious that any pattern of diversification discerned by this approach will be dependent on the system and extent of disaggregation. Although we retain the generic terms 'traditional' and 'non-traditional', we argue later that this is not a particularly clear or useful dichotomy.

We adopt the approach to new exports used by the World Bank. This defines any commodity which contributes more than some specified share of export earnings in a selected base period as 'traditional'. 'New' or 'non-traditional' exports are then those products which do not satisfy this criterion. The main merit of this approach is simplicity: the data are available and can be manipulated to give appropriate measures. It enables the immediate questions of changes in the concentration or diversification of exports to be addressed, allowing us to consider the problem of export vulnerability: a wider portfolio of exports presumably reduces the risks arising from international price and demand fluctuations. This was a major concern in the old trade and development literature and is still of concern.

There are two main problems with this approach that need to be addressed. First, the threshold share is arbitrary. Any good which has been exported consistently for many years, either at a level below the threshold or which for some reason has dipped below the threshold in the base period, shows up as a new export. Not only does this offend common sense but it also may mislead any analysis of the factors underlying the growth (or lack of growth) of new exports. It is plausible that factors which cause existing exports to grow are different from those that cause new exports to come into existence. We therefore distinguish between 'major' and 'minor' traditional exports, the latter being goods which have been exported consistently over the years, but in insignificant quantities.

We also categorize 'traditional' and 'non-traditional' according to whether exports are 'primary' or 'non-primary'. This is the view that is taken in Zimbabwean policy debates. We compare the results of the two approaches.

A second problem with the World Bank approach is that results will be affected by the level of aggregation. Obviously the more aggregated the figures the lower the potential number of new exports. At one extreme, when we aggregate all exports into one group, there can be no 'new' exports, only export growth. It would seem therefore that we need to disaggregate as much as possible to capture changes. Unfortunately, the more disaggregated the data, the more likely are statistical errors in the primary data. It may be clear that a particular product falls in the category 'food', or even 'milk', but it could be less clear whether it should be in 'Milk and cream of $\leq 1\%$ fat, not concentrated or sweetened' or 'Cream, other than sterilised cream of a f.c.b.w. $\leq 1\%$'. Since this classification is undertaken mainly by the exporter and entails a cost, it is likely to be done carelessly and inconsistently between one year and the next. For imports, where duty has to be paid, there may be an incentive to get it right, but in the absence of export bonuses for specific goods there is little incentive on the export side. Even if care is taken, it may not always be clear exactly how a product should be classified.

We undertake our analysis at the three-digit SITC level.

We concentrate on merchandise exports. However, there has been a noticeable rise in the importance of tourism as a foreign exchange earner in the 1990s. Between 1980 and 1984, earnings from tourism averaged 0.9 per cent of earnings from merchandise exports. It fell to 0.5 per cent between 1985 and 1989, but since 1990 has averaged 2.3 per cent. This increase is mainly due to the political change in South Africa, which has not only made Southern Africa a more attractive destination for international tourists, but has also led to a rise in the number of South African tourists visiting Zimbabwe. The decline of the Zimbabwe dollar with respect to the rand has reinforced this.

'Non-traditional exports': alternative definitions

The World Bank defines non-traditional exports as all three-digit export items other than the top ten in the base year. We refer to this measure as NTX2.

Since sanctions prior to 1980 mean that the data for 1980 are not representative, we have taken the average of 1981 and 1983 as our base period. We averaged the US$ value of exports in these two years, and defined the ten most important as 'traditional exports'.[2] They are listed in Table 10.7. Collectively they accounted for some 77 per cent of export earnings in 1981/3. We see that all the products are primary products, dominated by tobacco. They are not as diversified as they appear, since iron and steel products provide three of the ten SITC categories.[3] Table 10.8 provides some analysis of the composition of exports according to this definition. The share of non-traditional exports according to this definition, has risen substantially, from 23.6 per cent in 1981 to 37.9 per cent in 1996.

Table 10.7 Top 10 exports from Zimbabwe, 1981–3

SITC	Description	Share in 1981–3
121	Tobacco, unmanufactured, tobacco refuse	24.7
671	Pig iron, spiegeleisen, sponge iron, iron or steel granules and powders, etc.	10.6
27	Other crude minerals	8.6
263	Cotton	7.9
061	Sugar, molasses and honey	7.5
683	Nickel	6.0
044	Maize (not including sweet corn), unmilled	4.1
672	Ingots and other primary forms of iron or steel, semi–finished	3.5
682	Copper	2.2
676	Iron and steel bars, rods, angles, shapes and sections (including sheet plung)	2.1

Source: Estimated from data provided by the CSO.

Table 10.8 Traditional and non-traditional exports, World Bank definition (NTX2), Zimbabwe, 1981–97

	1981	1983	1985	1988	1990	1991	1992	1993	1994	1995	1996	1997
Shares in total exports (%)												
Traditional	76.4	78.0	70.2	72.6	68.6	65.4	64.0	52.8	63.1	56.5	62.1	56.5
Non-traditional	23.6	22.0	29.8	27.4	32.4	34.6	36.0	47.2	36.9	43.5	37.9	43.5
Annual growth rates of US$ values												
Traditional		–9.3	–6.7	13.9	–0.9	–21.1	–1.0	–13.8	58.0	–17.7	22.3	–11.1
Non-traditional		–13.7	13.6	9.9	8.8	–6.3	4.9	32.4	15.8	9.5	–0.9	12.3
Total Exports		–10.3	–1.5	12.8	1.9	–16.2	1.1	5.4	40.3	–6.8	12.8	–1.6

However, by this definition, there were a total of 137 non-traditional exports in 1981/83, 59 of which accounted for more than 0.1 per cent of total exports each. As a group, they earned 21.9 per cent of export earnings in 1981. It is not clear why we should regard these as 'non-traditional'; it would be more appropriate to call them 'minor traditional exports'.[4] The residual would be 'true' non-traditional exports (NTX4). Table 10.9 shows the results of this three-way categorization. Non-traditional exports, according to this last definition (NTX4), comprise a much smaller share of exports, but there is a sharper growth in their share.

Table 10.9 Traditional and non-traditional exports, significance definition (NTX4), Zimbabwe, 1981–97

	1981	1983	1985	1988	1990	1991	1992	1993	1994	1995	1996	1997
Shares in total exports (%)												
Traditional	76.4	78.0	70.2	72.6	68.6	65.4	64.0	52.8	63.1	56.5	62.1	56.5
Minor Traditional	21.7	20.4	23.7	22.1	24.8	22.3	26.9	32.4	25.8	30.4	24.5	27.9
NTX4	1.9	1.6	6.1	5.3	6.5	12.4	9.1	14.8	11.1	13.0	13.4	15.6
Annual growth rates of US$ values												
Traditional		–9.3	–6.7	13.9	–0.9	–21.1	–1.0	–13.8	58.0	–17.7	22.3	–11.1
Minor Traditional		–13.4	5.9	10.5	7.8	–27.2	19.8	24.1	17.4	9.8	–8.9	11.5
NTX4		–17.2	65.1	7.7	12.8	47.9	–29.3	53.4	12.0	8.9	15.5	13.6
All Exports		–10.3	–1.5	12.8	1.9	–16.2	1.1	5.4	40.3	–6.8	12.8	–1.6

Since there is no analytic basis for our criteria, it is somewhat arbitrary which definition we use. The choice of 0.1 per cent as a cutoff is as arbitrary as the choice of the top ten. Observe, however, that the top ten criterion can itself be recast as a significance criterion, the share of the tenth ranked product giving the cutoff level (2.1 per cent for Zimbabwe in 1981/3).

As is clear from Table 10.7, using NTX3, the definition of non-traditional exports employed for comparative purposes in the other African studies in this volume, reduces the number of traditional exports only by two. However, it changes the shares and particularly the growth rates more significantly than this because of the inclusion of tourist and travel receipts (see Table 10.10). Growth of these accelerated rapidly after 1991. This growth was probably affected more by the political changes in South Africa than by domestic reforms in Zimbabwe.

Although the different criteria change the share of non-traditional exports significantly, they do not change the story of the evolution of these shares. For instance, the correlation coefficient between the shares of NTX2 and NTX4 is 0.95. However, if one compares the growth rates of the US$ values, there is much less consistency. The correlation between the annual growth rates of NTX2 and NTX4 is 0.45. The change from NTX2 to NTX4 makes the growth rates for non-traditional exports more volatile. This is relevant for policy analysis, since it is the rates of change which will reflect responses to policy. We do not here run any regressions of non-traditional exports on policy variables, but it is clear that the results would depend significantly on which criterion we adopt.

Table 10.10   Traditional and non-traditional exports, NTX3 definition, Zimbabwe, 1981–97

	1981	1983	1985	1988	1990	1991	1992	1993	1994	1995	1996	1997
				Shares in total exports (%)								
Traditional	70.6	72.0	64.4	66.2	63.6	59.1	57.1	45.3	56.6	49.4	53.9	48.5
Non-traditional	29.4	28.0	35.6	33.8	36.4	40.9	42.9	54.7	43.4	50.6	46.1	51.5
of which:												
Goods	27.4	25.5	32.8	30.1	32.2	35.2	34.9	45.3	35.1	39.8	34.9	38.9
Tourism	2.0	2.5	2.8	3.7	4.2	5.7	8.0	9.4	8.2	10.8	11.2	12.6
				Annual growth rates of US$ values								
Traditional		–9.1	–6.9	14.0	0.2	–21.9	0.1	–16.3	61.3	–17.7	22.2	–10.6
Non-traditional		–12.5	10.6	11.4	6.0	–3.1	8.2	31.4	15.7	11.6	3.7	11.1
Goods		–13.7	11.3	10.2	5.6	–5.7	2.6	33.1	13.5	8.6	0.0	10.9
Tourism		2.3	3.1	22.6	9.3	14.6	37.5	23.9	25.5	23.2	16.6	11.8
Total Exports		–10.0	–1.3	13.1	2.2	–14.7	3.5	7.0	39.0	–3.9	13.3	0.0

Note: 'Tourism' is measured as all travel receipts recorded in the balance of payments.

Sources: CSO, supplied trade data; CSO, *Quarterly Digest of Statistics*, various dates.

Table 10.11 shows the growth rates for the alternative definitions of non-traditional exports. Over the whole period, NTX4 grew fastest, in part reflecting the small base from which they start. When we break the period into pre- and post-reforms, they continue to have the fastest growth rate but interestingly the growth rate after the reforms is lower than before. For all other definitions, growth rates pick up after the reforms.

Although there has been a rise in the share of non-traditional exports by whatever criterion we adopt, there is not a noticeable change after the 1990 reforms. However, as Table 10.11 shows, while the NTX2 measure suggests that the growth rates for both traditional and non-traditional exports were

Table 10.11   Period growth rates for alternative definitions of non-traditional exports, Zimbabwe, 1981–97

	1981–97	1981–90	1990–7
NTX1	10.0	8.1	11.0
NTX2	8.6	6.8	11.6
NTX3	8.9	6.3	13.1
NTX4	18.2	19.1	16.6

Note: The growth rates are estimated as the slope of $\ln NTX_i = a + bt$ fitted to the US$ values over the period.

higher in the 1990s than the 1980s, the NTX4 measure shows that the expansion of non-traditional exports slowed down after 1990. Insofar as these changes could be attributed to the reforms, they would accord with the view that the distortions inherent in a regulated economy work against comparative advantage; their reduction allows it to reassert itself.[5]

'Non-traditional exports': manufactured products

One of the objectives of ESAP was to expand manufactured exports, which is how non-traditional exports (NTX1) were defined by Zimbabwean policy-makers (GOZ, 1991). However, manufactured exports declined from US$537.2 million in 1990 to US$498.4 million by 1993. On average, the manufacturing sector exported 20 per cent of its output during the ESAP period compared to 19 per cent in 1990. Some of the reasons for the poor export performance of the manufacturing sector include the 1992 drought, poor external marketing, and poor infrastructure, particularly telecommunications (Muzulu, 1993; World Bank, 1995).

This view of non-traditional exports suggests that a different measure, centred around the primary/non-primary goods distinction, should be examined. Table 10.12 shows the results of grouping exports according to this criterion. We distinguish between agricultural and mineral primary goods and between agricultural-based, food, mineral-based and general manufactures.

Table 10.12   Zimbabwe's exports classified as primary and non-primary goods, 1981–97 (% shares)

	1981	1983	1985	1988	1990	1991	1992	1993	1994	1995	1996	1997
Primary	86.9	89.4	84.2	84.5	81.3	76.5	75.6	69.8	76.4	72.6	77.1	73.0
Agricultural	50.9	46.7	51.3	42.4	50.4	48.9	46.2	45.9	59.0	47.7	56.8	52.6
Mineral	36.0	42.7	32.9	42.1	30.9	27.6	29.4	24.0	17.4	25.0	20.2	20.4
Non-Primary	13.1	10.6	15.8	15.5	18.7	23.5	24.4	30.2	23.6	27.4	22.9	27.0
Agric.-based manufactures	1.4	1.8	3.1	2.7	3.6	5.6	4.9	5.4	4.9	5.6	4.7	6.0
Food manufactures	0.7	0.7	0.8	1.1	1.1	4.2	1.2	2.7	1.6	2.2	1.7	2.8
Mineral-based manufactures	1.8	1.9	1.7	1.9	2.2	2.2	1.9	2.4	1.6	2.4	1.7	1.6
General manufactures	9.3	6.3	10.2	9.8	11.8	11.5	16.3	19.8	15.5	17.1	14.8	16.5

At the broad level, this disaggregation shows a rising share of non-traditional exports, similar to that found previously. In 1981, primary exports accounted for 86.9 per cent of exports, by 1997, 73.0 per cent. Most of the decline emanates from the mining sector; the share of agricultural primary exports in fact rose slightly over the period. General manufactures account for most of the increase in the share of non-primary exports.

Although the period growth rate of both categories was higher after 1990 than before, the relative increase is greater for primary than non-primary (Table 10.13). As with the previous measure of NTX, this could be interpreted as showing that comparative advantage reasserted itself after deregulation. However, this measure makes clearer the tentative nature of this suggestion, since the dominance of agriculture in primary exports suggests the higher growth rate was due to the severe drought at the beginning of the reform period.

Table 10.13 Rates of growth of primary and non-primary exports, in US$, Zimbabwe, 1981–90 and 1990–7

| | *Period growth rates* | |
	1981–90	*1990–7*
Primary	*2.6*	*7.0*
Agricultural	2.8	9.6
Mineral	2.2	1.7
Non-Primary	*8.1*	*11.0*
Agriculture-based manufactures	12.9	11.6
Food manufactures	9.8	12.1
Mineral-based manufactures	5.5	4.2
General manufactures	7.5	12.1
Total	*3.4*	*7.9*

Note: The growth rates are estimated as the slope of the equation ln$y$ = a + bt fitted to the period.

This definition of 'non-traditional' derives from the traditional development literature and the debates around the Prebisch–Singer thesis. Unlike the World Bank definition, it is an analytical classification, based on presumed differences between the characteristics of the two groups and the behaviour of industries producing them. Much of its usefulness rests upon a presumed correlation between it and a classification based on income elasticities of demand. Primary commodities are assumed to have lower income elasticities than manufactured goods. We have not systematically undertaken an analysis of this correlation. However, some evidence on income elasticities for different commodities in various countries is available in McDougall (1997). Based on surveys of the empirical literature, income elasticities of demand are provided for 37 commodity groups (including 12 primary and 19 manufactured commodities) in 30 countries or regions. The range of the elasticities is the same for both groups, varying between 0.01 and 1.89. Processed food products tend to have elasticities similar to those for agricultural products (generally less than 0.7), while forestry, fishing and energy products have elasticities similar to other manufactured products (generally greater than 1.25). This suggests that the primary/manufactured distinction is not a good proxy for one based on income elasticities.

Furthermore, when we examine the individual exports for Zimbabwe, we find some primary products which cannot be regarded as 'traditional', in the sense of slow growing. As an example, consider SITC group 292 – 'Crude vegetable materials, n.e.s'. In 1981, it constituted 0.4 per cent of export values and was ranked thirty-first in importance. By 1993, it was sixth in importance, contributing 2.45 per cent of export earnings. Between 1981 and 1996 it experienced an annual average growth rate of 13.5 per cent in US$ values. However, included in this category is 'fresh cut flowers'. In 1981, just US$30 258 of cut flowers was exported. By 1996 this had grown to US$30 929 210, an annual growth rate of 46.2 per cent. In 1981, cut flowers constituted 0.6 per cent of the 292 group; by 1996 it was over 85 per cent. Thus, even though in this case the three-digit category shows some movement, we can see that it masks a much greater movement within the group.

Commodity concentration of exports

Our final analysis of the commodity composition of exports looks at measures of concentration and diversification. Various measures are presented in Table 10.14. There is no single index which captures adequately the various aspects of concentration and diversification. We follow standard practice by using the Hirschman index to measure concentration. However, this index is not particularly sensitive to changes in the smaller categories, so we supplement it with the Gini coefficient.

These two indices tell apparently contradictory stories. The Hirschman indices suggest there was falling concentration in the 1980s, followed by a rise between 1990 and 1992, since when the indices have fluctuated around a higher mean than in the 1980s. Over the whole period there has been a slight upward trend. However, the Gini coefficient shows a slight downward trend suggesting falling concentration. This contrast is because the Hirschman indices are more sensitive to changes in categories with large rather than small shares, while the Gini coefficient is more sensitive to changes in the smaller share categories.

Inspecting the frequency distributions (also shown in Table 10.14) gives a much stronger impression of diversification. The number of goods at the two extremes of the distribution have fallen, being sucked into the middle as it were. The number of 'significant' categories – those whose share of total export values exceeded 0.1 per cent – grew steadily from fifty-nine to ninety over the period. This is a crude measure of product diversification. The frequency distribution shows that much of this diversification was in the smaller categories; the number of products in the 0.1 per cent to 0.5 per cent and the 0.5 per cent to 2.5 per cent both doubled over the period.

Finally, the table also shows the share of the ten highest ranking exports for each year.[6] There has been a noticeable decline in their dominance, from around 80 per cent in the early 1980s to around 65 per cent in the mid-1990s. Again this suggests that there has been growing export diversification.

Table 10.14 Concentration and diversification in Zimbabwe's commodity exports, 1981–97

	1981	1983	1985	1988	1990	1991	1992	1993	1994	1995	1996	1997
Potential No. of Exports	154	154	154	154	154	154	154	154	154	154	154	154
No. > 0.1% total US$ value	59	56	65	71	71	76	81	86	86	88	87	90
Hirschman	0.330	0.317	0.324	0.301	0.304	0.366	0.384	0.314	0.362	0.305	0.374	0.307
Normalized Hirschman	0.230	0.212	0.228	0.207	0.210	0.284	0.307	0.231	0.285	0.222	0.299	0.225
Gini	0.737	0.745	0.742	0.735	0.724	0.716	0.720	0.649	0.713	0.671	0.701	0.665
% of Biggest 10	76.4	78.0	73.6	73.5	73.1	68.4	69.3	58.1	68.1	62.0	66.3	61.3
Numbers of Commodities												
less than 0.1%	78	87	82	75	75	71	67	61	63	60	60	56
0.1% to 0.5%	34	35	41	48	47	50	50	45	52	53	54	50
0.5% to 2.5%	17	13	17	14	14	18	25	36	26	28	27	34
2.5% to 5%	2	2	2	4	4	5	2	3	5	5	3	3
more than 5%	6	6	5	5	6	3	4	2	3	2	3	3
Total Number	137	143	147	146	146	147	148	147	149	148	147	146

Source: Estimated from trade data.

We conclude that, over the whole period, Zimbabwe's commodity exports have become more diversified. We would like to determine whether this process has been a smooth one over time or whether there is a 'structural break' around the time of the reforms. Unfortunately, the data do not allow us to undertake a sophisticated test. However, a simple t test performed on the Gini coefficients shows that the difference between the 1981–90 and the 1991–7 series is significant at the 1 per cent level. The share of the top ten appears to fluctuate around the mid- to low-70s between 1981 and 1990, decline over the next three years, then fluctuate around the mid- to low-60s. The period mean for 1981–90 is ten percentage points higher than that for 1993–7. Again this suggests that something happened after the reforms (and a brief transitional period) to reduce export concentration.

Country composition

Has the change in trade regime changed the pattern of export destinations? It is possible that a more open and thus more competitive regime forces firms to seek new markets, breaking down the lethargy of a protected system.

Table 10.15 summarizes data for export destinations. We see that the total number of markets has increased over the period.[7] The number peaks in 1992 and then levels off: there does not seem to be a structural break after the 1990 reforms. Given the limit on the potential number of export destinations, some levelling off is inevitable. We do not have comparative data to say what the 'natural' upper limit is.

Since some of these markets are very small, we also measure 'significant' markets using the 0.1 per cent criterion we used for identifying significant commodity exports. These have remained remarkably stable over the whole period.

None of the concentration measures show much action. The Gini coefficient is high, but does not change significantly. The Hirschman index gives a slight suggestion that there has been declining concentration of export destinations, with most of the downward trend being caused by 1996 and 1997. These measures are difficult to interpret, not least because there is no analytic guide as to what a 'big' change would be. Although it does not give a single measure, examining the frequency distribution perhaps gives a better picture. This is also shown in Table 10.15, where the number of destinations falling into each category have been converted to percentages for ease of comparison. Although these data show stability at the top end – suggesting there has been little diversification – there is considerable change at the bottom end. The number of small destinations has grown relative to middle-order countries. This suggests that while the major trading partners continue to dominate, there is instability amongst the smaller partners. This instability is not because of new partners coming in, but rather because of existing small partners moving down the ladder.

Table 10.15   Concentration and diversification in Zimbabwe's export markets, 1981–97

	1981	1983	1985	1988	1990	1991	1992	1993	1994	1995	1996	1997
Number	116	119	130	129	135	146	156	139	146	140	138	139
Sig. Markets	64	60	53	63	53	56	55	63	58	57	62	61
Gini	0.817	0.815	0.845	0.842	0.850	0.865	0.864	0.850	0.850	0.852	0.825	0.836
Hirschman	0.203	0.185	0.177	0.173	0.168	0.183	0.177	0.175	0.168	0.176	0.144	0.161
Top 10 (% Value)	66.6	65.5	68.1	71.6	67.2	68.3	65.7	67.0	63.8	66.7	59.5	63.8
Frequency Distribution: number of countries in each category as % of total												
less than 0.1%	44.8	49.6	59.2	51.2	60.7	61.6	64.7	54.7	60.3	59.3	55.1	56.1
0.1% to 0.5%	30.2	21.8	17.7	26.4	18.5	19.2	17.9	23.0	17.8	18.6	21.0	17.3
0.5% to 1%	7.8	10.1	8.5	8.5	6.7	6.2	4.5	10.1	6.2	8.6	7.3	12.9
1% to 2.5%	7.8	10.1	5.4	5.4	4.4	4.1	4.5	3.6	8.2	4.3	8.0	5.0
2.5% to 5%	6.0	3.4	6.2	3.1	5.2	4.8	3.9	3.6	4.1	5.7	5.1	4.3
More than 5%	3.5	5.0	3.1	5.4	4.4	4.1	4.5	5.0	3.4	3.6	3.6	4.3
	100.0	100.0	100.0	100.0	100.0	100.0	100.0	100.0	100.0	100.0	100.0	100.0

The number of trading partners is not as important as their relative size. This suggests an alternative method for gauging the importance of changes. We can categorize countries according to whether they are 'major', 'middle' or 'minor' export destinations. Then, using standard decompositions, we can see what contribution changing levels and shares of these categories have made to overall change in export earnings (see Appendix for details). Table 10.16 gives the results of such a decomposition. Between 1981 and 1990, the US$ value of exports grew by 14.4 per cent; 2.0 percentage points came from 'minor' market growth, 2.3 from 'middle' and 10.1 from 'major'. However, the 'share effect' of major markets was negative: if the only change had been the decline in the share of these markets that actually occurred, total exports would have fallen by 5.7 per cent. Between 1990 and 1997 a similar pattern occurred: major markets lost shares, while minor and middle markets gained. This shows the impact of diversification within the overall expansion of markets.

Table 10.16   Sources of changes in Zimbabwe's export earnings, 1981–97 (%)

	'Minor' markets				'Middle' markets				'Major' markets				Total
	(1)[a]	(2)[b]	(3)[c]	(4)[d]	(1)[a]	(2)[b]	(3)[c]	(4)[d]	(1)[a]	(2)[b]	(3)[c]	(4)[d]	
1981–90	0.1	1.6	0.2	2.0	1.3	0.9	0.1	2.3	13.0	–2.5	–0.4	10.1	14.4
1990–97	1.4	1.9	0.8	4.0	4.3	3.8	1.5	9.6	34.9	–5.7	–2.3	27.0	40.6
1981–97	0.6	3.5	2.1	6.2	5.4	4.7	2.9	13.0	54.9	–8.2	–5.0	41.6	60.9

Notes: [a] Level effect.
[b] Share effect.
[c] Cross effect.
[d] Total effect.

Table 10.17 shows the various destinations grouped into regions. The most noticeable trend in the 1980s was the decline in South Africa as an export market. This was primarily related to sanctions, but also reflected South African protectionism. Its place was taken by the European Union. Exports to SADC countries only increased in the late 1980s; in the 1990s they have not grown at all.

Table 10.18 shows the results of an experiment ranking export destinations according to their average GDP per capita growth rates over the period 1985–95. There are two ways of interpreting this classification. Looking at the shares in 1981–5 we get an *ex ante* interpretation: was Zimbabwe poised to take advantage of the high growth that was about to occur? Only 8 or 9 per cent of her exports were going to countries which had per capita growth rates over 5 per cent per annum in the following decade, while 23 per cent to 33 per cent were going to countries about to experience declining incomes. Alternatively, there is an *ex post* interpretation: looking back from the mid-1990s, had Zimbabwe hitched itself to economies which had grown? There was a slight increase in the share of exports going to the high growth countries. However, the share going to economies which had experienced negative growth rates also rose.

Table 10.17 Zimbabwe's export destinations by region, 1981–96

	1981	*1983*	*1985*	*1988*	*1990*	*1991*	*1992*	*1993*	*1994*	*1995*	*1996*
Africa	37.1	34.2	27.5	29.6	32.4	30.9	33.4	37.8	33.2	32.6	28.4
South Africa	21.6	18.5	10.4	9.6	8.9	10.2	13.6	14.3	11.8	12.6	9.6
SADC	10.9	10.4	11.6	15.7	20.0	17.3	16.5	19.1	18.5	17.6	16.8
Rest of SSA	3.4	2.5	5.2	3.6	3.3	2.7	2.8	2.5	2.7	1.7	1.8
North Africa	1.2	2.7	0.4	0.7	0.3	0.6	0.4	2.0	0.1	0.8	0.2
Europe	36.1	39.1	47.4	43.9	44.4	45.6	40.6	37.4	39.7	42.1	38.9
European Union	32.5	35.3	45.3	42.4	41.7	41.9	34.1	32.2	36.4	39.8	34.6
Rest of Europe	3.6	3.8	2.0	1.5	2.7	3.7	6.5	5.2	3.4	2.3	4.3
Americas	8.7	7.8	8.7	8.9	8.0	6.6	7.6	8.6	7.6	5.9	8.8
NAFTA	8.1	5.8	8.5	7.9	7.5	6.3	7.1	8.0	7.4	5.0	7.2
Rest of Americas	0.6	2.0	0.3	1.1	0.5	0.3	0.5	0.6	0.3	0.9	1.5
Asia	10.3	11.5	9.8	13.4	11.3	13.3	14.4	12.7	14.2	15.0	15.6
Former Eastern Bloc	1.7	2.5	3.3	2.3	1.6	1.5	1.6	0.9	2.8	2.0	4.6
Rest of the World	6.2	4.9	3.3	1.9	2.3	2.2	2.3	2.5	2.4	2.4	3.7
TOTAL	100.0	100.0	100.0	100.0	100.0	100.0	100.0	100.0	100.0	100.0	100.0

Table 10.18 Zimbabwe's export destinations classified by growth rates, 1981–96

GDP/cap growth rate		*Number*	*1981*	*1983*	*1985*	*1988*	*1990*	*1991*	*1992*	*1993*	*1994*	*1995*	*1996*
			% of Total Exports to these Countries										
High	> 5%	10	9.4	8.2	8.9	9.1	11.1	12.9	12.4	10.6	11.8	12.6	13.1
Medium	> 2%	23	15.8	20.0	23.0	20.3	22.5	22.1	19.2	19.9	18.9	22.7	23.2
Low	> 5%	32	34.9	36.1	42.1	44.2	38.9	38.5	36.1	36.9	40.3	37.2	36.5
Stagnant	> –0.5 to 0.5	12	4.1	2.7	3.0	4.2	5.4	5.2	8.3	6.6	5.2	2.6	4.7
Falling	> –5%	25	35.3	32.9	21.8	21.8	21.0	20.5	23.5	25.7	23.1	24.1	21.8
Collapsing	< –5%	14	0.4	0.1	1.1	0.4	1.0	0.7	0.4	0.3	0.7	0.8	0.6

Conclusions

Our analysis provides a descriptive account of the macroeconomic and institutional environment, followed by a statistical account of the trends in Zimbabwe's export patterns. The pattern seems to have changed, with both the commodity and the country composition of exports becoming more diversified over time. However, Zimbabwe's exports continue to be dominated by a narrow range of agricultural and mineral based products, being exported to a narrow group of countries. Such diversification as there is seems to be occurring at the bottom end of each distribution. It is difficult to assess the nature of this, since we have little evidence about processes of product and market diversification which might provide a benchmark.

This diversification could generally be interpreted as a good thing, since it reduces export vulnerability. However, the account does not allow causality to be inferred. While the climate for exports in general has, in some respects, improved, there is no particular evidence that non-traditional exports, however defined, were or should have been favoured over traditional exports. Although there is slight but inconclusive evidence to suggest that there was a break in the trend around the 1990, when the economic reform programme was introduced, we cannot attribute causality. The patterns we find could be statistical artifacts, arising from the non-analytical nature of the definitions used. They could also represent other influences, in particular the droughts. By dramatically cutting agricultural exports, droughts could give a spurious impression of greater diversification.

Further work needs to be done to sharpen the concept of non-traditional exports, if causality is to be identified. The approach we used is perhaps justifiable when undertaking cross-country studies, but is probably unsuitable for single-country analysis. We end by suggesting two directions in which future analysis might go.

We analysed the commodity and the country composition of exports separately from each other. This raises the problem of the exact definition of a 'product'. If we are concerned with the responsiveness of exporters to policy reforms, then it could be argued that a 'product' should be destination-specific. Is finding new markets for a 'traditional' export a less important or less likely response to liberalization than creating a 'new' export? If we regard A in Figure 10.1 below as representing a 'stagnant' exporter and D a 'dynamic' one, then both B and C are routes through which a firm – or a country – might shift from A to D. It could also be argued that, to the extent that there is segmentation of global product markets, diversification into different markets reduces export vulnerability in much the same way as diversification by product.

	Old Markets	New Markets
Old Products	A	B
New Products	C	D

Figure 10.1 Export routes

Our preliminary work on destination-specific export growth (not reported here), apart from demonstrating the difficulty of bringing order to such a large data set, suggests that the cells in Figure 10.1 can be ranked A, C, B and D, with D almost empty. Although this might be specific to Zimbabwe, it is probably inherent in the data – there is much more scope for expanding product range than destinations.

Finally, the proper definition of 'non-traditional' exports has to be addressed. The statistical approach does not concern itself with the characteristics of the exports: a new export is a new export is a new export. However, for a number of reasons we might regard the introduction of one type of export as more desirable than another, even if the export earnings from each are the same. Linkages with the rest of the economy, long-run growth prospects, transfer of technology and learning-by-doing effects will all be crucial in changing the growth process in a country. It is clear that the statistical approach does not concern itself with these characteristics. The primary/industrial dichotomy takes a naive view of them. There is no inherent reason why primary products as traditionally defined should confer any less dynamic advantages on the economy than do industrial products.

This suggests that a more qualitative approach to the definition of 'non-traditional' exports is called for. For such analysis, much more detailed analysis of the characteristics of production processes and intersectoral structures is called for. This suggests that country-specific microeconomic/industrial organization work is required; maybe sweeping cross-country analyses have reached their limit for the time being.

Appendix: decomposition of sources of changes in exports

The decomposition of the sources of changes in exports is carried out as follows.

Exports to each market were grouped according to the shares in 1981. 'Minor markets' are those with shares of less than 0.1%; 'middle markets' are those with shares greater than or equal to 0.1% but less than 0.5%; 'major markets' are those with shares greater than or equal to 0.5%. The share for each category in total exports was then calculated for each year. We then define total exports in US$ as:

$$X = \sum_i s_i X \text{ where } i = \text{minor, middle, major.}$$

Then:

$$\Delta X = X_1 - X_0 = \underbrace{\sum_i (s_{i1} - s_{i0})X_0}_{\text{share effect}} + \underbrace{(X_1 - X_0)s_{i0}}_{\text{level effect}} + \underbrace{(X_1 - X_0)(s_{i1} - s_{i0})}_{\text{cross effect}}$$

Notes

1. We would like to thank the Central Statistical Office for making data available to us and Mr Witness Zimbudzi for assistance in analysing the data.

2. For our analysis, we omitted Parcel Post and Special Transactions from our figures; the latter are primarily migrants' effects which were significant in the early 1980s because of the special circumstances of Zimbabwe's history. We also omitted gold exports (except 'non-monetary gold'), mainly because it is traditional to do so in Zimbabwe (a hangover from the Gold Standard days). Gold exports averaged 13 per cent of export earnings between 1980 and 1997, with no discernible trend.
3. This demonstrates how the level of aggregation affects the definition. If we regarded the three SITC 67 products as one, we would have to include more commodities and therefore the share of traditional exports would rise.
4. We would like to thank Gerry Helleiner for this terminology.
5. Although the NTX2 measure shows a rise in growth rates of both categories, the relative rise is greater for traditional than non-traditional, which could support the same view.
6. This should not be confused with the World Bank's 'top ten' definition of NTX, which takes the same products in each year. The measure in this table is more like a poverty head count.
7. The country classifications have been adjusted to take into account the growth in the number of countries in the world after the end of the Cold War.

References

Biggs, T., Shah, M. and Srivastava, P. (1995) 'Technological Capabilities and Learning in African Enterprises', World Bank Technical Paper No. 28, World Bank, Washington, DC.

Central Statistical Office (1998) Supplied trade data.

Central Statistical Office (various dates) *Quarterly Digest of Statistics*.

Chipika, J. T., Chibanda, S. and Kadenge, P. G. (1998) 'Effects of Structural Adjustment in Southern Africa: The Case of Zimbabwe's Manufacturing Sector During Phase 1 of ESAP: 1991–5', SAPES Trust, August, mimeo.

Davies, R. (1991) 'Trade, Trade Management and Development in Zimbabwe', in J. Frimpong-Ansah, S. M. Ravi Kanbur and P. Svedberg (eds), *Trade and Development in Sub-Saharan Africa*, Manchester: Manchester University Press.

Davies, R. and Rattsø, J. (1993) 'Zimbabwe' in L. Taylor (ed.), *The Rocky Road to Reform: Income Distribution, Politics and Adjustment in the Developing World*, Cambridge, MA: MIT Press, pp. 321–42.

GOZ (1991) *Framework for Economic Reform, 1991–1995*, Harare: Government Printer.

Knight, J. (1996) 'Labour Market Policies and Outcomes in Zimbabwe', Institute of Economics and Statistics, Oxford University, mimeo.

Lall, S., Wignaraja, G., Sellek, M. and Robinson, P. (1997) *Zimbabwe: Enhancing Export Competitiveness*, London: Economic Affairs Division, Commonwealth Secretariat.

McDougall, R. (ed.) (1997) 'Global Trade, Assistance, and Protection: the GTAP 3 Data Base', Center for Global Trade Analysis, Purdue University.

Muzulu, J. (1993) 'Exchange Rate Depreciation and Structural Adjustment: The Case of the Manufacturing Sector in Zimbabwe, 1980–1991', unpublished DPhil thesis, University of Sussex.

Reserve Bank of Zimbabwe (various dates) *Quarterly Statistical and Economic Review*, Harare.

SAPES (1996) 'Manufacturing Sector Survey' in Chipika et al. (1998).

Thomas, M. and Bautista, R. M. (1999) 'A 1991 Social Accounting Matrix (SAM) for Zimbabwe', International Food Policy Research Institute, TMD Discussion Paper No. 36, January.
UNESCO, *Statistical Yearbook, 1996*.
UNIDO, *Industrial Development Report, 1996*.
World Bank (1994) RPED Project.
World Bank (1995) *Zimbabwe: Achieving Shared Growth: Country Economic Memorandum*, Vol. I, Washington, DC: World Bank.
Zimbabwe Export Processing Zones Authority (1998) Pamphlets.

Index

Compiled by Auriol Griffith-Jones

Note: Page numbers in bold refer to Tables and Figures